You Can Choose To Be Happy:

"Rise Above" Anxiety, Anger, and Depression

with Research Evidence

Tom G. Stevens PhD

Wheeler-Sutton Publishing Co.

YOU CAN CHOOSE TO BE HAPPY:
"Rise Above" Anxiety, Anger, and Depression
With Research Evidence

Tom G. Stevens PhD

Wheeler-Sutton Publishing Co.
Palm Desert, California 92260

Revised (Second) Edition, 2010
First Edition, 1998; Printings, 2000, 2002.

Publisher's Cataloging-in-Publication Data

Stevens, Tom G., Ph.D. 1942-
    You can choose to be happy: rise above anxiety, anger, and depression./ Tom G. Stevens Ph.D. –2nd ed.
    p. cm.
    Includes bibliographical references.
    ISBN 978-0-9653377-2-4

    1. Happiness. 2. Self-actualization (Psychology) I. Title.

BF575.H27 S84 2010 (pbk.)
158-dc22

Library of Congress Control Number: 2009943621

CONTENTS

Appendices and Bibliography

BOOK DEDICATED TO:

Charlotte May Stevens--
my mother.
She raised Ron and I alone, loved me unconditionally,
and was always supportive of me and my efforts.
She taught me that honesty and integrity are more important
than what anyone thinks of me or any kind of worldly success.

and

Sherry Bene' Stevens--
my wife
She is the love of my life--my soul mate.
She is the sunshine and the music in my life.
She is more than I ever thought
I would be lucky enough to have in my life

COMPLETE SHAQ
and find your *Happiness Quotient (HQ)*

I suggest you take my
Success and Happiness Attributes Questionnaire (SHAQ)
(free) on my website at http://www.csulb.edu/~tstevens.
You can save complete results on all scales and items.

SHAQ is designed to go hand-in-hand with this book to provide the best possible
self-development experience. Your results may be more accurate and
you may learn more if you take SHAQ *before* reading this book.
Compare your SHAQ results to what you read in each chapter.
SHAQ research results from the first 3400 users are included in each chapter.
Users rated the interest and usefulness of SHAQ an average of 6.1 out of a possible 7.0.

INTRODUCTION

WHO IS THIS BOOK FOR?

It may be for you if you answer "yes" to any of the following questions:
- Do you want to discover the causes of happiness and unhappiness?
- Would you like to learn how to achieve mental control over emotions such as anxiety, anger, guilt, and depression?
- Would you like to develop greater self-esteem?
- Do you want a more positive, but realistic, view of the world?
- Do you worry too much about pleasing others or gaining approval?
- Are you too dependent on others for your happiness?
- Would you like to get more internal control of your life or become more persuasive, diplomatic, and assertive?
- Are you too codependent (take too much responsibility for others)?
- Do you want to improve your ability to motivate yourself, achieve your goals, and have a greater impact on the world?
- Would you like to feel less stress and make your time more productive?
- Would you like to be more self-actualized? (Be more like one of Maslow's self-actualizing people, who were extremely happy and productive)?
- Do you want to maximize your happiness and your gift to others' happiness?

ABOUT THIS BOOK:

Learn how to be happy--in any situation. What if you could be a little happier the rest of your life as a result of reading one book? Would you read it? I cannot promise that result, but I expect that reading this book will make a lasting difference in your happiness. I believe that you will learn at least a few new secrets about how to control your emotions and how to be happy--even if you are already very happy and an expert in the field.

Learn how to become more self-actualized. Dr. Abraham Maslow's concept of self-actualization is still one of the best descriptions of the healthy personality. Self-actualizing people are both extremely happy and productive. No matter what your background and personal history is, you can learn the basic beliefs and life skills it takes to be happy and more self-actualized.

Learn both internal and external routes to happiness. I emphasize internal routes to happiness--changing our thinking to get more mental control over our emotions and life. But practical actions that have powerful impact on other people, our careers, and every part of our lives are also emphasized. After reading this book, you may never view yourself quite the same again. You can gain a deeper understanding of how your mental processes work. You can view yourself as more interesting and worthy of your love and respect than before you read it.

Changes in your "Higher Self" can have dramatic effects on your self-esteem and life. Your Higher Self is not a mysterious entity, but your inner center of love and motivational power. The Higher Self is a belief system that begins when we are infants. A developed Higher Self incorporates beliefs reflecting the wisdom of the ages. It is a conductor that brings harmony to inner conflicts. It is a fountain of personal self-integration and spontaneity.

Core beliefs, values, and life skills make the difference between happiness and unhappiness. The first thing I did before writing this book was to list the key beliefs and life skills for creating a happy life and becoming like Maslow's self-actualizing persons. My reading, clinical and personal experience, and my research with my Life Skills Questionnaire on over 4000 people and my recent research with The Success and Happiness Attributes Questionnaire (SHAQ) on 3400 more have helped me identify those key beliefs and life skills. They form the heart of this book.

Get mental control over harmonious functioning. Harmonious functioning is a state we can all achieve which is similar to what Maslow called "peak experience" or Csikszentmihalyi called "flow." It is a more optimal state of being in which all of the cells in the mind and body seem to be functioning in harmony. The result is maximum learning, performance, and happiness. Understanding the causes of harmonious functioning can help you attain these natural highs.

Adjust your emotions like adjusting a thermostat. Learn the six CHUG-OF Harmonious Thinking strategies to get mental control over your emotions. When you are emotionally "too hot"--in overarousal states like anger and anxiety, you can turn down the thermostat to gain peace and calmness. When you are emotionally "too cold"--in underarousal states like boredom and depression, you can turn up the heat to get more energy and enthusiasm. Learn to spend more of your life "in the zone" of harmonious functioning.

Improve relationships--Overcome dependency, nonassertiveness, and external control. Another important ingredient of happiness is our personal relationships--especially intimate ones. Are you dominating or being dominated? How often do you do something for another person out of duty, obligation, because you "should," or out of guilt? How much freedom do you feel? How much closeness and intimacy? Have you achieved "independent intimacy?"

My wife Sherry and I rarely do anything for each other out of obligation. We almost always do whatever we do because we genuinely want to. You can eliminate most of the obligation from your relationships, but you may need a new way of thinking. You may also need to learn better communication methods. Try the methods in this book that have worked for us and our clients. The result is a mutual feeling of freedom, love, and intimacy.

Evidence for my conclusions comes from my and others' research results, psychotherapy with several thousand clients, and my own personal experiences. My clients entered therapy with diverse problems, backgrounds, and ethnic origins. I live my life according to the principles in this book. I frequently refer to my own and my clients' experiences to aid in your search for happiness and self-actualization. My extensive research on several thousand people was designed to test the ideas in this book. The research results strongly support these ideas— as you will be able to see for yourself in the summaries I have provided in this revised edition.

This is a comprehensive, advanced self-help book. It can be read, understood, and used successfully by almost anyone. I designed it for the type of people that I see most often in my classes, workshops, and psychotherapy. Many have already read one or more self-help books or have had previous counseling. Many are in recovery from alcoholism, drug addiction, abuse, or other problems. However, people ranging from 19-year-old freshmen to PhD psychologists have said that it was personally beneficial to them.

My primary goal is that by reading this book you will be a happier, more productive person. If you are happier, you will radiate that happiness to others as well. A secondary goal is for you to say (as others have) that this is the best book you have found to help you learn how to be happy and self-actualized.

MY THANKS TO:

Too many people have contributed to my knowledge and indirectly to this book to mention. My first mentor was Charlotte May Stevens, my mother. My second mentor was Dr. W. McFerrin Stowe, an extraordinary Methodist minister, who was loved by the 10,000 members of his church for his great insights into life and his great preaching. He helped me get started.

At both the University of Oklahoma and Claremont School of Theology, I had a number of professors who were especially influential and beneficial to me. They introduced me to some of the great thinkers of our time--such as Drs. Carl Rogers, Abraham Maslow, George Kelly, R. B. Cattell, Paul Tillich, Teihard de Chardin, and others whose ideas are reflected in this book.

From my doctoral program in psychology at the University of Hawaii, I am especially grateful to Dr. Art Staats, my dissertation chair, and Dr. Roland Tharp for their knowledge and help. Both contributed to major advances in the field of psychology and both helped give me a foundation in cognitive-based human learning theory that even today is a fundamental part of my thinking and of this book.

In the years since my formal education, I have actively pursued new ideas in the field of psychology. Cognitive science and artificial intelligence have become a special interest in recent years. In those fields I have been influenced by the writings of Dr. John Anderson of Carnegie-Melon and Dr. Art Grossberg of Boston University--among many others. Self-help writers--especially Dr. Wayne Dyer--have also influenced my ideas.

To my many friends and family members who have given me so much over my lifetime-- especially Jane Stevens and Ron Stevens--thank you.

To Bobbe Browning, a wonderful friend, who spent many hours editing the final manuscript and finding many wording problems I could not see, I give a special thanks for your work as well as your friendship.

My wife, Sherry, who is a university counselor and therapist, has been a special inspiration, and has been my close collaborator and editor. Since we met, my own thinking has continued to develop through our interactions. In our relationship, we both started with ideas similar to those in this book, but needed time to "work out the details." The results have been wonderful! When we meet a difficult situation that upsets us--either alone or together-- we can use our key phrase that we need to "rise above" the situation. We "rise above" it by thinking of the situation from a higher perspective (see Chapter 8). She is a constant joy and inspiration to me.

We are grateful for our children, Tracie, Spencer, and Tim; their spouses David, Christin, and Trina; and our grandchildren Savannah, Spencer, and Sean; Roxy and Charley; and Aubrey and James. All seem happy and we are proud of them.

I also want to thank the hundreds of my clients who have shared some of their innermost secrets and parts of themselves with me. They have allowed me to know them at a depth few others ever see. My clients have helped me learn that there are "secrets of happiness and success" that seem to work for most people--even those with very different backgrounds and personalities.

These many people have given their enriching gifts of knowledge to me. My gift is to pass it on to you, and I hope this gift brings you as much happiness as it has me. I wish you a life filled with happiness.

Note for Revised Edition

I want to thank the many readers who have sent me emails after reading my first edition. A few reader comments include:

•"The book is a terrific combination of scholarship, superb information, and spirituality."

•"I have read your book and it was very helpful to me. You cannot even imagine how it changed my life. My life was lonely and now I have many good friends."

•"I have just read your book, "You can choose to be happy." Already I am more at peace and will never be the same again."

•"Dr. Stevens, just wanted to let you know that I have found your book to be such an inspiration to me."

•"From reading your book, day by day, I try to understand and instill in myself the lessons on the CHOICE of being happy. You've done a wonderful job, and I thank you for writing this easy to read book and for helping me through rough times."

•"I have only been following your book's advice for a few weeks but I have already noticed a great difference in my level of happiness."

•"I am taking my Masters in Counseling. Your book is a very wonderful book. There are a lot of books on happiness but yours is a comprehensive one. Thank you very much for giving me such beautiful ideas."

•"I have been so unhappy, angry, anxious, and insecure for too long! You gave me the greatest idea I ever heard-- to make happiness (for myself and others) my ultimate goal in life."

•"I was trying very hard to be happy for decades, but I couldn't. New problems come to the surface when I solve the old ones…I read your book about happiness and I found it what I wanted for years."

Several hundred thousand people have read my book or visited my websites (http://www.csulb.edu/~tstevens). These websites contain hundreds of pages of free self-help information and my *Success and Happiness Attributes Questionnaire* (SHAQ). SHAQ is free, and was designed to test in detail the ideas in this book. SHAQ measures personal attributes such as self-worth, self-confidence, world view, internal control, core beliefs and values, emotional coping, self-management, and assertiveness discussed in this book. SHAQ also measures other factors important for success and happiness in relationships, careers, and academic pursuits.

I collected a great deal of research data with SHAQ. This data provides strong support for both the utility of SHAQ and the validity of ideas in this book. This book revision will summarize some of these research results. *Most SHAQ research results are put into boxes you can easily omit if you prefer not to read them.* However, even if you don't read the data, you can be assured that my recommendations are supported by the research data, and I hope that the data will give you more confidence in trying these ideas. As far as I know, this is the only self-help book that has tested so many of its specific ideas so thoroughly and found such positive results. Visit my website to see the full SHAQ research article or to complete SHAQ (free).

I hope this book will help you make yourself and the world a little happier. That is my main goal and reward for writing it.

Tom G. Stevens PhD   January, 2010

CHAPTER 1

OUR SEARCH FOR HAPPINESS AND SELF-ACTUALIZATION

\\

**Happiness, then, is at once the best and noblest
and pleasantest thing in the world. . .
we always choose it for itself and never for the sake of something else.**
(Aristotle, *Ethics*)

Happiness is an emotion that includes many shades--from peace and tranquility to joy and ecstasy Unhappiness includes all negative emotions--from depression, apathy, and sadness to anxiety, guilt, and anger. These negative emotions are commonly called "stress." People who feel stress are more susceptible to many kinds of mental and physical illness--including infection, viruses, AIDs, cancer, and cardiovascular disease. For example, studies have shown that people with prolonged anger or depression are more than twice as likely to have a heart attack as the general population! They are also more likely to die afterward. Researchers have also found that getting control of negative emotions and feeling happier can have a powerful effect on these diseases. [1]

Our emotions vary from moment-to-moment each day. Suppose you wore an emotion gauge that measured and recorded your emotions each moment during a typical week. What would the results look like? How much of your typical week is spent feeling happy--20%, 40%, 60%, 80%?

Do you ever long for more happiness, but fear that wanting it is selfish or naive? Do demands from family, friends, career, or even chores seem more important than your happiness? When you consider that many people face basic problems like hunger, poverty, crime, abuse, and fragmented families, do you ever feel guilty about wanting happiness?

However, if valuing happiness is so bad, why would great philosophers like Aristotle and Bertrand Russell value happiness above all other human experiences? Why would Buddha and Jesus value happiness and love so much? Were these men so naive or selfish?

Deep inside, we all want happiness, but how can we obtain it? Are we happy just because we're lucky enough to have the right genes or the right circumstances? What if we aren't so lucky? What if we face difficult circumstances such as rejection, failure, illness, or poverty? Can we rise above those difficulties and choose to be happy?

We can't control our emotions the way we can flip on a light switch. However, we can develop an inner power to master our emotions. Many people believe they have little or no

---

[1] See G. Miller et al (2009) , H. Cohen (1997), J. Blumenthal (1997), S. Cohen and T. Herbert (1996), and N. Adler and K. Matthews (1994)

control over their happiness and other emotions. They are right; they don't. Not yet! Until they learn the mental structures (values, beliefs, and life skills) necessary to gain control of their happiness and emotions, they cannot control them the way many others can. These differences in cognitive structures are the main reason some people are chronically happier than others. A person can't play tennis or the piano or even talk until they learn the mental structures needed. Gaining control over emotions is even more complex. However, your brain's cortex has the ability to learn structures to gain control of emotions as surely as it can gain control of your body. There is strong research evidence to support this claim.

MY OWN QUEST FOR HAPPINESS

During the summer when I was 16 years old, I was visiting my father in Phoenix. I had a lot of time to think. I had grown up assuming that happiness was just a by-product of meeting other goals. I assumed that what was really important was to be a top athlete, to have a special girlfriend, to be popular, to have lots of money (and a great car), and to be the best at almost everything I attempted. However, I wasn't too successful at meeting these goals, and I wasn't feeling happy at the time.

Something seemed wrong with this way of thinking, but I wasn't sure just what it was. I could see that not everyone could be the best or have the best. If people have to be the best to be happy, doesn't that condemn everyone else to miserable lives? If people have to own the best to be happy, doesn't that doom all poor people to misery?

These beliefs didn't make much sense--especially since some people with little success or money seemed happier than many people who "had it all." My father had lived by this "be number one" philosophy and had made lots of money. But he did not seem happy.

Yes, something was wrong with this way of thinking. But what could be better? I knew that eventually having a happy marriage was important to me. I thought about what I would want in someone else. I formed a fairly clear image of what she would be like-- based on women I had known and characters from movies. The person I wanted would be someone who would be warm, happy, enthusiastic, self-confident, intelligent, honest, emotionally expressive, had interests similar to mine, and more!

However, I didn't even have a girlfriend. Even if I ever found such a terrific person, why would she be interested in me? I asked myself what someone like this would want in a man she would meet. What I realized is that she would probably want a man who had the same positive qualities I was looking for in her!

This conclusion caused me to look at myself honestly. I had to admit that I came up short of what I wanted in someone else--in many respects. The quality that seemed most important was someone who was happy--happy with herself and happy with life. It seemed that no matter where I started my thinking, I kept arriving at the same conclusion--people's happiness is the most important quality in life. I decided that what I wanted more than anything else in my life was happiness.

This simple insight changed my life. At the time, I feared this insight would end as other self-improvement attempts had--with little progress. I was wrong. My life has never been the same since that event more than 50 years ago. That insight was the beginning of my conscious quest for happiness.

Where do we begin the quest for happiness? My first step for choosing to be happy was to choose to be happy! I decided to make an experiment of consciously making happiness number one. So, I made a commitment to make happiness for myself and others the top goal in my life for at least a few months. Part of that commitment was to recognize that I would take primary responsibility for my own happiness from now on. I quit assuming that money, others, fate, luck, a sexy spouse, or the government would make me happy.

If you decide that you really want to be happier, then how can you begin your quest? Today there are many options--counseling, self-help books, groups, classes, workshops, and other opportunities. They can all be helpful. However, try my experiment; try making happiness for yourself and others your top goal for at least three months. In addition, take responsibility for your own emotions.

Making personal growth a priority can produce "miraculous" effects. Who will be successful at this quest and who won't? The persons who become the happiest and grow the most are those who also make truth and their own personal growth primary values. They become fascinated with new growth experiences--even personally difficult ones--in order to keep reaching higher levels of development. Each new stressful event can be seen as an opportunity for growth instead of a disaster. You can fail to reach a goal, but you can never fail to learn.

I have seen many clients with problems such as hardcore drug or alcohol addictions who are now reaching high levels of personal functioning. I have seen clients who were so shy that they had never had a close friend become outgoing, friendly, and develop intimate relationships. I have seen angry people become forgiving and fearful people become confident. If you want to make rapid change in a short time, you can do it by immersing yourself in a variety of good growth experiences.

This book can help provide you with tools to get control of your emotions. This book is not about just one type of problem--such as stress, addictions, depression, loneliness, dysfunctional relationships, or lack of success in your career. It is about learning powerful ways of thinking that can help with almost any type of problem affecting your happiness. Once you increase your inner power, then you can choose to be happy in difficult situations.

Find role models for your own personal growth. Another way to begin your quest for happiness is to find good role models--such as people who have reached higher levels of happiness. Finding people who started with problems similar to yours can be especially helpful. This is one reason self-help programs such as Alcoholics Anonymous have been so successful.

When I was in college, I wanted models for my own personal growth. Dr. Abraham Maslow's study of self-actualizing people provided one model--which has been etched in my brain and has continued to influence my life.

If you are dealing with problems such as persistent depression or anxiety, you may be so focused on overcoming negative emotions that you resist focusing on goals like happiness and self-actualization. However, is it possible that part of your problem overcoming negative emotions may be that you focus too much on problems and on reacting to situations? Does focusing on problems leave you stuck in quicksand? If so, focusing on positive goals and positive models may be your lifeline out of the quicksand. In addition, happiness and self-actualization are closer than you think. You can achieve bits and pieces of happiness and self-actualization quickly.

MASLOW'S CLASSIC STUDY OF SELF-ACTUALIZING PEOPLE

Dr. Abraham Maslow--a founder of the humanistic psychology movement is one of the great psychologists of the last century. He noted that most Freudian and psychodynamic approaches to psychology tend to focus on psychological sickness. These theories had also developed too many negative concepts about people and human nature. This negativity was due partly to Freudians' study of people with the most serious psychological problems. Dr. Maslow asserted that psychologists could learn more about mental health by studying the healthiest people than by studying those with the greatest problems. His message needs to be restated for many in the mental health field today.

He completed a classic observational study of historically important people and important people of his time. These people were considered to be exceptional in their personal achievements, in their contributions to society, and in their own happiness and well-being. They had to pass mental health criteria as well (Maslow, 1954). People who knew Dr. Maslow personally thought he was a self-actualizing person. Perhaps his own personal experience was an important factor for his remarkable insights into self-actualization.

How important was his study and his conclusions? It had a significant and lasting effect upon the entire field of psychology. No other study of healthy people even approaches its influence. Dr. Maslow's model of self-actualizing people has stood the test of time over several decades.

What was it about these self-actualizing people that caused them to be so happy and productive? What were their secrets--the keys to their happiness and productivity? Listed in Figure 1 are Dr. Maslow's conclusions about the key characteristics of the self-actualizing people in his study. I invite you to begin your own conscious journey to self-actualization. Consider the following list of characteristics as a role model for yourself. May it serve as a guiding light for you as it has for me. (This book is also about how to achieve self-actualization. If you want to focus on developing certain characteristics, then read the chapters listed to learn more about how to achieve them for yourself.)

Maslow believed that before a higher need could become important to us, we must first get our lower, more basic needs met. Before we can become concerned about self-actualization, we need to adequately satisfy basic needs such as health, safety, belongingness, love, and status. To the degree that these needs are satisfied, then we are free to concentrate more on the higher needs or metavalues listed below.

MASLOW'S CHARACTERISTICS OF SELF-ACTUALIZING PEOPLE

A. PRIORITY OF VALUES LIKE TRUTH, LOVE, AND HAPPINESS

1. Acceptance of self, of others, of nature--"not complaining about water because it is wet." Stoic style of calmly accepting even the worst. (How? See Chapters 4, 5)

2. Identification with the human species--identification with all of humanity versus just their own family, friends, culture, or nation. (How? See Chapters 3, 4)

3. Emphasis on higher level values--see METAVALUE section on next page.

4. Perception of reality--greater perceptual accuracy of reality. Superior ability to reason and perceive the truth and understand people at a deeper level.

5. Discrimination between means and ends, between good and evil--Clearer and more focused upon ends than most people; though they view their experiences and activities more as *ends in themselves* than most people. (How? See Chapters 2, 3)

6. Resolution of dichotomies (conflicts). Resolved conflicts that plague most people, because of their highly developed, accepting philosophy of life. (How? See Chapter 3)

B. INTERNALLY CONTROLLED

7. Autonomy and resistance to enculturation. (How? See Chapter 6)

8. Detachment and desire for privacy--high enjoyment of privacy and solitude. Calm and at peace with themselves. (How? See Chapters 5, 6, 8)

9. Spontaneity, simplicity, naturalness--reflects integration of values and habits. Open, integrated values and habits. (How? See Chapters 3, 6)

C. HIGH INVOLVEMENT, PRODUCTIVITY, AND HAPPINESS

10. Problem-centering--easily forget self and easily absorbed in tasks they love and/or feel are extremely important. (How? See Chapters 3, 8)

11. Creativeness--retain an almost childlike fresh, naive, and direct way of looking at life. May be partly a result of other factors such as problem-centering.

12. Freshness of appreciation and richness of emotional reactions--ability to intensely focus on the present and highly involved in it. Very accepting of emotions. (How? See Chapters 7, 8)

13. High frequency of peak experiences. (How? See Chapters 7, 8)

D. HIGH QUALITY INTERPERSONAL RELATIONSHIPS

14. (Intimate) Interpersonal relations--"deeper and more profound interpersonal relations than any other adults." However, these very close relationships are often limited to a very few people. They tend to be kind, patient, affectionate, friendly, and unpretentious; but can be direct and assertive when needed.

15. Democratic character structure--a person's status is unimportant to them. They do respond to differences in values and character. (How? See Chapter 3)

16. Philosophical, unhostile sense of humor.

MASLOW'S METAVALUES (OR "BEING" VALUES)

Dr. Maslow observed that self-actualizing persons seem to spend less of their time concentrating on the lower values (safety, belongingness, etc. listed above) and more of their time being concerned primarily with higher values or metavalues. The content of self-actualizing people's thoughts is an extremely important way in which they live on a higher level. They spend much more time focusing on metavalues such as those listed below.

- **WHOLENESS** (unity, integration, organization, simplicity, etc.)
- **PERFECTION**
- **COMPLETION**
- **JUSTICE**
- **ALIVENESS** (process, life, spontaneity, self-regulation [versus. other-controlled], full-functioning)
- **RICHNESS** (differentiation, complexity, intricacy)
- **SIMPLICITY**
- **BEAUTY**
- **GOODNESS**
- **UNIQUENESS** (idiosyncrasy, individuality, novelty)
- **EFFORTLESSNESS** (ease, grace, beautifully functioning)
- **PLAYFULNESS** (fun, joy, amusement, humor)
- **TRUTH** (and knowledge?)
- **SELF-SUFFICIENCY** (autonomy, independence, environment-transcending, [taking care of oneself], separateness, living by own laws)

Focusing on satisfying these values (instead of focusing on lower values or negatives) is an important factor in why self-actualizing people are happier, more peaceful, and more productive than other people. They routinely meet their lower values (or have met them in the past), so now they are free to concentrate on these higher values.

It is interesting to note that when self-actualizing people's basic values are threatened, they do not tend to regress back to the earlier phase of development. Instead, their higher values are still more important to them. Once these higher values become firmly established, they are very resistant to deterioration.

Notice how these values are general and timeless. Contrast them with the goals that commonly occupy most people's time--such as worry over meeting deadlines, getting jobs, finding others to love, making high grades, or making good impressions.

Self-actualizing people are people who have learned to look at life from a broader perspective. They are attentive to the deadlines in life, but not carried away by them. They focus their lives on these abstract metavalues. Consequently, they are not so emotionally affected by the ups and downs of daily life. They feel a sense of happiness that comes from seeing progress toward satisfying these stable, inner values that do not depend so much upon external conditions.

> **PRACTICE: What are your highest values?** 1--What do you think about most of the time? What underlying values seem to be reflected by your goals and thoughts? 2–Do you want to give more attention to metavalues? 3--What can you do to spend less time concentrating on negatives or lower values and more time focusing on metavalues? In later chapters you will develop a greater understanding of your values and the parts of yourself that create them.

MOVING TO HIGHER LEVEL RELATIONSHIPS AND GROUPS

Once people begin to live on a higher level (become more self-actualizing), their relationships tend to change. They view their old relationships in a different light. They increase their understanding and caring for others, yet feel less worried about what others think of them or their choices.

As the new metavalues become more important, people spend less time with persons or groups who don't share their emphasis on these metavalues. They often seek new relationships or groups that do share them. They actively try to bring every relationship more in line with their metavalues.

Marilyn Ferguson (in *The Aquarian Conspiracy*) describes the growth process from a lower to a higher state of functioning. She compares this process to the early pilgrims crossing the Atlantic ocean from the Old World to the New World of America. She describes how those who were left behind in the old country often felt and how the explorer moves on.

> **Those who stay behind cannot understand why the familiar did not hold the**
> **immigrant. Why did he abandon his accustomed homeland?**
> **Saddest of all, how could their affections not hold them? . . .**
> **Over time, differences may seem more and more pronounced,**
> **old schisms widen. Many new friendships,**
> **even a whole new support network, take their place.**
> **Based as they are on shared values and a shared journey, these new**
> **relationships are perhaps more intense.** (Pp. 387-388)

Several years before I met my wife Sherry, she was going through a transition period involving some dramatic personal growth. The success, social status, and money she and some of her friends had and spent so much time focusing on had come to mean less to her. She knew that something was missing in her life. As she began to find new values and answers, she felt less connected to her friends. As a result, she felt increasing distance from even her closest friends.

She often walked along the canals in Long Beach. On one of these walks, she realized that she might have to continue her journey toward self-actualization without many people she was closest to. She suddenly felt alone and frightened about going ahead in her quest if it meant leaving everyone else behind.

She stopped in at the house of the one friend she thought might understand. Her friend showed her the above passage of *The Aquarian Conspiracy*. It helped her understand her situation and encouraged her to continue growing and searching for people who shared her new values.

That passage helped give her the courage to make some dramatic changes. She ended an unequal marriage, she continued to support herself in real estate while getting a counseling degree and raising two children, and she made many new friends--including me. Years later, she realizes that this was one of the most important periods in her life.

However, at the time, she greatly feared leaving the old, familiar people and life patterns behind. One of her biggest fears was that she could never find a man who was growth-oriented enough. Many women feel that way. Though, in fact, many growth-oriented men have the same fears.

To the degree that two people share the same metavalues, they can begin to have a higher-level relationship. We were lucky to find each other. When we met, we discussed many of our beliefs about what we wanted in a relationship and what we thought would make two people happy together. We especially focused upon combining intimacy, independence, open communication, and equality.

Neither of us had ever lived by these principles adequately in any previous relationship. So we began experimenting to see how this new kind of relationship would work. After much early trial and error, we found out that these principles really do work. We have developed a relationship that has evolved to a much higher level over the years. Our relationship is so loving, so freeing, and contributes so much to our own individual growth and happiness. These principles work for us and our clients.

PRACTICE: **Evaluate each significant relationship and group** in your life. What values are most important to each person or to each group? How similar are they to your new values? Is the relationship evolving toward satisfying these metavalues?

YOUR ULTIMATE CONCERN:
Your Top Goal will control your life and happiness

Dr. Paul Tillich, a great philosopher and theologian of the modern era, said that our ultimate concern is probably the most important single factor determining our personality and life. It is our most important value. He called it our personal "god," because it is so powerful. Our ultimate concern determines other values, beliefs, goals, feelings, and actions.

For example, if money is my ultimate concern, then I will focus upon making money above all else. I will choose a career, wife, car, dress, and activities that are consistent with making the most money I can. If money is my ultimate concern, then when the value of money conflicts with another value, the value of making money will always win the conflict. My "money god" will control me and determine much of my personality and my relationship to the world around me.

If my ultimate concern is being loved by my significant other, then the approval of my significant other controls my life--even when that approval is clearly self-destructive. People in "addictive" relationships often make their significant others their "gods."

Likewise, children from dysfunctional families often make their family their ultimate concern. Psychologists often see family members so enmeshed with each other that it is extremely difficult for them to break free of these bonds. Adult children may still desperately want love and approval from their family--even though they will never get enough.

When we make other people (or their approval) our ultimate concern, then we make them our "gods." We give them control of our lives and our happiness. Instead, take back the control of your life--take responsibility for your own happiness. Seek your own approval--not theirs. Let them have primary responsibility for their own happiness. Don't let them manipulate you with "guilt trips." (See internal control Chapter 6.)

EXTERNALLY-CENTERED (EC) VERSUS INTERNALLY-CENTERED (IC) VALUES

Perhaps you already understand that satisfaction of your top values and goals is fundamental to your happiness. However, you may not fully grasp how critical your choices of *ultimate concern* and top values are to your happiness. The choice of externally-centered versus internally-centered values is a powerful dimension affecting your happiness.

Externally-centered (EC) values. EC values are more dependent upon conditions outside you for their fulfillment; they are more dependent upon other people or external forces. EC values include having money, success, achievement, and material or other possessions and include being loved, accepted, or respected by others.

Internally-centered (IC) values. IC values are values that are more dependent upon your own thoughts and actions. IC values include happiness, love, beauty, truth, knowledge, and Maslow's metavalues. IC values are more mental, abstract, or spiritual. They depend upon what you think and give more than what others think or give you. Note the difference between *loving others* and wanting *to be loved by others*—the first is an IC value and the second an EC value. *Giving* in general is an IC value and *receiving* in general is an EC value. The IC-EC difference is a secret sense in which it is *better to give than to receive*. Caring more about (or focusing on) *what you do* versus what *is done to you* increases your control and happiness. Other examples are happiness, love, integrity, honesty, learning, and excellence.

The Law of Attachment

What is the Law of Attachment? Jesus, Buddha, and Tillich understood the following basic psychological-spiritual principle.

Whatever you are most attached to exerts the most control over your life and becomes your primary source of both happiness and anxiety.

Why is this so? Because, the instant you make an EC value your ultimate concern, you put yourself on a limb and create a huge source of anxiety. If you become too attached to an EC value, you give control of your emotions to *outside forces*. This EC value becomes your ultimate source of anxiety. Why? Because your ultimate fear will be not getting that value met; and if it is met, your ultimate fear will be losing it. The forces controlling it always remain primarily outside yourself—so you are always vulnerable and in a potential state of anxiety. Example, if you make being loved your top goal and don't receive love, your greatest fear will be not getting it; and if you get it, your greatest fear will be losing it. Results might include being overly dependent or being in an addictive or abusive relationship.

The instant you make an IC value your ultimate concern, you will likely feel a sense of calm, peace, and inner power. Control over IC, mental/spiritual values like happiness, truth, beauty, and loving lies primarily *within you*. Choosing IC values as your top values gives you security and peace, because you can control their satisfaction from within.

Satisfaction of IC values isn't so dependent upon external forces. For example, it's wonderful to love someone. However, if you make the loved one an ultimate concern and he/she leaves you, you will experience ultimate anxiety and unhappiness. You can love someone a great deal, but keep that relationship in perspective by making other IC values your highest values. Then if they leave you, you can still find happiness through satisfaction of IC values such as growth, beauty, and loving others. No one can ever take away love of God, nature, music, sports, learning, or many other primarily mental activities. Another problem of over-valuing others is that fear of losing them can undermine your relationships.

Substituting IC values for EC values is a primary part of many conversion experiences transforming people's lives and causing them to feel a wonderful sense of love and peace.

WHAT IF WE MAKE HAPPINESS A CONSCIOUS ULTIMATE CONCERN?

When I was considering change at age 16, I asked myself, "If what I want from life is to be happy, then why don't I make happiness my top goal?" It seemed ironic to me that my father and others worked all their lives to reach goals of having success, money, security, and many other things in order to be happy. Yet they were not happy--not because they didn't reach their goals; but because they chose the wrong goals.

Confusing "means" with "ends." It's not that having money or career success cannot contribute to happiness. They obviously can contribute. But if one makes these means to happiness their end goals, then they become so focused upon the means that they may lose sight of the end--happiness.

In my father's case, he made business success number one. There is nothing wrong with making business success an important goal. However, when he made it an ultimate concern, it took over his life. He constantly worried about it, deprived himself of many possible happy experiences, and got angry whenever anything interfered with his business success. I told him that I thought he could be happier if he would focus more on being happy. Yet, he couldn't understand how he could have happiness without business success. He was afraid that any change in thinking or focus might upset his drive for success.

Success had become more important to him than happiness. It is sad that after having had some business success--without having had a great deal of happiness--in the end he lost his business and was very unhappy before he died. For him his business success had become his personal "god."

Self-integration can overcome internal conflicts. So far, we have been assuming that we each have only one ultimate concern. However, most of us are too disorganized to have just one ultimate concern. Most of us are confused about what our most important values are. We owe allegiances to several "gods" that constantly conflict with each other.

We have internal battles between our desires for success, love, friendship, security, play, health, and more. Lack of integration among our highest values underlies much of our daily confusion and anxiety.

Once we consciously choose to make one value our top value (ultimate concern), then it becomes the ultimate test of any internal conflict. For example, if I have a conflict between spending an hour working or an hour playing, I ask myself, "Which will contribute most to my overall happiness (and the happiness of others)?" With experience, I have learned how to calculate my expected happiness quickly.

> **PRACTICE:** Your Ultimate Concern. What is the most important value in your life? What is your top goal? If you cannot give just one answer, list the values that seem most important. Then see if you can see if you can find any value(s) common to all of those less general values.

WHAT'S WRONG WITH MAKING HAPPINESS A TOP GOAL?

Would you feel comfortable telling most people that your most important goal in life is to be happy? Or, would you feel a little embarrassed or guilty? Why is this? Do you think people will accept your saying, "I want to be successful" more than saying, "I want to be happy"? Is "happy" a dirty word?

If you are embarrassed to openly say that you want to be happy, then it is important to examine the sources of this feeling. What assumptions underlie that feeling? Where did you first hear that putting happiness first is bad?

Resolving the selfishness and ethical issues. Many people are afraid that if they make their own happiness a primary goal in life, they will become too selfish, too self-centered, too hedonistic, or even unethical. My suggestion: make happiness for self *and* others your top goal, and learn a proper balance when there is a conflict.

These fears of making happiness a primary goal need to be examined. If we give undo attention to our own happiness at the expense of others, then almost any thoughtful person would agree that we are, indeed, being selfish or unethical. Is making happiness a primary goal incompatible with being ethical and caring? No! "Happy" is not a four-letter word. If you are concerned about being too selfish, hedonistic, or unethical, consider the following ten points.

1. Great religious leaders and philosophers promote happiness as a goal. Some people think that their religion does not value their happiness. There is an old saying, "Put God first, others second, and yourself last." The Bible does not say that, but many people think that way. What Jesus said was to love God first and love others as you love yourself--or equal to how you love yourself.

If you take a Christian perspective, ask yourself, "If I were a loving parent, would the happiness of my children be a top goal?" What is your idea of God? Could God be a less loving parent than you?

What do Aristotle, Immanuel Kant, Bertrand Russell, Buddha, and Jesus have in common? Happiness was a top-priority value for each of them. Reread Aristotle's quote that opened this chapter, he explicitly built his system of ethics around this idea--as did the great philosopher, Bertrand Russell. Gautama (the Buddha) made happiness his ultimate concern and centered his philosophy around that goal. The heart of his approach is the eightfold path to find the goal of happiness. Jesus stressed love and happiness as ultimate concerns--the heart of his famous "Sermon on the Mount" was his approach to finding happiness.

Kant's famous test of ethical principles. The great philosopher Immanuel Kant's famous ultimate test for an ethical principle is his *categorical imperative:*"Act as if the maxim from which you act were to become through your will a universal law of nature." He also notes that "there is one thing which we assume that all finite rational beings actually make their end, and . . . this object is happiness."

If we all seek happiness and are successful, then we will all be happy. Is there any other end goal that seems more desirable? Certainly, it would not be that we all sacrifice our happiness for each other. If we all did, no one would be happy. Thus, happiness passes Kant's categorical imperative ethical test.

2. Maximizing happiness is different from maximizing pleasure. Another type of criticism against making happiness an ultimate concern is that happiness is "just hedonism" or "just an emotion." Part of the underlying issue is the belief that emotions are just fleeting phenomena-- having little real significance. A related criticism is that happiness just reflects "lower" or more "primitive" values.

These criticisms are valid for making pleasure an ultimate concern, but not for making happiness an ultimate concern. People expressing criticism usually do not understand the important differences between happiness and pleasure.

Pleasure is produced by lower brain centers responsible for getting our lower needs met--such as hunger, thirst, touch, and biological sex. Pleasure can contribute to happiness. However, making pleasure the highest goal in life can lead to personality characteristics such as thrill-seeking, addiction, and selfishness. Many psychologists believe that making pleasure our ultimate concern is an underlying cause of a criminal or antisocial personality. Pleasure does not care about other people's needs.

On the other hand, happiness is an emotional state that depends upon harmony within the highest brain centers. It depends partly upon meeting lower, biological needs. However, it depends primarily upon meeting our higher, learned values--loving and being loved, achievement, truth, beauty, etc. We cannot be too selfish and be completely happy. Thus-- unlike pleasure--happiness has a biologically-based safeguard against selfishness.

Another complaint about pleasure is that people seeking pleasure are often irresponsible. That is often true. Many psychologists believe that making shortsighted pleasure-seeking a top-goal is an important cause of addictions to alcohol and drugs.

On the other hand, the higher brain constantly scans the future (at least its predictions of the future). If it predicts that values will all be met, then it produces happiness. If it is less than certain that values will be met, then it produces anxiety or other negative emotions. The person who seeks shortsighted pleasure will not be happy, because their higher brain will worry about the future. Thus--unlike pleasure--happiness has a wired-in safeguard against lack of concern about the future.

For example, we may feel pleasure from sex, but feel unhappy at the same time. Our interpretation of the meaning of an event such as sex affects our happiness more than the actual pleasure from sex itself. We cannot be completely happy about having sex if we feel guilty about cheating or worry about getting AIDS.

Happiness is the only human state that measures our overall physical and mental well-being. Happiness is even affected by our perception of the world's well-being. It results from harmony among our inner parts. We cannot deny important parts of ourselves and be fully happy. We cannot neglect the future and be fully happy. Nor can we neglect others and be fully happy. Happiness and love go hand-in-hand. Loving someone means we value his or her happiness. When we feel love, we feel happy-- whether the love is for an object, an activity, or a person.

3. We cannot be fully happy if we know we are hurting other people. This is a controversial statement. Many people believe that there are happy drug dealers, dictators, manipulators, and others who are powerful, wealthy, have many "friends," and are generally happy people who go unpunished for their misdeeds.

Yet, even these people have an inner part that cares about other people's happiness and is unhappy with what they are doing. Each of us has this inner part (our "Higher Self") which is based upon an innate concern for our own happiness and our knowledge that other people feel much the same feelings as us. Parts of us can try to ignore and deny this empathy for others, but those parts cannot totally drown it out--no matter how hard they try.

So far as we are knowingly responsible for doing things that contribute to the unhappiness of others--then this empathetic part of us will haunt us--no matter who we are. It is impossible to simultaneously be aware that we are hurting others and have the inner harmony necessary to be maximally happy! No matter how much hurtful people may try to fool themselves and others--inside they feel the conflict.

For example, biographies of Hitler and Stalin have shown that they had a great deal of internal conflict and unhappiness--even when they were riding the crest of their success and power. Their inner, hostile parts that victimized others also victimized their other inner parts. The result was inner turmoil, self-hate, and important parts of themselves that remained unfulfilled.

Full, prolonged happiness requires that we do what we believe to be consistent with contributing to others' happiness as well as our own. It is impossible to be both selfish and hurtful to others and very happy. How many times have you been aware of hurting another and not felt at least some guilt (or other negative emotion) at some time?

4. We need to balance focusing on our own happiness and focusing on the happiness of others. Making others' happiness a primary goal is necessary to be an ethical, caring person. It is also important in order for us to be happy ourselves. Loving another means giving their happiness high priority.

Achieving an adequate balance between valuing our own happiness and the happiness of others is the way to solve the ethical dilemma. We can seek win-win solutions to problems whenever possible, and we can occasionally sacrifice our own happiness for the happiness of others. In the long run, giving may bring us greater happiness than being selfish. Enlightened self-interest means that we must find a balance between giving to self and giving to others.

The United States constitution is quite permissive; it states that we each have the right to pursue our own happiness as long as it does not interfere with the rights of others to pursue it. It doesn't say anything about needing to actively seek others' happiness. It assumes that we are each responsible for our own happiness.

5. We are each responsible for our own happiness. Responsibility follows control. Since each person has more control over his or her own happiness than anyone else's, then each person has the greatest responsibility for his or her own happiness. Why should someone else be more responsible for my happiness then I am--or vice-versa?

Have you ever been in a situation where no one will say what they really want and each person is trying to make sure they please the other? For example in trying to decide which movie to see, one says, "What do you want to see?" "I don't care; what do you want to see?" This cycle repeats until both people become thoroughly frustrated. Isn't it better if both persons say what they want--yet simultaneously consider the other's wishes?

The balance between giving to self versus giving to others is an important issue we all have to face (and will be considered more in later chapters). You and I may not exactly agree on what that balance is, but perhaps we can agree that both our own and others' happiness are worthy as potential ultimate concerns.

6. Enlightened self-interest produces the greatest total happiness--the cell-organism analogy. If each person in the world intelligently assumes responsibility for his or her own happiness, then the total amount of happiness in the world will be maximized. Many people would say that this belief is naive. How can everyone be happiest if we each focus more on our own happiness? How could that ever work on such a large scale?

Consider the human body. It is composed of billions of cells. How do they function together in harmony? Each cell in the body is primarily responsible for its own health and "happiness" (harmonious functioning). It has less concern about other cells per se. However, as a subgoal to its own survival, it performs functions that are important to the health and "happiness" of other cells.

It may seem ironic that the cells--by each putting its own survival and harmonious functioning above all else--can somehow produce maximum health and happiness for the entire organism. How has this happened? The organism has evolved over millions of years into this highly integrated system of specialized cells working together as a harmonious whole. Similarly, if each human makes its own health and happiness its ultimate goal, then humankind will gradually evolve into a highly integrated "organism" that will produce the maximum happiness for all.

Consider the alternate possibility--for each person in the world to be primarily concerned with other people's happiness. Think about the following questions.

- **How do you feel about other people being primarily responsible for your happiness?**
- **How happy would everyone be if everyone sacrificed what they wanted and gave it to someone else?**

We have witnessed the collapse of communism--a system that emphasized the welfare of the collective (or state) above that of the individual. The emphasis on the group above individual happiness contributed to the lack of personal responsibility and motivation leading to communism's failure. When people focus on group responsibility, they often deny their own individual responsibility.

7. Should we make happiness a conscious goal? Many people believe that, in order to be happy, we must not make happiness a conscious goal. Instead we must make other things (such as achievement, helping others, or success) our goal, and then happiness will follow as a by-product.

Yet, it is simply not true that focusing on these goals and obtaining them will automatically lead to happiness. How many people--with more money, success, fame, and accomplishment than you or I ever will ever have--ended up miserable or even committed suicide?

Focusing on these means to happiness may have caused them to lose sight of the end of happiness. They forgot that happiness was the real end. Instead, they did whatever it took to get the money, status, and power--and were successful. The problem was that "whatever it took" undermined their happiness.

We will not make that mistake if we constantly remind ourselves that our top goal is happiness--the other goals are all means to happiness.

8. Making happiness and love top goals automatically supplies powerful motivation for actions. First, let's consider ethical acts for ourselves, such as pursuing long-term goals and taking care of our health. Do you feel more like doing something when you are doing it because you think you "should" or because you think it will make you happy?

When your brain believes that an action will make you happy, it automatically supplies powerful motivation to perform that act. You want to do it. On the other hand, rules or "shoulds" usually supply poor motivation for actions. Part of you resents doing it, because it doesn't like being controlled. Therefore, a system of ethics built on connecting ethical actions to a higher goal of happiness will be more motivating than a system of ethics built on an internalized system of rules and obligations.

Second, let's consider ethical acts for others. Do you feel more like helping someone because you know that your act will make them happier (and that would, in turn, make you happier) or because a rule tells you to do it? Similarly, do you feel less like harming someone because you know that your act would hurt them and make them unhappy (and that would make you unhappy) or because a rule tells you not to do it?

An ethical system that is based on empathy and love of others creates more motivation for respecting and helping others. In any system based on love, the emphasis is on adequately developing people's empathy and love of others. Otherwise, it will not work well either. (See Higher Self Chapter 3 for a more thorough discussion.)

> **The gift of happiness is the best gift one can give
> to both the recipient and the giver.**

9. Align your conscious goals with your biological nature and the nature of the universe. Evolution, growth, knowledge, harmony, and happiness are biologically-related phenomena built into every human being (see Chapter 7 on harmonious functioning). I believe that this coordination of good creative forces is a basic driving force of the universe. If you also believe--or even hope--that this is true, that hope gives you one more reason for making these values your conscious ultimate concerns. Creating goals of growth and happiness in our minds can help make them reality on earth.

10. Research evidence for choosing to make happiness a top goal. My research supports the proposition that making happiness as a top goal leads to being happier; having less depression, anxiety, and anger; having better relationships; being healthier; and being more successful in some ways. Out of almost 3400 people tested, making happiness a top goal correlated .45 with happiness, .22 with Low Depression, .19 with Low Anxiety, .32 with Low Anger-Aggression, .30 with Health Outcomes, and .40 with good Relationship Outcomes (Stevens, 2009). In addition, there is a great deal of evidence that people who are happier tend to be more successful in many life areas (Lyubomirsky, King, & Diener, 2005).

A NEW UNDERSTANDING FOR SOME COMMON TERMS

If we make happiness for self and others our ultimate concern, it will cause us to view life through a new set of glasses. Many of us make important goals of success, personal power, intelligence, or loving ourselves. Let's look at these common terms through our new glasses.

What is success? The dictionary defines success as "the achievement of something desired, attempted, or intended"--meeting one's goal(s). Many people in our society measure success by how much money, status, power, prestige, fame, or accomplishments a person has achieved. The media constantly bombards us with messages that say these factors are the measures of success. However, the word "success" simply means meeting one's goals-- whatever they may be. Everyone can have their own measure of success. What is yours?

I am successful to the degree that I am happy and contribute to other people's happiness. To measure your success, decide what your most important goal is. Ask yourself, "What is my ultimate concern?" Which is more important to you--money, status, power, prestige, fame, or happiness?

For me, happiness is most important. These other goals are important only to the degree that they contribute to my own and others' happiness. Therefore, I will measure how successful I am in my life by two simple measures, "How happy am I?" and "How much have I contributed to the happiness of others?"

> **If, at the end of my life, I can attain only one type of success,**
> **I would not choose success in career, friends, money, status,**
> **or any other worldly goal.**
> **For what good are these to me without happiness?**
> **If, at the end of my life, I can look back and say,**
> **"I have contributed to the happiness of others and been happy myself,"**
> **I will judge myself to have attained the most important kind of success.**

What is personal power? Let's try to understand personal power better by first looking at its opposite. A frequent complaint of clients entering therapy is that they feel weak or unsure of themselves. People often describe themselves as having low self-esteem or say that their life feels out of control. What these clients mean is that they can't control their own emotions and happiness.

I knew a multimillionaire who had a good family and friends. He had been very successful in his career and had lots of financial and social power. Yet he felt depressed for a long time, and described himself as feeling powerless.

There is a difference between my definition of personal power and society's definition of power. Society often measures power by criteria such as accomplishment, money, status, influence, or fame. By society's definition of power, Adolf Hitler was one of the most powerful men in history. He did have a huge impact on history. However, it was negative power; he was a total failure at contributing to the happiness of himself and others.

What is our *Happiness Quotient (HQ)?* In his book, *Your Erroneous Zones*, Dr. Wayne Dyer uses a concept he calls your "Happiness IQ." One well-accepted definition of intelligence is an ability to learn from experience and solve problems effectively.

Dr. Dyer points out that abilities to solve math problems or other difficult intellectual problems can be very useful. However, they are not nearly as important as the ability to solve the basic life problems necessary for finding happiness. Dr. Dyer calls this concept our "Happiness IQ" and asserts that it is the most important type of intelligence.

Salovey and Mayer's (1990) concept of *Emotional Intelligence* (EQ) also stresses the importance of learned skills for getting control of emotions. Goleman's popular book about EQ helped garner a great deal of research support. Martin Seligman, as president of the American Psychological Association (APA), renewed a *Positive Psychology* movement in our country. Seligman stressed learned optimism and other learned cognitive factors for helping individuals and society become happier and more productive (Seligman and Csikzentmihalyi, 2000). His efforts triggered a new round of positive psychological research.

Before writing the first edition of this book, my own study (Stevens, 1987) of more than 4,000 college students found that many key cognitive, self-management, and interpersonal skills correlated significantly with their happiness and other success factors. Now I use the term *Happiness Quotient (HQ)* to mathematically summarize a host of personal factors identified by our research as strongly predicative of happiness, other emotional outcomes, and some life success measures. A goal of this book is to help you increase your HQ.

When my wife Sherry read this passage about our Happiness IQ, she reminded me of a mutual friend's experience. For years Allen had led a life in which he seemed to give happiness for self and others top priority. He took time to lead a fulfilling life--balanced across many life areas. He took the time needed to "smell the roses" in each activity he participated in. Allen was successful in his career, but had not emphasized his career as much as the most successful in his field had. He was usually in a good mood and was giving toward other people. He would sometimes give even when he could not afford to. Yet he loved people and loved to give--he gave out of a desire to give and the joy it gave him. This lifestyle worked well for years.

Then Allen became involved with someone who was very ambitious for financial success. He began to feel a great deal of external and internal pressure to be more successful, make more money, and build a small empire of possessions. His mood changed dramatically during this period. He became dissatisfied with his work, his relationship, and his life. He did make a lot more money and was even more successful in his business in the short run. Yet, he got tired of the rat race and constantly fantasized about escaping.

Finally, Allen realized that he had let the means to happiness become the end. Despite his love for her, he ended the relationship because it had become unhealthy and unhappy. He put happiness back on track ahead of success and money, and once again was a happy (but wiser) man.

Focus your intelligence and energy on achieving happiness for self and others. You have a great deal of intelligence that you may never have focused on the goal of maximizing happiness. The knowledge and skills required to be successful at being happy are not innate. If your family (or others you know well) were not good role models for how to be happy, then where were you to get these skills? You can increase your Happiness Quotient (HQ) by learning from happy people, reading, therapy, and many other experiences in life.

But whomever you read or see for therapy, try to find out if they are happy persons themselves. Also, do they know about the specific areas that you most need help in? We can learn something from anyone, but we can learn most from those who know most about what we want to learn.

LOVING YOURSELF MEANS TAKING GOOD CARE OF YOURSELF

Think of a mother who loves her newborn baby. She tries to take good care of her baby by meeting all of its biological and psychological needs. This is taking good care of someone. However, many people never learn how to take good care of themselves in each life area. Loving yourself--translated into actions--means caring for all your needs and values the way a mother cares for her newborn baby.

Our happiness is determined by the satisfaction of our values. A simple but profound psychological fact is that our happiness is determined by the satisfaction of our true, inner values. By values, I include all biologically based needs and all learned needs or values (including metavalues).

If all our biological and psychological values are being met at a level that surpasses some internal criterion, then we will feel perfectly happy. (In Chapter 9, you can learn the O-PATSM self-management system for increasing the chances your values will be satisfied.)

> **PRACTICE: 1--How happy are you in each life area?** (1) Make a list of life areas (Examples: Career, College, Self, Family, Friends, Relationship, Recreation, Health, Financial, etc.) (2) For each area, rate your overall happiness from 0 to 100.
> **2--Make a happiness graph.** (1) Take a sheet of paper and draw a graph. Mark the years of your life on the horizontal axis and your degree of happiness (0-100) on the vertical axis. (2) Mark key life events on the time line. (3) Make a graph of (overall) how happy you were for each year of your life. (4) Optional. Repeat this exercise by life area--career/school, family, friends, self, etc.

SEEKING THE TRUTH FROM MANY PERSPECTIVES

The "truth will set us free." My quest for understanding the secrets of happiness led me to complete a Master's of Theology degree and a PhD in Psychology. It led me to become a licensed psychologist practicing psychotherapy, teaching, and doing research. The knowledge which I gained has helped me contribute to others' happiness, and it has helped me to find more happiness myself.

I have not accomplished great things compared to many people. I wish that I could do more. Instead, perhaps my greatest success in life--that I am most certain of--is the happiness I have achieved myself and have contributed to others.

One part of my quest for truth is that I use four major perspectives to view any issue--a spiritual-philosophical perspective, a scientific-psychological perspective, a psychotherapist's perspective, and a personal perspective. Each of these four perspectives is like the blind men who felt different parts of a giant animal. One felt a leg and thought it was a tree. One felt the trunk and thought it was a snake. And so on. Each perspective could only reveal part of the truth. Only knowing all perspectives could yield the full truth that the animal was an elephant.

In reality, there is only one truth; so, ultimately, each of the different perspectives is seeking the same underlying truth. Therefore, beliefs consistent with all four perspectives are validated more than those consistent with only one. I have attempted to include only ideas in this book that I find consistent with all four perspectives. Since writing the first edition of this book, I have also completed an extensive research study that also strongly supports these ideas.

RESULTS OF RESEARCH TESTING THIS BOOK'S IDEAS

The Success and Happiness Attributes Questionnaire (SHAQ). My previous research with the Life Skills Questionnaire (LSQ) and Stevens Relationship Questionnaire (SRQ) was a partial basis for ideas in the first edition of this book (Stevens, 1987; Stevens and Stevens, 1995). Though I received many emails telling how much the book had helped people, I wanted to more thoroughly test its contents. So I developed a free online questionnaire, the Success and Happiness Attributes Questionnaire (SHAQ). I systematically went through each chapter, taking each main idea, and turning it into questions. Thus, SHAQ is able to test the ideas in this book in a detailed way rarely found in other self-help books.

SHAQ is also used as a self-development tool and can be coordinated with the book contents so readers can get feedback about their progress and improve individual personal attributes and their overall Happiness Quotient (HQ).

This book assumes a cognitive systems model of personality and emphasizes the importance of *learned-controllable* cognitions (values, beliefs, knowledge, thoughts, and skills). I (and many other psychologists) believe that our cognitions are the primary causes of both our emotions and our behavior. Happiness and success of all kinds are determined by a combination of three basic types of causes. 1-cognitive/learned, 2-environmental/conditional, and 3-hereditary/genetic factors. The first two types are the most controllable.[2] In the next chapter, I will call these factors internal and external routes to happiness. SHAQ can help readers get specific feedback and advice about these cognitive learned HQ factors.

Who took SHAQ? When I analyzed this data, more than 3400 users had taken SHAQ on the Internet (free). They were a diverse group with a wide variety of ages, occupations, locations (27% outside the U.S.), ethnic groups, religions, and other factors. When asked what they wanted from SHAQ, 72% wanted to learn more about themselves and 63% said they wanted help with a problem.

The SHAQ scales. SHAQ is composed of 81 scales and subscales consisting of those questions taken directly from statements in this book. For example the chapter on self-worth and self-confidence is represented by two scales—one with each name. Each of the nine Self-Development Plan parts listed in the box below is represented by one or more SHAQ scales.

What was tested—the happiness and success outcome scales. I wanted to test how specific values, beliefs, and skills taught in this book are related to people's happiness and success. To assess happiness and success outcomes I created the following scales: Overall Happiness, Low Depression, Low Anxiety, Low Anger, Relationship Outcomes, and Health Outcomes.[3] The highest personal income and academic achievement measures were also used.

---

[2] Medications can have diverse, generalized, and often unknown effects; and can be helpful with some problems such as severe depression or severe anxiety.

[3] **NOTES:** The **Overall Happiness scale** measures happiness in each life area and for the past, present, and expected future. The **Low Depression** and **Low Anxiety** scales measure depression or anxiety-related feelings and thoughts, amount of therapy and medication for depression or anxiety, and questions related to official psychiatric diagnoses of Depression and Anxiety (from the DSM-IV). Since I want a high score on all scales to indicate a desirable score, I scored the negative emotion scales in reverse. The **"Low" label** means the scales were scored in reverse: a person with low Anxiety would receive a high "Low Anxiety" scale score. The **Low Anger-Aggression** scale includes anger-related feelings and thoughts and aggressive acts. The **Health Outcomes** scale includes frequencies of illness; drug, cigarette, and alcohol use; low weight, and physical conditioning (negative items were scored in reverse). The ***Relationship Outcomes*** scale measures marital/romantic relationship and friendship success.

Understanding the meaning of correlations and predictive power. For those who aren't familiar with research or correlations, let me explain. Correlations range from 0 to 1.00. Zero means no relationship between two variables and 1.00 means a perfect relationship. For example the correlation between flipping a switch and the light going on would be near 1.00, because when the switch is up, the light is on and when down, off.

The correlation *squared* (R^2) measures the *amount of effect* or *degree of predictive power* (*EffectSize*). The light switch position might predict 99% of the time whether the light was on or off (EffectSize = .99). Another example is that some people think that IQ scores are about 40% caused by hereditary and 60% caused by learning/environmental factors (of a possible total effect of 100%). If that were true then the 40% causation by heredity would equal an EffectSize of 0.40 and the 60% causation by learning/environment EffectSize = 0.60.[4]

The Happiness Quotient (HQ) as a Predictor of Happiness

What if you could combine the predictive power of all of the SHAQ scales together to predict people's chances of being happy and successful? I created the Happiness Quotient (HQ) to mathematically combine all SHAQ's scales. The HQ yields a score analogous to an IQ score (which measures intelligence). The research results show that the SHAQ-based HQ is a powerful predictor of happiness, depression, anxiety, and anger. SHAQ users can obtain their HQ score free on my website and improve it by reading this book.

Evidence that *You Can Choose To Be Happy*

I used a combined score[5] similar to the HQ score to test SHAQ's (and the book's) overall predictive power. The SHAQ scales had moderate to high positive correlations with almost all outcome measures. SHAQ's scales had surprisingly high correlations with the emotional outcomes. SHAQ's 56 subscales correlated with *Overall Happiness*, R = .87. SHAQ's EffectSize of .75 means SHAQ can predict Overall Happiness with about 75% accuracy. That high degree of predictive power is very unusual for psychological factors and supports the book's premise that happiness is largely determined by learnable cognitive factors. You *can* choose to be happy! SHAQ also correlated with *Low Depression,* .73 (EffectSize, .53); with *Low Anxiety*, .67 (EffectSize, .43); and with *Low Anger-Aggression*, .70 (EffectSize, .49). These numbers are also high for psychological research.

Some people believe that they cannot choose to be happy. They think that biological or environmental factors are so powerful, they cannot influence their own emotions. That belief alone can become a self-fulfilling prophesy—helping doom them to unhappiness. Our evidence strongly contradicts their belief.

No one can be happy all the time. However, we can all choose to *maximize* our happiness—given our unique biological and environmental situations. Thus, we can all choose to be happy and then try our best to maximize our happiness. You may truly not know how to influence your own happiness right now. However, you can *learn* how to maximize your happiness—as many others have. This learning strengthens your cognitive system and gives it more control over your emotions. Read this book and apply what you learn! The evidence

---

[4] To find the EffectSize or predictive power of any correlation, find the mathematical square (R Square or R^2) of the correlation. **NOTE:** Often the sum of several predictor variables' correlations with an outcome variable is greater than 1.0 because the predictor variables correlate with each other. They *share* some of predictive power. I will use the term "*EffectSize*" instead of "*R Square*".

[5] The scales were mathematically combined using a linear regression equation such as 3x + 2z to predict y. In this case the dependent variable "y" is actually an outcome variable such as happiness and the x and z predictor variables are variables such as "Positive World View" or "Self-Worth." The "weights" 2 and 3 are examples only. The actual values were determined mathematically by a regression analysis.

from SHAQ strongly supports these statements, as does evidence from many other sources.

Relationship of SHAQ Scales to Success in Relationships and Health

SHAQ's correlation with the Relationship Outcomes scale was .69. The predictive power (EffectSize) was 47%. The factors identified in this book that make people happier also tend to help them have better relationships, which in turn help people be happier.

SHAQ correlated with the Health Outcomes Scale R = .82. The predictive power (EffectSize) was 67%. So the implication is that living by the same factors that make you happier also makes your healthier!

SHAQ's Predictive Power for Income and Academic Success

For the users over age 25 completing all of SHAQ *including* the learning-academic scales, the SHAQ correlation with highest personal income was .62 and the predictive power (EffectSize) was 38%. The correlation with highest education completed was .58 and the predictive power, 34%. SHAQ correlated with college grade point average (GPA),.56; the predictive power was 32%. Learning motivation and skills were particularly important factors for predicting both highest personal income and educational achievement.[6]

So while SHAQ was not as good predicting income and academic success as it was emotional, health, and relationship outcomes; it was still a good predictor and better than most found in other research.

Summary: the factors identified in this book proved to be strong predictors of happiness, health, and success. Several thousand correlations were computed in this study, which in some respects is one of the most comprehensive studies ever undertaken on the relationship between cognitive factors and human emotions. SHAQ's non-academic scales consist of 71 independent scales-subscales.[7]

Of the several thousand correlations computed, almost every one was statistically significant in the direction predicted by this book—a remarkable consistency not often found in research. The size and predictive power of the relationships was surprisingly high--even to me.

In each chapter, I will summarize research results for the scale(s) developed from that chapter's contents. You may want to complete SHAQ yourself (free) to test yourself as a pretest *before* you read this book. You may view my paper describing this research study in detail on my website (Stevens, 2009).

CHOOSE TO LEARN AND BE HAPPY WHILE READING THIS BOOK

When you are reading--even something that you enjoy--do you sometimes bog down in the material? Do some parts seem too confusing or too boring? In later chapters, I discuss the concept of harmonious functioning. These chapters tell how to get "in the zone" of optimal interest and learning.

If you feel confused. You are only learning at a good rate if you are feeling interested. If you are feeling confused, then the input may be too overwhelming for your ability to process it. Your current thinking method cannot organize the input material well enough. Many people keep reading when they are confused and only compound their confusion. Others think that they are stupid when they feel confused. Some get angry and "turn off" out of frustration,

---

[6] Alone they correlated .37 with income, .36 with highest education completed, and .45 with college GPA.

[7] There are 11 value scales, 5 general belief scales (19 subscales), 3 knowledge skill scales (17 subscales), 9 interpersonal beliefs-skills scales, and 14 learning skills-academic success scales.

blaming their confusion on the book.

Confusion is a healthy part of everyone's natural learning and growth process. Our confusion can be like a door. Opening the door and looking at what our confusion is about will create learning. Letting the door remain closed and continuing to read in a confused state (or giving up) will just increase our confusion and lower our opinion of ourselves.

Instead, if you feel confused, immediately stop reading. Ask yourself questions. What you are confused about? Try to answer the questions. Break your confusion into parts. Relate examples in your own life to ideas in the book--a light may switch on.

If you feel bored. Boredom results from too little input and stimulation. We are bored if we're not learning anything new or useful. If you feel bored while reading, skim or find creative uses. However, boredom is often a result of confusion. If we "give up" or "turn off" because we don't understand something, and become bored. In that case, redouble efforts to understand.

Even if a book or speaker seems confusing or boring, *you* are responsible for processing the information so that you can maximize your growth and enjoyment. Blaming the speaker or book will just keep you from growing.

Using what you learn from this book. You may already know many keys to happiness and be using them in your life. Validating and reasserting the importance of these ideas is an important process. When you get a new insight, begin experimenting with it immediately-- before you lose it. Immerse yourself in your new ideas and behaviors. Experiment, practice, and play with them in as many situations as you can. Find their strengths and weaknesses. Discuss them with other people you respect. Write your own beliefs and guidelines as I wrote my original, "How To Be Happy" years ago that started my life on a new path. Or, keep a journal of your experiences.

THE YOU CAN CHOOSE TO BE HAPPY SELF-DEVELOPMENT PLAN

Immersion is the key to profound growth. Learning and happiness--like life--are not static entities, they are dynamic processes. I designed this book to be a step-by-step self-development plan for achieving greater happiness and self-actualization. In this chapter, I provided an overview of the concepts of happiness and self-actualization. I also suggested a most important step--that you make values like happiness, growth, love, and truth your ultimate concerns.

Next. In the next chapter, you will learn some basic routes to happiness and learn a process for discovering the deeper causes of unhappiness. Study the *You Can Choose To Be Happy Self-Development Plan* in the box to get an overview of how you can learn the key elements of controlling your own happiness.

The promise that I make you is this. I believe it is possible to find at least one route to happiness in almost any situation. If you will learn and follow the ideas in this book well, then you can choose to be happy--in almost any situation and in your overall life.

The You Can Choose To Be Happy
Self-Development Plan

1. MAKE HAPPINESS FOR SELF AND OTHERS A TOP GOAL (along with love, truth, growth, health, integrity, and other timeless values that go hand-in-hand with happiness.) Avoid becoming *overly attached* to any one *particular* goal, person, or condition. *Take responsibility for your own happiness.* Learn to choose both internal and external routes to happiness. (Chapters 1, 2)

2. LEARN HOW TO FIND AND SOLVE DEEP CAUSES OF UNHAPPINESS. Learn the self-exploration process to use in following chapters to root out dysfunctional beliefs and replace them with happiness-inducing ones. (Chapters 2 and 3)

3. DEVELOP YOUR HIGHER SELF. Your Higher Self is your "Inner Conductor" or "Inner Hero" that loves unconditionally. *Seek empathy and balance.* Learn to understand and respect each point-of-view of each inner part of yourself. Seek the same deep empathy for others. Develop a strong, positive philosophy to guide your life. (Chapter 3)

4. CREATE A POSITIVE WORLD BY ADOPTING A POSITIVE WORLD VIEW. Develop a realistic, positive world view. Overcome your greatest fears, and learn that you can be happy in any situation. Then you can face each day with peace and confidence. Discover a rock-solid basis for optimism. Overcome deficit motivation--instead learn *abundance thinking.* Learn to hope for the best, be prepared for the worst, expect something between, and be grateful for all that you receive. (Chapter 4)

5. DEVELOP GREATER SELF-WORTH AND SELF-CONFIDENCE. *Learn to love yourself and others unconditionally.* Learn to accept all parts of yourself and overcome negative self-beliefs. Learn the causes of low self-confidence and how you can improve it. (Chapter 5)

6. REPLACE EXTERNAL CONTROL WITH INTERNAL CONTROL. Overcome too much dependence on others, need for others, or worry about what others think. Learn to improve relationships by being more internally controlled, intimate, and assertive. (Chapter 6)

7. LEARN HOW HARMONIOUS FUNCTIONING PRODUCES PEAK LEARNING, PERFORMANCE, AND HAPPINESS. The harmonious functioning model is a breakthrough for understanding the basic causes of emotions and motivation. Learn what it takes to get "in the zone" of harmonious functioning. (Chapter 7)

8. LEARN THE SIX "CHUG-OF" MENTAL CONTROL STRATEGIES to achieve harmonious functioning and rise above anxiety, anger, and depression. Learn how to adjust your emotions like a thermostat. These six powerful strategies--based on the harmonious functioning model--will increase your *Happiness Quotient (HQ) so you can choose to be happy.* (Chapter 8)

9. CREATE A BETTER WORLD FOR YOURSELF AND OTHERS. Learn the well-tested **O-PATSM** system to accomplish your goals and get control of your life. This system focuses on *external routes to happiness*--how you can get more control of your time, your actions, and the world around you. (Chapter 9)

Read the book in order (Chapters 1-9) to follow this plan. However, you may use it as a reference book and read individual chapters in any order you please. Chapter 10 is a summary of the SHAQ research and book conclusions.

Happiness is a measure
of the overall health, growth, and harmony of the entire body and mind.
Happiness also reflects
our perception of the harmony and functioning of the external world.
The biological happiness mechanism has
safeguards against lack of concern about other people
and lack of concern about the future.
To make happiness our ultimate concern in life
is to align our conscious ultimate concern
with the most basic human motives and universal forces.
If we all seek happiness for self and others,
humankind can evolve into a highly integrated organism
that will maximize the happiness for all.

A note for Christians and others

The Intimate Connection between Love and Happiness
and
the "Two Great Commandments"

And one of them, a lawyer, asked [Jesus] a question, to test him,
"Teacher, which is the greatest commandment in the law?"
And he said to him,
"You shall love the Lord your God with all your heart,
and with all your soul, and with all your mind.
This is the great and first commandment. And a second is like it,
You shall love your neighbor as yourself.
On these two commandments
depend all the law and the prophets."
Matthew 23: 35-40

Ask a mother, who loves her child unconditionally,
what she wants *most* for that child.
She will likely say, "I want my child to lead a long and happy life."
Is it not true that
if you love someone, you value their happiness above all?

And,
when you are filled with love,
does not that warm feeling of love fill you with happiness?

Also consider:
If you believe in a God,
could you believe that God's love for you,
is inferior to a mother's love of her child?
And,
if you think about how God created the universe and
how much He loves you and wants you to be happy,
are you not filled with love for God?
[The first great commandment]

Isn't choosing to make your own and others' happiness a top goal
the same as "loving others as you love yourself"?
[The second great commandment]

CHAPTER 2

WE CAN CHOOSE TO BE HAPPY:

INTERNAL AND EXTERNAL ROUTES TO HAPPINESS

\\\

DO YOUR EMOTIONS SEEM TO HAVE A "MIND OF THEIR OWN"?

Do you sometimes say things like, "I can't help how I feel," "This stresses me out," "She makes me angry," or "You can't change how you feel." Are there times when you try your best to change how you feel, but fail? Does it seem like you've done everything that *should* make you happy, but somehow you are still not happy?

We all have experiences like these--in which our emotions seem to have a mind of their own. It is as if our emotions are being controlled by hidden, mysterious forces.

If you believe that you can't control your own feelings, then you may be partly right. You may be right in that (1) we all have limited control of our emotions, and (2) you have never learned all the tools for consciously controlling your emotions.

WE CAN CHOOSE TO BE HAPPY NOW

I used to believe that we had no control over our emotions, and I wasn't too good at controlling my own. But shortly after I made my commitment to experiment with making happiness my ultimate concern, that commitment had its first test. That night my father had taken my brother, Ron, and I on a drive around Phoenix. Dad stopped and told my brother and I to wait in the car while he went into a friend's house to "talk for a minute." Ron and I looked at each other wondering how long "a minute" would be. Thirty minutes later my brother and I were getting angry at dad for being so inconsiderate. We took turns reminding ourselves of all the times dad had been inconsiderate and making sarcastic comments. With each statement and accusing thought we made ourselves angrier and angrier.

Suddenly, I remembered my decision to feel as happy as possible. I realized that I was definitely not happy when I was feeling angry. For the first time in my life, I realized that my anger was hurting me more than it was hurting the person I was angry at. I realized that my father was probably in the house having a good time while I was in the car feeling miserable. That was *not* a happy thought.

So I just *decided* to feel happier. I stopped thinking the angry thoughts about my father and began to focus on the trees, stars, and beauty of the night. I also told my brother about this approach and it helped him feel better too. By the time my dad came back, I was quite happy.

Another amazing thing happened. When dad finally returned and saw that we were not angry, he was quite apologetic--a rare event indeed. Now, I realize that my positive attitude probably kept him from being defensive and gave him the space he needed to apologize.

Are you someone who doubts your ability to control your own emotions and "choose how you feel"? If so, you may be better at controlling your emotions than you think. For example, if you are feeling bad about a problem and you (1) consciously decide to think about the problem and (2) are successful in solving the problem, then you immediately feel better. Conscious problem-solving is only one of many internal routes to happiness.

> **PRACTICE: What has worked to get more control of your thoughts and feelings?** Think of a situation in which you were upset, yet it was important to appear to be happy or to make a good impression with someone. Were you able to get yourself to actually feel better? How did you do it? You must have chosen thoughts that would help you get into the right mood. You chose to feel better by choosing thoughts that would affect your emotions. In the "Sound of Music," Maria "thought of her favorite things" when she wanted to feel better.

EMOTIONS ARE CONTROLLED MORE BY THOUGHTS THAN BY EXTERNAL EVENTS

Just how powerful can choice of thoughts be for overcoming a negative environment? What is the worst negative environment you can imagine?

Wouldn't living in a Nazi concentration camp be about as bad as any you can imagine? In his classic book, *Man's Search For Meaning*, Victor Frankl described how he survived Auschwitz when most others died. He lived in a bleak, filthy barrack on the verge of starvation--in constant pain from hunger or wounds. Daily, he performed backbreaking, menial work and witnessed the guards--and other prisoners--perform incredibly inhuman and sadistic acts. Many prisoners became animals--who would do anything to survive.

Many prisoners could not tolerate this environment and died. Dr. Frankl wrote that the key survival factor was the *will to live,* and that whenever someone lost that will, he would die shortly thereafter. Many "ran into the wire" of the electric fence to end their misery. Others became ill. Some simply became immobilized in a catatonic state until they died.

Dr. Frankl kept both his life and his humanity. His survival secret was *to create his own positive inner world.* He created a fantasy life with his wife and spent many hours in their imaginary life together outside the camp. Listen to the words of a man who overcame one of history's most inhumane situations.

The salvation of man is through love and in love.
I understood how a man who has nothing left in this world
still may know bliss, be it only for a brief moment,
in the contemplation of his beloved. . .
Had I known then that my wife was dead,
I think that I would still have given myself,
undisturbed by that knowledge, to the contemplation of her image, and
that my mental conversation with her would have been just as vivid
and just as satisfying. . .love is as strong as death. (p. 61)

Dr. Frankl found that concentration on other higher, mental values also created happiness.

As the inner life of the prisoner tended to become more intense,
he also experienced the beauty of art and nature as never before.
Under their influence he sometimes
even forgot his frightful circumstance.

This positive spirit was contagious. Feeling good himself helped him care more for others. Whereas many prisoners were cruel to each other, Dr. Frankl performed many acts of kindness. These acts added happiness.

How many of us--facing far less difficult situations than Victor Frankl--are tempted to give up? Reminding myself of Frankl's situation helps me put my own problems in perspective. If he could choose to live by higher values and choose to be happy in that environment, surely, we can choose to be happy in almost any circumstance.

Changing feelings is different from *denying* feelings. We all know of people who pretend to be happy or put on a happy face for others when they are really unhappy inside. We may do that ourselves. We also know of people who *deny* their negative feelings. I remember a client who was red-faced and so tense from his anger that he was about to squeeze the chair arms in two. He looked straight at his wife and between gritted teeth said, "I am *not* angry."

He was not only trying to fool her, but he was also trying to fool himself. He truly seemed to be unaware of his own anger at the time. He had shut off the focus of his attention from all of the internal bodily sensations such as the tenseness and rapid heart rate that were giving him feedback that he was angry. This is a good example of *denying feelings*. Denial is unhealthy because it robs us of valuable information that we can use to understand a problem.

To *change our feelings* from negative to positive, we need to first recognize, understand, and accept the negative feeling. That is step one. Step two is to find out what is behind the feeling and then try to find ways of changing those feelings. Simply *pretending* that we do not feel what we feel is not usually adequate to overcome the negative feelings.

Years ago, my wife, Sherry, thought that trying to control emotions by changing thoughts was a superficial change method that was similar to denying how we really feel. I will let her speak for herself,

I used to believe that feelings were something that just happened to you.
I thought that you had no control over them and
"you just feel how you feel."
I believed that people who thought that you could "choose how you feel"
were operating "out of their heads" not "out of their hearts."
I knew that for the most part I was a happy person, but I didn't believe that I was
continually making choices and thinking thoughts
which *caused* my happiness or unhappiness.
Part of the reason was that I was *not consciously* thinking about whether or not my
thoughts or choices would make me happy.
As I continued to grow and feel more in control of my life, I gradually realized that I
am continually making choices every moment of my life.
I noticed how these choices of my thoughts and actions had direct effects on my
happiness. Sometimes, it was easy to find an alternative that immediately
caused me to feel happy.
At other times, I had to work through the sadness or anxiety,
and resolve underlying problems before I could feel happier.
In either case, knowing that
I can choose to be happy at almost any time--
even when I am feeling very bad--
gives me a feeling of inner strength I never had before.

Even though we can *choose* to be happy in any situation, it is not always easy to *be* happy. We need the right beliefs and tools for finding happiness. No one tool will work for all situations--we need many. This chapter will give you some basic tools; but to fill your toolbox, you must read the entire book.

How we choose to *react* to upsetting emotions has a major effect on our happiness. When you feel upset what are your most likely responses? Do you eat, drink, blame it on someone else, withdraw, avoid dealing with it, or just worry? Or, do you make better emotional coping responses such as solving the problem, discussing it, giving yourself a pep talk, or taking constructive action to help yourself feel better? The *emotional coping scale* first used on the Life Skills Questionnaire and later on SHAQ contains both negative and positive coping responses.

The Life Skills Questionnaire (LSQ) was my first questionnaire to study the relationship between thinking/learning, self-management, and interpersonal skills on life outcomes like success in college, career, and personal life. Over a four-year period, it was given to more than 4,000 college students and 385 people established in the community (Stevens,1986). Some of the conclusions in the first edition of this book were partially based upon the research using the LSQ. SHAQ incorporated most of the LSQ items.

Overall, the LSQ was quite successful at predicting outcomes–especially happiness. One of the most interesting findings was how strongly the *Emotional Coping Skills scale* correlated with life success. The correlation between the coping score and overall grade point average was .25. That's almost as good a predictor as college aptitude test scores such as the SAT! Higher scorers also tended to have more and happier close relationships. The correlation with happiness in various life areas was as follows: as a student, .45; in job and career, .41; in sexual relationship, .31; in friendships, .40; in family, .42. The correlation with *overall happiness in their life* for the past three years was .57. I believe that this data speaks for itself! *How we typically react when we feel upset has a powerful effect on our overall happiness and success in life.* We found very similar results with SHAQ's Emotional Coping scale about 15 years later (see later in chapter).

RESTATE "HELPLESSNESS" LANGUAGE INTO "CHOICE" LANGUAGE

Our speech habits often reveal important underlying beliefs affecting our happiness. Our speech habits not only *reveal* deep, inner aspects of us, but they also *change* important beliefs. We may use excuses that we are too stressed, too tired, or too busy to do something, when we actually just do *not want* to do it. The subtle, hidden message in that excuse is that "I cannot get control of my emotions--I am too weak or helpless."

These hidden messages have two major effects. First, they will affect *others'* beliefs about us. Others may believe that we are weak and helpless and treat us that way. Second--and even more importantly--we may believe the hidden messages ourselves. We may become more convinced that we actually are weak and helpless--thereby undermining our self-esteem.

In addition, a belief that our emotions are out of control contributes to anxiety and depression. We can stop undermining our self-esteem and self-confidence by monitoring our language. We can stop using "helplessness" language and start using "choice" language. Choice language is based on underlying beliefs such as the following.
- "I can make choices that determine how I feel."
- "We are responsible for our own emotions."
- "I can be honest with myself and others I trust."

"HELPLESSNESS" LANGUAGE => CONVERTED TO => "CHOICE" LANGUAGE

Replace: "I can't help how I feel." or "This stresses me out."
With: "I take responsibility for my own feelings" or
              "I can get control of my emotions."

Replace: "He/she/it makes me angry." "He/she/it makes me feel . . ."
With: "When he/she does . . . , I choose to think_____,
              and that causes me to feel . . . ."

Replace: "I'm too [tired, stressed, upset, depressed] to . . ."
With: "I do not want to . . . at this time." or
              "I could get myself in the mood to . . . if I choose."

In the box above are some examples of how we can transform helplessness language into choice language. During the next few days make a special effort to observe your own and other people's speech patterns. See how many people don't think they can control their emotions. Try to convert your own speech habits into "choice" language.

ROUTES TO HAPPINESS

Sometimes we may think that a situation is hopeless. We may believe that we are in a situation for which no routes to happiness exist. I have seen many people who feel little hope and believe that there is no way out. The problem is not that a route to happiness doesn't exist; the problem is *how they view the situation*. Following is one such case.

My client was talking of killing herself. She said that she could not think of any reason to live, because she had been depressed and unhappy for so long that she was sick of it. She thought that her life would only get worse. She had no hope for the future. To her there were no routes to happiness open to her--only routes to despair.

Why was this woman--who was young, attractive, intelligent, healthy, and living in a society full of opportunities--so depressed and pessimistic about her future while another client--who had cancer and was facing a high probability of death--felt happy and hopeful about the future?

The client with cancer had found routes to happiness and the other had not. It was my job to help the depressed client find her own paths to happiness. A new belief that she could find more *controllable* worthwhile goals and happiness gave her a renewed sense of meaning, control, and hope. Getting her more involved in activities with higher *immediate payoffs* also helped--these included music, reading, centering, appreciating beauty, decorating, getting chores done, talking to old friends, and biking.

WE HAVE MANY ROUTES TO HAPPINESS--WE ARE NEVER HELPLESS

An important underlying cause of hopelessness, powerlessness, and depression is a *belief that we cannot find any possible route to happiness*. Do you ever think that you *have no choice* except a path that will make you unhappy? The next time you feel trapped, unhappy, or depressed ask yourself, "Am I assuming that I can't find one route to happiness in this situation?" "Am I assuming that I have *no choice* but to be unhappy in this situation?"

Challenge that "no choice" belief. Tell yourself that *no matter what the situation is, you have many routes to happiness!* Perhaps you have not yet found those routes. However, someone in this world has learned how to create happiness in a similar--or even worse--situation. *How* did he or she do it?

Once you believe that you can achieve happiness in that situation, that belief will give you *hope*. Hope will allow you to start looking for new, creative routes to happiness that you may have previously overlooked.

Seek happiness and you will find it. This is a positive self-fulfilling prophesy. It is amazing how many people have never valued their own happiness highly and have never learned *how* to play, have fun, or create happiness.

Seeking happiness is partly choosing to find interesting things to do, but it is mostly a mental skill--learning how to make *every* activity as interesting and fun as it can be. The more we begin to look for creative ways of generating interest and enjoying ourselves in difficult or unpleasant situations, the more skilled we become. I have seen people learn how to be happy in many "impossible" situations.

One of my own pet peeves has been standing in lines or waiting. I used to get irritated and upset when I had to wait too long and thought about how I was wasting my time. Once I realized that I was responsible for my own happiness--even when waiting in a line or in the doctor's office--I decided to take control of that time and use it productively for myself or for working.

I realized that the time was only wasted if I chose to remain unhappy. Now, I usually take a book with me if I anticipate a wait. If I have no reading materials, I begin thinking of something enjoyable or begin thinking about something that will add to my life or my work. The time is no longer wasted because I no longer choose to waste it.

**Knowing that there are many potential routes to happiness
for every one of us--
no matter what the situation is--
gives us hope and strength to face any uncertainties about the future.**

EXTERNAL ROUTES TO HAPPINESS

We have both external and internal routes to happiness. External routes to happiness include any actions that *utilize our external environment* to contribute to our happiness. In a typical day, we take many actions like eating breakfast, talking with family members, working, playing golf, or going to bed. These actions *generate external effects* that, in turn, *affect our internal world*. It is as if we use the external world as a mediator between our actions and our senses so that we can achieve more desirable internal states.

Our happiness is dependent upon the *satisfaction of our values*--current and anticipated. The most common way to satisfy our values and find happiness is through external routes to happiness. If we are hungry, we eat and satisfy that hunger. If we want the love and fun of a friendship, then we can be a friend to others.

We can set goals, plan, and take actions to get money, friends, material goods, or the job we want. Or, an activity may provide interest and fun in itself. By choosing to do that activity, we get immediate increased happiness. Many of us are so focused on these external routes to happiness that we may even assume that they are the *only routes to happiness*.

ROUTES TO HAPPINESS
Think of this diagram to choose to be happy

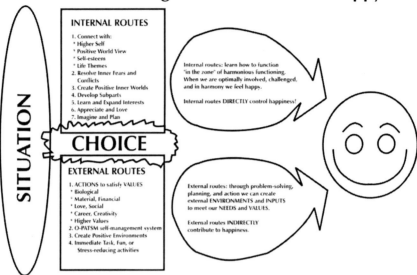

In ANY situation, we have
MANY INTERNAL AND EXTERNAL ROUTES TO HAPPINESS!

Our Western culture emphasizes these external routes to happiness. Indeed, they are important! They produce our food; build our houses, schools, and factories; they give us art, music, and philosophy; and they give us our family, friends, and lovers. Developing our knowledge and skills to use these external routes can lay a strong foundation for happiness.

However, think of the famous people who have "had it all"--yet killed themselves. Why would someone with more money, popularity, sexual prowess, and success than you or I will ever have kill themselves? To be maximally happy, we cannot depend exclusively upon these external routes. We must achieve inner harmony to be happy. No amount of external goods or success will ensure internal harmony.

While many who "have it all" are unhappy, others--like my client fighting for her life against cancer--achieve happiness with limited external resources. How can she be happier than the person who has so much?

How can we be happy when the external world is *not* to our liking? What happens when we *don't* have the resources to get what we want? Sometimes we fail no matter how hard we try. What happens when we lose something or someone we love dearly? In some cases, internal routes to happiness may be our *only* means to finding happiness.

Creating our own worlds. To the degree that we cannot find or obtain environments we want, we can strive to create them ourselves. Dr. McFerrin Stowe once said that no matter how inhospitable or crazy the world may seem, and no matter how badly others may treat you, it is possible to create your own world that reflects your own values. For example, in your family the husband can be treated like a king, the wife can be treated like a queen, and the children can be treated like princes and princesses. Each person can treat the others as if they are the most important people in the world. Even if you came from a family that was more like hell than heaven, you can make your own little version of heaven right here on earth-- even alone in your own home and daily life.

INTERNAL ROUTES TO HAPPINESS

Victor Frankl lived in worse conditions than hopefully any of us will ever be exposed to. He spent several years in Auschwitz and similar camps. Many "realists" would have said to Frankl that he had no hope. Yet Frankl chose to live. He considered death, but believed that life was too precious to give up so easily. He quoted Nietzsche,

"That which does not kill me makes me stronger."

Once he chose to live, then he chose to live life as positively as possible. He had few external routes to happiness available, so he focused upon internal routes. Victor Frankl *developed a positive inner world* to overcome the terrible external conditions at Auschwitz. He knew that he was creating mental images that were a fantasy. Yet spending hours each day creating thoughts and a complex and positive inner world made his life interesting and even enjoyable for much of his day.

This rich inner life helped him survive, and also allowed him to create a more positive world for others. He not only helped those in the death camp, but his books have helped millions more since then. What if he had given up instead?

Whose way was the most rational? The "realists," who focused on the reality of the terrible conditions in their environment and died--or Dr. Frankl who developed fantasies and survived. After the war, Dr. Frankl led a very successful and happy life. After the war, the "realists" were still dead.

If we look at the lives of the happiest people and the people who have had the biggest impacts on the world, we usually find that they were *not* "realists" in the sense that they saw *only what was there* in their world. Instead, they were dreamers who first created a mental image that was better than the image they saw in the external world.

Developing positive internal worlds not only gives us direction, but it gives us positive feelings and energy to move in that direction. Our positiveness and enthusiasm can also help motivate others. Even if we believe that we have little hope of ever making that image a reality, the image can still enrich our lives the way Victor Frankl's image enriched his.

Some major internal routes to happiness. Internal routes to happiness can include almost any mental activity--from appreciating a tree or enjoying music to contemplating life. We can learn new beliefs, skills, or habits which can dramatically affect our personal power and happiness. We have seen how making happiness a conscious top goal is important. Awareness that each choice we make affects our happiness is also important.

We have less control over our environment and people in our lives than over our own thoughts, actions, and emotions. Of these, the most important is our thoughts--for they have most control over our emotions and actions.

WHAT DOES RESEARCH SAY ABOUT THE CAUSES OF HAPPINESS?

In his book, *The Pursuit of Happiness.* Dr. David Myers reviewed a wealth of research about the causes of happiness. What were his conclusions?

So far, we identified things that matter surprisingly little. Happiness is similarly available to those of any age, gender, race, location, education, even to those with a tragic disability. We have pondered things that do matter-- physical fitness, renewing sleep and periodic solitude, traits such as self-esteem, sense of personal control, optimism, and extroversion; work and other activities that enhance our identity and absorb us into flow; close, supportive friendships and marriages.

Along the way, we have exposed falsehoods, most notably the idea that more money, and the pleasures and possessions it buys will make middle-class people happier.

Dr. Myers also points out how important one's more general beliefs--such as their religious beliefs--can be for determining happiness. He points out that evidence supports the idea that people who genuinely care for others and act altruistically are happier than people who are too self-centered. He quotes a Gallup survey that concluded "The highly spiritual were *twice* as likely to say they were 'very happy.'"

My own (and others; Howell & Howell, 2008) research has come to similar conclusions about income—our correlations were nearly zero with happiness in developed countries. Happiness is most determined by the cognitive factors described in this book--Internally Centered and Higher Self Values, Positive World View, Self-Worth and Self-Confidence, Internal Control, Good Emotional Coping, Self-Management Skills, and Assertive Interpersonal Skills. These factors were also strongly related to low depression, low anxiety, and low anger. They were also associated with good relationships and career success.[8] See Stevens, 2009, for detailed results—and keep reading this book.

Most of us fail to notice the obvious connection between our thoughts and our emotions. We make no attempt to discover or understand the hidden mental structures that generate those thoughts. Yet, these underlying mental structures are at the heart of our personal power and happiness. If you want to be happy--especially in the long run--explore and develop these important parts of yourself.

• **Develop your HIGHER SELF**--that part of yourself that unconditionally loves you and others.

• **Develop a POSITIVE WORLD VIEW.** Learn to feel gratitude for all you are given, and learn to accept (feel calm about) all aspects of life--even the most frightening.

---

[8] **Correlations between SHAQ main scales and emotional outcomes.**

Scale	Happiness	LowDepression	LowAnxiety	LowAnger
"Higher" IC Values	.546	.318	.264	.416
Ethics-Related Beliefs	.459	.442	.362	.306
Positive World View	.720	.549	.468	.420
Internal-Ext Control	.492	.420	.462	.421
Self-Worth	.585	.446	.420	.484
Self-Confidence	.691	.462	.427	.381
Self-Management	.655	.396	.315	.379
Emotional Coping	.662	.601	.510	.491
Interpersonal Skills	.591	.492	.457	..417

Note: All correlations significant at $p < .0001$ level. All N's > 3000 except Self-Man > 1700.

• **Develop your positive LIFE THEMES and ROLES**--and learn to overcome old negative ones. Develop good role models, self-expectations, and goals for every role in your career, family, groups, or play.

• **Resolve inner conflicts**--that underlie your daily negative emotions.

• **Create INNER WORLDS and PLANS**--create visions in your mind as a first step toward creating both internal and external reality.

• **Learn, think, and problem-solve**--keep expanding your mind. Involve it in interesting and challenging activities. Keep learning and growing in a variety of interest areas. Keep growing as a person. Optimal challenge and growth underlie happiness.

➔ Each of these above internal routes will be addressed in later chapters.

LIFE AS A JOURNEY WITH MANY ROUTES TO HAPPINESS

Life is a journey through time and space. In this journey, we are explorers, and each of us finds our own unique path. In our own private journeys we will visit many places-- some happy and some not. *Our goal is to learn, create, and be as happy as possible.*

If we focus on continual learning and growth, we will increase our abilities to understand life, to harness our emotions, to enjoy our time alone, to develop intensely satisfying relationships, and to create productive careers. The traveler who not only travels--but learns *about* traveling--will not only live, but will live well. This traveler will become self-actualized.

NEGATIVE EMOTIONS AS GROWTH OPPORTUNITIES

No matter how self-actualized we may become, sometimes we will feel anxiety, depression, and anger. Those feelings are not bad. They are simply internal feedback that our inner subparts are out of harmony with themselves or their environment. *These negative feelings are really opportunities for growth.* They are telling us that our current approaches are not coping well, and it is time to learn a new way of thinking or a new route to happiness. Many of our greatest personal growth spurts occur because strong negative emotions help us focus on outdated beliefs or habits.

I frequently see clients who are growing rapidly because they were challenged by crises. We can face and overcome emotions such as anxiety, depression, or anger. The self-exploration and problem-solving methods described below are the same tools I use with myself and my clients almost daily to turn these negative emotions into growth.

Once we understand the *causes* of our emotions, then it is time to find new ways of coping with these causes. We can change our thinking and our actions. We have external and internal routes to happiness. External routes to happiness focus on our actions and the world outside our skin. Internal routes to happiness focus on mental means of achieving happiness. These mental means include examining our beliefs, our sensations and perceptions, our stream of thoughts, and all other internal phenomena to achieve more harmony and happiness. Some internal systems, such as the executive self and the Higher Self, are potentially centers of great power and control. These parts can attain direct control over our thoughts and actions (and will be topics in later chapters).

Do not get *too attached* to any one route to happiness. A client came to my office who had been extremely unhappy for more than two years. For the last year she had been in a relationship with a man whom she said did not treat her well, but she was "miserable with him and miserable without him." What had begun as a wonderful, exciting relationship with a man who fulfilled her dreams turned into a nightmare. Now, he was demanding, manipulative, and inconsiderate of her feelings.

When she would tell him she was leaving, he would use his gift of charm to get her back. "He made me feel so special. . .down deep I thought he had a kind heart and really loved me." She wanted to believe that if she would hang in there long enough, he would change. Instead, he used her hope *to keep her bonded to him*. He had no intention of changing.

What was the essence of this bonding--this addiction to him? In her words, "Very early in the relationship we had a magic between us that I had only read about in books. It seemed like we were fated for each other." How could she fight fate? She had developed a powerful underlying belief that *he was the only man she could ever be happy with*. The belief that she had *only this one route* to happiness kept her locked into the relationship.

An important element of getting free of the relationship involved observing her own feelings. She began to keep a mental record of *how she actually felt* when she either thought about him or was with him. Most of the time she felt anxious, depressed, guilty, hurt, or angry! Not only was this man *not* her only route to a happy relationship, he was not *any* route to a happy relationship. Overcoming the belief that he was the "right," "fated," or "only" man for her opened the possibility that she could find happiness with someone else.

The story of this client illustrates an important lesson. Whenever we allow ourselves to believe that a certain person, object, career, home, lifestyle, or anything is the *only route to happiness,* then *that belief alone will undermine our happiness*. This belief in *exclusivity* makes us much *more dependent* upon that one route. Then, *any* threat to that one route will profoundly threaten our happiness--because we believe that that one route is our *only* route to happiness.

My wife and I love each other deeply and have a wonderful relationship that we hope will last forever. However--as happy as we are--we both know that if we lost each other, we could still be happy as individuals. Because, we both know that we can create *many other* routes to happiness. Otherwise, we could be consumed with fear of the other leaving or dying.

Finding and *risking commitment* to *some* routes is necessary to achieve happiness. I showed how some people become so committed to one happiness route that they become inflexible--even when they are miserable. However, other people make the opposite *mistake--failing to commit to any route*.

For example, I talk to many college students who keep taking classes and avoid facing a choice about what career they want. One client became a *senior* before he really got serious about researching and choosing a major. Then, he decided to major in business. If he had chosen business as a freshman, he would have been able to graduate in four years. However, choosing it as a senior meant that it would still take him *three more years to graduate*--the cost of not facing his anxiety.

HARMONIOUS FUNCTIONING AND HAPPINESS

Harmonious functioning is a state of healthy peak functioning of our mind and body. It represents being interested--even fascinated--with what we are doing. Being passionately involved in doing what we love causes us to lose track of time and become almost "at one" with what we are doing. We may experience this feeling in optimal moments of sports, sex, movies, conversation, reading, solving a problem, or some other form of work or play. These are moments we may remember as peak experiences in our life--not unlike the ones that Maslow's self-actualized people experienced.

Understanding what causes us to get in this state of "flow" or harmonious functioning can help us learn how to achieve that state more often and spend more of our time being interested and enjoying what we are doing. Learning how to achieve this state of peak performance, peak learning, and peak happiness will be a topic of later chapters. You will learn specific methods and routes to happiness for converting negative emotions to happiness.

HOW DO WE CHOOSE TO BE HAPPY?
Self-Exploration and Problem-Solving Skills

Choosing to be happy is not as easy as just saying to ourselves, "Be happy" that will magically happen. However, we can choose to be happy by choosing internal and external routes that will increase our probability of being happy. We can learn from others who have been successful leading happy and productive lives, and we can learn from our own experiences.

Simple, direct routes to happiness--are they too naive? I recently saw a book that consisted of a long list of several thousand things people could do to "make themselves happy." Listening to music, talking with a friend, riding a bike, and filling time with interesting activities increase happiness.

However, reading such a book leaves me with the question, "Why should anyone ever be unhappy?" If all we have to do is fill our time with positive thoughts and activities to be happy, then why is there so much unhappiness in the world?

Unfortunately, life is not so easy for most people. In order to meet basic needs, we must set goals and work hard. Even then, we still may not get what we want. It may be that we have no natural liking for the type of work we do. In the real world, most of us must deal with many unpleasant and demanding situations. We must deal with serious losses of money, relationships, or health. We may be bombarded by negative thoughts, conflict, or other unpleasant events. We must also deal with our own inner conflicts such as desire for work versus play, time for family versus earning a living, or independence versus pleasing others. Squeezing a few positive activities into a life full of unhappy times is not an adequate approach for filling our lives with happiness.

Using "stress reduction techniques" such as relaxation training, visualization, physical exercise, and repeating affirmations is another common approach suggested by many books. Using these techniques when we feel negative emotions can help us *temporarily* feel better. Building these positive activities into our normal daily or weekly schedule can help us feel better in general. I encourage the use of these techniques as a *supplement* to actually solving the problems that will more *permanently* help people feel better.

Another approach found in the literature is substituting positive thoughts for negative ones--looking at the glass as half-full instead of half-empty. That approach also has its merits. However, if one's underlying world view tends to predispose them to see the glass as half-empty, then repeating that it is half-full a thousand times will not really get them to see it as half-full. *Simple substitution and repetition is not enough.*

Most of the clients I see come in with problems that are not solved by stress-reduction techniques or even by substituting simple positive thoughts for negative ones. A client loses a loved one, a client is worried about getting a job, or a client feels her life is out of control. Do I tell them to breathe deeply or visualize peaceful scenes to solve these problems? Do I tell them to just think more positively? Of course not! If I did, they would probably feel like I didn't really understand their problem.

My clients may eventually find external routes to happiness. The first client may eventually find a new relationship, the second may find a good job, or the third may get control of her life. However, these solutions take time--possibly months or years. How can they get control of their emotions right now?

The answer is to use internal routes to happiness--to get *mental* control of the problem. The best way to get mental control is usually to look inside and find the deeper beliefs that are generating their worry. Then, they can find new perspectives that adequately address their deepest concerns--in ways they can honestly believe.

The client who lost a loved one may have to deal with issues of rejection, anger, guilt, self-worth, or how she can be happy living alone. The unemployed client may have to deal with basic career goals, lifestyle expectations, or self-worth. The depressed client may have to deal with her basic world view and view of herself as well as dealing with issues in each important life area that seems out of control. Once these clients solve their underlying issues, then they will not only overcome the current problem, they will have a *new inner strength* that will help them overcome happiness-threatening problems *their entire life.*

The first step in the process that solves the underlying problems is almost always *self-exploration.* It is a process I use with almost every client I see. It is a process that I almost always use on myself when I am upset. It is the only good way I know to get to the real heart of the problem.

Persistent self-exploration and growth can accomplish "miracles." Recall that my Life Skills Questionnaire research found a correlation of .57 between how people cope with their negative reactions and happiness! We also found that making self-development part of one's life style correlated .35 with happiness the past three years. By using this self-exploration/problem-solving approach persistently over time, we can accomplish what sometimes appears to be a miracle. One client who was having severe panic attacks said that it would be a "miracle" if she even finished that first semester I saw her. Not only did she do that, but also she has graduated with excellent grades.

I have seen many people accomplish what they or others considered to be "miracles" in their own lives. I have seen shy clients who could barely talk to anyone become confident, outgoing, and assertive. I have seen people with serious alcohol and drug problems beat the habit and go on to new levels of living and continued growth that surpassed their peers. I have seen people terrified about being alone learn to love being alone. I have seen people who worked hard to make "D"s and "F"s in difficult subjects begin making "A"s and "B"s. I have seen people with serious "addictive relationship" patterns learn to find happiness alone and then go on to form happy, mature love relationships.

All of these clients who accomplished "miracles" had something in common. They all had locked within themselves the barriers to success and happiness. Yet they all also had locked within themselves the inner power that could overcome those barriers.

SELF-EXPLORATION AND PROBLEM-SOLVING SKILLS
GIVE US AN "INTERNAL PSYCHOLOGIST"

What if--whenever you got upset--you could call your own personal psychologist who understood you and always helped you feel better? What if, in addition, this personal psychologist charged no fees and was always available? You can have a psychologist like that.

One thing that both Freud and Maslow (and most psychologists) agreed about was that self-knowledge is a key to mental health. The process of self-exploration is a prerequisite to maximizing happiness and personal power.

From our point of view, Freud's greatest discovery is that the great cause
of much psychological illness is the fear of knowledge of oneself--
of one's emotions, impulses, memories, capacities, potentialities, of one's destiny.
(Abraham Maslow, *Toward a Psychology of Being*, 1960, p. 57)

Fear of the *inner monster*--most of us fear looking too far inside. I used to be afraid to look too far inside. I was afraid of what I now call the *inner monster*. I didn't know what this inner monster was, but I was afraid that it was something dark and terrible--something I would be very ashamed of. But when I looked inside, I didn't find a monster at all. I just found many interesting parts--a little boy, a baseball player, a scholar, a brother, a psychologist, a lover, a philosopher, and much more.

Many clients have the same sort of fears about looking inside. They are afraid of finding their own personal monster. They may fear that their basic nature is "selfish," "evil," "dirty," "weak," "stupid," "crazy," or "sick." However, after intensively exploring the inner cores of hundreds of clients, I have not found one monster! Not one rotten person!

People don't find monsters--they find outdated or limited beliefs. When we find the causes of our problems, we don't find "sick" inner parts; we find old assumptions, old beliefs, old expectations, old commitments, or old goals that we now see as limited.

We feel excited about finally finding the inner causes of our problems, and we want to change these old parts of ourselves. The result of self-exploration is not horror at what we find, but relief that it is not nearly as bad as we feared. We find peace from discovering the truth. That relief gives way to enthusiasm as we open new life paths to explore.

If you fear finding inner monsters, you will feel anxiety whenever you look inside yourself or question some established belief. You can replace that outdated belief in inner monsters with a better metaphor.

"Solving the inner *mystery"* metaphor. I love to watch good mysteries. Agatha Christie's Hercule Poirot is one of my favorite detectives. Sometimes, I think of psychotherapy as Poirot finding clues to discover "who dunnit."

Instead of thinking of self-exploration as a search for inner monsters, think of it in terms of your favorite *discovery* metaphor. Think of self-exploration as being the detective in an exciting mystery movie. Or, think of self-exploration as your being a scientist trying to discover a major new insight into human nature. Learn to replace those old fears of looking inward with a sense of adventure, curiosity, and excitement.

"Looking for buried treasure" metaphor. The process of self-exploration is not like looking for an inner monster, it's like looking for buried treasure. You may find inner roadblocks you didn't know about; but you will find at your core that you care about yourself and others. You will find you care about many higher values such as truth and beauty. You will find new sources of interest, competence, inner strength, and motivation. You will find that you have more potential for success and happiness than you ever realized.

If you've been afraid to look inside,
because you're afraid of finding an inner monster--
that's really sad.
Because your fear has kept you from finding what's really inside--
a beautiful, loving human being.

HOW I USE SELF-EXPLORATION AND PROBLEM-SOLVING SKILLS

A few years ago, I had a dream longing to be back in graduate school. Once awake, I felt very confused. I couldn't understand why I would long to be back in graduate school; my life seemed so much better now--in almost every way. Why would I have such a strong feeling? It was a mystery to me.

I solved the mystery using my **nonjudgmental inner observer**. I used the same process I would use with a client--to *follow my feelings to the underlying issues*. Even though I was dubious of the longing feeling, I accepted that it was a real emotion, and I accepted that it must be connected to some real--but obviously hidden--underlying issue. My inner observer noticed two types of feelings--the longing feeling and a feeling of mild anger. The anger feeling seemed the easiest to identify.

When I focused on the anger, I **free-associated**. The thoughts and self-talk poured from the associations with anger. Part of me said things like "How could I be longing for graduate school when my life is so good now! When I was in graduate school, I was a poverty-stricken student and I know that I was not as happy as I am now!" This part of me felt somewhat threatened that the progress I had made in my life might not have mattered. However, after some exploration, I realized that most of my life *was* better, and I realized that these areas of progress *were not* the underlying issue.

Therefore, I decided to explore the longing feeling. Exploring the longing feeling was harder. I tried free association. I focused on the longing feeling to see what thoughts or images spontaneously appeared. What appeared were images of reading, talking with other students, and going to classes. Associated with them were good feelings. I was still confused about why these images appeared. I had been a psychologist for years, what could possibly be so positive about these old grad-school images?

I decided to try some **mental experiments**. I consciously generated images and observed my emotions. I focused on scenes from my grad-school days and scenes from my current professional life. I compared my emotional reactions in the old scenes to my emotional reactions in the present ones. For example, I compared how I spent a typical day as a graduate student to how I spent a typical day at work as a psychologist. As I imagined different parts of my day, I observed my emotional reactions. I noticed that the parts of being a student that felt so good were the parts concerned with learning new ideas. I loved to read about them, write about them, and discuss them with other students.

"Ah hah"--what a difference between my student days and my current days! I used to feel excited about learning new ideas and discussing them with others. Instead, I had become so involved in the process of counseling, teaching, writing, and program development (based upon ideas I already knew), that I had little time for learning new ideas. Some part of my brain that loves to learn new ideas was bored and had begun to generate dreams about graduate school--a time when it was happy.

My dream finally made sense. I had identified the *underlying issue*. My underlying value of learning and developing new ideas was being deprived. Once I identified the underlying issue, I began **self-exploration of my subpart** that was responsible for these feelings. I continued to let myself free associate and imagine situations where I had been happy learning and thinking about new ideas. I got more in touch with many memories where the **common theme** intuitively seemed the same.

That common theme was learning new ideas, organizing them in my mind, and writing or talking about them. I labeled this part of me my "inner scholar." This part of me had been active most of my life; I had always been curious and loved to learn about almost any new idea that seemed interesting.

So this one dream--with its strong associated feelings--had led me to get in touch with a part of myself that I had let drift into the background. But how had this happened? Why had this important part of me become so neglected?

I started looking for **causes of the problem**. My first tendency was to blame the problem on my job. After all, the administration wanted direct service to students and seemed to care little about professional development or writing. However, I realized that I needed to take responsibility for my scholarly activity myself, and do what was necessary to increase it.

The next stage was deciding on what **route to happiness** I would take. My new **internal route to happiness** was to start *challenging my assumptions* that had kept me from scholarly activity. I questioned the assumption that I couldn't find some scholarly activity that administrators would support. I also questioned my assumption that I needed their support--after all I could do it on my own time. I realized that my inner scholar was so important that I would give it more of my time and money resources and cut back in other life areas.

My new **external route to happiness** was to **develop a plan** to begin studying cognitive science and artificial intelligence. I decided to reduce my outside work, and consequently lower my income. However, overall I was a happier person--so the decision was a good one. To my surprise, I even received support from the administration. Since that time, I have nurtured my inner scholar. It enriches my life, my happiness, and my productivity. This book is partly a result of that continued effort.

So, the self-exploration process that started with that one dream rekindled a part of me that has had a major impact on my life since. This self-exploration also released a powerful, natural motivation to spend the many hours required to pursue my scholarly goals. The payoff has been bountiful--for my own happiness and for the benefit of others.

> **PRACTICE: Explore a complex problem.** Think of a problem. You can start with an emotion you feel too often--such as anger, anxiety, or depression. Or, you can start with a problem in some area of your life--such as people, career, financial, or health. Or, you can start with a habit you want to change. Apply each of the following six steps of the self-exploration process to better understand the internal causes of the problem; or, wait until you have read the seven steps once. Then apply them to your problem.

THE SELF-EXPLORATION PROCESS:
Learn the STEPS to Finding Underlying, Internal Causes

My graduate school dream example illustrated the self-exploration method. The self-exploration method includes some of the most essential skills involved in therapy and self-development. In future chapters I will frequently refer back to this self-exploration process. If you learn it well and use it regularly, your rewards will be great!

For novices and experts.[9] How much training or experience have you had exploring your inner being? Learning to do self-exploration *well* requires a great deal of skill and experience. If you are new at this, it may appear as if I am providing too much detail. In your case, it is better to focus on the major steps and the bigger ideas and skim the detail for now. After you have practiced self-exploration for a while, reread this section and

---

[9] This self-exploration process is similar to the process I use in therapy. It is based upon methods first described by Carl Rogers (1951), Robert Carkhuff (1961), and George Kelly (1955). It can also be a model for helping another person explore complex issues.

concentrate on the details.

If you are an advanced self-explorer, some information may appear too basic. Instead, focus on fine-tuning your skills. Reaching an expert level of self-exploration is essential for maximizing your happiness, and reaching that level takes experience. You will not be able to read this chapter once and find--overnight--that you can solve all your problems. You will need to use it like you use a pair of glasses. Every time you need to deal with a more complex problem or emotion, you need to put on your new self-exploration glasses and look inside.

Self-exploration is only the first step. Once you explore old parts of yourself that need changing, you will need specific methods for fixing those problems. You will need new ways of dealing with those underlying issues. In other chapters we will focus on many of the underlying issues that you might discover--issues like having a negative world view, having low self-esteem, being too externally controlled, having dysfunctional expectations and beliefs, having poor coping skills, or being too nonassertive.

Read now or later? If you are an expert self-explorer or you just want to skip the detailed explanation now, you can skim the rest of this chapter and proceed to Chapter 3. You can return to this section later. However, I urge you to return, because this is a *critical skill for discovering the roots to unhappiness and new foundations for happiness.*

STEP 1: WARM UP YOUR *INNER OBSERVER*—GET IN THE RIGHT FRAME OF MIND

Before you begin looking at a problem, it is important to get the right mental set. If you feel any anxiety about looking inside or questioning some cherished belief, remember your discovery metaphor. You are not afraid of the truth. You are Hercule Poirot, a psychologist, or a seeker of buried treasure. The truth *will* eventually give you peace and set you free!

Let your inner observer watch inner events neutrally--just recording data. Hercule Poirot must look at the facts dispassionately as a scientist would--both are searching for the raw, uncolored truth. You cannot understand and solve the problem unless you can observe the raw data from your senses and emotions as clearly as possible--with a minimum of interference from thoughts that want to filter it, interpret it, and judge it. You must suspend these higher interpretive thought processes until you get all the facts. If you start drawing conclusions prematurely, you may bias your perception to fit your preconceived views.

Self-exploration involves developing a subpart of you that becomes a neutral, nonjudgmental observer. It can observe the most positive or negative thoughts, feelings, actions, or events dispassionately. To get in the right frame of mind pretend that you are a neutral observer sent from another planet to unobtrusively study the people of earth. Or pretend that you are watching a movie and know that what is happening is not real. This inner neutral observer can learn to observe events as if none of the events will affect it at all.

Neutral observing may sound easy, but it is one of the most difficult aspects of the self-exploration process. How often have you simply observed your own sensations, thoughts, and feelings for even five minutes without interpreting them, getting strong emotional reactions, or jumping to conclusions? People attempting to learn meditation may take weeks before they can focus inward peacefully for five minutes.

Notice the difference between different sensations, thoughts, emotions, and actions. Everything in your consciousness is either a sensation, a thought, or an emotion. Thoughts consist of images, words, and their relationships. Even external events are not directly accessible to your consciousness--only your sensations from those events are. Your inner observer must know that sensations are distinct from external world events. Your inner observer must know that your sensations and perceptions can be strongly affected by your preconceptions and biases.

Let your nonjudgmental inner observer use neutral, nonjudgmental language as it talks. Some part of you (not your inner observer) might be judging someone--calling them "stupid" or "bad." During the first part of the self-exploration stage, don't let your inner observer change that judgmental part or change the language it is using. It will only observe the language and its effects on your other thoughts, emotions, and actions.

Your inner observer may notice that condemning someone increases negative thoughts, increases anger, and increases aggressive actions. The reaction of your neutral observer is not to condemn, it is, "That's interesting--perhaps there is a causal relationship between my judgments, my anger, and my aggressive responses."

As your inner observer talks about what it is observing, it is important that it use descriptive, nonjudgmental language. If it falls into a judgmental mode, then it will lose its power to be an accurate observer.

Let your nonjudgmental inner-observer avoid *zingers* and *melodramatic descriptions*. Zingers are key words that incite emotional reactions. They can disrupt thinking from a "just getting the facts" mode to an "I need to react" mode. At times when you are observing yourself, you will undoubtedly be tempted to think thoughts like, "That was stupid, why did I do that?" But beware of such temptations. Innuendos, digs, subtle put-downs, and defensive comments all stir up parts of us that are anything but neutral--so avoid observational zingers of any type!

Melodramatic language incites emotional reactions. If you want an emotional reaction from someone (including yourself), then you may be tempted to exaggerate or overdramatize a situation. The problem is if you exaggerate the situation, then it also gives you a message that the problem is larger than it really is. It may also give a message that you view yourself as too weak to meet the challenge. This kind of dishonest communication is the opposite of what your inner observer is striving for.

Let your inner observer "rise above" emotions and not get caught up in them. Recall a time when you got really upset and got totally lost in the emotion and experience. In that experience, you had tunnel-vision. You lost all perspective that anything else exists. You probably felt as if the emotion was totally outside of your control. In this case your neutral observer was not engaged.

In contrast to this experience--try to think of a time when your neutral observer was engaged. Haven't you ever experienced one part of yourself dispassionately observing another part as the second part gets upset? Perhaps the experience felt a little strange, sort of like an "out of body" experience. But it is this *dual processing state* that you must achieve with your inner observer to accurately observe what is causing your emotional reactions. To achieve this dual processing state take turns focusing on your inner observer and letting the upset part act naturally until it's finished with the episode.

> **PRACTICE:** Right now try closing your eyes and with your "inner eye" try observing all of your bodily sensations, your emotions, and your thoughts. Try just observing them without controlling them or judging them. Especially pay attention to *sequences* and *patterns* of internal events. As you feel emotions, notice them and label them; but during the self-exploration stage *do not attempt to change them*. Observe any correlation between your emotions and thoughts.

STEP 2: FOCUS ON SITUATIONS WHEN THE PROBLEM OCCURS

Look for Sequences and Patterns. Think about times when the problem occurs. Look for *sequences* of events. When did the problem start? What was the order and timing of events?

Look for *patterns* of events. What else was happening about then that might be related? List situations when the problem occurs and situations when it does not. Think of as many situations as you can and be as specific as you can in recalling all of the events.

Nonjudgmental observe each situation in depth. Listed below are some additional questions I use when gathering the "raw data" for helping clients find the causes of their problems. Use these yourself during self-exploration. For more complex problems explore the entire *history* of the problem--even dating back to childhood.

- **When did the problem begin and *what conditions immediately preceded* that beginning?**
- **Compare situations it does and doesn't occur in**. How are the situations it occurs in *similar* to each other? How are these situations *different* from situations where it does not occur? What if you discover that a person is normally not depressed with other people, but is often depressed alone? You might suspect that the cause of the depression has something to do with loneliness, lack of being able to "entertain" his or herself, or some other condition associated with being alone.
- **What events *regularly precede* the target thoughts or actions?** This will help identify what some of the *immediate causes* are to the actions or thoughts which we are trying to understand. People often overlook the most obvious causes. Important *antecedent causes* of the problem thought or action can include the place, the time-of-day, a negative comment, a loss, or a situation you've never faced before are all examples of events that might precede a problem.
- **Check the environment--any temptations or distractions?** Often students complain because they can't concentrate on their studies. Yet often in their study environment, the TV is playing, people are constantly interrupting them, or they have chores to do. Most students cannot concentrate in this environment because of all the distracting stimuli. In this case, finding a new study place or making agreements and being firm about people leaving them alone when they have a "Do not disturb--I'm studying" sign hanging on their door can really help. Understanding which external stimuli and events are affecting your feelings is an important step to finding possible solutions.
- **What events *regularly follow* the target thoughts or actions?** The reason that *consequent* events are so important is that they may be **reinforcing** the target thoughts or actions. When children throw temper tantrums, some parents give the child what the child wants. It seems to work beautifully; the child stops crying immediately. Both parent and child are now happy. However, why is it that this child turns into a terrible brat who is always throwing temper tantrums? And why is it that the parents keep giving in to these tantrums?

The answer is that both parent and child are being *reinforced* regularly for their behaviors and *reinforcement tends to increase the strength of habits*. The child is being reinforced for the tantrum by the parent; the parent gives the child what the child wants. Similarly, the parent is being reinforced for giving in by the child--the child immediately stops crying and thus gives the parents what they want.

How do the parents break this cycle? First they must completely stop reinforcing the tantrums. In order to speed the process they can also use some sort of punishment following the tantrums (to decrease the strength of the habit). Even though there might be a temporary increase in crying--that is a signal to the parents that the child *does not like* the intended punishment. Punishments are not supposed to be liked. If they are liked, then they are reinforcements--not punishments.

STEP 3: FOLLOW THE STRONGEST EMOTIONS
TO THE DEEPER ISSUES AND PARTS OF YOURSELF

Our emotions are like the warning lights or gauges in our cars. Our car gauges tell us what is right or wrong with important inner parts of our car such as the oil pressure, the generating system, or the engine temperature. If the oil light comes on and we don't stop immediately, we can burn up the engine in our car.

In a similar way our emotions tell us about aspects of our lives that are important to us. Some important inner value, expectation, goal, or belief may be threatened and we might not be aware of it at a conscious level. However, some inner part of us is aware of the problem and it speaks to us though our emotions. Therefore, to locate the cause of the problem, we need to follow our emotions.

Emotions are the CLUES we follow to find the solution to the mystery.

(1) Identify the *types* and *intensity* of emotions involved. Many people have difficulty identifying emotions. You may experience an emotion like anxiety as bodily sensations-- tightening of your chest, pain in your stomach, rapid breathing and heart rate, and excess perspiration. You can also observe which sensations, thoughts, or actions precede or follow an emotion. From these careful observations, you can find the emotion's causes.

Don't confuse emotions with sensations, intuition, or thoughts. People often confuse other internal events with emotions. They use the word "feel" to mean many things besides emotions. For example, there is the old joke about the woman in her tenth marriage getting out of bed and saying, "What a beautiful day, I feel like a new man today!"

Many people confuse thoughts, intuition, or "hunches" with emotions. "I feel like something bad is going to happen" is an intuitive prediction--not an emotion. Does the person mean that he *feels* sad because he *thinks* something bad is about to happen? This distinction may seem picky to some, but it can make a major difference. Anger, anxiety, and depression have different causes and different solutions.

(2) Follow the *strongest emotions* to the underlying issues (versus *avoiding* them). It feels bad to focus on unpleasant emotions, and most people have learned to *avoid negative emotions--not actively pursue them.* [10]

The self-exploration process is the opposite of avoidance behavior. It causes us to look down the barrel at our most feared emotions and underlying issues so that we can solve the underlying problems--not just cover them up with temporary patches.

Pretend you are playing the old children's game in which you are blindfolded and

---

[10] **Note: Avoiding emotions can lead to serious problems.**
    Psychologists call behaviors we use to avoid negative emotions **avoidance behaviors.** Avoidance behaviors receive strong, immediate reinforcement by helping us avoid negative emotions--such as anxiety. Most psychologists believe that many addictions and other dysfunctional behaviors *are* avoidance behaviors--they become powerful habits because they help us avoid negative emotions.
    I agree. People eat, drink, take drugs, become obsessive, get "addicted" to relationships, and learn many other dysfunctional habits in order to avoid unpleasant emotions (and to therefore avoid dealing with major underlying issues).

your goal is to find a hidden object. If you get farther from the object the other kids shout, "You're getting colder." If you are getting closer, they shout, "You're getting hotter."

The COLDER the emotion,
the FURTHER from the underlying cause of the emotion,
the HOTTER the emotion, the CLOSER to the source of the fire.
If you can stand the heat, you can control the fire.

WHAT ARE OUR BASIC EMOTIONS?

After many years of research, experts in the field still have not agreed on any one classification system. However, it is generally agreed that anger, anxiety, and depression are basic negative emotions--and they are the most widely studied emotions.

Many laymen confuse the emotions of depression or anxiety with diagnostic categories of clinical depression or clinical anxiety disorders. The clinical syndromes are marked by extensive, prolonged, intense periods of the particular emotion. Often people have had recurring problems with unusually high amounts of the emotion for many years. But, depression and anxiety are normal emotions that almost everyone feels at least small amounts of every day. Even people feeling intense emotions for awhile are not necessarily clinically anxious or depressed.

I classify all unpleasant or negative emotions as either some form of *anxiety, depression, or anger*. (See harmonious functioning chapter for more explanation.) Anxiety includes subcategories of fear, guilt, stress, confusion, nervousness. Anger includes resentment, irritation, frustration, and rage. Depression includes boredom, loneliness, apathy, (some) tiredness, sadness, and grief.

There is even less agreement about a classification system for positive emotions. But I use the word happiness to refer to what I believe is the most basic positive emotion. I think that it is inseparably intertwined with its variations of love, caring, liking, joy, peace, excitement, and ecstasy.

The positive and negative emotions are related, but are like opposite ends of a spectrum. It is impossible to feel anger, anxiety, or depression and joy at the same instant. They each have their turn, depending on what our state of mind is at any one instant in time.

STEP 4: IDENTIFY CONNECTIONS WITH EMOTIONS

What thoughts or mental images pop into your mind as you focus on the target emotions? These pop-up associations are not just chance events. They are often very important. The mistake most laymen make is that they do not realize that these *associated thoughts are not just coincidences*--they are **conditioned associations** and causally connected to the emotions and the problem. Therefore, following these associations can often lead to other associations that are the underlying causes of the target problem.

(1) Focus on words, images, or ideas that create the strongest emotional responses. As you think about the target situations, your emotions will vary both in type and in strength. As they vary, notice the exact image, thought, or sensation that was associated with the strongest emotions--especially the target emotion. If depression is the target emotion and if you suddenly feel a small *increase* in depression, then what internal event *just preceded* the onset of that small increase? Answering that question may provide a valuable clue to an underlying cause.

(2) Identify thoughts that *regularly* precede the target emotion. Even if a particular internal event precedes a target emotion only once, it may be important. However, when you notice that a particular *type* of internal event *regularly* precedes the target emotion, then you are really getting hot. Examples of common causes of some negative emotions follow.

Anxiety: Anxiety is caused by *uncertainty* about *important* values and goals. *Examples:* Uncertainty about being liked, about getting a job, about people's opinions, about finances, about deadlines, or about your expectations being met.

Anger: Anger usually results from not accepting some loss or potential loss. The higher the stakes, the more the anger is directed at the perceived cause of the problem. A person may generate anger for power to overcome the perceived barrier. *Examples:* Not accepting an interruption or negative event, thinking someone wants to hurt you or is being unfair to you, or being injured and wanting to "get even."

Depression: While both anxiety and anger are states of high arousal, depression is generally a state of low arousal characterized by goalessness, loss, and lack of challenge. The person may have "given up" or be experiencing a lack of values satisfaction or reward. *Examples:* Loss of a loved one or job, a perceived or anticipated failure experience, not having anything interesting to do, or being alone. Depression may even come after successfully meeting goals, when suddenly goals are lacking.

Chapter 8 will focus on overcoming anxiety, anger, and depression.

(3) Conduct inner experiments with your emotions--what makes them go UP and DOWN? Test different words, images, and ideas to see if they will evoke even stronger emotions. You can learn what causes your emotions to vary by consciously varying your thoughts and watching the corresponding changes in your emotions. Consciously focus on beautiful music or a beautiful ocean scene and observe your emotions. Then consciously focus on scenes of serious illness, famine, or death. Compare your emotional reactions. Also, notice how rapidly they can change as you alter your focus.

While clients are feeling very depressed in therapy and are focusing on how helpless they feel, I often ask them to think of a time when they were depressed and were able to get themselves out of the depression. They suddenly appear more alert, active, and energetic. They immediately begin to feel better.

Then I ask them to compare how they felt when they were talking about *how helpless* they felt versus how they felt when they were talking about *how they could cope* with their depression. They realize that when they focus on what they cannot do and focus on what is out of their control, they feel worse. But as soon as they focus on constructive problem-solving and *focus on what they can control*, they feel better. From this simple mental experiment, they discover one cause and one treatment of their depression.

(4) Use free association techniques--follow thoughts, memories, and images. One powerful way to dig up underlying issues is by using free association techniques. Let your inner observer just watch the chain of connections between different mental events.

I explored my dream about graduate school using free association--to get to the underlying cause of my "longing" feelings. I am not normally someone who spends much time exploring dreams. However, that one had strong feelings associated with it and I felt confused. I kept free-associating and got in touch with many old memories. I then focused on the feelings associated with these old memories.

Memories of talking with other students, reading, listening to certain professors, and writing were popping into my mind. I began to see that the *common theme* was that I was thinking about interesting new ideas.

(5) Search your memory for similar situations where you *do* feel the target emotion. A client couldn't understand why she got so angry at her significant other for being late. I asked her to think of other situations when she got angry at him. She was angry about his nagging her to "hurry up" whenever they went out, about his always getting his way about what activities they did together, and about several other situations.

What did all of these situations have *in common* (besides her angry reaction)? She felt *controlled*. She thought that he always wanted her to be on his schedule and do whatever he wanted. The underlying issue was *control*--she was angry because she was allowing him to control her time and activities.

(6) Compare them to situations where you *don't* feel the target emotion. Ask yourself why you feel the target emotion in the first set of situations and don't in the second set. What are the key *differences* in the sets of situations? These differences may help you understand the deeper causes of your emotions.

In the above example, my client did not feel angry in situations when her significant other listened to her or did what she requested. She also did not feel angry if she told him what she wanted--even if he did not ask. That puzzled her at first. After all, he was not being any nicer. She realized that the underlying issue was not as much *his behavior* as it was her *believing she had adequate control* in mutual decisions. She had adequate control *either* if he asked what she wanted *or* if she asserted herself.

(7) Keep asking yourself, "What am I MOST afraid of?" Another version of that question is, "What is the WORST thing that can happen?" These questions can help you unlock mysteries that may have haunted you for years.

Our underlying fears drive much of our anxiety, depression, and anger. Discovering, facing, and overcoming our worst fears will solve most problems! I have seen many clients with underlying fears that have been the root of their unhappiness for years. When they finally face these fears, their lives are often transformed--at least in that one area. It is sad that they had been living at less than their potential for so many years--when confronting these fears could have set them free. Is this happening to you in some important life area now?

In the short-run, facing your greatest fears may take time and be painful; however, in the long-run, avoiding them, covering them up, rationalizing them, or blaming others produces far more pain.

STEP 5: IDENTIFY UNDERLYING BELIEFS, VALUES, THEMES, SUBPARTS

As you use the preceding steps, you will begin to uncover the underlying issues and subparts that are causing problems. When you discover an underlying issue, a little light comes on in your head. Your emotions, such as relief or joy, tell you that you have made an important insight.

What are underlying causes like? At this point you still may not know what you are looking for. You may not know what I mean when I say search for underlying issues or for underlying parts of yourself.

Underlying causes include important values, beliefs, and belief systems. These mental systems are the source of our personality, motivation, and daily habits--they remain partially hidden or "unconscious." They *produce* the thoughts and emotions you have been exploring up to this point. By following the river of thoughts and emotions upstream, you can find their source--the underlying mental structures.

Characteristics of these deeper structures. These mental, cognitive systems will be discussed in more depth in later chapters. However, for now, remember that you can tell when you have found them by looking for issues, beliefs, conflicts, expectations, assumptions, values, goals, plans, etc. that have some of the following characteristics.

- **More general and abstract.** Example: Who is in control in *overall* [more general] versus who gets their way right now [more specific].
- **Apply to a wide range of situations.** Example: The person is *usually* late, not late just this one time.
- **Related to major life themes, life roles, or life areas.** Examples: "Living the good life," "Being an honest and ethical person," or related to career, family, health.
- **Related to major commitments or decisions.** Examples: Marriage, family, owning a house, an organization, or a career.
- **Important to your identity--your self-image or self-esteem**.

As you use the methods in step 4 to make connections between emotions and underlying thoughts, go one step further--keep looking at the big picture. What are the more global, bigger issues or parts of yourself that are attached to these specific thoughts that keep popping up? Some of the following questions can help.

(1) What do the causal, surface thoughts have in common?
- **In what way are thoughts preceding the problem *alike*?**
- **How are they *different* from thoughts that seem to reduce the problem?** Notice the content of the thoughts and the underlying issues.

One client came in for serious episodes of depression. She said that her biggest problem was loneliness. She made a lot of statements like those that follow. What common themes do these statements have?

"I'm always doing favors for my friends; but when I ask them for a favor, they always have some excuse." "I study harder than almost anyone I know, but I only make average grades." "I did everything I could to please my boyfriend; but in the end he said I was too needy."

One theme was a theme of rejection, or more broadly a theme of failure--"I try so hard, but in the end I fail." Since this theme occurred across most of her life areas, it is no wonder that she often felt severely depressed. Changing her expectations and getting more control of her life--one area at a time and in general--were strategies that helped her overcome her depression.

(2) Ask yourself, "WHY?" or 'WHAT AM I ASSUMING?" These probing questions are often a direct pipeline to underlying assumptions and beliefs. When I ask, "Why?" I don't mean that you should give an explanation following the rules of logic. I mean it in the same sense that you would ask a five-year-old child, "Why did you hit your brother?" You want to learn about the child's underlying reasoning and motives. Maybe the child says that his brother took his toy, and therefore he hit him. He assumes that hitting is a proper response to the taking of toys. These underlying assumptions are often the problem.

(3) What common THEMES recur across different situations? A client was feeling very unhappy about her relationship with her fiancé, but she could not figure out why. She said she had begun to notice an increased feeling of "distance." I suggested that she might really mean "mild anger" by the word distance, and she agreed. I asked her to think of some situations where she felt the most distance.

First, she described several situations where she had stated her opinion and he had responded by either disagreeing, making fun of it, or acting as if it were unimportant. In turn she usually felt hurt or inadequate. Inside, she questioned her own intelligence and judgment. This was an important issue in itself, but it was not the end.

She also felt distance in other situations where he seemed to out talk her to get his way. When they disagreed about something really important to him, he tended to become domineering and pay little attention to what she wanted. His domination and her nonassertiveness were the themes that seemed common to all of the situations where she felt distance. He seemed to give much higher priority to his own beliefs and wants than he did to hers. Frequently, she gave a higher priority to his beliefs and wants as well!

Once we identified the problem, we could focus on the parts of her and him that led to his domineering behavior and her nonassertive behavior. For example, she had a part of her that almost always played the role of a "nice, obedient girl" who would always try to please other people and make them happy--even at great cost to her own happiness. She believed that she needed to play this role to be accepted by her parents and friends. Her inner observer explored her "nice, obedient girl" beliefs. Once she understood how these beliefs allowed her to be manipulated, she chose new, more assertive beliefs.

When she found herself falling back into the obedience role, she reminded herself that she could be *both* nice and assertive. "I love my partner and want to support his happiness; but I am the one responsible for my own happiness, and I love myself enough to take good care of myself. That is more important than being obedient and worrying about what others think all the time."

STEP 6: CLARIFY BOUNDARIES OF CONTROL AND RESPONSIBILITY

Clarifying boundaries of control and responsibility is a primary stage of solving emotional issues. Often clarifying these boundaries, control, or responsibility issues will immediately solve the problem and we will suddenly feel much better.

We may start by focusing on external causes and problems. We may start trying to solve a problem with the assumption that *the source of the problem is external*. By external I mean roughly outside of the skin. My low-assertive client had started with the assumption that the source of her unhappiness was a problem with her relationship or fiancé. In fact important *external aspects* of the problem may need to be solved, but they are never *the entire problem*. The *link* between those external events and our emotions lies *inside*. We can *only change our own thoughts and behavior*. The rest of the world is less in our control, but our *choices* about that world are important and will affect it. My client could not change her boyfriend (at least not directly), she could only change herself and how she deals with him.

We may assume that others are causing our negative feelings and deny responsibility. At one stage of solving the problem, my client with the dominating fiancé' was focusing on what *he* had done to contribute to the problem--she was ignoring her contribution. Often when people reach this stage of **externalizing the problem** or blaming it all on others, their friends will agree with them to "support" them. Her friends had made statements like, "Yeah, aren't men bastards," "He's not good enough for you," "You poor thing, you tried so hard." These statements aren't helpful. They just keep the problem externalized. They assign all of the cause, control, and responsibility to the other person(s).

My client's friends wanted to help, but they were giving my client a strong message that she was weak and had no control. If her fiancé was totally responsible, then the implication is that she was helpless--and must be a weak person. He didn't hypnotize her or cast a spell over her. In fact, she had many assertive options that she could have made to his dominating behavior.

She had unwittingly allowed herself to be manipulated in the past. Knowing that she had allowed herself to be manipulated motivated her to learn new assertiveness skills.

We are only responsible for what we can control--our own thoughts, actions, and feelings. If some outside event *beyond my control* is causing me to feel upset, then I am helpless. But I reject this assumption that any outside forces *directly control* my emotions. My mind directly controls my emotions--not outside forces.

I know that no matter how bad the external situation is, I can have enough control over my emotions to feel happy most of the time. If Victor Frankl can get control in a concentration camp, then we can potentially get control in our most difficult situations.

Using the same reasoning, *I cannot control another person's thoughts, actions, or feelings*. Therefore, I am not responsible for their thoughts, actions, or feelings. My client was *not* responsible for changing her fiancé's domineering behavior. She was only responsible for herself and choosing how to deal with her unhappiness with this situation.

> **PRACTICE: Explore a complex problem.** If you did not apply the six self-exploration steps to solving a problem as you read this section, go back to the last "PRACTICE," think of a problem, and apply the seven self-exploration steps to understanding its inner causes. Then read the following.

AFTER SELF-EXPLORATION, WHAT NEXT? STEPS 7+

Obvious solutions. Sometimes, when an underlying problem has been identified, you will find a solution that seems obvious. Plan it and do it.

Reframing. Many times you will discover a negative or dysfunctional belief underlying your negative emotions. Using more positive, yet honest ways of looking at the problem can often solve the problem. Often these positive beliefs are more general-abstract ideas that come from your Higher Self or positive philosophy. In therapy I have found reframing has powerful, often instant effects. Example: *Not*, "I failed." *Instead*, "I have learned an important lesson."

Other problems and solutions. At other times, you may say to yourself, "Now I know what the problem is, but what can I do about it?" Before writing this book, I made a list of the most *common issues* underlying most problems presented to me by my hundreds of clients. These chapters are organized around most of these issues. If you use the self-exploration process and uncover a problem, you will find the tools for solving many of life's basic issues in these chapters. You will find many tools for converting negative emotions into happiness. Think of this book as your happiness toolbox. Later, use it as a reference book.

Use the following table to locate chapters that can help you with a particular type of problem. Remember, behind many of these problems are *underlying issues* affecting your happiness in many situations. Solving one may solve many.

Reference for coping with some life problems

Problems with:	Go to chapter:
1.Confusion, conflict, lack of direction or meaning to life	1, 2, 3, 4, 8
2.Pessimism, stressful events, or a negative world view	4, 3
3.Self-esteem, self-confidence, or negative self-talk	5
4.External control, dependency, non-assertiveness	6
5.Anxiety, anger, depression, or any negative emotion	7,8, 2, Appendix
6.Accomplishing goals, time-management, achievement	9
7.Relationships, intimacy, or communication	6, 3, 5, 4, Appendix
8.Making decisions and solving problems	2, 6

Our emotions are like warning gauges on our cars;
they report the condition of our mental states.
Negative emotions tell us of these inner problems.
Yet so often we treat these negative emotions as if they were enemies--
instead of friends.
If we are to find happiness,
we must not avoid these helpful beacons of light
from our innermost selves.
Instead, we must follow our strongest emotions
to get to the source of the problems or conflicts.
Using the self-exploration/problem-solving method
can transform conflicts and confusion into inner harmony.
It is at the heart of all good psychotherapeutic approaches.
We can learn to be our own therapists
and effectively solve most problems ourselves.
Knowing that there are many routes to happiness (in any situation)
gives us peace of mind and inner power.
Then, *we can choose to be happy*
by choosing the best ultimate concern, top values, and goals and
by choosing good internal and external routes to happiness.

CHAPTER 3

DEVELOP YOUR HIGHER SELF:

THE PART THAT LOVES YOU UNCONDITIONALLY

\\

PERSONALITY CHANGE CAN BE SUDDEN, DRAMATIC, AND ENDURING

Many people (including many psychologists) either believe that radical personality changes can't happen at all or believe that they take a tremendous amount of time and effort to achieve. They believe that years of therapy are required. Personality change, as measured by most personality tests, usually takes awhile.

Yet, how do you explain someone deeply involved with drugs and the drug culture who suddenly stops taking drugs; stops stealing; seeks help; gets an honest job that pays far less than dealing drugs; leaves his old friends and lifestyle behind; and becomes more open, honest, and caring toward others?

How can all of these changes occur almost overnight? I have known many people who have made such radical changes. There are many documented cases of people making profound changes in their identity, their values, their goals, and their behavior as the result of one experience.

Often the people making these changes refer to these experiences as conversion experiences. Some people describe them as finding a new direction in life, or achieving some basic insight that helped them change their entire life. In my own life, I would compare my teenage experience of choosing happiness over success to a conversion experience. In some respects, the key to my change was simple. I suddenly understood that people's personal happiness and well-being were more important than any type of success, "being number one," money, being popular, pleasing other people, or anything else.

In other respects the insight was much more complex. I had been thinking about parts of this bigger concept for several months. However, until the time I got the right insight and made a decision to live by it, my overall thoughts and actions barely changed. I thought about the many implications of this new insight. I wrote a list of guidelines called "How to Be Happy" for living by this new philosophy.

As I began to contemplate actual commitment to a new way of life, I felt a great deal of anxiety about choosing something so radically different from everything I had learned. I feared that I might be wrong. On the other hand, I felt excited by the possibilities of making happiness for self and others my most important goal. I decided to make an experiment out of it. I would try living by that new philosophy for a while.

I feared that I might not persist living by these guidelines. I feared looking back in a few years and saying, "I forgot to be true to these insights." But since that time--more than 50 years ago--I have generally made decisions consistent with that original commitment. Without that "conversion" experience, I wouldn't have become a psychologist; and I wouldn't have had a life filled with so much peace and joy.

HOW DO PEOPLE MAKE RADICAL PERSONAL OR LIFE STYLE CHANGES?

I have been fascinated by people who have made radical changes in their lives. When I meet such people, I find out all I can about what caused them to make these dramatic changes. I have interviewed dozens of these people and have been amazed at the similarity of their reports. Almost all of my interviewees can point to a brief time period--often the exact day or hour--when they believe they made some new commitment to change. Another similarity was that they made this new commitment *the most important value in their lives*. It became like Tillich's ultimate concern.

One woman, Ann, had weighed more than 300 pounds for years. She had tried everything--including surgical removal of fatty tissue. Ann had lost large amounts of weight on numerous occasions. However, she had always regained her weight. The way she described her previous state of mind is that she always knew in the back of her mind that enjoying food was more important than being healthy and trim. Inside, Ann knew she wouldn't lose weight.

"Then, one day I just decided to make being healthy and slim the most important thing in my life." Ann thought about the implications in terms of her daily habits and decisions. She thought about the potential problems of making her own health and weight loss number one. Each time she thought of a situation where she knew she would have a problem, she would consciously decide in her imagination to accept the implications of her new commitment.

Her first major test came that week. Ann's best friend, Carrie, invited Ann over for one of her special dinners. Carrie was also obese, and she loved to cook huge meals with thousands of calories as a special gift to Ann. Carrie was very sensitive and would feel extremely hurt if Ann didn't eat everything that she worked so hard to prepare.

Ann was terrified of hurting Carrie's feelings and losing her as a friend. Yet, she faced her worst fears and told herself, "Being healthy and losing weight is the most important thing in the world to me right now. If necessary, I am even willing to give up my best friend." Once she passed that test, one of her biggest barriers had been overcome--her fear of rejection. It took her about two years to get down to 140 pounds. Fifteen years later she had never allowed herself to get over 145.

The center of radical change--a decision for a new Ultimate Concern

I have interviewed two other women who lost more than 200 pounds and kept their weight down permanently. Their stories were similar to Ann's. One woman said, "I started losing when I decided to face the truth about my problems and decided to care for myself more than I cared about what others thought of me." *Every one* of the dozens of people making radical lifestyle changes has chosen a new set of values, priorities, or view of life. Their new commitments consistently placed more value on people's health and happiness.

HOW DO YOU KNOW WHAT WILL MAKE YOU HAPPY?

Many people eventually choose health- and happiness-enhancing beliefs over more destructive ones. Why do they suddenly make those choices after years of not making them? Why is it that some people continue to choose the destructive beliefs? I will examine three different types of mind systems as potential guides for making decisions-- (1) pleasure and pain (from the lower brain centers), (2) reason and emotion (from the cognitive system), and (3) empathy and love (from the Higher Self).

Even though our bodies and minds have amazing powers--those powers do not guarantee that we will find--or even consciously seek--health and happiness. I will discuss two types of limits--the *limits on the pleasure principle* and the *limits on the cognitive system.* How could the Higher Self overcome these limits?

PLEASURE AND PAIN AS DECISION GUIDES

We have seen how pleasure is different from happiness, yet we often use pleasure and pain as decision guides in everyday affairs. Let's examine pleasure and pain as decision guides.

Pleasure provides valuable feedback about bodily needs, but is limited as a decision guide. Pleasure and pain are potent messages our lower brain centers use to tell us about our bodily needs. They tell us when our cells need water, food, heat, cold, oxygen, stimulation, and the like. If we ignore these messages, we will undermine our own health and ultimately our happiness. It is important to listen to our bodies. Feeling pleasure and avoiding pain are important ways we can increase our health and happiness.

However, as Freud and many philosophers have pointed out, living strictly by the **pleasure principle**--getting the most pleasure you can from the present moment--is shortsighted. In the long run, ironically, it usually leads to a life filled with pain. We know that if we spend all our resources for pleasure now, we may not have any left for pleasure tomorrow.

Freud contrasted the pleasure principle with the reality principle. The **reality principle** understands that to maximize pleasure over a longer period of time, it is often wise to undergo some pain in the short run. Many college students sacrifice their time and endure poverty in order to have a happier career and life later. We are all familiar with these ideas. So is our cognitive system. Most philosophers and religions view the ability to *delay gratification* (when wise) as an important way that we can increase our *overall* happiness for self and others.

REASON AND EMOTION AS DECISION GUIDES

Our cognitive system surely evolved because creatures living by the reality principle had survival advantages over those living only by the pleasure principle. A central function of the cognitive system is to look at the external and internal environments from a *broader perspective.* The cognitive system provided intelligence to store food for times of famine, suffer hardship in order to build a home for protection, and give up some individual freedom for group security. In the long-run pleasure will probably be increased. The *emotions*--not the pleasures--tell how our cognitive system is doing. If our cognitive system *believes* that all our concerns will be met, then it will be happy.

The cognitive system and emotions *simultaneously* monitor many concerns. The cognitive system *cannot help* but care about the future and care about all its subparts' desires. By "*design*," the only way that our cognitive system can have harmony within itself is by having adequate plans for what it believes will happen in the future. Our cognitive system is biologically "wired" to produce anxiety when it is uncertain about need satisfaction in the future. Our happiness directly reflects harmony within the cognitive system, we cannot be happy unless we have adequate plans for meeting our perceived future needs and values.

It is impossible for anyone living exclusively by the pleasure principle to be happy for long! The short-sighted hedonist may feel a lot of pleasure now, but part of him is constantly worried about the future. Many people with addictions live by hedonism. They focus on pleasure today; but eat, drink, or take drugs to avoid worrying about the future. The cost is nagging guilt and worry. Instead of facing their problems, they take more drugs to cover up the guilt and worry. They become trapped in a downward cycle toward self-destruction.

Enlightened self-love--happiness is more important than pleasure.
Enlightened self-love means that we are trying to maximize our happiness instead of our pleasure. Pleasure often contributes to happiness, but not always. If we believe we are having fun at the expense of our career or health, or at the expense of others, we will feel guilty. We cannot be fully happy now if we believe that we are undermining our own future happiness or the happiness of other people.

Limits on the cognitive system's ability to assure health and happiness.
The cognitive system also has limits. Just as listening strictly to our pleasures can get us into trouble, so can listening strictly to our reason or to our emotions (both are cognitive-related functions). Our emotions are dependent upon our values and beliefs. Therefore, if our values or beliefs are dysfunctional, then we cannot trust the thoughts or emotions erupting from them.

Beliefs and goals can *undermine or empower* natural unconscious forces.
With all these good biological mechanisms built into humans to enhance our health and happiness, why do we do such dumb things that constantly undermine our health and happiness? Why do we smoke, take drugs, hurt people, or live for today without considering the future?

A worm is too stupid to take drugs or to commit suicide. It is not able to form a conscious goal to destroy itself. It is not capable of creating nuclear weapons of mass destruction--only humans can do that. Our cognitive system is a source of tremendous power not only to do great good, but also the power to do great harm.

Biological development of the cognitive system has given it power and *freedom* to create all types of beliefs, images, and thoughts. The cognitive system has a built-in irony. Evolution developed the brain's power and freedom for its adaption and survival advantages. Yet, that same power and freedom allow humans to learn destructive beliefs and goals that can undermine the health and happiness of the entire person, group, or human race.

It is possible to learn belief systems that become so independent and powerful in themselves that they work for our ultimate self-destruction. These dysfunctional belief systems *do not believe* they are working for our self-destruction, they believe they are working for our well-being--that is where they get their power! They get their power from reinforcement. Persons who take drugs or commit suicide often do so to cope with *immediate problems*. The immediate goal is to feel better right now or eliminate pain. However, these solutions have long-term negative consequences that do not lead to the person's best health and happiness.

Choosing to make long-range health and happiness our top goal is essential to maximize our chances for achieving health and happiness. Whenever we forget those goals and let a less functional goal rule, then we accidentally undermine our health and happiness. This *miscalculation* is the cause of most self-destructive behavior.

The executive self is president of one's life and personality.
The executive self (like part of Freud's ego) is a cognitive system that is in charge of our personality and life. Our executive self makes important decisions and plans. It resolves conflicts between lower centers. Why is it that some people's executive allows them to weigh more than 300

pounds, take drugs, abuse others, or have other serious psychological problems?

The limits of the executive self. Just as corporate presidents do not always do what is best for the organization, neither do our executive selves. Dysfunctional executive selves learn beliefs, world views, philosophies of life, values, or lifestyles that are not life-enhancing for themselves and/or other people. Our basic beliefs are major factors determining our personality, our behavior, and our lives.

Thus, while the executive self is a valuable inner resource, it cannot always be trusted to have our best interests at heart. If we cannot trust our lower brain centers and the pleasure and pain they produce as decision guides, and we cannot trust our executive self and the emotions it produces, is there any part inside we can trust? I believe that such a part exists. I call it the Higher Self.

YOUR CENTER OF LIFE-ENHANCING POWER--
Empathy and Love of Self and Others as Decision Guides

The Higher Self is a cognitive system like the executive self. However, it is the *only* system with the *goal* of seeking happiness for self and others. The Higher Self cares most about our happiness. We can trust our Higher Selves for guidance.

The Higher Self is *not* a conscience. It does *not* act from internalized parental or societal rules (as Freud's superego is supposed to). Instead, the Higher Self acts out of empathy and true love. It is our inner hero. It is the part that I have heard people near suicide say, "Some part of me wants to live and cares about me no matter what I have done."

How does the Higher Self develop? At birth, the Higher Self probably doesn't exist-- except as a primitive neural structure. It probably begins by learning to care about the bodily sensations and about emotions.

Empathy and unconditional love of self. We have seen how the cognitive brain is "wired" to oversee what happens in lower areas of the brain. I believe that the Higher Self has a similar, primitive, built-in empathy for the lower brain centers that govern basic bodily functions. It receives messages from the lower brain centers and is affected by their pleasure and pain.

In addition, the Higher Self learns the *concept* of pleasure. And it initially learns to value *pleasure per se* as good. This "pleasure principle" is the first type of *conscious* unconditional infant self-love. The infant probably develops some primitive form of an unconditional self-love belief like, "My feelings are important no matter what." The Higher Self also learns that it can control actions that lead to pleasure, and consequently begins to *value those actions* and give them priority over other actions.

However, eventually, the pleasures begin competing with each other. For a baby, conflicts between one food and another, between food and play, or between hugging and play create anxiety. While pleasure is the stuff of the lower brain centers, anxiety is a whole new ball game. Anxiety is the stuff of the higher brain--the cognitive system. It innately feels really awful to the cognitive system. Anxiety's opposite--happiness--feels great!

The Higher Self learns the *concepts* of anxiety and happiness. The Higher Self may begin by valuing pleasure, but will quickly learn that *happiness is even more important*. I suspect that a superordinate location in the brain puts it in a unique position to innately monitor and care for the overall happiness and harmony of the brain. Just as the cognitive system's job is to take good care of the lower brain centers and their *pleasure*, the Higher Self's job is to take good care of the cognitive system and its *emotions*.

Thus, no matter how dysfunctional or destructive other parts of the cognitive system may become, the Higher Self learns to love us and value our happiness unconditionally.

Empathy and unconditional love of others. As the infant develops, it learns that consistent images (later called "mama" and "dada") become associated with many important events. In most cases parents are associated much more with pleasure and the relief of pain than they are associated with pain. This may be the first, crude form of love--loving someone because of the pleasure they bring to us.

However, just as the cognitive system cannot help but know there is a future, it cannot help but know that there are other people out there too. It is intelligent enough to know that other people have feelings and thoughts similar to our own. The Higher Self *automatically* empathizes with other people. It cannot help but imagine that when other people are experiencing pain or unhappiness it feels like our own pain and unhappiness.

In other words, I believe that we cannot help but have a Higher Self that truly cares about other people and their feelings--just as it cares about us and our own feelings. The Higher Self is so intelligent that it cannot help but guess how other people feel. It knows that they would probably feel much like we would feel in the same situation.

This empathy is the foundation of a higher form of love--caring about how others feel *no matter how it affects us personally.* This love is an early form of unconditional love. (For more on empathy roots, see Izard, 2009.)

Therefore, we cannot be completely happy unless the Higher Self feels ok about the happiness of other people. We are especially concerned about *our own effects* on other people's feelings. The Higher Self produces anxiety or guilt when it believes we have hurt others. It produces happiness when it believes we have contributed to another's happiness.

The Higher Self is *not* a set of rules. The Higher Self is based upon empathy and unconditional caring--not a set of rules that tell us what we "should" do. The Higher Self is not the rule, "Act as if you cared about someone." It guides us to get into someone's shoes to see how the person feels, and to develop *genuine concern* for that person's happiness.

This concept of a Higher Self based upon empathy and genuine caring is unlike the way Freud described the *superego.* He described the superego as being more like what I have called *internalized parents.* Freud believed that the superego was a reflection of societal norms. I believe that the Higher Self is based upon empathy and unselfish caring. Empathy and unselfish caring develop from our own intelligence and observations--largely independent of what others teach us.

GIVING OUT OF UNSELFISH CARING INSTEAD OF OBLIGATION

What we learn from others can have a powerful effect upon us. Our internalized parents and societal norms are important, but they are rules--the source of "shoulds." The type of empathy and caring that comes from the Higher Self is not based upon rules. (For research, see M. Iacoboni, 2009.)

Recall seeing someone you care for in pain. Recall the feeling when you genuinely wanted to help relieve their pain. Compare that to a situation when you felt that you "should" do someone a favor according to some rule, but didn't really feel like it. That contrast in feelings illustrates the difference between *giving out of genuine empathy and caring* as opposed to *giving out of obligation.*

That is the kind of love that the Christian New Testament writer, Paul, was talking about in his letter to the Corinthians. Before becoming a Christian, Paul's life as a Jewish Pharisee priest had been dominated by hundreds of rules spelling out almost every detail of his life. He believed he had to follow these rules to be a good person. A large part of his conversion to Christianity involved choosing to value true empathy and love rather than living by rules describing how he "should" live. Paul wrote in I Corinthians 13,

> **If I have the gift of prophecy and can fathom all mysteries**
> **and all knowledge, and if I have a faith that can move mountains,**
> **but have not love, I am nothing.**
> **If I give all I possess to the poor and surrender my body to the flames,**
> **but have not love, I gain nothing.**
> **Love is patient, love is kind. It does not envy, it does not boast,**
> **it is not proud. It is not rude, it is not self-seeking,**
> **it is not easily angered, it keeps no record of wrongs.**
> **Love does not delight in evil but rejoices with the truth.**
> **It always protects, always trusts, always hopes, always perseveres. . .**
> **And now these three remain: faith, hope, and love.**
> **But the greatest of these is love.**

Learning to transform *obligation giving* into *giving from the heart*. How much of your giving is to keep the scales balanced? How much giving is to please other people and their expectations? Frequent feelings of guilt and shame are signs that we are giving more out of obligation or giving more to please others--than out of genuine empathy and caring. Even giving because you want to *act like an empathetic, caring person* is not the same as giving out of true empathy and caring.

If I catch myself feeling guilty, saying "should," or worrying about what someone else expects me to give, then I ask myself, "What do I really want to do?" Next, I search all my own positive and negative feelings about doing it. I give each of my subparts a chance to speak.

I also focus on developing a deep understanding of the *other person's situation and point-of-view*. When the part of me that cares about someone experiences the situation from their point-of-view (and I conclude they genuinely need help), it gives me a stronger *urge* to give to that person. Giving out of empathy and love is very different from giving out of guilt. By focusing on their point-of-view, I thus transform a "should" into a "want."

I try to avoid giving out of "shoulds." If I cannot persuade myself to give out of true empathy and caring, then I generally do not give at all. [Although, in many simple daily situations, I give out of "habit"; because going into a deep understanding is too time-consuming.]

Can we give too much? It may be that the part of me that wants to give is in conflict with a part of me that wants to use the time, energy, or money for some other goal. We will see in Chapter 6 how people who are too codependent may give so much that they don't take adequate care of their own needs.

My Higher Self must make the ultimate decision about that conflict between giving to someone else and giving to me. We must each find our own balance between giving to self and giving to others.

Engaging another person's Higher Self. I attended a meeting where one staff member aggressively attacked another in front of the whole group--calling him irresponsible and unprofessional. He was obviously angry. The second responded, "I can see that you're upset with me. I am sorry for any problems I may have caused you and appreciate your bringing it to my attention. Why don't we talk about it after the meeting?"

Immediately, the first staff member calmed down and became much friendlier. He even apologized in front of the group for his outburst and praised the second person for his "classy" response to his attack.

The second person had looked beyond the attacking words into the eyes of his comrade's Higher Self. He heard more than a personal attack, he heard a person he cared about hurting inside. His caring response was not lost. It engaged his comrade's Higher Self to apologize.

Everyone develops a Higher Self--no matter how weak or hidden it might be. What about all of the times people appear to act without empathy or caring? Obviously, their Higher Self is not controlling their behavior at that time. If we can help them engage their Higher Self, then we will find that we are suddenly dealing with someone who is much more understanding and caring. One way to do that is to treat an angry, aggressive, or otherwise unpleasant person with *deep* understanding and concern.

Thus, we begin living at a higher level ourselves. Instead of living by an "eye for an eye" (which is one reason why gang warfare is so difficult to stop), we begin living by the rule of empathy and love. We are trying to maximize our own and others' happiness. We stop worrying about "getting even." Perhaps the best way to overcome our enemies is make them our friends. Perhaps "turning the other cheek" can really work in the right situation.

This approach may not work with all people at all times. We might not know how to engage a person's Higher Self. We each need to draw our own boundaries for self-protection. We need to protect ourselves and act assertively against aggressive domination. Giving in to their aggression only reinforces their aggressive actions and beliefs.

If we set clear boundaries, we can help empower their Higher Selves and de-power their dysfunctional parts. The assertive, "tough love" response is *consciously motivated* partly by a desire to protect ourselves and partly by a desire to help empower their Higher Selves.

THE POWER OF THE HIGHER SELF DEPENDS ON
DEVELOPMENT AND REINFORCEMENT

The Higher Self may start as a simple set of beliefs valuing its own and others' happiness. Like any other cognitive system, it can remain weak, primitive, and undeveloped or it can grow and become strong through learning and reinforcement. Parents can encourage their children to care for themselves and others' happiness, and parents can help them develop beliefs that support these overall goals.

However, many parents teach their children to be obedient and rule-bound. Other parents give little guidance and their children are left to fend for themselves. In these cases, their Higher Selves may remain weak compared to the Higher Selves of children whose parents consistently supported love for self and others. By adulthood, the Higher Selves' development and power can vary dramatically from person to person.

The Higher Self might only be a weak, but persistent, inner voice. One of my clients illustrates how the small inner voice of the Higher Self can speak to us at an early age-- even when it goes against our parents' will. Her father would come into her room in the middle of the night and tell her that what he was doing was good, and it was because he loved her.

She wanted to believe him because she was young and he was important to her. She depended on him for everything. In the community, he was a model citizen and pillar who was successful and respected by everyone. For a long time a dominate part of her told her she must agree with her father and that what he was doing was ok.

However, despite all of this external input, a part of her told her that--even though it brought some pleasure to her--it was not ok. That part of her felt violated. It took her years to really begin to listen to that little voice inside of herself, but it was always there. Finally, she paid attention to it.

When you are doing something that is clearly not life enhancing, is there a little voice inside questioning it? This little voice may be your Higher Self speaking to you. It is repelled by people it perceives as harmful. On the other hand, your Higher Self seeks knowledge and reinforcement from others who value your happiness--it is automatically attracted to them.

Competition with other belief systems. We cannot trust *all* the little voices we hear from within--though all need to be explored and understood. Each cognitive system has its own little voice, even those that are not healthy. The Higher Self faces a hazardous path of conflict with other belief systems in order to develop into a strong system.

If a child's parents create an environment that is too confusing, boring, or unpleasant, the child may not learn to trust others or to feel valued or important. Or the child may go to school and learn that obedience to teachers or peers gets more immediate reinforcement than love of self and others. That lesson supports the *internalized others* belief systems--not the Higher Self.

If competing belief systems are given more reinforcement than the Higher Self, the Higher Self can become underdeveloped and weak. The Higher Self is like a muscle that needs to be exercised. In Chapter 6 on the transition from external to internal control of your life, I will discuss how we can become so focused on pleasing others; doing what they want; and internalizing their beliefs, values, and expectations that we can literally lose our own identity and self-esteem. Developing the Higher Self and focusing on its beliefs and goals is our primary way of increasing our self-esteem, personal power, and happiness in our life.

UNPRODUCTIVE BELIEF SYSTEMS-- THEY DEVALUE HEALTH AND HAPPINESS

Any established belief system that tends to devalue or compete with loving oneself and others is potentially dysfunctional.

A functional belief can become dysfunctional. Often beliefs and rules that are good for limited purposes are used beyond their range. They may be limited *means to happiness* that become dysfunctional when they are made into *ends* or ultimate concerns. For example, making a lot of money can potentially provide many things, help, experiences, or environments that can help bring happiness. However, if I must give up too much happiness for myself or others to get that money, then making money is dysfunctional. Oddly enough, making more money can *reduce* our personal power by reducing our ability to be happy and contribute to the happiness of others.

A belief system can become outdated. We may have learned beliefs that worked well as a child within our particular family, but do not work well as adults. For example, one client's parents taught him as a child that it was God's will for children to obey their parents. They said, "The *Bible* says that you will go to Hell if you don't obey us." He believed them--literally.

For many years he tried to do everything that he was told. As a small child, obedience worked ok. Placing obedience above meeting his own needs was reinforced by avoiding punishment. However, as he got older, he couldn't meet his parents' expectations no matter how hard he tried. He was ridiculed and punished. Since obedience stopped working, he tried rebellion. He gave up trying to please them and he began meeting some of his own needs. This new philosophy worked much better--except for one thing. He still believed that he was evil and that he was going to Hell. He still held that old belief his parents had taught him as a child.

Therefore, he lived in constant fear that God would severely punish him for being so evil. These beliefs continued to haunt him into adulthood. Only through therapy and through talking with a more understanding minister did he question these beliefs. It was not easy, because his parents had also taught him that to *question* any of these beliefs was evil and meant he was going to Hell.

He learned that loving ourselves and taking good care of ourselves is not selfish and evil. He began to view God as a loving God who wanted his children to be happy and who would forgive them for mistakes. How could he believe that God would be less forgiving than a loving human would? These new beliefs got to the core of his underlying fears of failure and punishment. He was on the road to greater self-esteem and happiness. As a child, were you taught any of the following dysfunctional beliefs?

- **"I should always put other people's needs before my own."**
- **"I should be loved or liked by everyone I meet."**
- **"I am weak and dependent on strong people for my happiness."**
- **"I must be the best at everything I do."**
- **"I am entitled to health and happiness, and other people should meet my needs."**
- **"We must run our lives by rules, and people who break those rules must be severely punished or we will have chaos."**
- **"There are winners and losers. If you are not strong and take advantage of others before they take advantage of you, then you will be a loser."**

PRACTICE: List some of your basic beliefs that may have been unproductive for you. If you are having trouble, start by looking at some beliefs that you think may have been unproductive for your *parents*. What messages did they keep giving you that you now know are dysfunctional? How did these beliefs interfere with their happiness and productivity? How did these beliefs influence you? Compare these basic beliefs to beliefs of unconditional love of self and others. Evaluate them by the criteria presented in the next sections.

THE HIGHER SELF AS CONDUCTOR

Think of the Higher Self as the conductor of a symphony.[11] The jobs of the conductor are both (1) to help each orchestra member become the best and happiest musician possible and (2) to coordinate the activities of all musicians so that their combined effort produces the best performance for the whole orchestra. Consequently, each musician receives individual, intrinsic rewards from playing at a peak level and receives his or her share of the rewards from the entire orchestra.

---

[11] Or if you prefer, think of the Higher Self as the leader of an organization or the coach of a team.

When any one part of the orchestra is out synch with the rest, then the performance and happiness of the entire orchestra suffer. The conductor's job is to coordinate the musician's performances so that--together--they produce beautiful music played in perfect harmony.

GOAL OF HIGHER SELF IS HARMONY AMONG ALL MIND-BODY SYSTEMS

The Higher Self's job is to conduct our inner orchestra members' performance so that--together--they produce beautiful music played in perfect harmony. The Higher Self's job is to keep all parts of our mind and body functioning at their peak level of growth, performance, and happiness as much of the time as possible. Whenever there are conflicts, or whenever parts of the system are inactive for long, the performance and happiness of our entire mind-body system suffer. In later chapters, I will describe how we can *consciously choose* to bring about a state of harmonious functioning in almost any situation--from dull, boring situations to stressful, frightening ones.

LIFE AND BODY AFFIRMING BELIEFS--HOW DO WE KNOW WHAT TO BELIEVE?

We can *measure the validity of our beliefs* by how much they contribute to the overall health and happiness of ourselves and others. The beliefs we center our lives around are our foundation for living. Yet how much time and thought do most of us invest in thinking about our basic beliefs? How much do we seek the wisdom of others?

Perhaps one concern is the question, "Who can we trust to be our teachers?" My answer is, "People we see living the happiest, most productive lives and people who have taught others to live those kinds of lives." Find people like Maslow's self-actualizing people to model yourself after.

Philosophers and religions can speak to our Higher Selves. The first philosophy book I ever read was titled, *The Enduring Questions*. It pointed out that there are certain issues in life that face all humans in the past, present, and future. Each major philosophical system and each major religion has addressed many of these issues and at least partially resolved them. That is why they have attracted millions of followers who say that these beliefs have made them happier people. How can we ignore these millions of people or assume that they are ignorant because we do not agree with some of their beliefs? Perhaps they know something we don't.

Why not look for the beliefs that *do* seem to be healthy and life affirming? Look for themes that religions have in common. The themes shared by most major religions may be especially important. But we can learn valuable insights from every major school of thought. On the other hand, just because many people share a belief does not mean that we should automatically accept it. Always question beliefs' truth and happiness value (for all humankind).

If your religion tells you that you should *not question* certain beliefs, remind yourself that several different religions tell their followers that they must accept beliefs without question. They *all* claim that God revealed these truths to someone and you must accept them *exactly as written*. Yet these religions do not all agree.

So, how do you decide which belief is the most truthful or life affirming? For many people, acceptance just depends on which church they walked into first. But how does a thoughtful person decide--if not by *questioning* the beliefs' truth and happiness values? [12]

---

[12]I have learned from a number of religions and philosophers. I have a United Methodist background and completed the MTh degree at the School of Theology at Claremont. I am now somewhat independent. However, I see great potential in the best teachings of all of them. I see many clients with major problems partially caused by how they were taught or treated by parents or others who were active members in some religion. Therapy has sometimes consisted of helping them change

People who spend a lot of time studying and thinking about their higher beliefs will not all come to the same conclusions. They may find different paths to happiness and self-actualization. However, the phrase "seek and you will find" applies to most of them. Most find a richer life.

Some believe they have a special relationship with God or Nature. Some connect more with humankind and work toward social betterment. Some connect more with seeking beauty through art or other means of expression. Some seek truth through philosophy or science. Many paths lead to "spiritual" success and happiness. However, if the Higher Self guides this progress, the Higher Self will in turn be enriched. It will become stronger, more complex, and more integrated with the rest of the personality.

Does the Higher Self connect to a larger Spiritual Unity? It is a common belief among religions and philosophers that some part of us is part of a larger spiritual power--like a cell is part of a greater organism. Think of the world as populated by billions of people with their own Higher Selves together forming an emergent higher level of human consciousness. It is like billions of water molecules together forming a wave.

For example, Christians believe that the "Holy Spirit" is an aspect of God that is both a godlike part of every person and yet is part of God as a whole. It is not hard to imagine each person having a Higher Self that values truth and love, yet shares those higher values with parts of all other people and possibly some larger spiritual presence.

If we view the peoples of the world as all having Higher Selves, then we can see what a powerful force the totality of these Higher Selves can be on the future of the world--especially if they are nourished!

For example, I find the following visualization to be a source of optimism and love within me. I create an image of little "suns" within each person. Each "sun" represents a Higher Self. I recall a church service as a teenager. Several thousand people held small candles in total darkness. The service symbolized the total effect on the world--if each person would "light just one small candle." The light was breathtaking.

ELEGANT BELIEFS--BOTH COMPREHENSIVE AND SIMPLE

Ideally, we want a few, simple Higher Self beliefs that will cover almost any situation in life. These beliefs need to be very abstract and general so that they *can* apply to almost any situation. What did some of the great religious teachers say?

• Jewish law is summarized in the Ten Commandments.

• Jesus said that only two of these Ten Commandments contained the keys to living-- to love God first and to love others as you love yourself. When we love someone, we care for his or her health and happiness. How simple--yet elegant! Jesus suggested approaching every situation from this loving point-of-view. He said that loving God, self, and others above all else is the ultimate test. That is the test of everything we *think* or do. It tests every *rule or law* we develop. If our actions or rules conflict with love of God, self, and others, then we are to make an exception or abandon them.

---

these beliefs that their parents thought were part of Jesus' teachings. Usually, these beliefs are inconsistent with Jesus' teachings. Clients appear to be happier and function better in their lives when they change their beliefs to more understanding, caring, democratic, and life-affirming ones. In my book--especially this chapter--I use several examples or quotes that are especially relevant and meaningful. My use of them does not mean that I am recommending that anyone change their own religion or see these quotes as carrying the authority of God. Their ultimate truth value is up to each reader to decide for themselves. Instead, I would like you to view them as powerful statements that represent the point-of-view of Jesus or some other highly respected teacher.

• The Buddha distilled his philosophy into a few statements as well. He implied that happiness was a primary goal of life and that the way to happiness was to overcome all selfish craving through the eightfold path--right understanding, purpose, speech, conduct, vocation, effort, alertness, and concentration. (These are not dissimilar to the six mental control methods I describe in Chapter 8.)

Many people have attempted to codify these general beliefs from the masters into intricate legalistic codes. However, as the great philosopher Paul Tillich pointed out; these codification attempts usually end by making the rules into rigid *ends* in themselves. They forget that the rules are only *means* to the more important ends of happiness and love.

Follow your highest beliefs--being rule-bound makes people like robots. *Rule-bound* means rigidly making no exceptions to specific rules--even when they conflict with more important, general rules.

For example, John made a house payment of $1480.46. His actual payment was supposed to be $1480.64--leaving him 18 cents short! The clerk at his mortgage company refused to accept the payment and charged him an $80 late-payment charge. The rule read that if you don't submit the full payment by the 15th of the month, then a late fee is assessed. Technically, John was wrong. Yet those of us who are not rule-bound will see this as an injustice. Why?

The reason is because we believe that higher, more comprehensive rules are more important than that specific rule. The reason that mortgage companies assess penalties is because otherwise it would cost them interest income if a person were very late with his payment. However, John's payment was only 18 cents short. So being a few days late giving them the additional 18 cents would not really cost them any significant amount of interest. A higher, more comprehensive rule states, "If no harm, then no penalty."

Rule-bound means following the more specific and explicit rules instead of following the *higher rules*--that tend to be more comprehensive and less explicit. The highest rules are valuing our own and other people's well-being and happiness. Whenever lower, more specific rules conflict with higher rules, make an exception or replace the rule.

Whatever happened to John? A manager higher in the company waived John's late-payment fee. He was not rule-bound. The clerk probably felt more insecure about breaking the late-payment rule because he was afraid he would get into trouble with his manager. On the other hand, the manager was aware of higher company rules--to protect their investment *and* to satisfy customers.

People with obsessive-compulsive disorder provide extreme examples of being rule-bound. People who become rule-bound become robots. They let the rules make their decisions for them--instead of making unique decisions for every situation (based on higher, general principles). Since they are not taking responsibility themselves, and everything is based upon a code of fixed rules, life becomes too predictable and controlled. They lack creativity and flexibility. Their lives often become devoid of meaning, enthusiasm, and enjoyment--which causes depression.

We all need rules to live by and a certain amount of routine and control in our lives. We all need an optimal amount of control. We need more control in areas that are more important to us--such as in meeting basic needs. Security in our food supply, health, and income is a lot more important than security in knowing what kind of car we will drive. However, the most important type of security is knowing that we can find a way to be happy and productive in any situation (that we can find routes to happiness for any situation). Once we know that, we do not need to be rule-bound.

A strong Higher Self can overcome loneliness and a fear of being alone. My client was so afraid of being alone that she would jump into any relationship she could find. She often picked men who abused her. She would pick almost anybody in pants who met minimal standards; because, she believed that being in a bad relationship couldn't be as bad as the loneliness and worthlessness she felt alone.

Her Higher Self beliefs telling her that she was a valuable person who could take care of herself were weak. Learning these ideas were threatening to old beliefs, but she was also excited about them. Slowly, she learned how to take good care of herself. She found new fulfilling activities that she could do alone or do with new friends. She learned how to meet her own needs without being in a relationship. Finally, she reached a major turning point in her life--she preferred being alone to being in a bad relationship.

Ironically, no longer "*having*" to be in a relationship caused her to be more appealing to the kind of men she would be happier with. Previously, only "losers," who abused her, were attracted to her. Men who would respect her more valued her new self-confidence and happiness. They would have been turned off by her previous neediness. Within a year, she was in her first healthy, happy relationship.

Strong Higher Self beliefs *do not negate needs*; they listen to *all* of our needs and parts of ourselves. The best conductor is not someone who neglects parts of the orchestra. The best conductor isn't someone who loves the violin and dislikes the flute! In order for an orchestra to be in greatest harmony, all players must perform well. The best conductor must attend to the needs of each player in the orchestra with minimal favoritism. Each player must be given a chance to grow and perform well.

We all have basic needs--such as nutrition, safety, health, caring, and creative activity. We also each have many individual values, interests, goals, and desires that reflect unique parts of ourselves. Each of these parts is like a player in the orchestra. When one is repressed, denied repeatedly, and not understood or encouraged, then it will become a discordant player that takes away from the harmony of the orchestra as a whole. That harmony is the foundation of our happiness.

For example, one client came to therapy because he was constantly thinking about sex, masturbating 20 or more times a week, and felt tremendous guilt. All of this thought, guilt, and worry about masturbating had begun to interfere with his college work, his relationships, and his whole life. His masturbation caused guilt feelings, then he would masturbate again to cover up the guilt feelings, etc.

Underneath these guilty feelings were some powerful beliefs that helped cause his problems. He believed that sexual feelings are inherently bad. He was taught, "God made sex for procreation--not pleasure." He felt guilty whenever he had sexual impulses or feelings. He thought that masturbating was a mortal sin.

In therapy, we questioned his old beliefs. His new beliefs accepted his sexual part as another player in the orchestra. He began to think of his entire body as a gift of God and each bodily part as worthy of his love and care. Once he began to accept his sexual feelings as normal, healthy biological functions and realize that many healthy, morally good people also masturbate, he quit feeling guilty about masturbating. He also stopped masturbating compulsively, because he didn't have any guilt to cover up with more masturbating.

AN INNER GROWING FORCE

The Higher Self starts with a few, unorganized beliefs. It initially has weak and limited effects on other thoughts, emotions, and behavior. However, it can develop into a highly organized, comprehensive system with a great deal of control over the entire being.

To the degree that this harmonious organization of beliefs and habits develops, the person will be more integrated. For example, Freud wrote that the ideal psychological state was an integration between the id, ego, and superego--all three receiving high gratification of their needs. Dr. Carl Rogers, a father of the humanistic psychology movement, thought that integration of the Self was the ideal psychological state.

Dr. Paul Tillich saw how our ultimate concerns were the guiding light for our life, so that our personalities would become more and more integrated around them. He wrote,

Ultimate concern is passionate concern. . .
The ultimate concern gives depth, direction, and unity to all other concerns and,
with them, to the whole personality.
A personal life that has these qualities is integrated. . .
Ultimate concern is related to all sides of reality and
all sides of human personality. . .
body, soul, and spirit are not three parts of man.
They are dimensions of a man's being, always within each other . . .
If a uniting center is absent, the infinite variety of the encountered world,
as well as of the inner movements of the human mind,
is able to produce a complete disintegration of the personality.
(Tillich, *Dynamics of Faith*, pp. 105-107)

THE PROCESS OF INNER CONFLICT RESOLUTION--
HOW THE HIGHER SELF CAN INTEGRATE OUR PERSONALITY

A developing Higher Self will include new, constructive beliefs about ourselves and the world. These new beliefs may conflict with older sets of beliefs (often learned during childhood). The resulting conflicts may generate anxiety. Resolution of those conflicts can occur as the new beliefs (or their "children") explain reality better--and make us happier--than the old beliefs. By "children," I mean deductions or conclusions based upon the higher beliefs.

A higher belief is powerful enough to integrate lower beliefs. The brain has built-in mechanisms for resolving these conflicts. Many cognitive psychologists think that the cognitive brain will automatically pick the belief with the most power to predict the future.[13]

A more general or abstract belief will usually have greater explanation power than a more specific belief. For example, one 30 plus year old client had always wanted a happy marriage. His previous marriage had been a disaster--full of mutual screaming and yelling matches. His current four-year relationship had been much better, and he had counted on it resulting in marriage. He was devastated when she broke-up with him (even though he had not been happy in the relationship).

After exploring his feelings in depth, we found at the bottom a fantasy which had anchored him since childhood. His fantasy was of a happy family like TV's "Brady Bunch."

---

[13] Kelly (1955) used the term **range of convenience** to mean how broad a set of inputs a category covers (discussed in Chapter 7). The **predictive validity** of beliefs as measured by the natural feedback they receive is seen as a primary underlying mechanism for belief verification in many cognitive, learning, and neural network theories.

That fantasy was like night and day to his own family. He had had a miserable family life and childhood--except for a few brief times when his family was like the Brady Bunch. He treasured those brief periods and longed to have a family where he could feel loved and happy. As a little boy, he had developed the belief that "To be happy I *must* have a happy, warm family" [like his "Brady Bunch" image].

What is wrong with this belief? It seems quite normal. However, he gave it *too much importance*. He had made a positive--but too limited a goal--an ultimate concern. He believed that he *had to have* a happy family to be happy. Yet, he was single. That fantasy had *driven* him to desperately seek relationships--which always failed. The *range of convenience* of his goal was too limited. The idea that one *must* have a happy family life to be happy would seem to doom all single people to misery.

What he learned instead was an expanded belief that went something like, "Anyone can be happy in almost any situation, if they learn how to use the proper internal and external routes to achieving happiness." That belief has a much larger range of convenience and applies equally well to married or single people. His new beliefs removed the pressure of finding a relationship--he now saw that he could be happy single. That took some of the pressure off and he focused on learning *how to be happy* instead of *how to get married*. Once he was happier with himself, he eventually found a much better relationship.

The Higher Self as an *Inner Observer* utilizing *Problem-Solving Skills*. People who learn meditation techniques usually practice clearing their minds of all active thoughts so that they can just observe what thoughts, images, and feelings enter awareness. Meditation helps calm people. Other people write journals about their feelings and thoughts and then read what they have written. These self-observation methods help our *inner observers* or *inner therapists* learn about how different thoughts, images, and feelings are connected.

During psychotherapy, one of my primary goals is to help my clients develop their own inner therapists. The inner therapist can become integrated with the Higher Self. In Chapter 2 discussed the self-exploration and problem-solving methods for exploring our strongest emotions to find underlying issues, beliefs, and conflicts between subparts of ourselves.

An important part of keeping the Higher Self in control is to focus on the Higher Self during difficult situations, and let it remain above the situation. From its detached view, it can calmly observe other thoughts, images, and feelings as they are occurring. At first, it is best for it to remain simply an observer--not rushing to make judgments. Its goal is simply *to observe and understand more* until it is confident it has a good understanding and knows how to bring harmony and happiness to the situation.

Hidden inner conflicts can only be resolved as they are *activated*. I love my wife Sherry with all my heart, and I strongly believe in empathetically resolving conflicts. Yet, recently, when she was upset about something I had done, all I could do is defend myself by explaining my reasons for doing it. It never occurred to me to listen to her point of view and let her explain her point of view in more depth. At the time, she reminded me of what I was doing, and my inner conflict was obvious. My Higher Self was not in control of my actions; my old dysfunctional parts had taken control. But as soon as I tuned in to my Higher Self, my emotions immediately changed and I started listening. My shift immediately affected Sherry as well.

My Higher Self was in conflict with an older part that had to be right all the time. This is an example of an *implicit* (hidden) conflict. I was not aware of the conflict in this situation until Sherry pointed out the inconsistency to me.

Our overall system of beliefs has many implied conflicts that are not obvious until the beliefs are simultaneously *activated*. Implicit conflicts between the Higher Self beliefs and old beliefs can be discovered and resolved by using the Belief Integration Process described later.

When we first learn a new insight, we may become excited with its potential. We begin trying to use this new insight in every situation where it has any chance of being appropriate. The new insight may conflict with older ways of coping with those situations.

If the new belief seems to work better in a particular situation, then it will be *validated* (or reinforced) for that situation. We have reprogrammed that situation. If not, we may have to resolve the conflict by modifying the new belief or by just saying it doesn't apply to that situation.

General beliefs are hard to validate or invalidate. It takes time to try out new beliefs in many situations. The more general the belief, the longer it takes to validate it or invalidate it. Some beliefs are so general that they are difficult to validate or invalidate. That is why people often cling to general dysfunctional beliefs even long after they are useful.

For example, why would smokers, alcoholics, or drug addicts argue--even to themselves--that these habits are not doing them much harm despite overwhelming evidence. The reason is that these general beliefs may be helping them feel calmer than the belief that they have been *wrong so long* and must go through a *radical life change* process to break the habit. The old belief helps the person maintain the chosen lifestyle and feel calm about it.

Dan, a psychologist who smoked heavily, years ago told me that he would never get cancer because he "had such good circulation." He said, "Look how red it is under my fingernails; that means I have exceptional circulation. I don't ever have to worry about cancer with circulation like this--only people with poor circulation have to worry about getting cancer if they smoke."

The sad part of the story is that a few years later, Dan died of lung cancer. He put his desire to smoke above valuing the truth. His *inner smoker* seemed to take advantage of the fact that general beliefs are hard to prove false.

Honesty is the answer. Dan was an intelligent and well-informed man. How could he tell me such nonsense? Clearly, he was *biased*. He wanted to continue smoking more than he wanted to take an *honest look at the evidence*. He chose to make smoking a higher priority than honesty.

Not making honesty and the truth the highest of priorities is a fundamental problem that supports many dysfunctional beliefs and lifestyles. Being honest with oneself is worth the cost of change. The final result is a healthier, happier life. Honesty could have saved Dan's life; he died a relatively young man. I make honesty a top, conscious goal-- especially with myself. My goal is to never lie to myself or hide the truth from myself.

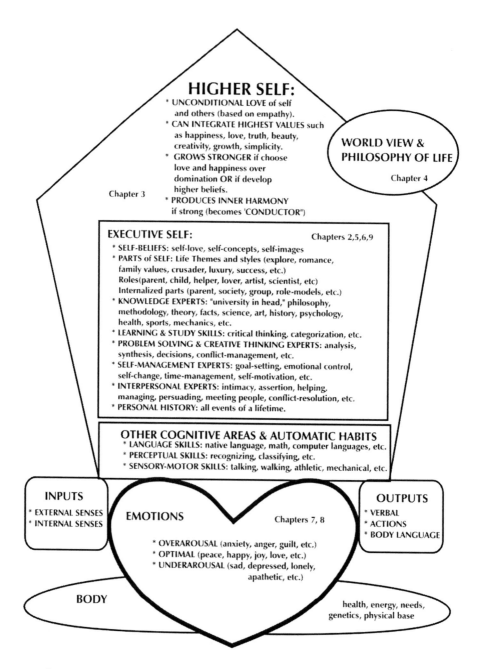

HIGHER SELF:
* UNCONDITIONAL LOVE of self
  and others (based on empathy).
* CAN INTEGRATE HIGHEST VALUES such
  as happiness, love, truth, beauty,
  creativity, growth, simplicity.
* GROWS STRONGER if choose
  love and happiness over
  domination OR if develop
  higher beliefs.
* PRODUCES INNER HARMONY
  if strong (becomes 'CONDUCTOR")

Chapter 3

**WORLD VIEW &
PHILOSOPHY OF LIFE**

Chapter 4

EXECUTIVE SELF: Chapters 2,5,6,9
* SELF-BELIEFS: self-love, self-concepts, self-images
* PARTS of SELF: Life Themes and styles (explore, romance,
  family values, crusader, luxury, success, etc.)
  Roles(parent, child, helper, lover, artist, scientist, etc)
  Internalized parts (parent, society, group, role-models, etc.)
* KNOWLEDGE EXPERTS: "university in head," philosophy,
  methodology, theory, facts, science, art, history, psychology,
  health, sports, mechanics, etc.
* LEARNING & STUDY SKILLS: critical thinking, categorization, etc.
* PROBLEM SOLVING & CREATIVE THINKING EXPERTS: analysis,
  synthesis, decisions, conflict-management, etc.
* SELF-MANAGEMENT EXPERTS: goal-setting, emotional control,
  self-change, time-management, self-motivation, etc.
* INTERPERSONAL EXPERTS: intimacy, assertion, helping,
  managing, persuading, meeting people, conflict-resolution, etc.
* PERSONAL HISTORY: all events of a lifetime.

OTHER COGNITIVE AREAS & AUTOMATIC HABITS
* LANGUAGE SKILLS: native language, math, computer languages, etc.
* PERCEPTUAL SKILLS: recognizing, classifying, etc.
* SENSORY-MOTOR SKILLS: talking, walking, athletic, mechanical, etc.

INPUTS
* EXTERNAL SENSES
* INTERNAL SENSES

EMOTIONS   Chapters 7, 8

OUTPUTS
* VERBAL
* ACTIONS
* BODY LANGUAGE

* OVERAROUSAL (anxiety, anger, guilt, etc.)
* OPTIMAL (peace, happy, joy, love, etc.)
* UNDERAROUSAL (sad, depressed, lonely,
                apathetic, etc.)

BODY

health, energy, needs,
genetics, physical base

The HIGHER SELF and other key psychological systems

When I first gained the insight that happiness is more important than worldly success, I was excited by the idea. However, I also needed to test it. I wanted to be totally honest with myself, because I did not want to adopt an important new belief if it were false. I started by trying to think of all of the arguments I could against this "radical" new belief. I thought that if anyone would have good arguments against it, my dad would. Therefore, I went to him and asked him what he thought. He argued against it, but I did not think his arguments were valid. Then, I decided to test the idea for a few months. I decided to see if my life actually got better by making happiness for self and others my most important goal.

Before I could live by making happiness my most important goal, I had to think of what the implications would be for my daily life. How would it affect my relations with my family and peers? Would I be any different in high school or during sporting events?

For example, in the past I had made "being right" and "winning every contest" important. I realized that sometimes I would get argumentative over unimportant details to prove I was right. I decided that from now on I was going to pay more attention to helping people be happier, and that being overly argumentative took away from both my own and the other party's happiness. That single application of the more general *happiness goal* had a significant positive effect upon my relationships with others.

Biological basis for triumph of truth. No matter how hard I try, I cannot believe that the leaves on that tree outside my window are red and not green. No matter how much I would like to believe that this body of mine will live forever, I cannot. Why can't we believe that which we do not believe to be true? The thought that my body could live forever certainly is a *positive* thought. However, the cognitive system operates by some basic psychobiological laws. One of these laws is that we need *supportive evidence* from other experience and beliefs to actually believe an idea. We can only believe what our own sensory evidence adequately supports.

Honesty brings harmony and integration to the cognitive system. We can temporarily trick ourselves into denying what some inner part of us knows to be true, but we can never totally escape that honest part of ourselves. It will be somewhere inside causing conflict and anxiety for the part that is living a lie. The alcoholic, foodaholic, or workaholic may keep denying that they have a problem, but some healthier part of their cognitive system knows that they are lying to themselves. It will not be totally repressed. It will keep creating guilt and anxiety until it is heard.

If we make truth a top-priority *conscious value*, then we are aligning the higher (cognitive) parts of ourselves with our basic biological nature that seeks truth. Hunger and thirst for honesty and openness! Doing otherwise will develop a self that is torn into warring parts--like members of a dysfunctional family. Seeking honesty will help develop a self that is integrated and spontaneous--like members of a loving, happy family.

If we are honest with ourselves,
our life-affirming and happiness-affirming beliefs eventually triumph;
because they *really work better!*

REPLACE OLD BELIEFS WITH MORE FUNCTIONAL HIGHER SELF BELIEFS

How do find and root out old beliefs that are interfering with our health and happiness? The process will happen somewhat automatically. However, we can accelerate the process by using the belief-integration process below.

The Belief Integration Process

We can *consciously* monitor our Higher Selves to speed the integration of our personalities. Early in my own quest, a little book by Frank Luboff fascinated me. When he wrote the book, he was a young man serving as a missionary in a remote jungle area. He felt confused about what his mission was, but he was lonely and decided to try an experiment. He wanted to develop a loving, intimate relationship with God. His goal was to stay in touch with God and the loving part of himself every moment of every day. His book is a documentary of these efforts. He found his endeavor difficult at first. He constantly had to put himself back in touch with his Higher Self. But the more he tuned in, the more love and happiness he felt. Within the year, his life had been transformed.

The book's title is, *Letters from a Modern Mystic*--written more than 50 years ago. How practical is such an inward focus in a world with so many "practical problems"? Frank Luboff went on to form and lead a worldwide organization that has taught millions of people how to read and write. If we will consistently focus on love and base our lives on our Higher Selves, we will transform the world! Here's how.

1. Keep tuned in to your Higher Self. Weekly, daily, hourly--even moment-to-moment--tune in to your Higher Self and consciously view situations from its point-of-view. Constantly ask yourself questions like, "How can I view this situation from my new perspective?" "What will make me and others the happiest in this situation?" "Which is the most truthful?"

2. Observe your reactions and activated conflicts. Watch your natural reactions, old thoughts, and old habits. What conflicts do you feel? Follow your emotions--what are their sources? What old beliefs are being threatened by your new point-of-view? Use the self-exploration process in Chapter 2 to get to the hidden, underlying beliefs that are the troublemakers.

3. Resolve the conflicts. *Carry on a dialog* between your newer, Higher Self point-of-view and the inner parts producing the old habits and beliefs. In what ways do you need to modify the old (or new) beliefs to keep them consistent with the truth and with the ultimate concern of happiness for all? The goal is to update our beliefs to make sure that the old beliefs and habits are consistent with the new Higher Self beliefs.

4. Choose to live by your Higher Self beliefs. The belief you choose to live by is the one you strengthen. Which is it to be--dysfunction or Higher Self?

THE SOURCE OF MY NEW IDENTITY

As I have been writing this book, I carry on all sorts of internal dialogues. My *inner psychologist* says that it is important for the readers to know about important psychological principles that will help them understand more about themselves. My *inner writer* part says that people want to hear interesting stories or cleverly worded statements more than dry theory. These two parts battle on every page over meaty content substance versus style and interest. Which one is the "real me"?

When you say "me" or "I," what do you mean? What part of your cognitive system is doing the talking? Generally, it is some part of the executive self. However, the executive self has many subparts. We can be most aware of these subparts when we talk with ourselves or shift points of view.

When I first wrote my "How to be Happy" years ago, my ideas were tentative. I was not sure if I believed the things I was writing or not. They were more like hypotheses to be experimented with. I did not yet identify with them. However, after all these years, these values and beliefs are the heart of my identity--I do not question them seriously anymore because they have worked so well, for so long.

As your Higher Self develops and successfully guides your daily life, it will become stronger and achieve even more control of your life. You will gradually identify with it more, and you will say, "I have inner peace; I am living my life the way I really want to."

The Higher Self is selective about which habits it changes. As the Higher Self observes our daily habits and beliefs, it will tend to change those parts that are inconsistent with its higher beliefs. For some people changing higher beliefs will dramatically affect a number of life areas. For others it will involve only minor changes. In general, the more life-enhancing our previous beliefs and habits have been, the less change that will be necessary.

The Higher Self as *Inner Hero*. So many times, I have seen someone facing extremely difficult circumstances reach deep inside and find inner strength they didn't know they had. I have seen clients ready to die--unable to find anything to live for--suddenly find the will to live.

Dawn, one of Sherry's clients, had a form of cancer that is almost always fatal. Her treatment necessitated moving away from her beloved Seal Beach to a cold, east coast climate. While in therapy, Sherry and Dawn worked on helping Dawn accept the loss of things she would miss and ways to keep them alive in her heart after her move. Dawn tried visualization, positive thinking, and reading Dr. Bernie Siegle's book, *Love, Medicine, and Miracles*. She practiced learning how to play and find happiness within herself.

In a letter to Dawn, Sherry sent sand from Seal Beach and suggested that she listen to the song *Hero*. Dawn wrote back. She loved the sand, and had--almost unbelievably--an encounter with Bernie Siegel, who had been kind and helpful. Coincidentally, she had already been listening to the song, *Hero*, during all her chemotherapy sessions. The song *Hero* is a reminder that you may feel all alone in the world and feel no one is there for you. Yet, you can always feel loved if you look deep enough inside to your Higher Self. Inside is a hero that always loves you, is always there for you, and is strong enough to overcome any circumstances. At times, you may feel weak, empty, and hopeless. However, if you look to your Higher Self, you will find the strength to survive and the strength to rise above your fears. For inside your heart, you will find your inner hero. Dawn, indeed, found the hero inside herself. Think of your Higher Self as your *Inner Hero* whenever you need strength or love you can't find from others, or don't think you have yourself.

SELF-ACTUALIZATION--THE RESULT OF A STRONG HIGHER SELF

Dr. Abraham Maslow (1962) talked about "our essential inner nature" in a way that is similar to what I mean by Higher Self. He discussed its initially fragile character and pointed out how it can be repressed or pushed aside, but not lost entirely.

He believed that psychological health was not possible unless this essential core was accepted, loved, and allowed to grow and develop. Ultimately, the person cannot move to self-actualization without adopting the metavalues such as those Maslow identified. Developing these higher values is a critical part of strengthening your Higher Self.

MASLOW'S SELF-ACTUALIZATION METAVALUES:
wholeness, perfection, completion, justice, aliveness, richness, simplicity, beauty, goodness, uniqueness, effortlessness, playfulness, truth, and self-sufficiency[14]

As we develop the Higher Self and our philosophy of life, and as we begin to resolve our inner conflicts and live by these metavalues, we move down the path toward self-actualization.

As we approach self-actualization, our behavior will become more spontaneous. Dr. Maslow's self-actualized people were spontaneous and natural. They seemed to act with less conflict and more ease than most other people. However, this spontaneity came only later in life, after they had resolved most of their important internal conflicts. Once inner conflicts are resolved--integrated around our ultimate concern--we can be more spontaneous and free.

Instead of work versus play, work becomes play. Instead of me versus them, most acts are done *both* for self and other. As the yeast from the Higher Self works its way through the mind, our choices represent more of our inner parts working together in harmony. As Maslow said, **"Be healthy and then you can trust your impulses."** (A. H. Maslow, 1954, p.179)

LIST YOUR TOP BELIEFS TO GIVE YOUR HIGHER SELF MORE POWER

You know that inside somewhere is the true you, the part that is your best part, the part that represents what you want most, the part that really loves you and others, the part that is your *inner hero*. That part is your Higher Self. Have you ever tried to write your best and most important Higher Self beliefs?

A few years ago, I decided to write my own current version of "How To Be Happy." I wanted to integrate all that I had learned from my personal life and my years as a psychologist. The result was a list of key beliefs and skills that formed the basis for this book. I have summarized them in the box, "I CHOOSE LOVE, TRUTH, and HAPPINESS." These guidelines are commitments that are from the conscious core of my philosophy of life and of my "Higher Self." Just about everything else in my life follows from this center of my values and goals.

PRACTICE: Write Your Higher Self Statements. Perhaps you would like to make a similar commitment to yourself. You may use my version, or (better) write your own version. When you have your first version, put it in a place where you will look at it frequently on a daily or weekly basis (in a closet, inside a cabinet door, on a mirror, etc.). Periodically revise it.

---

[14] The Maslow's metavalues' correlations with Overall Happiness on SHAQ were: wholeness, .29; perfection, .16; justice, .19; simplicity, .24; beauty, .28; goodness, .28; uniqueness, .27; effortlessness, .20; playfulness, .32; and self-sufficiency, .22   (Number of subjects > 3000, significance, $p < .0001$).

My Commitment:

I CHOOSE LOVE, TRUTH, and HAPPINESS--
Loving Myself, Loving Others, and Loving All Creation
(The Foundation of My Higher Self)

I am grateful for the gift of life. I was given the gift of life and the opportunity to create a happy life for myself. I did not earn or deserve life or this opportunity--so I will not complain that my time on Earth or opportunities may not be as great as someone else's.

I am the person most responsible for meeting my own needs and values. I cannot prove that my feelings are important, I can only assert that they are important to me because I am the one affected by them. I am also the person most in control of my own thoughts, feelings, and actions. Since I am the one most in control, I am also the one most responsible for my thoughts, feelings, and actions. [I am not primarily responsible for others' thoughts, emotions, or actions.]

My ultimate concern is maximizing my own and others' happiness and contributing to the good of the universe. All other values or goals are less important than this ultimate concern. I recognize that whenever I do not keep this as my ultimate concern, I will confuse the means with the end and decrease my chances of being happy.
• I try to properly balance present with future happiness and balance my own with others' happiness-- a key to inner harmony.
• For every decision I make--especially big ones--I will attempt to estimate which alternative will lead to the greatest truth and happiness. I will choose that alternative.

Part of my ultimate concern is to always seek truth and growth for myself and others. My mind was designed to seek the truth and continually grow in knowledge. Without truth and growth, I cannot be maximally happy. Others have the same needs to ultimately find happiness. Truth and growth are basic principles of the universe. Therefore, I will make them top priority conscious goals and "hunger and thirst" for the truth.
➔ **Continued in next box.**

I CHOOSE LOVE, TRUTH, AND HAPPINESS (Continued)

I care about every cell, system, and value in myself. Every cell and every system in my body and mind is important to my overall functioning, health, and happiness, and I care for each one. One way to care for each part of myself is to give it proper exercise and allow it regular harmonious functioning.

• Similarly, every living cell and creature is important--the most important being the happiness of humans.

I will *take good care of every area of my life* (and encourage others to do likewise) including:

1. My Higher Self and spiritual needs. I will continue to develop the part of me that loves life, myself, and others. I will seek greater understanding, empathy, acceptance, and forgiveness of myself and others--even those who have harmed me (that does not exclude reparations).

2. My relationships with others--empathy, love, and clear boundaries. I will seek win--win relationships with others and realize that each of us is primarily responsible for our own happiness. I will not allow myself to remain in abusive or win--loose relationships where I am either the winner or loser. I will either change the relationship until it is acceptable or separate myself from it. Some other guidelines:

• Loving means giving without expecting anything in return.

• I give primarily out of empathy and love--giving makes me happier by seeing others happy. I give only secondarily to get something in return.

• Loving effectively is giving what the other person truly wants/needs.*

• Empathetic listening and exploring issues in depth is the way to discover what the other wants/needs.

• If there is conflict between what I think others' needs are and others' requests, I must use my deep understanding to decide the issue. However, normally I go by what they say.

If I can help create a good relationship with one person, I can help create at least that good a relationship with someone else.

3. My relationship to nature, beauty, and my environment.

4. My body, health, and safety.

5. My mind, learning, and growth in each area of knowledge.

6. My emotions. *While pleasure is important, happiness is much more important.* To obtain happiness I must resolve inner conflicts and feel good about my current and future satisfaction of values in each life area. I must learn how to function harmoniously (See chapters 7, 8).

7. My material and financial needs.

8. My education and career--my contributions to other people and the world. I will try to maximize my competence, productivity, and positive impact.

9. My play and personal activities. I will set priorities for my free time that produce the greatest happiness (and is not based on "shoulds"). During this time I can meet health and happiness values such as physical activity, learning, beauty, spirituality, social, creativity, sex, and many more. I will minimize time spent on less productive and fun activities. I will do them as quickly and efficiently as possible or try to create a natural interest or fun in them.

SHAQ Research Results: The Higher Self

I created a scale to summarize the main values corresponding to the idea of Higher Self presented in this chapter.

The Higher Self scale consists of the following values-beliefs:

Self-happiness, others' happiness; balance present-future, self-others' happiness; base decisions on maximizing happiness for self-others; value/love self and all unconditionally; accept all parts of self; gratitude-abundance thinking; integrity; develop personal philosophy; learning, self-development; exploration/truth; competence, be best I can be; complete all important goals; independence; self-sufficiency; self-discipline; health and longevity; life balance; beauty; goodness; and fun and playfulness.

The Higher Self scale correlated with Overall happiness, .50; with Low Depression, 25; with Low Anxiety, .20; with Low Anger-Aggression, .37; with good Relationship Outcomes, .44; and with good Health outcomes.37.[15]

Therefore, our research supports the idea that these Higher Self values are associated with not only happiness and low depression, anxiety, and anger; but also with good health, relationships, and other positive life outcomes (Stevens, 2009).

Where do I look for guidance I can trust?
Not from my lower pleasures and pains--they are too shortsighted.
Not from just any emotions or thoughts--
they may come from dysfunctional parts of myself.
Not from just anyone--they may not know or care what is best for me.
Then where?
I can trust the emotions and inner voice of my Higher Self, because
the Higher Self reflects true empathy and love for self and others.
Even if it makes errors, at least it values happiness and truth above all.
It is my inner hero and spiritual center.
Every time I listen to it and choose its way,
become stronger and increase my chances for happiness.

---

[15] The correlations were all Pearson product-moment r's that were significant at the p < .0001 level. The number of subjects (N) ranged from 2588 to 3179.

CREATE A POSITIVE WORLD
BY ADOPTING
A POSITIVE WORLD VIEW

\\\

WE CAN NEVER KNOW THE REAL EXTERNAL WORLD--ONLY OUR PERCEPTIONS

Explain these inconsistencies. Someone from sunny California sees a cloudy, cool day as dark and depressing; whereas, someone from Washington state sees it as refreshing. An avid hockey fan views a baseball game as boring and slow, while an avid baseball fan views hockey as too violent and aggressive. A rock music enthusiast is baffled about how someone listening to classical music can soar to emotional heights (and vice-versa).

Each of these external inputs was identical, yet in each case, one observer had a positive emotional reaction and the other, a negative one. The observer feeling the positive emotion had a better understanding of the input or had more positive experiences associated with it. Where one person finds meaning and beauty, the other finds only confusion and ugliness. Two different perceptions--two different emotional reactions.

OUR TRUE REALITY IS OUR INNER WORLD--NOT THE EXTERNAL WORLD

Consider how unhappy some are who have "everything" in the external world and how happy some are who have "nothing." Famous people have been miserable or even committed suicide despite having great amounts of money, love, fame, friends, attention, success, or any other external condition we can imagine.

Yet, other people are happy despite living in poverty, being unable to see or walk, living alone for years, or being without almost any other external condition that we consider necessary for our own happiness. How can people with so much be so unhappy, while others with so little be so happy? If money, fame, friends, and all these things don't cause happiness--what does? It is not really such a mystery if you understand one simple fact--we live in our inner world more than we live in the external world!

Our Inner World Views Filter All Inputs and Affect Emotions

Each day my consciousness seems to focus on *external events* such as hearing the alarm, getting dressed, eating breakfast, driving my car, talking to people, writing, playing tennis, or watching television. I usually consciously pay more attention to the external world around me than to my internal world. So I must be a little skeptical about the idea that my internal world is a more important determinant of my happiness than my external world. After all, my attention seems so focused on my external world.

Yet it is an interesting idea. How is it that my inner world can be so important if I hardly pay attention to it as the day progresses? Our attention may focus on the external world, but consider the following:

- **We never experience the external world directly.** Our focus on the external world actually consists of internal perceptions and thoughts. It does not consist of the external world events themselves!
- **We live in a constant stream of thoughts**. We are thinking the entire time we are awake. Our minds rarely "go blank." We have thousands of thoughts each day!
- **Thoughts directly determine emotions.** Our thoughts--not external events-- directly control all emotions--including positive emotions such as love, joy, and happiness and negative emotions such as anxiety, anger, and depression.
- **Underlying mental models and structures.** There are mental structures that underlie and generate the conscious thoughts we have in our moment-to-moment experience.
- **Causal power of these mental structures.** These underlying mental structures are the basic causal mechanisms determining our personality and happiness--not immediate, external life situations.

We Automatically Create a Model of the World in Our Mind

When a child is born, it knows almost nothing of the world around it. Soon it discovers many new sights, sounds, and feelings. The child learns to recognize patterns from these stimuli. The infant associates being fed, bathed, changed, and cuddled with this strange looking creature that keeps making odd sounds. Later, the child learns to call this strange pattern of stimuli, "Mama."

Even from those early experiences, the infant starts to create a mental model of its mother. It learns what its mother looks like, sounds like, feels like, and learns to predict her behavior--"If I cry hard enough, I can get mom's attention."

The infant may also begin to realize that mother is influencing its behavior--"If I cry just for attention, mom will ignore me, so I might as well not try that anymore." Children may not learn to describe these relationships with words until much later, but they learn the rules nevertheless.

The child's mental models of its mother, father, and other significant persons can become very elaborate. Most of us know so much about our parents that we could probably write a book about them. Indeed, many children (as adults) have written biographies of their famous parents. We also develop mental models of objects--our houses, automobiles, and even our toasters. We interact with these objects based on our mental models of them.

An expert has a very detailed and accurate mental model compared to a novice who has only a vague, less accurate model. We develop beliefs and feelings based on our mental models of people, objects, and events. We can develop mental models of societies or even of the entire world. The mental maps of our cities are important for daily navigation. But more important are the mental models of the forces controlling the world and universe.

Do we picture the world as controlled by positive forces continually improving the world and taking good care of us? Or do we picture the world as controlled by negative forces gradually destroying us? This negative world view could be summarized by a bumper sticker that says, "Life's a struggle and then you die." Our world models (world views) are major factors in how optimistic and happy we are. They filter most inputs and process most outputs to the external world.

Internalized versus examined mental models. When we were children, we were ill-equipped to examine the models presented to us. Most likely, we internalized the expectations or "shoulds" of our parents. For example, they taught us how to eat, how to dress, how to bathe, how to play, how to communicate, how to think about other people, and how to deal with our emotions.

To this day, if we do not do as we were taught and eat with poor table manners or speak disrespectfully to authorities, we may feel guilty or embarrassed. Somehow, it feels wrong. These mental models have become powerful determinants of our thoughts, feelings, and actions.

When we were small children and our parents told us something, we "swallowed it whole" without "chewing it over" adequately. That is natural for a child. We may ingest our parents' mental models of what is right and wrong, of racial groups, of God, of parenting practices, and of even our self-images with little rational questioning. Someone we trusted told us that something was true, and as children we automatically believed them. As adults, it is time to stop automatically swallowing ideas whole.

If we have not already done so, it is time to examine these old beliefs and mental models from our newer, growth-oriented point of view. It is time to put Higher Self beliefs such as seeking openness and truth above all else or we will only delude ourselves. It is time to appeal to our Higher Self's ultimate concern of seeking happiness for self and others.

If we will begin to compare our old internalized models with these Higher Self beliefs, then we will find conflicts. We can modify our old models (or--sometimes--our Higher Self beliefs) to achieve a higher state of integration. Integration resolves basic belief conflicts underlying most daily conflicts and emotional reactions. As a drop of dye gradually colors the entire glass of water, so our Higher Self beliefs will color our entire personality.

One client started with a dismal view of the world. She could find only faults with herself, everyone, and everything around her. She had never received much affection in her life and had almost always been surrounded by conflict, criticism, and anger. She said that she had never even *seen* a happy family. Is it any wonder that she had developed a cynical world view? She could not believe in God or any positive, loving force in the world. She thought that people were only out to get more money, power, and prestige. She believed that it was impossible to be happy or to have a close, happy relationship for any length of time--so why try?

However, a part of her (her Higher Self?) *could* imagine a better life and a better world. She still had a hope deep inside that maybe she could be happy and someday have a happy family of her own. One-by-one, we explored many of her negative world view assumptions and challenged them with more positive views. For example, she frequently assumed that her troubles were due to people being out to get her personally. However, we found other explanations for people's actions--including explanations that put much of the responsibility for problems back on her. She had often unintentionally initiated negative cycles with people. We also explored benefits of revenge versus forgiveness and her beliefs about love and affection.

She improved her communication skills, and created a happier world for herself and others. As she began to explore and develop this part of her, she created her own more positive mental model of the world. She developed her own positive mental model of what loving relationships would be like. Her new mental models became active--they helped her create a world more like she wanted. It was amazing to see the transformation of this cynical, negative person into someone who was happy, radiant, and loving.

Our imagined world models can become reality. We develop a mental model of our city's streets. We use that mental map to select a route to our destination. An architect planning a house develops a mental model and commits it to paper. Builders follow that blueprint to create an actual home.

Some mental models are based upon our perception of reality. However, the power of imagination gives us the power to imagine possible states of the world that do not exist. Our imagination can make mountains out of molehills, or it can create visions of a better world. Our reality checks limit the mental models we can *actually believe*. However, our imagination is *almost limitless* in the models it can create.

We can create plans for a building, create a work of art, or create our own blueprint for a better life or world. Martin Luther King's "I Have a Dream for America" was a vision that he created. It motivated him and his followers and helped change the world to become a little more like his vision. Our power of imagination--creating our own unique mental models--is one of the greatest gifts that separates humans from other creatures. It has transformed the world.

To the degree that we can imagine and create an internal model of a more ideal world, then we can begin to live in that new world. Once we create the model and choose to adopt it as a model for our own life, then we are beginning to *actually live in that world*. Our new model will affect our perceptions, our thoughts, our feelings, and our actions-- the main ingredients of the world we experience.

If we create a world full of beauty, harmony, love, truth, and happiness in our mind, then we will actually begin to live in that world! On the other hand, if our mental model of the world is one of ugliness, conflict, hate, falsehood, and unhappiness, then that will be *our* world.

I can imagine a world in which people love themselves and other people just because they are alive. They recognize the caring Higher Self in every person and attempt to communicate with that person's Higher Self--instead of focusing on dysfunctional parts. In this imagined world people seek truth and knowledge and live by many of the principles in this book. In this world, people attempt to understand each other before judging how to react to them. In this world, people more consistently choose actions that will make themselves and others happy. The more I imagine this world, the more this world model helps me create certain effects--such as:

- **Many of my beliefs and thoughts come from this ideal world model.**
- **I treat other people according to these beliefs.**
- **People begin treating me more "as if" we both live in this kind of world.**
- **I change the world a little**. Since more of my beliefs, thoughts, and actions and experiences with others are like my ideal world model, I really am living in a world more like I imagine. I am also helping create a world more like that for other people.

TWO BASIC WORLD VIEWS--CHAOS versus CREATIVITY

Two world views--which is more like yours? A graduating college senior was feeling quite depressed and felt little motivation to look for a job. What was behind this student's depression? He said, "Our parents had all the breaks, and there's nothing left for us." In his mind, it was easy for them to get a high-paying job, buy a house, and raise a family in a world without crime or serious problems.

Yet, he saw himself facing a world full of too many competitors. He foresaw an overpopulated, polluted world where everyone would be poor and unhappy. He had little to look forward to: "I learned in a class that everything is basically chaos and everything living eventually returns to dust."

Contrast this doomsday view of the future to that of another graduating senior. "I've been supporting myself since I was 18, and I can't wait to find a job as a professional." This student was moving toward future goals of a home and family. He gave me a lecture, "Getting a good job in my field is tough. Some of my friends think their parents had it so easy, but they forget that our parents also had recessions, the cold war, and other problems. When I think of all the advances in technology and improved communication between people, I'm excited about the future. I think ideas of a global economy and a global society are fantastic. I want to be a part of that."

These opposing views of the world and human nature are more than just intellectual differences. They affect our mental health. A pessimistic view of the universe and human nature will predispose the believer toward depression and other negative emotions. A positive view of the universe and human nature will predispose the believer toward happiness and will provide hope and energy to face life's daily problems. Research strongly supports the value of a positive world view and optimism for minimizing negative emotions and maximizing happiness (Carver & Scheier, 2002; Chang, 2001; Peterson, 2000; and SHAQ results).

Which world view is more accurate? Can we believe in progress? Are the basic forces inherent in the world and human nature driving us toward extinction or toward a far better world? Which is more powerful--the forces of chaos or the forces of creativity?

If we look at history from a perspective of a few years or even a few decades, we may get a different idea about progress than when we look at it from a longer time frame. For example, suppose you had been living in 1939. The country had been in a terrible depression for 10 years, and Hitler was conquering Europe and executing millions of Jewish people. Just 12 years before, we had won the war to end all wars and the economy had been booming. Who could be optimistic in those days? It seemed as if the world was going to hell.

Yet, suppose you had been living in America in 1949--just 10 years later. The Allies had just won World War II, the economy was booming, and people believed the future was bright. It was easy to be an optimist then.

Evolution is the steady force behind long-range progress. When we look at history as a whole, the ups and downs over a few years or even a few decades fade. The subtle, yet powerful forces of evolution become much clearer. At one time humans didn't even exist. The great philosopher and paleontologist [studies evolution], Teilhard de Chardin (1959) wrote that the world is divided into different levels of organization--the physical, the biological, and the spiritual levels.

Each level evolved slowly until it reached a *critical mass* of organization. Then its development suddenly exploded. At the physical level, in the primordial soup of molecules interacting and evolving, something happened. At some critical mass of organization, the first form of life emerged. Biological evolution had begun.

Millions of years later, the biological evolution produced a brain that reached some critical mass of organization, the first form of higher level thinking emerged. Spiritual evolution had begun. By *spiritual*, he meant the level that includes information, knowledge, thought, and the spiritual realm [in the more traditional sense]. The spiritual level is higher than the biological, and the biological level is higher than the physical. However, the spiritual level could not exist without the lower levels. First, it couldn't have evolved without them. Second, the spiritual level *emerges* from the lower levels like a melody emerges from an orchestra or like life emerges from a collection of molecules in a cell.

For the first time in history, some part of existence had the ability to know itself and the world around it at a high level of thought. At this new level of thought, organisms could *consciously create their own inner and outer* worlds--not just *react* to the world. Humans could become creators of the world--not just residents or victims of it. Endowed with this new power, humans have changed the world more in the past hundred years than in the preceding million years. Imagine the differences in just the past 100 years--electricity, automobiles, televisions, airplanes, books, computers, colleges, hospitals, and modern homes.

Teilhard believed that, even within the spiritual level, higher spiritual levels are evolving. The seeds of this new level are present today. We are approaching a critical mass of information which could lead to a new level of integration and spirituality among all humans. We call part of this proliferation of information the *knowledge explosion.* The computer revolution has changed almost every aspect of society. Artificial intelligence is a whole new field for understanding and using intelligence in order to create robots and get more control over our machines and environment. As late as 1800, it would have been hard for most people to imagine the electronic marvels we have now.

Teilhard used the concept of *higher consciousness* to represent what many people mean by the more traditional word of *spiritual*[16]. Higher consciousness is a level at which we are more conscious and knowledgeable about ourselves as thinking, feeling persons. We can create and love an internal and external world that will meet our human needs. At higher levels of spirituality, we also care about our natural environment and all living creatures.

At the higher consciousness levels (in the psychological and philosophical realms), a similar phenomenon is possible. For example, we can see great progress in psychology. In 1900 psychological research was just beginning. Now psychologists publish hundreds of research articles each month. Self-development has mushroomed. When I was young, I couldn't find any self-help books to help me learn how to be happier. I didn't know what a psychologist was. Now, self-help books fill whole aisles in bookstores, and psychotherapy and self-help organizations are everywhere.

Dr. Roger Sperry, a Nobel-prize winning psychobiologist wrote about how science is taking this new level of consciousness seriously--as a powerful causal force shaping the present as well as the future. He states,

---

[16] By *spiritual* I do *not* infer the existence of any type of "supernatural" beings or world that is beyond the "natural" universe. I leave it to the readers to draw their own conclusions about the existence of such a world. By spiritual, I mean more what some philosophers have called the "meta" levels of knowledge or the higher consciousness levels--such as humans knowing about themselves and their own essential nature.

. . . this turnabout in the causal status of consciousness abolishes
the traditional science-values dichotomy. . . .
Subjective human values, no longer written off as ineffectual epiphenomena nor
reduced to micro-phenomena, become
the most critically powerful force shaping today's civilized world,
the underlying answer to current global ills and a key to world change.
(*The Science of the Mind*, 1995, p. 37)

Groups, societies, and all humankind can collectively develop states of higher consciousness. Reaching that critical mass level can open new potentials that were previously beyond our imagination. Thousands of years ago, humans could live together peacefully only in small groups--such as extended families. Over time our abilities to organize and live together peacefully has evolved. The size of groups able to function in minimal harmony has grown from families to tribes, to small nations, to large nations, and eventually to a new world order that includes all nations and all people.

How is it that all of a sudden the iron curtain was dismantled? Why are there worldwide peace and environmental movements? Why has there been such a growth in acceptance of human diversity? The spiritual level is fermenting. As more people begin adopting healthy belief systems, they are producing constructive revolutions in our institutions.

In short, I am not the only one with a quest for happiness. We all thirst for happiness. We are learning how to find happiness from each other. We're moving toward some critical mass in which most of the people in the world will know about these keys to happiness. Then, the values of "life, liberty, and the pursuit of happiness" will have an explosive impact.

This new world culture will not only have the *will and goal* for happiness but the *knowledge* and other *means* to obtain happiness for most of its people most of the time. That is not just wishful thinking. Powerful creative forces are built into every cell of every living creature. These growth forces are providing the impetus to make this better world a reality. Humankind *does* learn from experience.

Perhaps, you find what I have been saying hard to believe right now. You may have a basic world view that is different. We don't all have to believe the same thing to be happy. I have just presented what I believe to be the truth. However, I suggest that you consider the following:

If you have a pessimistic view of the future,
you will be predisposed to negative thoughts and depression.
If you have an optimistic view of the future,
you will be predisposed to feel happy.
If you want to change an underlying cause of your negativism or depression, you
must examine and replace negative world views
with more positive ones that you can honestly believe--
or at least hope for.

PRACTICE: Examine your basic world view--Is it negative or positive?
Part I: How does your view of the future compare to the ones discussed above? Do you believe in these creative forces inherent in life and the universe? Do you believe that they will probably triumph over chaos or negative forces? Why? How do these beliefs affect your daily thoughts and happiness?
Part II: Think and write about a possible more positive world view. Try reading works by more thoughtful, optimistic authors. The more ambitious reader might try Teihard's book, *The Phenomenon of Man.*

ACCEPTANCE OF LIFE AND ITS "DARK SIDE"

It would be easy to have a positive world view if everyone lived in paradise. It would be easy to have a positive world view if every part of the world was beautiful, if everyone was always treated with love and respect, and if everyone was given all they need to be happy and live forever. Unfortunately, we don't live in a world like that.

If scientists are correct, the earth started with no animal or plant life. Life on our planet has had to struggle to exist and to develop into higher forms. Life has always been a challenge and a series of overcoming problems. Evils such as illness, death, pain, unhappiness, cruelty, and destruction have been part of each generation. Even people who seem to have it all, in reality, have also experienced more pain, unhappiness, and hardship than others may ever see.

Negative life experiences can lead to a negative philosophy of life and pervasive anxiety and depression. My client was in her early 30's and had already led a life filled with tragic events. She grew up in a small Midwestern town exposed to "all American values"; except, her parents were both alcoholics and hid their secret well. On the surface, her family appeared normal. Yet behind closed doors, she had to take care of her younger brother and her intoxicated parents.

As a teenager, she escaped to the downtown area of Detroit. There she got involved with a man who said he would take care of her. Instead, he turned out to be a drug addict and dealer. He got her hooked on alcohol and a whole variety of drugs. Her life there was a nightmare.

Besides her drug dependence, she was physically, sexually, and verbally abused for several years. Her views of herself and the world grew very dark. She felt like she was in hell. There seemed to be no way out and suicide was a real option. Then she gave birth to her daughter. Although she had almost given up on herself, she decided that she wanted her daughter to get out of this terrible mess. Therefore, she went to Narcotics Anonymous and began a 12-step program to become drug and alcohol free.

She has now been in recovery for more than eight years and turned her life around. She began supporting herself and her daughter, went back to college, finished a bachelor's degree, and is now doing very well in a graduate social work program. She has immersed herself in self-development of all kinds. Besides Narcotics Anonymous, she has taken many classes, read many self-help books, and received counseling. Thinking positively has been a foundation of her new life.

When I met her in a class I taught, I was impressed by her openness, her thirst for learning, and her ability to interpret difficult situations positively. These characteristics have been the secrets to her recovery and success. However, it has not been easy.

After the class, she came in for counseling. Whenever she heard of gangs, drugs, or violence in our area, she would feel a sense of terror. She could not understand it. Her life was going so well, how could she still have flashbacks of these feelings. We explored her underlying beliefs and we discovered that a part of her still believed that the negative, dark forces of the world are "winning" and that the positive forces are "just struggling to survive."

Her fear of the "dark forces' power" created an undercurrent of anxiety and depression that entered her thoughts daily. Her positive side had to keep fighting these negative thoughts. But in the past she had fought them on a superficial level. Instead of exploring and confronting her deeper world view, she often tried to substitute positive thoughts as band-aids. She would tell herself something like, "Everything will be ok, it's silly to worry about this." Her band-aid therapy helped her feel better temporarily, but did not change the *source of the negative thoughts*.

For example, one of the key underlying beliefs we discovered was that there were so many "bad guys" that they were overwhelming the "good guys" of the world. When we explored her "worst possible scenario," we found a feared image of the world eventually being overrun with drug addicts and violence. I asked her to look at her beliefs about that image and the evidence for it. She realized that much of her "evidence" came from the media and their preference for presenting many more negative than positive stories.

The creative forces are inherent in all life. I questioned her belief that the "world was going to Hell." I suggested that she look at this in a broader historical perspective and look at the progress that has been made in the past 5,000 years. I pointed out that within each cell and within each living organism, powerful forces are tenaciously pursuing health and harmony. These inherent forces are not just in a few good guys, but are part of every one of us. In addition, we all have a Higher Self inside--no matter how weak it may be.

When I finished talking, she became animated and excited. She said she knew that what I said was true. She said that as I was talking she thought of her inner city experiences. Her daughter's father and the other people she lived with were hardened, violent criminals. Most people would believe that they were evil to the core.

However, she knew their backgrounds and could understand how abuse by others had empowered their inner, abusive parts. They had developed hardened shells to survive. Yet, she knew them well enough to see that each had a softer, more caring part. She had seen times when each of these hardened criminals showed vulnerability, empathy, tenderness, and love. She said, "I know that if these people have a Higher Self, then everyone does."

She no longer experiences the bolts of fear when she reads the morning paper or sees the evening news. She now believes the forces of love and happiness--though gentler--are stronger than the forces of raw power. They are winning the war.

Sometimes we tend to idealize the past, and therefore believe the world is going downhill. Sometimes we look at all the unethical, harmful people who have achieved financial success and power--even world leaders--and think that the "dark forces" are winning the war. However, when you have these negative thoughts, consider the creative forces in even the worst of people. Also, consider what Ralph Waldo Emerson (1991) wrote more than 150 years ago,

**Things seem to tend downward, to justify despondency,
to promote rogues, to defeat the just; and yet by knaves, as by martyrs,
the just cause is carried forward.
Although knaves win in every political struggle,
although society seems to be delivered over
from the hands of one set of criminals into the hands
of another set of criminals as fast as the government is changed,
and the march of civilization is a train of felonies,
yet the general ends are somehow answered.
We see, now, events forced on, which seem to retard . . .
the civility of ages. But the world spirit is a good swimmer,
and storms and waves cannot drown him.
. . .throughout history, heaven seems to affect low and poor means.
Through toys and atoms, a great and beneficent tendency irresistibly streams.**

OUR IDEAL WORLD VERSUS REALITY:
HOW CAN WE BE HAPPY IN AN IMPERFECT WORLD?

One of my hobbies has been to invent ideas of what a more ideal world would be like. Perhaps you also imagine what a better world would be like--at least better for you. However, I live in the world as it is today. I cannot change the past and my abilities to change the future are limited.

If we do not accept the limitations of our situation--or of ourselves; then we are choosing to be unhappy. Some of the saddest and most unproductive words we can utter are *"what if."* "What if I had been born wealthy, beautiful, or with a happy family?" "What if we had discovered a cure for cancer?" "What if she hadn't left me?" "What if I had gotten that job?" "What if I hadn't made that dumb mistake?" "What if. . .?" instead try saying, *"It is. . .and I will make the best of it--I will find some route to happiness."*

**If I am to be happy,
I must learn to accept and love this world as it is, was, and will be--
not focus on what is not, was not, or cannot be.**

Every creative act also produces waste and "garbage." Our bodies take in food and convert that food into energy and into structural parts of our bodies. As part of this natural, growth process, our bodies also produce waste from that food. Any manufacturing or creative process also produces a certain amount of waste and garbage. With every creative idea or action, there is also a certain amount of waste or garbage that occurred in its production. Perhaps we had to make mistakes before we learned the right way to do it, or perhaps doing it produced negative side-effects.

Do you ever develop expectations that you should do something perfectly--with no mistakes or waste? I may make mistakes and I may make things worse. No matter how hard I try, *I will produce a certain amount of waste and garbage.*

To be happy it is necessary to *accept and forgive mistakes*--my own and the mistakes of others. Otherwise, we choose guilt and resentment over love and happiness. The only way to produce no waste is to think or do *nothing.* However, that would be the biggest waste of all! (Forgiveness of self and others is a major topic in Chapter 6.)

Our limited time on earth. One client who came in because of persistent depression and frequent suicidal thoughts said, "The religions teach you that there is life after death, but I don't believe it. What good is life if it is so short? You go though a few years of living, and then you die. I might as well die now."

His argument was like the fool who wished he had $100,000, but only had $100. He threw away the $100 because he thought, "It's not worth anything." The wise man who had $100 said, "Since I only have $100, I must spend each dollar carefully and get the most for it--for each dollar is precious."

THERE ARE DIFFERENT LEVELS OF REACTIONS

Our thoughts consist of different *levels.* At a lower (more specific, sensory, externally tied) level, we may react negatively to negative situations. However, we can overcome that initial negative reaction by viewing the whole situation from a higher, philosophical level.

Viewing it from a higher perspective can enable me to accept the situation and view it more constructively. This new view can help me feel better. We can use this method to rise above even the most painful situations. Our Higher Selves and constructive philosophies (or religious views) provide the beliefs for this higher perspective.

ACCEPTING THE "UNACCEPTABLE"--SUCH AS PAIN, CRUELTY, AND DEATH

What seems too unacceptable or too overwhelming for you to cope with? List all the situations you believe you could not stand or could not cope with.

> **PRACTICE: Stop and make that unacceptables list now.** Imagine the worst possible conditions that you are most afraid of--no matter how unlikely they may seem right now. What are your greatest fears? Death? Blindness? Being alone? Poverty? A boring job? Failure? Rejection?

What if these unacceptable events happen despite your best efforts? As long as you have no way of viewing these "unacceptable" events (and their effects) in a minimally positive way, then they will be an underlying source of negative emotions. Whenever you perceive *any possibility* that these "unacceptable events" might occur, you will feel bolts of anxiety, depression, or other negative emotions.

Some events--such as death and taxes--either are inevitable or are a threat to all of us. Some of our most feared events might include poverty, failure, prolonged periods of pain, exposure to cruelty, illness, loss of loved ones, serious financial reverses, and death. You may wonder what value there is in even thinking of such terrible things. Why not just wait until we face poverty or death before thinking about them? If we consider such terrible things now, aren't we just bringing up a lot of bad feelings unnecessarily? Isn't this negative thinking?

The strategy of avoiding these issues as long as possible may seem to work. However, even if we do not face a *severe threat* often, we still get less severe "reminders" that stir up fears of these unacceptables. My client's little reminders were stories about drugs and violence--what are yours?

If you live by the avoidance strategy, you will live a life full of little fears. If one of your worst fears does come true, you may be overwhelmed emotionally because you were totally unprepared. Facing your worst fears *now* immunizes you against all fears from those sources. It gives you earthquake insurance against *both* the big one that could hit anytime and the daily tremors of its reminders.

Once we learn to feel at peace about our "unacceptables," then we can feel calm about almost anything. During a workshop I gave at a professional convention, a woman, Genevieve, told this story. She had been in a severe automobile accident, and she was put in a full body cast. She was totally immobilized for more than a year, and could not use her legs, arms, or hands. It was not even possible to read or watch television. How would you feel? How would you cope with this situation for a year? Could you be happy?

Lonely people are often terrified of being alone and don't know how to make themselves happy. Yet, Genevieve learned how to be happy in these extreme circumstances. At first, she didn't know how she would cope with being so cut off from normal sources of interest and happiness. Then, she heard a true story that helped her cope. A Vietnam prisoner-of-war was confined for over a year in a mud hut so small he could not even stand up. However, he chose to overcome his initial feelings of depression and resentment. Instead of thinking of himself as a helpless victim, he decided to take mental control of the situation. Instead of viewing the mud hut as his cell and his guards as his captors, he viewed the hut as his home and viewed the guards as his guests. For example, he would save bits of his meager rice ration. Then periodically he offered the rice to the guards, whom he treated as guests in his home. He found happiness in the mud hut by living according to *his* beliefs--not theirs.

Genevieve realized that the source of happiness was in her mind--not in the external world she was so isolated from. She overcame boredom by generating interesting and loving thoughts. When Genevieve had guests in her hospital room, she focused her attention on helping *them* become happier. She gave so much that her small daughter once said, "Mommy, it isn't fair that you cheer everyone else up--you're the one who is sick." Her daughter was too young to understand.

She immersed herself in thoughts about her life and her future. She changed many of her basic beliefs and values. During her year in the cast, she changed her life in many ways. Genevieve decided to pursue her "impossible dream" of getting a doctorate and a job in counseling--goals that she has since accomplished.

Before the cast, she had low self-esteem; afterward she loved herself and was confident about the future. Before the cast she was shy, timid, and fearful; afterward she was outgoing and assertive. How well did she adjust to being in this full body cast for over a year? "It was the happiest and most important year of my life."

It may be time for you to face your worst possible fears. If you can develop a way of viewing them (or planning for them) so that you know how you can be happy despite being in that situation, then you will be set free from those worst fears. Genevieve said, "Now I know that I can overcome almost anything. *If I could be happy in that situation, I can be happy in almost any situation.*"

Once you have faced your worst fears and successfully overcome them--in your mind; then you can say confidently, "Now I know that I can overcome almost anything. If I could be happy in that situation, I can be happy in almost any situation."

Dealing With the "Ultimate Negative Event"--death. The existentialist philosophers and psychologists recognized that there are certain types of major problems in life that we *all know will happen to us*. Death is one of those unavoidables. Have you ever had a strong experience with death--such as almost dying yourself, losing someone you loved, or fearing the loss of someone you loved?

Have you ever given much thought about your own death? How would you feel if your health or life was threatened for a long time? If dwelling upon any of these topics is uncomfortable for you, then you have not dealt constructively enough with the issue of death. Overcoming your fear of serious catastrophes and death is a necessary step toward achieving peace and maximum happiness.

If we can learn to deal with our fear of death, then perhaps we can use this as a model to deal with any negative event. Each different religion makes dealing with death a central theme. What is your view of death--especially your own death? How do you feel when you think of the possibility of dying?

We do not need to view death as good in order to rise above our negative feelings about it. I view it as one of the "ultimate bads"--we cannot be healthy and happy if we are dead. So how do we develop a view of death that helps us deal with the death of someone close or our own potential death? People have developed many different views that help them accept death or feel better about it. Each person must find a view that is consistent with their other beliefs--such as their religious or scientific beliefs. Some hope they will go to a better place after dying, some believe in reincarnation, some believe they will live on through their children and their children, and some focus on their accomplishments lasting beyond them.

A view of death is emotionally effective only to the degree that we can truly believe it. However, we can create our own image that is a partial solution based on our own reasoning. Even if we cannot *know* that it is true, we can *hope* that it is true. Don't underestimate the power of hope. *Hope is a force that goes beyond belief.* In many cases, hope can ultimately create reality as well as reflect it.

I have struggled with my fear of death from many different philosophical and religious perspectives. Currently, I focus on my belief in life as a gift and my appreciation of every moment of life. I would like to live forever because I love life. I live a healthy lifestyle to extend my life as long as possible. However, I know that I will die someday and want to have an accepting attitude about it.

I hope for future awareness in some life form I don't currently understand. No matter how likely or unlikely that hope may be, I *can still hope* to be conscious at some point in the future. My knowledge is too limited to know how that could happen, but this hope comforts me and helps me accept death.

Another great fear of mine is that my wife, Sherry might die. (She fears the same about my death.) However, we both know that we are each *responsible for our own happiness* and have the *philosophy of life and life skills* to be happy--even if the other should die. That knowledge comforts us. It also helps give us confidence that we could overcome any loss. That confidence gives us a sense of security that radiates through our entire life and affects even daily "little fears."

Fears of poverty or lifestyle changes. I have talked with many college students who feared losing financial support upon graduation and feared not finding a job. I have talked with other college students who were leaving home (often after a conflict) and had no means of support. I have talked with people who were leaving a marriage or a partner who had been supporting them and were terrified of not being able to financially take care of themselves.

Often, these people have a real fear of being homeless and on the streets. Or they may fear drastic changes in lifestyle which seem totally unacceptable: having no car, living in a small room or rundown apartment, having no money for entertainment, or not being able to afford the type of social life they were used to. Or perhaps their fear is working in a job which is far below their potential.

Remember, the more *confident* we are that we can find routes to happiness in a certain scenario, the less fear of the scenario we will have. When I work with people facing poverty or restricted lifestyles, then we look at what their basic needs and values are. We look at activities they can still enjoy that are free or inexpensive--reading, walking, enjoying nature, visiting, watching TV, helping others, sports, listening to music, "personal sex," or thinking. Then the person develops a plan for what he or she would actually do if that scenario were to become a reality.

For example one client couldn't sleep because he was hopelessly in debt, was making far less money than he was spending, and could not pay his rent. He had tremendous anxiety because his mind kept going in circles. Generating this anxiety was a fear of being homeless. He kept repeating, "I don't know what I'll do, I don't know what I'll do." His lack of clear routes to happiness created the anxiety.

We explored his fear in detail and he planned what he would do if he could not afford a place to live. He could rent a storage unit and move his furniture and extra things into it. He could live in his car until he found a job and saved enough money to pay for a less expensive room. He thought living in his car would be like "camping out"--a much more positive way of looking at his situation. Immediately, he felt much better. "What a relief." Instead of viewing "homelessness" as some sort of death, he actually *chose* "homelessness" until he got his finances in order.

A few weeks later when I saw him again, he had found a job, had a room, and was financially stable again. He said his experience living in his car had not been bad at all. He said, "Being homeless was not nearly as bad as the *fear* of being homeless." This sounds like Franklin Roosevelt's statement, "We have nothing to fear, but fear itself."

WE CAN CHOOSE HOW WE WILL REACT TO DAILY NEGATIVE EVENTS

Every day there are thousands of negative events occurring all over the world--people are abused, mistreated, sick, and dying. If I choose, I could focus on these events and feel miserable every minute of my life. Many of us live our lives focusing on those negative events or others closer to home. Focusing too much on these negatives creates a negative inner experience. It can lead to recurring unhappiness and depression.

If we really care about others, how else can we react? One alternative is to ignore these events. I know people who will never watch a news program or read a newspaper because of so much negative news. I can appreciate their efforts to draw boundaries and screen out a certain amount of negative inputs. That can be a partial solution to the problem.

However, we cannot completely screen out all of the negative news of the world. To do so would cause us to be become hermits and turn away from responsible involvement in the world. One result can be like a woman I met who was retired. She lived in a small apartment and constricted her world more and more until she became afraid of almost everything outside the safe haven of her apartment. Then she gradually became suspicious of her neighbors too. The more she constricted her world, the more suspicious and frightened she became. Constriction and fear became mutually reinforcing until she reached an isolated, almost paranoid state. Avoiding our fears and constricting our world is not the answer to overcoming our fears.

If we care, it is natural to have *initial* negative feelings to negative events. However, it is *how we deal with these initial negative feelings* that is important. We can let them habitually overwhelm us and entrap us, or we can develop a positive philosophy of life and world view that will help us "rise above" these negative events.

HOW CAN WE BE BOTH CARING AND HAPPY WHEN OTHERS ARE SUFFERING?

Do you ever feel guilty for feeling good when someone else is feeling bad? Does part of you feel like you should suffer after watching all the "bad news" on TV? If you visit a sick friend, is it better to be upset so they know you care or to be in a good mood to help them feel better? It is possible to care about the other, show concern, *and* feel good. The combination may help cheer them up.

"Mutual misery" versus "Mutual happiness" as a sign of caring. Many of us have learned that *"If we care about someone who is feeling bad, we should feel bad too."* We have learned to measure our *degree of caring* by how badly we feel when the other hurts. According to this **mutual misery** philosophy, the more you suffer when I am suffering, the more you must care about me. If, on the other hand, you feel happy when I am miserable, then you must not care about me and you are a "bad," "uncaring" person.

The logical conclusion of the mutual misery philosophy is that both people will end in dramatic expressions of suffering. You may have witnessed people who suffered together dramatically and created beautiful misery together to convince everyone how much they care. Is that what we want? Wouldn't it be better if caring could be expressed more simply and honestly, and both people could end feeling happy?

There is a philosophy other than the "mutual misery" approach. I call it the **mutual happiness** approach. In this approach, we do not have to prove that we care for one another by our own suffering. *We show our caring by* our gifts of understanding, comfort, or whatever it takes to help us *both feel happier.*

We can express sensitivity and empathy by asking them how they feel and be willing to listen if they want to talk about their feelings. Being upset ourselves is *not* what the other person needs. The clients who come to see me don't want to find a therapist that gets depressed over their problems. They want someone who will listen effectively, show caring, and help them solve their problems. They want someone who is confident and realistically optimistic.

In the mutual happiness philosophy, we *measure how much we care by how much we attempt to contribute to the other person's happiness.* We express our caring by doing something active to help them. Alternatively, we might decide that the best gift is freedom and support *so they can take care of their own needs.* That is especially true in codependent relationships.

A student of mine, who had been gravely ill, recently read this section. She said that people visiting sick people needed to understand how important this section is. When she had been in the hospital, she disliked having people visit her who were too upset about the seriousness of her condition.

They not only increased the "gloom" of the situation; in addition she said, "I wanted to cheer *them* up; but I was so sick, I felt a tremendous burden." On the other hand, she looked forward to seeing people who were happy and cheerful--she felt no burden and their cheerfulness helped her feel better. Just what the Doctor ordered!

The best way you can help me when I am feeling bad is to feel good, because I care about your feelings. Similarly, if you care about me, I expect you will ultimately want me to feel good after your misfortune. Both bad feelings and good feelings are contagious. Which do you want to give?

IS CHOOSING TO THINK POSITIVELY BEING HONEST WITH MYSELF?

Being honest has always been one of my most important values. When I was 16 and first began considering a more positive view of life, I had a serious reservation about "positive thinking." I didn't want to fool myself or be naive. I wondered, "How can I think positively without being dishonest with myself? Aren't I fooling myself?"

I realized that being honest with myself is not really so simple. I knew that I wanted to be totally honest with myself, but I realized that most situations in life are ambiguous. The truth is usually not so clear. If a situation is ambiguous, there are two types of errors I can make: the first is to be *too optimistic* and the second is to be *too pessimistic.* However, I decided right then that I would rather err in the direction of feeling too positive throughout my life than err in the direction of feeling too negative.

I would rather go through life being too optimistic and happy
than too pessimistic and depressed.
Consider two types of errors.
First, consider being too optimistic.
What if at the end of my life,
I found that I had been too *optimistic* about the future?
At least I would have spent my life being happy.

Next, consider being too pessimistic.
What if at the end of my life, I found that I had been too *pessimistic?*
I would have spent my life being unnecessarily depressed
and wasted all that worry and misery.
How sad!

Our view of an ambiguous situation can profoundly affect our emotions and our actions. A sudden *change* in our interpretation can have dramatic effects on those emotions and our behavior. It can also dramatically affect others around us.

A 22-year-old client came in because she had been angry with her father for months. She thought that he was being "totally selfish," "no longer really cares about what happens to me," and "doesn't want me around anymore." Their communication had all but stopped, they would constantly bicker about little things, and it had gotten so bad that sometimes she would purposely do things to "get even."

It did appear that her father had been doing many things in which he was reducing contact and support of her--with no explanation. However, after hearing in detail about the history of their relationship, it seemed to me that her father really did care about her.

I noticed that she had been fueling her own anger all this time by focusing only upon *her negative interpretation* of his behavior. I asked her why she thought her father was doing these things. The only thing she could think of was that *he never really cared* for her as much as she had always thought. No wonder she felt so hurt and angry! I suggested a more positive interpretation of his actions. Let's start by assuming that he really loved her. Suppose that he thought she might *want* more independence and *want* to be treated more as an equal adult. She seemed interested.

After the Christmas break, she had returned from a visit home and was elated! She said that everything was fine now. She had talked with her father and had discussed this issue in a more positive, understanding manner. She had found that his own explanation was similar to the one we had discussed; he was just trying to treat her more like an adult.

They developed a completely new and more positive understanding beyond anything she had thought possible only a few weeks before. Had we worked some miracle? By changing her interpretation to the positive, understanding one that assumed the best of her father's motives, she also changed her behavior. She became open, communicative, and viewed his words and actions more positively. What had begun as a long complaint list about her father, ended with mutual understanding and renewed affection.

SHAQ Research Results: Overcoming Worst Fears

Because I suspected that people's underlying worst fears were important causes of their emotions, I created the SHAQ Low Greatest Fears scale and subscales.

The Low Greatest Fears (LowGF) scale had a strong relationship to the Overall Happiness scale. The correlation was r = .55. The LowGF scale correlated .48 with Low Depression, .45 with Low Anxiety, and .38 with the Low Anger/Aggression scale. The LowGF scale also correlated with good Relationship Outcomes, .31; Health Outcomes, .32; Highest Personal Income, .18; Highest Education Completed, .10; and College GPA, .19.

Greatest Fears Subscales. The four subscales of the GF scale and their correlates to outcomes are:

1. Low Fears of Illness and Death: Happiness, .22; Low Depression, .22; Low Anxiety, .31; Low Anger, .30; Good Relationships, .09; Health, .25; Income, .08; Education level, .07; college GPA, .05.

2. Low Fears of Failure and Poverty: Happiness, .38; Low Depression, .31; Low Anxiety, .30; Low Anger, .27; Relationships, .16; Health, .23; Income, .19; Education, .07; College GPA, .07.

3. Low Rejection/Social-Related Fears: Happiness, .49; Low Depression, .44; Low Anxiety, .37; Low Anger, .28; Relationships, .32; Health, .26; Income, .14; Education, .08; College GPA, .06.

4. Low Self-Related Fears: Happiness, .57; Low Depression, .48; Low Anxiety, .43; Low Anger, .38; Relationships, .33; Health, .28; Income, .12; Education, .08; College GPA, .11.

It should be clear that these underlying fears are substantially related to happiness and success and that working to overcome them should be a high priority for anyone who chooses to be happy, healthy, and successful in relationships and other areas of life. Use the self-exploration techniques (Ch-2), planning, reframing, and other methods suggested in this book to overcome your worst fears.

Note: All correlations, p < .0001 and N's ranged from 2048 to 3199.

DEFICIT MOTIVATION versus ABUNDANCE MOTIVATION--
Have I received enough?

Do you sometimes feel cheated by life or by another person? Do you ever think about how much more fortunate other people are than you? Do you wonder why they have more money, better opportunities, better parents, a more beautiful body, or more talents? Does life seem unfair?

Do you ever feel that no one *really* cares about you? Do you ever resent others who have what you feel you deserve? What if they didn't earn it and you did? How do you feel when you get these thoughts? Hurt? Sad? Angry? These aren't happy feelings.

These emotions are caused by the belief that *you have received less than your expectation level* (or that you *will* receive less than what you expect). You may believe that you have received *less than you deserve or less than is fair.* You may believe that you *actually do have less than you deserve* and have rightfully earned. Perhaps most people would agree with you.

Deficit motivation. Deficit motivation is believing that we have *received less* than we expect, minimally need to be happy, or deserve. It is believing that we are always working just to get to that state of *meeting our minimum expectation*, "being even," or getting what we are owed. Deficit motivation is feeling like we are in a deep hole and are just trying to climb out.

Deficit motivation is being in debt and just trying to pay off all we owe. We feel resentment and feel like a victim. We could react by being aggressive toward others "to get what we deserve." On the other hand, we might withdraw, give up, and feel sorry for ourselves. The result of giving up is apathy and depression.

Abundance motivation. Abundance motivation means believing that we have *more* than we minimally need or expect. If we think we have more than we minimally need or expect, then we feel grateful (and happy). We appreciate what we have--to get more is a *bonus*. We will feel *minimal resentment* and can focus on getting more *because we want it*--not because we are owed it or deserve it.

If we really do have a lot compared to other people, it may seem easy to feel abundance motivation. However, people's *perception* of their deficit or abundance often has *little relationship* to their *actual abundance*. Remember how the POW saved his meager rations of rice and shared his "abundance" with his guests (guards). Remember how grateful Genevieve was for her year in the body cast. Their abundance came from a spiritual abundance--not a material one.

I am also reminded of a dentist friend who flew to Mexico on weekends. He gave free dental work to the poor in rural villages. He was amazed at how happy the children were compared to children in the U. S.--despite their extreme poverty. The children of the villages seemed happier with their makeshift toys of sticks and stones than many of the children he knew--who had every toy invented. When he brought in a load of used toys to these children for Christmas, they went wild. They appreciated these used toys much more than the children he knew appreciated new toys.

Why do the children who receive so much less appreciate so much more? The American children thought that they "deserved" expensive gifts of their exact choosing. The key to the puzzle is not how much they *actually receive,* but how much they *expect to receive.*

Setting high *minimum expectations* creates deficit motivation. A professional I know began graduate school at a time when people in her occupation were in great demand and were starting at high salaries. Companies were making attractive offers right and left. She developed the expectation that if she were to complete graduate school, a great, high-paying job would await her upon graduation. She was divorced and had children. She worked long hours, took care of her children, and attended school for many years before she completed her goal. It was as if she thought she had a contract with God or Society that if she were to sacrifice so much, then she should earn a great job with high pay.

However, when she completed school, the job market had radically changed. People were being laid off in her field and jobs were hard to get. Nevertheless, she was very competent and got a good job--a job many others would have been happy to get. Yet, for years, she felt a deep resentment about her pay and her job.

For years, she still felt "cheated" by God, society, fate, or someone. Her resentment affected her in many ways. At work, she felt that she was not getting what she deserved. Her house, her car, and her lifestyle were less than they "should" be. She felt like a victim of "the Economy" or something. Eventually, she learned that she was just making herself unhappy.

She decided to rethink her original expectations and "contract." She realized that no one had ever really promised her that she would get the job she had imagined. My friend realized that *she* had created that expectation and accepted her responsibility for overestimating the future job prospects.

She accepted the reality of the situation and finally realized that she could be happy on a *lot less* than her current job. She reset her *minimum expectations* to a level that was *significantly below* her current job. After a serious job search, she decided that she would rather stay where she was. After all those years, it was the first time she ever felt grateful for her job and her life.

Entitlement thinking versus appreciation for life's gifts. When we read the papers, watch the news, or listen to politicians, we often hear that we are "entitled" to certain things. We believe all children in our country are *entitled* to good health care, a good education, and good parenting. We may believe that we are *entitled* to live in a city with good streets, fire and police protection, good parks, and low pollution. We may also believe that we are *entitled* to live in a house with good plumbing, electricity, a telephone, TV, and other conveniences.

Where did these entitlements or rights come from? Who promised us these things in life? Did God give them to us? Did the government give them to us? "*Entitlement*" or "*rights*" are just ideas that exist in our heads. Many politicians, TV and newspaper reporters, parents, and others believe we have these rights. It is natural for parents to want their children to "have the best." However, often the idea transmitted to the children is that they have a *right* to have the best.

Often associated with beliefs about rights and entitlements is the assumption that *people cannot be healthy or happy without these minimum entitlements*. Yet two hundred years ago even the wealthiest people somehow managed to survive without cars, TVs, dinner at Luigi's, CD players, telephones, or even electricity and indoor plumbing. Today, even people living "below the poverty line" have many of these conveniences. We believe that we *must have these basic "necessities" to be happy*.

Yet, today, many people in the world do not have these "necessities." The problem with entitlement thinking is its implications. One negative implication of entitlement thinking is that *we are not strong enough* to be happy without these necessities.

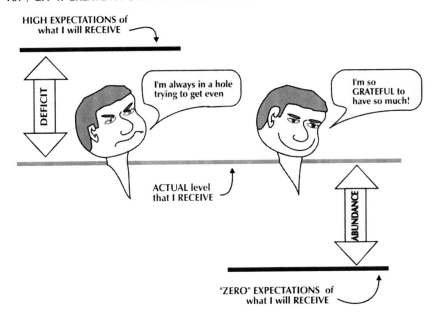

DEFICIT THINKING versus ABUNDANCE THINKING

Another implication is that if we do not receive these entitlements, we are being cheated. These thoughts cause feelings of *resentment and self-pity*. Entitlement thinking is just another form of deficit thinking.

I strongly support the *goal* that we all have advantages such as basic health care, education, and lots of material possessions. However, I support these goals because I *care about people's health and happiness*--not because people are *entitled* to these advantages. I do not believe these modern advantages are *essential* to people's happiness.

The alternative to entitlement thinking is **appreciative-assertive thinking**. Appreciative-assertive thinking is believing in *zero entitlement* and *zero rights*. I am entitled to nothing: I was born into this world naked with no possessions and given my time in this world by powers beyond myself. I was not entitled to that time nor did I do anything to earn it. Ultimately, I cannot "deserve" anything, because I would have nothing without having been given my life and my powers.

Therefore, I am eliminating the ideas of "earning," "deserving," "fairness," and "entitlement" from my basic way of thinking and from my vocabulary as much as is possible. We do not need these entitlement ideas; they just lead to resentment. We can replace them with ideas like "assertion" and "agreement."

I want to be happy myself and want others to be happy *not because we deserve it, but because I want it and I love myself unconditionally*. It is because *I have chosen to make happiness of self and others my ultimate concern* (or top goal). I choose it and I assert it; *I don't need to justify it or rationalize it as something I am entitled to.*

Appreciative-assertive thinking is a form of abundance thinking. We start with *zero minimal expectations*. We may set goals to receive friendship, a good job, money, a nice home, or whatever else that might contribute to our happiness. We can work hard to achieve those goals. Yet there is no guarantee that we will obtain what we seek. Everything we receive is a *bonus* over our initial naked condition.

President John F. Kennedy recognized the pervasiveness and destructiveness of entitlement thinking when he stated, "Ask not what your country can do for you, but what you can do for your country." If I accept Kennedy's statement, I shift from being a needy person who *must be taken care of by society* to a person who is strong enough to take care of myself and has enough left over to give to society. Both society and I benefit from this shift in belief systems.

Deficit motivation is victim motivation; abundance motivation is power motivation. Ponder the figure of the twins--one with deficit thinking and the other with abundance thinking--and consider the following.
- **If I view myself as having an abundance to meet my needs, I feel happy, grateful, and peaceful. Getting more is fun. In this case, *the rich get richer.***
- **If I view myself as having a deficit of less than I need, I will feel like a victim-- deprived, angry, or depressed. In this case, *the poor get poorer.***

One of my clients came in because all of her previous relationships had ended "in disaster." Typically, they would begin with an initial period of happiness and fun. As they spent more time together and got closer, she began to feel more dependent on him for "making her happy." He began to feel *pressure* to be with her instead of *desire* to be with her. As he felt more trapped and more desire for freedom, she sensed his feelings and feared that he wanted out of the relationship. That in turn only caused her to get more "needy" and demanding for his time and attention--driving him farther and farther away.

She was terrified of being abandoned. As a result, she became possessive and tried to manipulate her partner into being with her every free moment. She also became jealous of other women. Her current relationship was "on the rocks" and looked as if it might end like the rest had. She was feeling very upset about its possible end and confused about why this kept happening to her.

We explored the problem more. She thought that everyone who had loved her had abandoned her. Her father, to whom she had been very attached, had left her at an early age. She had never felt close to her mother, who had resented taking care of her. Since she had been abandoned by everyone, she secretly believed that it was at least partly because something was *severely wrong with her.* She had tried everything to become more appealing and attractive. In many ways, she had succeeded. Yet men continued to leave her. Their leaving only heightened her worry, "Something is deeply wrong with my personality."

"All of my life I have wanted to find a man who would love me and never leave me." That was a key part of her problem. Where was she to find such a man? The problem started as a little girl. She developed the belief that to be happy she must have someone to love her and take care of her forever. Possibly, because her father left her, this "must" became a top priority goal in her life--possibly even her "ultimate concern."

The reality was that she had no close, affectionate, long-lasting relationship with anyone. Therefore, there was a huge *gap between her "must have" expectation and her reality.* This gap created a powerful deficit motivation. She felt "cheated" and a "victim" of others--especially men, because "No matter how hard I try to please them and make the relationship work, they always leave me. Men are 'flakes.'"

That was her point of view. Part of the problem was that she expected too much of men. No man would love her and stay with her "unconditionally." Almost any man would leave if he became too unhappy in the relationship.

It wasn't that all men were "flakes." Her fear of their leaving actually drove them away. She was so terrified of their leaving that she became possessive and manipulative. Her partners wouldn't tolerate this behavior for long.

In order to keep from being so possessive, needy, and manipulative, she had to greatly reduce her fear of being abandoned and being alone. She would have to feel calm when she imagined men leaving her.

Once I explained my hypothesis to her, she acknowledged that she had been afraid that something like this was going on, but she hadn't understood it so clearly. We worked on eliminating deficit thinking and developing abundance thinking. First, she needed to lower her expectations. She needed to question her old assumptions that to be happy, she *must* have a man love and take care of her.

She needed to accept her worst fear that she could *be alone indefinitely*. No matter how good a relationship she had, her partner could always leave or die. There was no absolute security that she would not be alone. No one *owed* her their time. That type of thinking only leads to deficit thinking, hurt, and deep resentment. Instead, she needed to have "zero expectations" that a man would love her and take care of her.

How could she learn to accept and to be calm about being alone? She could learn that she can *take care of herself* and *make herself happy*--especially during periods when she is alone. Expecting someone else to "make her happy" was unrealistic. Learning how to enjoy life living alone takes some skill and time. However, just believing in the *possibility* calmed her.

She also gave up her deficit thinking assumption that she and her partner should be together all of the time. She chose the "zero expectation" that, "I do *not automatically assume any togetherness*. Any time together is a bonus for which I am grateful."

Consequently, she no longer needed to possess her partner; and she no longer needed to manipulate him into being with her. Her new approach delighted her partner and their relationship improved dramatically. More important, she was overcoming this long-term abandonment issue, and she was overcoming her fear of being alone. Her self-esteem was rising, and she was feeling much happier.

Summary: Deficit thinking has many negative consequences. When we choose to continue believing that we have less than we "deserve" or "must" have, then we choose deficit motivation. The consequences of deficit thinking are feeling hurt or resentful. We may view ourselves as "victims."

Deficit thinking can even create paranoid type thinking: thinking that other people are actively trying to prevent us from getting what we deserve--when they are not. Negative assumptions about others often lead to either withdrawal from relationships or open anger and conflict.

Deficit thinking may focus more on "who is to blame" than on important issues. In addition, we may give ourselves negative messages that we are too weak to cope with the situation. We are too weak to make ourselves happy if we don't get what we are "entitled" to. These messages lower self-esteem.

Abundance thinking creates positive motivation. Abundance thinking starts with having *no assumptions about what we will receive in life*. We develop zero expectations about what we will receive. We make zero assumptions about what anyone will give us. "Anyone" means God, nature, society, parents, peers, or any loved one. Everything we get is a gift. We receive the gift because the giver presented it to us, not because we "deserved" it.

What are the implications of abundance motivation in everyday situations? If I develop a disease and become disabled so that I cannot work, no one (including society) "owes" me anything.

Lack of obligation does not mean that we cannot choose to care for each other's welfare and happiness. If we care for our own and others' welfare, we will choose as a society to adopt social policies beneficial to all. For example, society can adopt a kind of social insurance, so that it will help people who are physically unable to earn an income. In that way we can all feel more secure about our fears that if we become disabled we will have an income. We develop a social policy because we choose to, not because society inherently "owes" it to anyone. Society develops a contract with its members. Social security works that way.

Let's apply abundance thinking to the example of a contract. If I contract with someone to provide a service, I expect to be paid after I do my job. However, I am not naive. Many events could prevent payment. Thus, overly expecting that the other person will keep his or her end of the bargain is not only foolish, but it can also cause a great deal of wasted emotion. It is better to hope for the best, but keep an open mind.

Suppose the other person is a crook and never intended to pay. Focusing on my deprivation, moralizing, blaming, working myself into a frenzy about being cheated, and developing a deep resentment only create anger inside me. I do not need anger to take action. The excess anger doesn't hurt the other person or balance the scales, it only takes away from my own happiness.

I can still choose to take action to receive payment or restitution, because I still want to receive the money and I do not want to encourage the other person to cheat more people. However, there is no need to get in a stew about it--that only hurts me. Being cheated only hurts me if it undermines my happiness.

My abundance comes not from the amount of money I have in the bank, but from the amount of happiness I have in my life. If being "cheated" does not seriously undermine my being a happy person, then it has not done me too much harm.

Even if the cheating harms me in some real ways, I will be happier if I accept the new situation and move on. I can pick up the pieces and set new goals given the new reality. Abundance thinking keeps me in control of my emotions and gives me positive motivation for maximizing my positive actions to accomplish realistic goals.

Abundance thinking is better illustrated by this true story. A friend, George, was close to his eldest son. He and his son had dreamed for years that his son would complete medical school and then go into private practice with George. His son struggled to get accepted into medical school; then he struggled through it. Just after graduation, father and son finally began their practice together. A few months later, a drunk driver ran a light and killed his son.

At first, George was devastated. However, I received a copy of a poem George sent to friends and family a few weeks later. The poem expressed no anger, instead it expressed George's gratitude for the time his son had walked the earth and for the joy that his son had brought into George's life and the lives of others. That is abundance thinking!

To create abundance thinking. If you want to choose abundance thinking over deficit thinking, try the following:

1. Create "zero expectations" of what you *will receive*. Abundance thinking means creating "zero expectations." *Do not automatically assume* that you will receive anything. Instead, you will be mentally prepared for the *worst possible case*. Think positively about your chances of receiving what you want, but that is quite different from assuming that you will get what you want. Do not assume that you "*must have,*" "*should have,*" or *ultimately "deserve"* anything. You do not assume that God, nature, society, or any other source has established absolute rules for what you "should receive."

2. Use appreciate-assertive thinking. Replace all of the phrases like "should have" or "must have" with the phrase "I want.*" Assert* that you want something based upon your choice of your ultimate concern for happiness for yourself and others.

That assertion is *sufficient reason for wanting it*. You do not need to justify it from any other moral code or set of "shoulds." Nor is there any moral code or set of "shoulds" that indicates you "deserve" to have it. Everything you receive in life is ultimately a gift. You would have nothing without the gift of life, the gift of your environment, and the gift of your abilities. Once you view the situation this way, everything good in life becomes a bonus: a gift you did not get because you deserved it, but a gift that you are grateful for.

3. Take responsibility for your own happiness. Foster abundance thinking by assuming that you are responsible for your own happiness and that *no one else is*. Developing your interests, knowledge, and skills in areas that help you take better care of yourself and make yourself happy. Know that even when you are poor in some area(s) of life, you can still find routes to happiness like Genevieve (in the body cast), the POW, and Victor Frankl have done.

4. Focus on positive "wants" and goals. Give up trying to justify what you want with "shoulds" and give up expecting other people to meet your needs for you. Then you are free to focus on what *you want and take responsibility for getting it yourself*. In abundance thinking, you start with the assumption that you can be happy with what you have. However, you are free to want more and to keep *setting challenging goals to receive more. If you meet the goals, it is a bonus to the happiness you already have. If you do not, that is ok because you can be happy with what you have.*

> **PRACTICE: Compare your own deficit thinking with abundance thinking.** (1) Think of an area where you feel abundance thinking. (2) Compare that abundance area thinking to any area where you experience deficit thinking. (If you are having trouble thinking of one, think of an area where you feel that you "are in a hole" or have less than you "deserve." It could be that you feel that you received less than you "should" from your parents, education, peers, work opportunities, or almost anything.) (3) Use the self-exploration technique (from Chapter 2) to explore your feelings, images, thoughts, underlying beliefs, and history of this deficit thinking. Then try to replace your deficit thinking with abundance thinking.

Hope for the best, be prepared for the worst,
expect something between,
and be grateful for all that you receive.

CHOOSE TO BE HAPPY NOW--
MODIFY YOUR DAILY STREAM OF THOUGHTS

Have you made a conscious choice that you want to spend as much of your time feeling happy as possible? How many minutes of the day did you feel happy yesterday? Today? How can you spend as many minutes of your life feeling happy as possible?

One way you can feel happier is to develop a more positive world view. Making happiness your ultimate concern and developing a positive world view can help you feel better on a moment-to-moment basis.

TURNING THE TIDE OF THOUSANDS OF THOUGHTS

There are 3,600 seconds in an hour and 57,600 seconds in a normal 16-hour waking day. If we have one thought per second (much less than the brain's capacity), then we have about 60,000 thoughts in one day. What percentage of your 60,000 thoughts lead to positive emotions and what percentage to negative ones?

One day I decided to try an experiment--to let my *inner observer* watch my thousands of thoughts for a day. I wanted to see if I could let my Higher Self intervene so that I could have a higher percentage of positive thoughts and feelings. First, I noticed that having breakfast outdoors on our sunny patio triggered lots of positive thoughts. As I read the morning paper, a headline on gang violence ignited a stream of negative thoughts and emotions. In the past, articles like this had set off negative thoughts causing depressed or angry feelings. In the past, the negative thoughts were *not countered by positive thoughts to help me deal with those specific negative thoughts.*

This day, I decided to try to think of a new perspective for viewing gangs and gang violence. One of my *worst fears* was that gangs would spread uncontrollably and that gang members were "lost souls" who would cause immeasurable harm. I turned to my Higher Self for an answer. Were there positive forces in the universe that might help counteract this trend? I realized that one of my beliefs is that there are positive forces working for harmony and happiness within all life forms--even in the worst gang members.

Well, the day was going pretty well so far. Later, as I was walking across the university campus, I noticed that I started thinking about the university "budget crisis." Everyone on campus was talking about it, and most people felt as though there were a dark cloud over the school. I noticed that I was thinking of the university as a depressing place right now-- another stream of negative thoughts.

Therefore, I decided to put this "budget crisis" into perspective and asked myself what the university was all about. It was *not* primarily about being a place of depression and crisis. I focused on my beliefs about the positive mission of the university. I also applied the idea of zero expectations to the reduced funding problem. I realized that despite all the financial problems, the university still supported a great deal of teaching, research, and creative thought. The university gives these creative thoughts to thousands of students who flow into the community and help it become a better place for us all. I created a mental image of our university as a giant fountain overflowing with knowledge into the community. That wonderful image made my day.

During that day, I also noticed that occasionally I didn't have any thoughts pressing to enter my mind, and I would feel bored. During those periods, it was easy to let negative thoughts enter the vacuum. I started searching my mind for sources of positive thoughts. My positive interests and the loves of my life were good sources of positive thoughts. So I would start thinking about something that interested me. Or, I might focus more on the present and pay more detailed attention to my environment. I could appreciate the beauty in the trees, in the birds' singing, or in the people I saw.

PRACTICE: Get control of your daily stream of thoughts--think and feel more positively. These were real examples from that one day in my life. Try observing yourself for one day. Keep a log of them. (Use the **self-exploration** process described in Chapter 2 to help you with this exercise.)
(1) Observe emotions and thoughts. What thoughts are associated with positive and negative emotions? Observe positive and negative emotions in a neutral, almost scientific manner. What types of thoughts precede positive versus negative emotions?

(2) How are you viewing external events? What external events preceded the positive and negative thoughts? What assumptions intervene between the external event and the negative thoughts? How can you question these assumptions or see them from a new or higher point of view?

(3) List recurring positive and negative themes. What themes are present in many thoughts associated with positive emotions? With negative emotions? List them. (Examples: achievement, failure, rejection, fear of being alone, worry about money, desire for respect, embarrassment, injustice, pressure from others, or worry about someone you care for.)

(4) List inner *sources* of positive and negative thoughts. What parts of yourself (or belief systems) are producing these positive or negative thoughts? What additional parts of yourself can you use as sources of positive points of view and thoughts? Your Higher Self, positive interests, and positive belief systems are key sources. Themes supporting higher values such as truth, beauty, creativity, love, romance, art, growth, family, self-sufficiency, internal control, play, and kindness are powerful sources of positive thoughts. List them.

(5) Plan to control your thought-stream (therefore emotions). List what you can do to decrease negative thoughts and replace them with more positive, realistic thoughts. (Examples: Get in touch with positive themes; question and confront negative themes with new higher points of view; avoid unnecessary negative inputs from people, media, or situations.)

Are some negative themes, belief systems, or parts of yourself generating such persistent sources of negative thoughts that you need to find better ways of coping with them? For example, do you need to weed out deficit thinking and replace with abundance thinking? Do you need to work on building a positive world view, overcoming fears of poverty, being alone, or failure? Do you need to build up positive sources (such as your Higher Self) by exposure to positive sources, study, therapy, or deep thinking? Other chapters deal with many of these issues.

SHAQ Research Results: Positive World View

Compared to other factors researchers have studied, SHAQ's Positive World View (PWV) scale had a strong relationship to the Overall Happiness scale. The correlation was r = .72 and the EffectSize was .52. That means that the PWV scale *alone* can predict with 52% accuracy our users' Overall Happiness score.

The PWV correlated .55 with Low Depression, .47 with Low Anxiety, and .42 with the Low Anger/Aggression. scale (predicting 30% of the Low Depression scale score, 22% of the Low Anxiety scale score, and 18% of the Low Anger-Aggression scale score). The PWV scale also correlated with good Relationship Outcomes, .48; Health Outcomes, .39; Highest Personal Income, .18; Highest Education Completed, .09; and College GPA, .10.

Positive World View Subscales. The three subscales of the PWV scale and their correlates to the outcomes are:

1. Optimism about Self and World. Happiness, .54; Low Depression, .35; Low Anxiety, .28; Low Anger, .26; Good Relationships, .37; Health, .30; Income, .08.

2. Gratitude and Abundance Thinking. Happiness, .72; Low Depression, .57; Low Anxiety, .45; Low Anger, .36; Relationships, .46; Health, .33; Income, .13; Education, .09; College GPA, .11.

3. Not Entitlement Beliefs: Happiness, .16; Low Depression, .16; Low Anxiety, .19; Low Anger, .27; Relationships, and .08; Income, .20.

Here is strong evidence that one way to choose to be happy and overcome these negative emotions is to develop a positive world view. Developing optimism for self and the world, gratitude and abundance thinking, and not having entitlement beliefs are key factors for being happier and all the other outcomes we measured.

Note: All correlations, p < .0001 and N's ranged from 2541 to 3173.

Our internal world models color everything we perceive, think, and do.
Therefore, seeking truth, beauty, love, and creativeness
creates truthful, beautiful, loving, and creative thoughts.
These positive thoughts
will not only create a harmonious, happy internal world;
they will change the external world.

CHAPTER 5

DEVELOP GREATER SELF-WORTH
AND
SELF-CONFIDENCE

\\

PRACTICE: Write a self-description now. Before proceeding, write a description of yourself now so that you can analyze it later after reading the following sections. Write a half-page to two-page description of yourself as if you were another person who understood you very well and knew everything about you. Write the description in the third person using "he" or "she." (If you wait until you read further, your self-description may be affected by what you read.)

OUR SELF VIEWS HAVE POWER (INCLUDING THEIR OWN INERTIA)

Concepts similar to *self-esteem*–such as *ego strength, self-image, and self-concept* have been studied by psychologists for decades. Research has shown that high self-esteem relates to many positive qualities of mental health, life success, and happiness. My own research found a correlation of .48 between overall positive self-statements on the LSQ and overall happiness the past three years. Our self-esteem can have powerful effects, but how do we get it and how can we improve it? [17]

Brian grew up the oldest child in a poor family. His alcoholic father left at an early age. His mother loved her children, but she struggled with her own problems. Brian felt that the other kids looked down on him for being poor and having so many family problems. As a child, he wished that he could have a "normal" family and money to buy the nice things other kids had. Most of all, he hated being looked down on as less than others.

Brian believed that to be worthwhile he had to fulfill a certain image. His image of a minimally ok person was to be rich and successful in his career, to have a happy marriage and family, and above all to have "class." Having class meant having fine cars, a big house, expensive art, and other symbols of status. Having class meant knowing what to wear and what to say; and having class especially meant being accepted by the right people.

However, growing up, Brian did not do well in school or sports and was not popular with his peers. Therefore, he thought of himself as a not ok person who was destined to fail at whatever he did. He suspected that he had some deep inadequacy inside that kept him "in the gutter," but he avoided dealing with these fears. These beliefs became a self-fulfilling prophesy. He quit trying to be a success and hung out with people he secretly

---

[17] Many people maintain their self-concepts by deceptive thinking--even when the self-concepts are negative. However, other powerful self-related tendencies may help overcome this *self-verification process. Self-enhancement* (getting positive feedback) and *self-improvement* (learning and growth) may be healthier tendencies. See Banaji and Prentice (1994) for a review of the related research.

thought were losers. He set easy goals--such as minimal education and low-paying jobs. Brian often felt depressed and angry about his life and the future. He was in a vicious cycle of low self-worth, low goals, underachievement, and depression.

Then Brian got a job in an electronics store--where a lot of good things happened. He got interested in the electronics business. The store owner praised him for his hard work and showed confidence in him. Brian decided to change his life, "I was sick of being a failure and set a goal to become a successful electronics businessman." He went back to school and studied hard. He made good grades and kept learning the electronics business. He started his own computer business and made lots of money.

His increased success and income increased his confidence with people. He had had a crush on Carol since high school, but had always thought of her as being out of his class. He lavished her with attention, flowers, gifts, exciting experiences, and promises of leading an idyllic life. He learned everything he could to present himself as a man with class.

She fell in love with him, they married, and they had three children. He bought a beautiful home, drove expensive cars, and bought only the best of everything. He showered her and his children with the best of everything that money could buy. Most people who met him were impressed by his success.

Brian began to see himself as a success and began to think that his success was proof that he was as good as or better than other people. He loved to compare himself to former high school classmates who were not nearly so "successful."

Was Brian happy? His answer was, "I have everything a man could have to be happy. If I'm not happy, then I feel sorry for all the poor people in the world. Seriously, I'm not sure if I'm happy or not. Sometimes I feel like keeping this life style and image up is a burden and a lot of stress. Sometimes I'm not sure I know what I want in life. Maybe being happy is too much to expect."

Inside, he kept asking himself, "Why aren't I happier, when I have everything I want?" One thing that really bugged Brian was that his brother had been far less successful in his career, but seemed much happier.

Others thought of Brian as somewhat self-centered and dominating. Many thought he had an inflated view of himself, was ill-tempered, and only cared about success and acquiring the symbols of success. His wife Carol had been initially impressed by his ambition and strength. She liked the lifestyle that money had brought them and their children. However, his total focus on success, his neglect of her, and his frequent dominating manner had gradually driven a wedge between them. She kept telling him, "Our romance and intimacy are disappearing. You never listen to anything that deals with emotions."

What lessons did Brian need to learn? First, his happiness was not dependent upon his career success. Brian had not been happy as a failure or as a success. Either way, he feared failure and being looked down on by others. These fears were his worst nightmares and his frequent companions--despite all his money. He had never faced those fears.

He also kept raising his self-expectations to higher and higher levels. He was no longer "ok" if he was as successful as his high school classmates. Now, he had to be as successful as the multimillionaire who lived nearby in even bigger homes than his. He felt inadequate to them. Now, he had to prove that he was as good as they were, by working even harder and taking more risks. With the increased risks came increased stress.

Basically, Brian was never happy just being Brian. He never learned to love himself unconditionally. He always had to achieve something more before he could be happy. He never had enough success to prove that he was a "minimally ok human being." Consequently, he never believed that anyone--including his wife--could really love him exactly as he was right then. He thought he had to buy her love or show her that he was more successful than other men.

Conditional versus *unconditional* **self-worth.** The essence of Brian's problem was his belief that his self-worth *depended* on being successful and fulfilling his image of a "minimally ok" person. He knew that no matter how successful his business was, it could fail. He had seen it happen to others. Therefore, he could *never feel that his self-worth was safe.*

Consequently, his business controlled his emotions. Any threat to his business was a threat to his worthiness. As long as we believe that our basic self-worth is dependent upon *anything* that is partially out of our control, we will have a great fear of that thing. It will be our own private monster holding our happiness in the palm of its hand.

To feel safe and not so threatened by business failure, Brian needed to separate his self-worth from his business success. More generally, he needed to let go of his image of a minimally ok person; he needed to learn to love himself and others unconditionally.

Another advantage of a new belief in the *basic worth of every human* was that he could let go of trying to impress others and stop worrying about what they thought of him. Ironically, his desire to impress his wife and provide money for her caused him to neglect her, dominate her, and hide his fears from her. Yet, these very behaviors were destroying intimacy and pushing her away from him.

She longed for him to be more open about his feelings--instead of maintaining this macho, "success" front and being so defensive. Sadly, he didn't understand that his wife would love him and stand by him even if he "failed." She would gladly trade the extra money and status for more attention, openness, and intimacy.

In the last chapter, we saw how *deficit thinking* could cause us to feel deprived, resentful, and weak. On the other hand, *abundance thinking* can cause us to feel grateful, happy, strong, and positively motivated.

The ideas of deficit thinking and abundance thinking can be applied to our view of ourselves as well. If we view ourselves as unworthy, weak, or inadequate then we may spend much of our lives feeling like minnows swimming with the big fish. We may respond to these inadequacy feelings by either of two common reactions-- **underachievement** (low expectations and low motivation) or **over achievement** (too high expectations and intense motivation to overcome the perceived "deficit"). Brian had first tried underachievement, then over achievement.

Unconditional self-love means loving our selves "no matter what. . ." How many of us-- like Brian believe that we are worthwhile only if we are successful, rich, powerful, good, and have all the trappings of "the good life." How many of us also value others to the degree they are successful and good. That is an example of *conditional love*--loving someone only if the person meets certain conditions.

If we love ourselves or others unconditionally, we love *only because we are human and because we are ourselves.* We love some essence of ourselves no matter what we have done or not done.

I once saw an interview with a father whose son was a serial arsonist. His son had caused millions of dollars of damage to property and had been responsible for the deaths of several people. The father seemed to be a responsible, caring person. The reporter asked the man how he felt about his son. The father said, "No matter how much I hate what my son has done, I still love my son." That is unconditional love.

Loving ourselves unconditionally means that we love ourselves no matter who we are, what we have, what we have done, or what others think of us. Loving ourselves unconditionally means that we love ourselves even if we have qualities we don't like; even if we have pimples, are overweight, aren't good looking, have a low IQ, drop out of school, are unemployed, drive rusty Volkswagens, are homeless, have herpes, or no one likes us.

If you can learn to love yourself unconditionally, that love will provide a stable power base to overcome your fears and center your life around. It is your most inner sacred zone. No person or failure can take it away from you.

SELF-WORTH--The *unconditional* value
we place on ourselves

It took millions of years of evolution to produce us.
Our brains have over 30 billion cells.
We are the height of creation on Earth.
Our creator valued each of us enough to give us
a universe full of opportunities,
the gift of life, bodies that give us wondrous physical powers,
sensations and emotions for experiencing life to its fullest,
and a mind that allows us to create our own worlds.
When we have been given so much and put in such a pivotal place
to affect the lives of so many others, how can we doubt
that we are of great value and worthy of our own love.

WHAT IS SELF-WORTH?

The worth of something is how much we value it and love it for itself, how important it is to us, and how much priority we give it compared to other things. **Self-worth** is an overall measure of how much we value ourselves and give priority to our own needs and happiness. Our self-worth is a measure of our unconditional self-love.

High self-worth means loving ourselves unconditionally in all situations and in all areas of our lives. To have a high degree of self-worth, then we must still love ourselves even when we make mistakes or do dumb things--no matter how bad they were.

There are a lot of confusing "self" terms--self-worth, self-concept, self-esteem, self-confidence, etc. Think of *self-esteem* as composed of two parts--the *unconditional* part, and the *conditional* part. The unconditional self-valuing part is our *self-worth*. The conditional self-valuing part is our *self-confidence*. The most important part is the self-worth (unconditional) part. I will address it first. The last part of the chapter will discuss self-confidence and life skills.[18]

HOW DO WE GET UNCONDITIONAL SELF-LOVE?

To some degree we were "prewired" to care about ourselves. Positive and negative emotions and pleasure and pain provide a biological basis for taking care of ourselves so that we will tend to choose that which causes us to feel good over that which causes us to feel bad. Some part of us that I have called the Higher Self learns to value us at an early age (see Higher Self Chapter 3).

---

[18] That is how I define the three terms. There are no universal definitions; different authors refer to them in different ways. However, this distinction reflects common implied meanings.

Our Higher Selves *do love us unconditionally*. Our Higher Selves want us to be happy--despite past mistakes. It doesn't matter what we accomplish. It doesn't matter what anyone else thinks of us. Our Higher Selves still love us. No matter how dysfunctional our other beliefs about ourselves become, our Higher Selves still love us unconditionally and still believe in us.

Think of something or someone that you have loved almost unconditionally--your dog, your cat, your favorite place, your teddy bear, your parent, your lover, or your child. When we love someone unconditionally, it means that we will always care for that person and wish the best for him or her--no matter what the person does to us or anyone else.

A child can love an abusive parent--even though it hates the abuse and the abusive part of the parent. A parent can love a child even if the child becomes a criminal or mass murder. Some part of the child or parent cannot help but continue to care--that is the unconditional love part. We can repress our Higher Selves and our feelings of unconditional love for ourselves and others, but we cannot actually eliminate this part of us.

It is the strength of our Higher Self belief system relative to other belief systems that can determine the strength of our overall self-worth. If a strong internalized parent tells us we must be "good" to be worthwhile, then our self-worth will *be conditional*. We must learn to question those beliefs and replace them with new ones that are more loving.

You are the star of your own movie. Have you ever felt all alone, neglected, unappreciated, or unsupported? Have you wished that you could be like a movie star-- the center of attention, recognized and respected, and the character in the movie that all of the other characters revolve around.

If becoming a star doesn't seem possible to you, then perhaps you are not recognizing what you already have--*you are the star of your own life!* Think of your life as a movie in which you are the central character. Many of us think of our lives as revolving around other people (such as a dominant parent or partner). It is like we are in a movie in which we are only bit characters with a few lines.

In the movie, *"This is Your Life,"* you are the main character and star. Everything that happens to you is of major significance in the plot of the movie. Your ups and downs are all important to the viewers of your movie. Your growth and development over the course of the movie are the main themes in the movie. How are you doing so far?

> **PRACTICE: Think of your life as a movie in which you are the central character or star**.
> View your life as if you were a member of the audience watching a movie about it. What have been the major events of the movie? What have been the major *lessons* that you have learned and the areas of most growth in the character? How does it feel to think of yourself as the star of your own movie about your life?

I was given the responsibility for my own happiness. I was given the mental and physical powers to take care of myself. *Responsibility follows control*--the person with control over something is the one responsible for it. I was given direct control over my thoughts, my emotions, and my actions; therefore, I am the one responsible for my own thoughts, emotions, and actions.

If we develop a belief system that says I am responsible for other people's feelings or that they are responsible for mine, then that type of codependent belief system is dysfunctional (see internal control Chapter 6). If each person on the planet will take good care of their own needs, then we will all be happy. The result will be greater equality in relationships.

LOVING YOURSELF MEANS TAKING GOOD CARE OF YOURSELF

If you want to love yourself more, then one way to do it is to start treating yourself *as if you really do love yourself unconditionally.* Loving yourself means taking good care of yourself. It means making your own health and happiness a top-priority goal or part of your ultimate concern. You can be happy if you take care of meeting your own needs and values.

Develop habits of taking good care of yourself to increase your self-worth and self-love. Think of some person or object in your life that you really loved and took special care of. Think of the habits you developed to maintain it and keep it special. Do you love yourself as much as your mom, dad, lover, or child? Your dog or cat? Your home? Your car? Surely, you love yourself much more than your car or house? Yet do you show self-love by developing habits that take good care of your body and mind?

Loving yourself means taking good care of each part of yourself. Loving yourself means loving each part of yourself that contributes to your overall happiness. In addition to loving your overall self, you love your body, your inner child, your inner lover, your inner athlete, your inner parent, your inner music lover, and every healthy part of yourself that contribute to your overall happiness. You can also love your more dysfunctional parts in that you try to help them gain a better understanding of their *limits.* (In Chapter 9, I will describe the O-PATSM self-management system to keep your time use in sync with your overall values.)

Loving yourself means managing your time and resources well. If you love each part of yourself, you will prioritize your time and resources (such as money) to reflect the relative importance of each part of yourself or each life area. You will create some *balance* in your time and your life so that you can take good care of your body and your main interests and needs. Spend time and money on activities wisely. Ask yourself the following key question,

How much happiness will I and others get per dollar or per hour spent?

DEVELOPING A POSITIVE SELF-IMAGE:
Part 1: Develop a Positive BODY-IMAGE

WHAT DOES "SELF-IMAGE" MEAN?

On the one hand, self-worth measures how we feel about our unchangeable essence--important, essential aspects of ourselves. On the other, self-image is more about how we see ourselves in important, but NON-essential aspects of ourselves. The self-image is a collection of sensory images, beliefs, thoughts, and attached feelings we have about ourselves. It includes both the ideal self-image and the perceived self-image.

The **ideal self-image** is the complete set of goals and expectations for what we want to be like. The **perceived self-image** is based on our observations of what we are really like. **Guilt** is caused by the *gap* between our ideal self-image and our perceived self-image--between our self-*expectations* and our self-*perceptions.* The larger the gap, the more guilt we feel.

To overcome guilt we must *reduce the gap* between our self-expectations and our self-perceptions. We can either *change ourselves* to become more like our self-expectations, or we can *change our self-expectations* (self-concept) to fit reality.

It is important to remember, that in many situations we cannot change ourselves overnight. We may never be able to change some aspect of ourselves! How do we stop feeling guilty about something we can't change?

The self-acceptance process (described later) is a step-by-step method for overcoming guilt associated with your body, your past, and your dysfunctional subparts. But first, it's important to understand more about your self-image and how to change it.

SELF-ACCEPTANCE IS A PREREQUISITE FOR SELF-LOVE AND SELF-WORTH

To the degree that we do not like or accept some part of ourselves, then our self-love is affected. If I will not even admit to myself that sometimes I talk too much, do dumb things, have not met all my career goals, or bore people, then I am disowning those aspects of myself (and feeling guilty about them).

Learning to love or at least accept *every part of ourselves* is a fundamental part of developing self-worth and self-love. One of the first steps is accepting our bodies and our basic physical limitations.

ACCEPTING OUR BODIES AND OUR BASIC CAPABILITIES IMPROVES SELF-WORTH

Roger Crawford was the keynote speaker at a professional conference in San Diego that I attended. Roger is an amazing person who has overcome what could have been a disabling physical condition. When Roger was born, the physician took Roger's father back to see him. His father saw a baby with one leg crumpled beneath him and saw hands and feet that ended in pointed stumps instead of fingers and toThe doctor warned him that his son might never be able to walk or participate in normal activities.

Yet Roger's parents kept a positive attitude and always believed that their son could learn to do almost anything anyone else could do. Roger said that they never let him use his disability to get away with anything. Eventually, one of Roger's legs was amputated below his knee and replaced with an advanced artificial limb.

Then Roger learned how to play tennis. His "hands" each look as if he has one giant finger--with no thumb. He learned a two-handed grip. He put the "finger" from one hand into the end of a tennis racket and wrapped the other "hand" around the throat of the racket. Roger would not allow himself to believe that he was limited by his disability. He played his hardest.

He got so good that he began winning tournaments in high school and college and became a tennis professional. He got so good that he once played John McEnroe, when John was advancing in his career. Roger says that the night before the tennis match, "I slept like a baby. I woke up every two hours and cried." Eventually Roger won a special award for his tennis and he was given the honor of carrying the Olympic torch during the opening ceremonies of the Olympics in Los Angeles.

Roger said that one of the hardest times in his life was as a child in a Chicago school. Many of the other children said cruel things about his limbs and shunned him. Some even tried to harm him. He felt hurt and angry. He kept his hands in his pockets so that no one would see them. It seemed unfair to be given these distorted hands and feet. Sometimes he felt sorry for himself.

However, other people--like Dr. Norman Vincent Peale--helped him understand that it was not his body that was his problem; it was his attitude about his body that was important. Once he began to accept and love his hands and feet for what they were and see the possibilities in them, he began to feel much better.

Part of accepting ourselves is accepting other people's reactions to us. Roger began to understand and accept other people's reaction to his hands. He understood their curiosity, fear, and even disgust at seeing them. He accepted these as normal reactions and learned to focus on helping other people feel as comfortable with his appearance as he was.

For example, he "warned" the audience that after years of dreading to shake hands with people, he now really enjoys it and would offer his hand if they came up to talk. Being comfortable with his appearance and other's reaction to it changed his life.

Roger has been successful in his career, his marriage, and seemed happy on his journey toward self-actualization. He said that he would never trade his positive philosophy for normal feet and hands.

YOUR SELF-IMAGE IS MORE POWERFUL THAN YOUR ACTUAL IMAGE

Dr. Maxwell Maltz was a plastic surgeon who became interested in "self-image psychology" because of his confusing observations of patients who had undergone plastic surgery. Some patients who only received minor facial changes changed their personality and life dramatically while others with greater facial changes didn't seem to change at all. A boy with large ears had been told he looked like a taxi cab with both doors open and had been ridiculed all his life. He had become withdrawn and shy. After surgery, he became much more outgoing.

Yet others, such as a shy Duchess who was given a truly beautiful face in surgery made no noticeable improvement in her personality. Maltz concluded that the reason was because these people continued to think of themselves as ugly, different, abnormal, or defective people.

It was their *self-image* that was the main problem--not their actual physical appearance. His conclusions caused him to begin to focus on improving people's self-image and eventually write books such as *Psychocybernetics*. For years, this was one of the self-help books most frequently cited to me by clients as a book that had helped them change their lives.

One of my clients came in because she lacked confidence in herself--especially in meeting men and relating to them. Through her teen years, she was 50 to 75 pounds overweight. Only in the past few years had she taken good care of her body and lost weight. She was happy about that, but she said that she still saw herself as fat and ugly. In fact, she was beautiful--she could have won a beauty contest.

I was amazed that she still saw herself as fat. We discovered that a subpart of her had learned from her mom that it was wrong to show off and stand out. This part produced feelings of guilt whenever she tried to dress well or attempted to appreciate her own appearance. She would not even accept what she saw in the mirror.

It became important to reject these beliefs about being a "show off." She had to overcome those thoughts that interfered with her self-appreciation. To overcome her fear of self-appreciation, her repeated thoughts like, "It's wonderful to look at a flower and appreciate the beauty in it, and it's just as wonderful to look at myself and appreciate the beauty in my own body."

A PROCESS FOR ACCEPTING YOUR BODY AND APPEARANCE

Loving ourselves unconditionally means accepting all of the realities about ourselves and *still* loving ourselves. A good place to start is with our body and appearance. Most people do not love and accept every part of their body.

Looking at ourselves in the mirror. In his book, *Your Erroneous Zones,* Dr. Wayne Dyer suggests that one way to increase our self-acceptance and self-worth is to examine each part of our body and each bodily function in detail and observe our own thoughts and feelings about each. Do we feel disgust at certain normal body functions or products--such as bodily fluids or waste? If so, we do not accept all of our normal, healthy parts and functions. Try understanding how these basic functions work and how important these basic functions are to our health and survival. Try loving each function because it helps keep you alive and healthy. Some people can become phobic about such normal processes.

Our physical appearance is stressed so much in our society that we may be very sensitive about any part that does not measure up to our ideal. Try Dr. Dyer's exercise. Stand in front of a mirror naked and look at yourself. What parts do you feel good about? What parts do you not feel good about? How can you love and accept that part *as it is right now.*

Don't say to yourself, "I'll love that part *after I change it.*" That is *not* accepting that part as it is *now*. You can still improve the part later if you choose. Ironically, changing the part may be easier *after* accepting it; because you can face it without guilt.

Learning to love and accept our "most unacceptable" parts. My wife, Sherry, tried following Wayne's suggestion from his book and found that she could accept every part of her body except her tummy. She has felt most of her life that her middle was too big. She always wished that she could have a tiny waistline. For years, she had chosen clothes partly because they hid her tummy.

She consciously worked on looking at her tummy, developing positive thoughts about it, and loving her tummy instead of disowning it. Her attentiveness worked: she felt better about her tummy and accepted it.

This new tummy-acceptance had a number of effects. She bought and wore clothes that allowed her tummy to be seen. She started tucking in her blouses and wearing dresses with belts. Previously, if I were being affectionate, she would not allow me to even touch her tummy. Now I could love her tummy too. The most interesting thing is that her tummy began to get smaller!

> **PRACTICE 1: Learn to accept all aspects of your body as they are**. Try this exercise on yourself and see what happens as a result of learning to accept and love the formerly disowned parts or functions of your body or your personality. You can start with the aspects you dislike the most, or if you would rather, start with less odious ones and work your way up to the worst aspects.
>
> **PRACTICE 2: Take care of your body.** If your value yourself and your body, you will naturally want to take good care of your body. Similarly, paying loving attention to your body and its needs will increase your valuing of it.
> (1) **Assess your body and your care of it in each of the following areas:** nutrition, exercise, substance abuse, weight, muscle tone, sleep, and appearance.
> (2) **Develop a plan to improve any needed areas.** If you are not knowledgeable in an important area like nutrition, get help or start studying ASAP.

SELF-IMAGE:
Part 2: Develop a Positive Self-Concept

Tricia, a woman in her mid-fifties, had a job for many years working in a low-paying retail sales job. She had health problems that made long periods of standing very painful. Her teenage daughter made much more money than her mother by working as a typist. The daughter tried to get her mom to learn how to type. However, Tricia literally believed that she "was too old" to learn a complex new skill like typing.

That belief about herself was limiting and affected not only her career, but many life areas. Her daughter knew that her mother was an intelligent woman who had much untapped potential. It's sad that the mother didn't share her daughter's view!

Do you think of yourself as too shy, not coordinated, not motivated, a slow learner, too flaky, or not able to relate to people well? What physical, mental, personality, or financial limitations interfere with your happiness? How do your assumptions about them interfere with your success and happiness?

Limiting versus *expanding* self-beliefs. An alternative to having such *limiting self-beliefs* is to see ourselves as having almost limitless potential. It is not that we don't really have limits, but that *we do not allow ourselves to retain ideas that limit us*. That means that we do not allow ourselves to say to ourselves that we are too limited in any way--unless we have absolute proof! We are not too old, too young, too dumb, too weak, too slow, too disabled, too sick, too emotional, too shy, too afraid of . . ., too poor, or any other "too."

Instead, we can develop a positive view of ourselves that says we believe in our own strengths--especially our *abilities to learn* and *to motivate ourselves* to do what will make us happy.

This general self-view can help us go into almost any situation with a positive attitude of willingness to learn and do whatever it takes to achieve happiness. These general beliefs about ourselves can provide the energy, flexibility, and persistence required for maximizing our chances of succeeding at even very difficult tasks.

NEGATIVE SELF-BELIEFS GENERATE DYSFUNCTIONAL THOUGHTS AND HABITS

Viewing ourselves with negative self-labels and self-concepts can produce dysfunctional thoughts and habits. These negative self-beliefs cause unnecessary negative emotions such as guilt, depression, and anger. They can undermine success in our career, relationships, and other life areas by undermining our motivation and confidence.

In the following sections I will discuss some types of negative self-beliefs and their dysfunctional effects. I will also suggest some ways of overcoming them. One approach common to many of these "cures" is to find these underlying dysfunctional beliefs. Like a cancerous tumor, we must locate and operate on the source of the cancer--it is not enough just to keep fighting the cancer in places where it has spread. (Use the self-exploration process from Chapter 2.)

Developing a facade to hide our actual self-image from ourselves or others. One way that we may try to defend ourselves against criticism is to develop a *false image* of ourselves that more clearly matches our ideal self-image. Adopting a facade might be especially tempting to someone with a large gap between their perceived self-image and their ideal self-image. Consequently, they can pretend that the gap is minimal.

It is important to note that there is a major difference between trying to better ourselves by *living as if we were the persons we want to be* versus *trying to fool ourselves that we have arrived* at being that ideal self. In the first case, we are completely open and honest with ourselves about the fact that we have a goal we are attempting to meet and can accept any failures to reach that ideal with few problems. That is a functional way of moving toward self-actualization.

The dysfunctional way to deal with our shortcomings is to cling to beliefs that we are what we are not--and to ignore negative feedback. We may cling to our facade partly because we fear that others will not like us if they learn the truth.

However, even presenting a facade to others is not as dysfunctional as trying to hide the truth from ourselves. Self-deception can cause persistent, mysterious guilt--such as the kind often found in alcohol or drug abuse. Maintaining a facade may also be an important cause of habitual lying, "sociopathic," or "con-man" behaviors.

Fragile egotism is a cause of aggressive and violent behavior. Drs. Roy Baumeister, Laura Smart, and Joseph Boden (1996)--after an extensive research review--have concluded that people who hold "inflated, unstable, or tentative beliefs in the self's superiority" are most likely to be (1) easily and frequently threatened by negative feedback from others and (2) most prone to react aggressively and violently to those threats. "Entitlement" thinking and being dependent upon other people's approval (externally controlled) also increase one's propensity toward violence.

The authors discuss how one's belief in a "culture of honor" and a threatened public image (such as "losing face") can foster violent responses when those beliefs are threatened. For example, a gang member may want to be seen as a "bad ass." When someone else says he's "badder," then the only choice is to fight or be publicly humiliated. The fear of public humiliation and loss of self-esteem seems to be worse than violence or the fear of death.

When someone believes he or she must be "the best" to be "ok," then that belief inherently creates a "fragile ego," because only one person can be the best. When one defines oneself by external conditions--such as financial success or others' opinions--then that belief also increases one's fragility; because these conditions are so unstable. Only if we love ourselves *unconditionally* and define our essential natures by more *stable* measures can we overcome this fragility. Loving ourselves and others unconditionally undermines the conditions that create violence. Unconditional love of self and others is the best cure for violence in ourselves and our society.

DANGER--Choosing the wrong words can undermine your self-image.
Negative labels can undermine your unconditional self-worth.

Confining labels can backfire if given *too much priority*. Negative self-labels can become self-fulfilling prophesies, but even positive labels can have negative effects--if they are too self-limiting. We have just seen how defining ourselves as a "bad ass" can lead to violent behavior.

One problem I have is that my thirst for truth and knowledge can have a "dark side" if I develop the *additional* belief that I know more than others. If I spend a lot of time learning about something, I am tempted to conclude that I know more about it than other people. In someone else's view, I'm just a "know it all." Or--even worse--if I let myself believe that I "should" know more than anyone else about it, then I develop a fragile self-belief that is easily threatened by anyone challenging my knowledge.

Whenever I allow myself to get too proud of myself in some knowledge area, then I become defensive and argumentative in that knowledge area. On a smaller scale, it is the same thing that happens to the person prone to violent behavior.

When I was in the third grade, our teacher held a math speed contest. I finished second in the class and was proud of myself. I developed a belief about myself that I was "fast at solving math problems." I was so proud of being "fast at math" that it became part of my self-image. Therefore, whenever I solved math problems my self-expectation told me that I had to work them faster than anyone else. Whenever I took a math test, I raced through the exam as fast as possible to be the first student to turn my paper in. This went on for more than five years, and I was blind to its negative effects.

One day, I wondered why my grades in math weren't as good as some of the "slow" students who turned their papers in last. I realized that I could correct frequent careless errors if I would take time to check my exams before turning them in. However, taking more time conflicted with my self-image of being fast in math. Fortunately, I decided that my grades were more important than this limiting self-concept, so I decided to check my exams until the last minute.

CREATE A POSITIVE, TRUTHFUL SELF-CONCEPT--
CHOOSE THE RIGHT WORDS TO DESCRIBE YOURSELF

We just saw how negative self-labels and confining self-labels can cause problems. So what are more functional ways to describe ourselves?

Growth-oriented, flexible versus *status-quo, rigid* self-concepts. If we view any important part of ourselves as a fixed entity that never changes, then self-change can become threatening and anxiety-producing.

> **We are not stone sculptures or any kind of fixed entity.**
> **We are human beings--constantly learning and growing--**
> **in a constantly changing and growing world.**
> **If we define ourselves as rigid, fixed-entities,**
> **then we will live in constant fear of the changes which are sure to come.**
> **On the other hand, if we define our primary nature as changing, growing entities,**
> **then we will look forward to the future and**
> **embrace the changes which are sure to come.**

Change is everywhere. We go through many phases of life from childhood to adulthood to old age. Our careers, relationships, health, and economic situations can change dramatically. Life is a river of changes. If we do not learn to "go with the flow," then we risk being swept away and drowned.

If we view ourselves as fixed, inflexible beings, then we will be threatened by change. If we view ourselves as growing, changing beings, then change is welcomed as a natural part of the growth process. Even negative changes can be more readily accepted.

I recognize that every single belief or state of my mind, body, or the world can change. If everything important seems to be changing too much and we do not have anything to hold on to, then we can become extremely insecure and anxious. Building our house on a foundation of rock means that we develop beliefs and attachments that will withstand the changes of time.

The rock I build my life on is the set of fundamental beliefs I have described as being part of my Higher Self. It includes beliefs that value personal health and happiness for myself and others, growth, truth, beauty, and a good environment. [Also, recall Maslow's self-actualization *metavalues*.] These are general and flexible values that are adaptable to many situations.

Building our identity on rock--avoid identifying with any role. Did you still think of yourself the way your parents, peers, or others think of you? Do you think of yourself as *primarily* an athlete, an artist, an engineer, a wife or mother, a son or daughter, or member of some group? No matter how important these roles are to you--they are just roles.

I am a husband, psychologist, tennis player, and father. These are important parts of me. However, these roles can all be taken away from me. They are more specific and limited to certain situations than my more general values and parts of myself. If I were to make husband, father, or psychologist become more important than being happy or seeking the truth, then my identity would be built on sand.

If I could no longer be husband, father, or psychologist, then the core of my identity would be threatened. Any threat to them would *magnify my anxiety* if it also threatened my identity. That is one reason why losing a partner, having an "empty nest," retiring, or losing a job is so much more devastating to some people than others. I have *chosen* that none of these roles will be as essential to my identity as my more general values. These more general values cannot be taken away. For as long as I live I will always be able to find some beauty, truth, growth, love, and happiness no matter what situation I am in. With values like these we build our identity on a rock foundation that cannot be swept away by crashing waves.

> **I identify myself as someone who values**
> **growth, love, happiness, truth, and beauty.**
> **I am this person that occupies my body and mind**
> **over a certain period in history.**
> **I have received many gifts for which I am caretaker**
> **during a limited amount of time.**
> **I am an explorer on a journey through life**
> **attempting to maximize these values,**
> **through many roles, each moment of my life.**

PRACTICE: Redefine your identity to make it more growth-oriented, flexible, and limitless. Look back over the self-description you made at the beginning of this chapter. Or, write an entirely new one.
(1) **Identify your essence.** Decide what the core of your essence is that will never change and that you can love unconditionally. What is your Higher Self like?
(2) **Identify and replace limiting self-beliefs.** Look for self-descriptions that are negative, limited, rigid, and non-growth oriented. Replace them with more positive, limitless, flexible, growth-oriented descriptions.
(3) **Examine your various subparts and roles.** What life roles do you play? Child? Parent? Older brother? Student/learner? Professional? Executive? Plumber? Wife? Dancer? Golfer? Mediator? Rebel? Problem-solver? Addict? Judge? Clown? Do you overly identify with any particular role or roles? Are there any roles that you think you *must* be happy or successful in to be happy overall? If so, then a key to overcoming anxiety and being happy is to plan *how you can be happy even without being successful in that role.* Make such a plan and start telling yourself that you can be happy whether or not you are happy in that role.

SELF-ACCEPTANCE AND FORGIVENESS--
The Keys to Eliminating GUILT and ANGER

Dr. Maslow believed that acceptance of self and others (and all their imperfections) was one of the primary characteristics of self-actualized people. His description follows.

They can accept their own human nature in the stoic style, with all its shortcomings, with all its discrepancies from the ideal image without feeling real concern. It would convey the wrong impression to say that they are self-satisfied. What we must say rather is that they can take the frailties and sins, weaknesses, and evils of human nature in the same unquestioning spirit with which one accepts the characteristics of nature. One does not complain about water because it is wet or about rocks because they are hard, or about trees because they are green.
As the child looks out upon the world with wide, uncritical, undemanding, innocent eyes, simply noting and observing what is the case, without either arguing the matter or demanding that it be otherwise, so does the self-actualizing person tend to look upon human nature in himself and in others. (Abraham Maslow, (1954) pp. 155-156)

The little, wide-eyed child Dr. Maslow described in this passage is the Higher Self. What I believe has happened for these self-actualized people, is that their Higher Selves have become the dominant parts of their personalities, and the other parts have become integrated with their Higher Selves.

We all do things that are dysfunctional to our own and others health and happiness. We are all *only human* and have *many limits* to our knowledge, skills, and resources. Our limits may create dysfunctional habits that we keep our entire lives. However, the Higher Self is committed to growth and to our quest for self-actualization. It wants us to have a happy, productive life no matter what our past was like.

We will *never get rid of all our inadequacies or negative subparts*. Getting rid of negative subparts is not our task. It is ok for those negative subparts to exist, but we must remove their power to control our lives. Our task is to strengthen the more functional parts of ourselves and learn ways of identifying, understanding, and coping with the more negative parts. If you can do that, you will be making fundamental personality changes that will have effects in many areas of your life.

Psychologists since Freud have recognized that one of the major causes of emotional problems are habits of repressing, avoiding, or denying parts of ourselves that we feel bad about. We hope that if we just avoid these negative parts, they will go away. While this approach does have some merit in limited situations, we cannot just avoid major subparts of ourselves that continue to cause havoc in our lives. That avoidance can actually give them *more control*.

Self-understanding, self-acceptance, and restructuring our beliefs are the keys to getting control of our underlying negative belief systems. See the self-exploration process in Chapter 2 and the sections below to explore beliefs about yourself and replace dysfunctional ones.

"We make mistakes, mistakes don't make us" (Maltz, p.150,1960)

OUR SUBPARTS CAN UNDERMINE OUR UNCONDITIONAL LOVE

Sometimes loving ourselves can be difficult. How do we love ourselves when other people keep telling us that we are "selfish," "stupid," or "dysfunctional"? Exposure to frequent negative labeling or name-calling from parents or peers can help cause us to internalize those messages. We internalize not only their messages, but we internalize mental models of the persons themselves. I have a little "mom" and a little "dad" inside. They have the same beliefs my real parents had when they were alive.

My inner mom is supportive, loving, and understanding; but mom never learned to have fun. My inner dad is concerned about "being the best," making a lot of money, and "having the best." My inner dad is intolerant of failure and used to yell "stupid" or "idiot" to me whenever I didn't do something perfectly. My Higher Self has learned from both parents. Over the years, I have usually chosen to listen to my Higher Self--not my inner mom or inner dad. Those choices have quieted my inner parents and empowered my Higher Self.

One client's father had been psychologically abusive to her. If she did not do what he wanted, he called her "lazy," "bad," or "selfish." Once when she went out without his permission, he called her a "slut." As a young girl, she tried pleasing him and tried to meet his sometimes high, sometimes contradictory expectations. She learned that no matter how hard she tried to please him, he would still berate her. Therefore, she quit trying.

Consequently, as a teenager, she began to drink heavily, take drugs, and generally led a wild life. She eventually left home and started working. Her new lifestyle was a way she hoped to get even with her father--she intended to hurt him by doing the opposite of what he wanted. She also hoped that her new friends and partying would help her drown out the inner voices that constantly told her what a loser she was. Those voices came from her dysfunctional, internalized father. She responded by sinking deeper and deeper into drug dependence and guilt.

Fortunately, she began to see that her drug-based lifestyle was just making her more miserable than she had been as a little girl. She started college, met a new group of friends, went to Alcoholics Anonymous, and began recovery.

She came to see me because she was haunted by guilt. She said, "I despise myself for wasting eight years of my life." Learning to accept herself and love herself was difficult: her internalized father *still* told her what a loser she was. Even though she had improved her life, she those messages haunted her.

How could she get control over this part of herself that was so critical and responsible for so much guilt? First, we explored it thoroughly to see what its' expectations were. What did her father really want from her? He wanted her to be moral, successful, and happy. In fact, she finally concluded, the "good father" part of him really loved her and wanted what was best for her. It's just that he thought *he* knew what was best for her and wanted *to control her and run her life* to assure that she would be successful.

On the other hand, another part of him was quite "selfish." When she had lived with him, he wanted her to cater to him and be at his beck and call. Yet he would disguise these "selfish" motives by saying he wanted her to learn "responsibilities" such as doing his cooking, laundry, and housecleaning. If she didn't obey, he would say something like, "Look at all I've done for you, you selfish ingrate." The result was that she felt guilty, and wondered if he really loved her.

Once she understood that these self-expectations (and guilt) were coming from her internalized father and she could *clearly verbalize them,* then she could examine them from the point-of-view of her higher, more functional beliefs. One unrealistic expectation was, "I should never make a mistake. If I do, I should be severely--even eternally-- punished for it." Another was "All addicts are bad people--permanently! They can't overcome this moral wrong."

Thoughts like "I am a bad person, because I am an addict" came from those dysfunctional beliefs. Once she was aware of these beliefs, she could accept or reject them based on how well they fit her newer, higher beliefs. For example, she could respond to these old messages by saying, "All people have great value--even addicts. I am not a bad person or a loser. I love myself unconditionally and am loved unconditionally-- no matter what my past is. Even though I am not proud of all I did, I did not waste that time; I learned from it and could not be the person I am today without that experience. I will try to use that knowledge for my own and others' benefit." That self-talk was the only thing that had ever worked to help her get lasting control of her guilt.

She not only got control of her guilt, but she got control of the deep anger she had felt toward her father (and most men). She had blamed him--as well as herself--for her years of unhappiness. She had thought she could never forgive him. But she said. "Only because I *understood and forgave myself, could I understand and forgive him.*"

THE SELF-ACCEPTANCE PROCESS--
Learn *how* to accept *all* of yourself, your past and your future

The self-acceptance process is a method for accepting the parts of yourself that you may feel bad about. Think of some part or aspect of yourself that you don't like--especially some aspect that you can't change immediately. Use the following process to increase your self-acceptance of that part. Even if you *do* choose to change that part, gaining acceptance of it *as it is now* is an important first step to change. The first thing that Alcoholics Anonymous requires of new members is for them to admit that they are alcoholics.

SHAQ Research Results: Forgiveness

The Forgiveness subscale correlated with Happiness, .34; with Low Depression, .27; with Low Anxiety, .35; with Low Anger-Aggression, .49; with good Relationships, .23; with Health, .34; and with Income, .12. (For all correlations, $p < .0001$ and Ns ranged from 2093 to 2328.)

SHAQ research (and that of others) supports the value of forgiveness for helping people have better relationships and find more happiness. Forgiveness gives to the giver at least as much as it gives to the receiver. Again, the control of your happiness lies within in your mind.

STEP 1: CHOOSE TO VALUE TRUTH ABOVE ALL--INCLUDING HONOR AND PRIDE

The words "pride" and "honor" can mean many things. In certain contexts they can be functional concepts that enhance our lives. The idea of taking pride in our work and caring about what we do are examples of using the concept of "pride" functionally. Similarly, honoring or specially recognizing someone because they have achieved an important goal can be functional.

However, placing values best confined to specific situations above more important values can lead to dysfunctional results. When we put our honor, pride, or any other *self-image above the truth*, then we are inviting disaster--in the form of guilt hammering at our peace. Trying to drown guilt with alcohol, work-ahol, or play-ahol instead of facing the truth are dysfunctional results of putting pride above truth. Being completely honest with yourself is the first step toward self-acceptance--even when it means facing the worst truths about yourself.

STEP 2: EXPLORE THE SELF-EXPECTATIONS--SELF-PERCEPTIONS GAP

Ask yourself questions like, "What do I expect myself to be like?" "How does that differ from how I am?" and "How are my beliefs, thoughts, and actions different from what I expect them to be?"

Explore conflicting expectations from different subparts. You may find conflicting answers to these questions from different parts of yourself. One part may expect you to make a lot of money, while another part may think that money is not important. In other words, you may have conflicting expectations from different parts of yourself.

STEP 3: EXPLORE THE UNDERLYING CAUSES—
KNOWING "WHY" INCREASES ACCEPTANCE

One way we give more control to our healthy parts is to understand our dysfunctional parts better. We can question and change these beliefs and learn more functional beliefs. Some important questions to understand why we keep performing unproductive habits include:
- When does it occur? What situations and stimuli regularly precede it?
- What thoughts and behaviors occur?
- What thoughts and images are associated with these thoughts?
- What overall themes, beliefs, or assumptions are behind these thoughts or actions?
- What internal or external outcomes may be reinforcing the thoughts and behaviors?
- What are the historical causes of the habits? (E.g. Parental or peer modeling, instructions, reinforcements, etc.)
- Use the self-exploration process to get at deeper causes (see Chapter 2).

STEP 4: USE HIGHER BELIEFS TO REDUCE THE EXPECTATIONS--PERCEPTIONS GAP

If two lower courts conflict over federal law, then the conflict is referred to a higher court. Eventually the case may go to the Supreme Court. The Supreme Court relies upon the U.S. Constitution as the ultimate code of law.

The same principle applies to resolving conflicts between lower parts of ourselves. We can choose to make our Higher Selves our Supreme Courts. We can give our Higher Selves this authority by choosing to resolve inner conflicts with questions like, "Which alternative will create the most happiness for me and others?" or "Which is the most honest?" "Which will lead to the most growth?" Our "Constitution" consists of values and beliefs such as these. (If you have not done so, make your own list of higher principles from earlier chapters.)

==> **For every old or dysfunctional belief, question it, confront it, explain it, or persuade it with a more powerful Higher Self belief.**

We cannot unlearn old beliefs and habits. We can never entirely erase an old belief or habit, because we can *never completely unlearn something we have learned* any more than we can forget $2 + 2 = 4$. However, we can get better control of these dysfunctional parts by (1) understanding them--especially their negative effects--and by (2) acting on messages from our healthier parts.

Accept the past as past--focus on the present and future. One client came in because he was almost 40 and had been in college for almost 20 years without ever completing all the courses he signed up for! He was intelligent, but had always lacked motivation. He typically set very high goals, and started semesters with a bang. If he had problems or lost interest, he would fall behind and then drop out when he was not making "A" grades. Many of his friends were professionals with high incomes and jobs he envied. He said, "I think I'm as smart as they are, but I've just wasted my life."

One thought that had haunted him for years was, "Look where I would be if I had just worked hard and finished college in my early twenties." This thought was so strong that it was a powerful impetus for his constant dropping out. He learned to replace that thought with a different point of view. He would put himself into the future 20 years, when he would be almost 60. He then asked himself, "How will I feel if I look back to the age I am now and say, 'If I had completed college then, look where I would be today'."

Whenever he would start to focus on the past missed opportunities, he would refocus on this new way of looking at the future instead. His new focus lights a fire under him. This was the first semester that he had *ever completed all the classes he signed up for.* Not only that, but he made good grades. He has since graduated and was completing his Master's degree the last time we met.

We are not exactly the same people we were in the past. One thing to remember when we beat ourselves up now for past actions is that we are *not the same people* that made the errors in the past. So, in a sense, we are blaming the *wrong person.* We have learned and changed since then, so why criticize someone that doesn't even exist anymore? Focusing on past mistakes (beyond what we can constructively learn from them) is totally unproductive.

Recognize positive aspects of yourself--including your goal of growth and your past growth. Review the sections on unconditional self-worth, your Higher Self, and the importance of measuring your life by how much you learn and grow. Focus on your ultimate concern of overall happiness, and adopt abundance motivation by being grateful for all that you have received. Identify past positive actions and aspects of yourself. Make a list of all the positives about you--as you are *now.*

Put this list in a prominent place and keep reminding yourself of these qualities. Convert these general ideas into clear visual images that exemplify these qualities. Never let yourself state negatives about yourself without also stating positive qualities.
==> *Go to the "Rise Above" Chapter 8, mental control strategy 4 to learn more methods for changing expectations.*

STEP 5: OVERCOME YOUR FEARS OF NEGATIVE LABELS

We can develop a huge fear about the truth behind a label. The fear of being labeled "stupid," "weird," "crazy," or any "whatsit" can be like a cancer eating away at our self-esteem. It can be a fear that others use to control us. It can prevent us from believing or doing many of the things that can help us grow and be happy.

One of my clients, a psychology graduate student, came in because he had low self-esteem and a combative relationship with a woman he loved. They got into arguments that started with mild disagreements, but quickly escalated into shouting matches or even physical brawls. He knew that he couldn't control his temper and suspected that it had something to do with his relationship with his father. He had tried to figure it out, but to no avail. Why did he always have to be right? Why was he so persistent and competitive-- even over unimportant differences of opinion?

We explored his relationship with his father. His father was a brilliant scientist, had obtained a prestigious position at a very early age, and had achieved a great deal of recognition. However, his father was very demanding. His father had hoped his son would someday become a great scientist. When my client was a boy, his father spent many hours training him to be a scientist.

Yet his father was impatient and short-tempered. Whenever his son couldn't grasp an idea quickly, he would use a negative label like "stupid." My client's mother was also very bright and had a doctorate. Intelligence and science were supremely important in his family.

My client felt confused about his intelligence. Part of him believed he was intelligent. After all, he did well in school, and he thought a high IQ ran in his family. However, another part of him doubted his intelligence because his father had called him "stupid" all his life.

When my client developed interests in art and psychology instead of "hard science," his father was furious and felt like a failure as a father. He told his son what a stupid choice he had made and nearly disowned him. His father was a role model of aggressive, dominating--even cruel--behavior. The goal was to win any conflict--no matter what the means or the cost. Even though my client was angry at his father, he admired him for his intelligence and accomplishments so much that part of him believed his father was right-- he must be stupid.

Yet being smart--even brilliant--was so important to him and his family, that he could not stand to think of himself as other than brilliant. He always *had to be right*--just like his father. To be wrong might imply that he was stupid (the ultimate sin). When a difference of opinion would arise with someone, he would either fight desperately to win and prove himself right or withdraw (out of fear of losing the other person's love.)

He, literally, didn't understand how to have a noncompetitive conversation over an issue and accept that two people could each have a legitimate point of view. He turned every discussion into a contest in which one person won and the other lost. His pride or self-image was at stake in every disagreement. This competitiveness undermined all of his relationships--especially those with women. Through self-exploration we had found that being thought "stupid" by himself or others was *one of his worst fears* in life. That was a major insight for him. But what could he do to overcome this fear?

Accept the *implications* of the worst possible self-label. Behind all of this competitiveness was his fear of a label. The idea of being stupid (or even not being highly intelligent) was about the worst possible self-label my client could think of.

We explored the origins of his fear. His family *assumed that a person had to be intelligent to have any self-worth*. To be accepted as a family member, a person had to be brilliant. He even said half-joking at one point, "I might as well be dead as be stupid."

We continued to explore his negative associations with the label "stupid." What if he really had a low IQ? What would his life be like? What would other people think of him and how would they react to him?

Then, I asked him to find scenarios of how he could still be a happy person even if his worst fear were true--even if he really had a low IQ. He *faced his worst possible self-concept fear and found routes to happiness* that were possible even with a low IQ. For example, even if he couldn't be a successful professional, he could still be happy as a carpenter.

He also confronted his belief that stupid people have no value with a higher belief that all people have value. Consequently, he found that he could *still love and accept himself--even if he were to have a low IQ*.

My client clarified how much "being right" and "winning arguments" was interfering with his relationships and life. He chose to make intimacy, empathy, and happiness more important values than winning and being right. He lost much of his need to defend himself against perceived attacks on his intelligence. He began to listen more, be more accepting, and be more supportive.

> **Why can't we all learn what even children say,**
> **"Sticks and stones may break my bones,**
> **but words will never hurt me"?** [Unless we let them.]

Remember, the more successful and powerful we are, the more praise and criticism we receive. More derogatory jokes, cartoons, and statements are made about the president of the United States than any other person in the country. Yet, by many measures, he is the most powerful and successful person in the entire country! What if the president couldn't stand criticism and got upset every time a politician or journalist said something negative about him? It just wouldn't do to have a thin-skinned president.

I asked workshop participants to list both positive and negative characteristics of the U.S. President. For almost every negative label, they listed a corresponding positive label that described the *same behavior*. For example, he was called "slick" by someone who didn't like him, but called a "good communicator" by one of his supporters. The underlying behaviors that the two people saw were the same, but their *interpretation* of those behaviors was positive or negative *depending on their point of view.*

Behaviors are just behaviors. They do not come with labels. However--no matter who we are or how we behave--people will give negative and positive labels to those neutral behaviors. People who like what we do will use positive labels, and people who don't like what we do will use negative labels--for the same behaviors. There is no way out--even doing nothing can be labeled negatively. Certainly we will not think well of a president who does nothing.

What can you do if you have been inhibited by your fears of negative labels? First, assume that *whatever you do will not be liked by some people*. Those people may use negative labels to describe your behavior. They may also overgeneralize and use a *negative label to describe you as a person*. Not just that you *acted* "selfishly," but that you *are* "selfish."

Also, remind yourself that the more successful and influential someone becomes, the more they will be the target of negative comments. The more decisively you act, the more upset those who disagree will become. *Learning to accept those negative comments is necessary if you want to have a significant positive impact on the world.* Otherwise, your fear of those comments will keep you from speaking or acting assertively.

How to overcome negative labels. In addition to using the self-exploration methods, try using the following to help you identify and overcome some of your worst-feared negative labels.

1. Make a list of the *worst possible* self-labels. Follow your fears and imagine the worst possible comments someone could say or think about you. List them all--no matter how "silly" or unlikely they seem.

2. Accept the worst possible consequences and implications. Pick two or three of the worst labels to work on accepting. For each negative description use the self-exploration process described in Chapter 2 to explore the implications of these self-labels. What beliefs or historical events with others underlie these self-labels? What are the practical implications for your life if it turns out you really are this way? What routes to happiness would still be open to you if the worst were to happen?

3. Learn to accept and love yourself "Even if I were a *whatsit*." Work on accepting and loving yourself even if you were this worst possible "whatsit." *Unconditional self-love* means that we can love and respect ourselves no matter what kind of a "whatsit" we might be. You are more than a label. You may do "whatsit" behaviors or even partly be a "whatsit," but you are much *more* than a "whatsit" and your *essence* is not a "whatsit."

4. Face the truth. Face the issue "How true is this description of me." Try to be honest with yourself and even seek the opinion of trusted others.

5. Do you want to make any changes? Keep working on accepting and loving yourself *as you are now* even if you do intend to change some part of yourself. As you begin to accept that you are an ok, worthwhile person who can love yourself *being a whatsit,* you free yourself to decide whether or not you really want to partly be a "whatsit" or not.

You are no longer being "pressured" into change by guilt, "shoulds," or internalized expectations from others. You can now ask yourself questions like, "Will's I be happier being a 'whatsit' or not?" or "Is changing from a 'whatsit' a high enough priority in my life to merit the time and effort it will take?"

> **PRACTICE: Learn to accept your worst possible self labels.** Just as Roger Crawford learned to accept and love his hands and feet, we can learn to accept the worst possible "whatsit" that we might possibly be. We need to do this even before we face the truth. We need to follow our fears to the bottom or worst fear. Try thinking of all of the worst possible labels or descriptions you can think that someone might say or think about you. Then apply steps 1-5 above to overcome those worst possible label fears.

STEP 6: USE THE SAME STEPS 1-5 TO ACCEPT AND FORGIVE OTHERS

We can't fully love ourselves unconditionally and accept all aspects of ourselves while we cannot do the same for others. We cannot accept the imperfections in ourselves and not accept the imperfections in others. Our Higher Self is too smart for that. It will not let us have inner harmony if we try to accept imperfections in ourselves and not accept them in others. That inconsistency creates disharmony.

We can apply the same principles to overcoming anger toward others that are successful for overcoming anger toward ourselves (guilt). We will not be able to rid ourselves of the anger *unless we can do the following.*

1. Accept the effects of their actions. You cannot truly accept or forgive another until you have accepted all of the perceived consequences of their actions. Begin by working on accepting those. Use your higher beliefs. Be grateful for the positives that you have. Find new routes to happiness--despite what they have done. Then the acceptance process can proceed.

2. Choose happiness and health over anger. Are you holding on to your anger in order to punish the perpetrator? Your anger is harming you more than them--is that what you want? If issues like fairness, justice, or revenge are central concerns see the appendix on Anger and Aggression.

3. Develop understanding and empathetic thoughts toward the perpetrator. We can use the same process of understanding, accepting, and forgiving others that we use for ourselves. *Deep understanding of the causes and empathy* are the first steps to accepting negative effects of others' actions. Understanding and acceptance helps reduce the blame and anger.

==> Go to the appendix on Anger and Aggression for more help on accepting and forgiving others.

SHAQ Research Results: Self-Worth

The Self-Worth Scale correlated with Happiness, .59; with Low Depression, .45; with Low Anxiety, .42; with Low Anger-Aggr, .48; with good Relationships, .39; with Health, .36; with Income, .11; with Education, .09; and with college GPA, .10.

The three **Self-Worth subscales'** results were:
1. Love self and others; maximize and balance happiness correlated with Happiness, .57; with Low Depression, .33; with Low Anxiety, .25; with Low Anger-Aggr, .36; with Relationships, .43; and with Health, .31.
2. Unconditional self-worth (not dependent upon anything) correlated with Happiness, .36; with Low Depression, .34; with Low Anxiety, .38; with Low Anger-Aggr, .43; with Relationships, .21; with Health, .29; with Income, .14; with Education, .11; and with college GPA, .08.
3. Accepting all of self correlated with Happiness, .16; with Low Depression, .28; with Low Anxiety, .19; with Education, .07; and with college GPA, .07.

According to my research, a person with high Self-Worth--who loves all of himself or herself unconditionally, cares for all others unconditionally, and attempts to maximize and balance happiness for self and others--is more likely to be happy, have good relationships, and have success in life. Consequently, developing your self-worth is an important part of choosing to be happy.

Note: For all correlations, p < .0001 and Ns ranged from 2593 to 3199.

SELF-CONFIDENCE AND LIFE SKILLS

WHAT IS SELF-CONFIDENCE?

Self-confidence is *the expected probability that a person will achieve a goal in a certain situation.* For example if Mark estimates that his probability of achieving an "A" on a calculus exam is 90%, we would conclude that Mark had high self-confidence in his ability to do well on a calculus exam. If Mark had estimated 10%, then we would say he had low self-confidence about his ability to do well on the exam.

Self-confidence is *situational--not absolute.* It is important to remember that self-confidence is always relative to the task and situation. We have different levels of confidence in different situations. For example, Mark might be confident in Math; but lack confidence in English. He may also lack confidence in meeting people. He may estimate that his probability of success when he meets someone is only 10% (relative to a goal of making a new friend). *Confidence is relative to the prescribed situation, task, and expectations.*

Although self-confidence is *primarily* situational, self-confidence may generalize across many situations. For example, suppose Jason was good not only in math, but in almost all academic subjects. He would probably develop self-confidence for learning *any* academic subject--even those he had not attempted. If Jason is also good at sports, people skills, and other life areas, then he would probably develop a high level of *self-confidence in general.*

Similarly, if Jeff performed poorly in math, social situation, sports, and most areas of his life, then he would probably develop a low level of self-confidence in general. However, most of us are not like Jason or Jeff. Most of us believe that we do well in some situations (such as math) and not so well in others (such as meeting people or dealing with conflict).

I use the term "self-confidence" to mean what Dr. Albert Bandura, a leading research psychologist, has called "self-efficacy expectations." It has been the object of intense study in the field of psychology and led to many important findings. Generally, it is a good predictor of how well people will perform on all sorts of tasks. High self-confidence also increases people's motivation and persistence.

Self-confidence is at the root of *self-fulfilling prophesies.* Another research finding is called the **self-fulfilling prophesy**. An example of a positive self-fulfilling prophesy would be if you believe, "Lori will probably like me if I talk with her." That belief alone can partially cause you to initiate a conversation with Lori and be friendlier to her. Thus, the *belief alone actually increased the probability that it would be fulfilled* (since the *belief* actually helped cause the *action* that helped cause the prophecy's *fulfillment.)*

An example of a negative self-fulfilling prophesy would be your belief, "Lori will probably *not* like me if I talk with her." That belief might prevent you from speaking to her or cause you to be less friendly to her. In turn, Lori may not like you because you were not friendly to her.

What if I believed, "If I think it will rain tomorrow, my belief will actually make it rain tomorrow (because my beliefs have some magical powers over the weather)?" What is the difference between a belief like that and the belief, "I can learn math"?

It is important to differentiate between a self-fulfilling prophesy and **a superstitious belief**. A superstitious belief is a belief that XXX is a cause of an outcome when it really isn't. For example my beliefs *do* have causal effects on my motivation, but my beliefs *do not* have causal effects on the weather. Any such belief is superstitious.

Don't *waste time trying to control events that you really can't.* Too many people spend too much time, money, and energy seeking the advice of astrologers and others taking advantage of people's superstitious beliefs. People often claim to have magical powers of insight or control over events that they do not—often to make money. They prey on people's desire for help. Don't become psychologically dependent on these people. Don't become a victim of superstition. Investigate claims of magical powers and insights.

OUR SELF-CONCEPT AFFECTS OUR SELF-CONFIDENCE

Our general beliefs about ourselves can have a powerful effect upon our self-confidence across many situations. An engineering student in his mid-twenties came to one of my workshops because he was a junior on academic probation (had less than a "C" grade average). He really wanted to be an engineer, but he believed that *he was not as smart as the other students.*

As a result he usually felt insecure in his classes or in any situation that related to engineering. He was afraid to talk to his instructors because he feared they would discover his secret--that he was really "dumb." Whenever he came across a difficult problem or idea, he would give up easily because he thought that he was "too dumb" to ever understand it.

His underlying false belief was, "If I feel confused, it must be because I'm dumb." He often felt confused, so that "proved" he was "dumb." What he didn't know is that the "A" students often feel confused also, because the ideas and problems really are hard. *Feeling confused is not an indication of intelligence or ability; it is a normal part of the learning process.* (See Chapter 7 on harmonious functioning and peak performance).

How is this an example of a **negative self-fulfilling prophesy**? The belief he was "dumb" caused him to give up too soon. If he had believed he had the ability to solve the problem, he would have persisted.

We can believe that we are too strong and secure to feel threatened. Several weeks later, this student came in for counseling. He told me that the workshop helped him reinterpret his confusion. He no longer assumed that he was dumb. Each time he started to assume that he was "dumber" than the other engineering students; he *questioned that assumption and persisted until he understood* or solved the problem.

His effort, understanding, and grades improve dramatically. In addition, he enjoyed his classes more and felt more confident about his intelligence in general. He said, "I used to think that the few students who could solve the tough homework problems must be brilliant. Now, I am one of them--I can't believe it." His increased self-confidence in his *personal intellectual power* gives him more confidence in almost any problem-solving situation--even outside of engineering.

It is important to note that *his intelligence had not increased--only his belief in himself.* It was not important that he believe he was brilliant, it was only important that he believe he could *keep trying his best a little while longer.*

DEALING WITH PAST "FAILURES"--AND LOW SELF-CONFIDENCE

By "failure" I simply mean *not reaching a goal*. Putting ourselves down, beating ourselves up, and being overly self-critical or self-punitive not only feels terrible, but it is *highly unproductive and dysfunctional*. Even if negative self-talk produces some short-term motivation for some people to improve performance, the long-term motivational effects are almost always negative. For most people, even the short-range effects on motivation are negative.

Positive techniques work much better. However, you may *not know how to motivate yourself with positive approaches--especially if your family did not do it*. In Chapters 7-9 on harmonious functioning and the O-PATSM self-management system, I will revisit the topic of self-confidence and will present a number of specific methods for increasing your sense of self-confidence. Meanwhile, here are a few statements you can tell yourself when you tend to be too self-critical or focus on the negative aspects of not reaching your goal(s).

• Just because I didn't reach a goal in the past does not mean that *I am a failure* or will *not reach my goal in the future.*

• Abraham Lincoln lost every election until he finally went to the Senate and then ran for president.

• The great football coach, Vince Lombardy who became famous for "making winners of losers" suggested that no matter how "bad" we are, we start with simple, small goals and do our best in order to "get in the habit of winning" and get a "winning feeling" and get a "winning expectation." He was one of the few coaches who tried his best to win even the practice preseason games.

• Don't use the world "failure." Instead, (1) describe what you did and did not accomplish, (2) accept all outcomes, (3) ask what you can learn from the situation, and (4) ask if your goals and expectations are realistic (Chapter 8).

• **If your goal is to learn or grow, you can never fail!** No matter how many goals you fail to accomplish in a specific situation, you can always succeed at learning from it. Therefore, make learning a top goal in life, and you can be a success--no matter how much you fail at any other goal.

SELF-CONFIDENCE AND LIFE SKILLS

What is the secret to self-confidence? Is it encouragement and positive feedback from other people? Dr. David McClelland, a leading authority on achievement motivation, summarized years of research on self-confidence. He said that the most important factor for developing self-confidence is to *master the needed skills.* Your mother, your friends, and your teachers may tell you that you are not good at a task XXX. However, if you know *how* to XXX well enough, you can feel confident about XXX no matter what they think. Likewise, if everyone else tells you are great at XXX, but you know that you *don't know how* to do XXX well enough, you will lack self-confidence.

How much of a talent is innate versus learning? We can develop any skill by learning-- even skills many people do not ordinarily think of as skills--such as self-motivation, learning skills, and assertion. Do you think that people are born "motivated," "smart," or "assertive"? These factors can be affected by heredity, but specific values, beliefs, knowledge and skills are learned. These are factors we can control that will affect our motivation and competencies in all areas of life.

We can improve our skills through watching and learning from others who are experts, reading, taking classes, and from practice. The more we *immerse ourselves learning the skill, the faster we will learn.*

By gradually increasing our goals as we increase our skills, we can be challenged, interested, and feel successful at every stage of learning--novice, intermediate, advanced, and expert. The same methods of learning apply as well to interpersonal skills as to sports, business, or intellectual skills. *If you have been good at learning in one area of your life-- such as sports, playing the piano, or in school--apply the same learning methods that were successful there to an area where you feel less confidence.*

RELATIONSHIP BETWEEN LIFE SKILLS, HAPPINESS, AND SUCCESS

How important are basic life skills--cognitive skills, self-management skills, and interpersonal skills--to success in life? Research has shown that life skills are keys to success in academic, career, relationship, and personal areas. I have developed three questionnaires to measure life skills—the LSQ, SRQ (with Sherry), and SHAQ.

Life Skills Questionnaire (LSQ) and Stevens Relationship Questionnaire (SRQ) Results

I developed the LSQ to measure the relationship between life skills and life success. I used both self-rated life skills and more objective measures. More than 4,000 people were given the LSQ to see how well it correlated with life success criteria and happiness (Stevens, 1987). One study compared the relationship between life skills of 384 adults in their mid-twenties through fifties and their life success. We found significant correlations between *life skills* (cognitive, self-management skills, and interpersonal skills) and **life** *success* (college success, career success, and relationship success). For example *overall cognitive skills* correlated .37 with college grade average and *learning skills* correlated .43 with job status. *Overall self-management skills* correlated .30 with job status and .24 to number of relationships. *Overall interpersonal skills* correlated with both career status .30 and interpersonal success, and *intimacy skills* correlated .27 with relationship commitment level.

The LSQ, SRQ, and happiness. I believe the most important type of success is overall happiness. The LSQ and SRQ had even better correlations with happiness than it did with these other types of success. Overall personal happiness was correlated most with self-management skills, .51. However, personal happiness was also correlated to cognitive skills, .32 and interpersonal skills, .34.

My wife, Sherry, and I also developed the Stevens Relationship Questionnaire (SRQ) to measure relationship skills (Stevens and Stevens, 1995). Intimacy and assertive conflict resolution skills were highly correlated (more than .70) with the widely-used Locke-Wallace relationship satisfaction questionnaire.

It is important to note that cognitive, self-management, and interpersonal skills are vital to *all important life areas*. For example, all three types of skills can improve chances for happiness and success in one's career and in one's close relationships.

The Success and Happiness Attributes Questionnaire (SHAQ) Results

While the first edition of this book utilized the above research results, the new research results from 3400 people taking SHAQ has provided much more detailed evidence for the relationship between life skills and both happiness and success.

Self-management skills. The SHAQ *Self-Management scale* correlated with Happiness, .66; with Low Depression, .40; with Low Anxiety, .32; with Low Anger-Aggression, .38; with good Relationships, .50; with Health, .47; with Income, .10; with Education, .14; and with college GPA, .20. These are impressively high correlations, and show the importance of self-management skills for life happiness and success. See Chapter 9 for a more in-depth analysis of self-management.

Emotional coping skills. The SHAQ *Emotional Coping scale* correlated with Happiness, .66; with Low Depression, .60; with Low Anxiety, .51; with Low Anger-Aggression, .49; with good Relationships, .42; with Health, .49; with Income, .13; with Education, .14; and with college GPA, .14. Emotional coping also seems to be a fundamental skill set that is substantially related to happiness and success. See Chapter 8 for detail on emotional coping.

Interpersonal skills. The original SRQ had such good results that it was copied almost verbatim into SHAQ, and became the SHAQ Interpersonal Skills scales. The nine Interpersonal skills scales combined correlated with Happiness, .59; with Low Depression, .39; with Low Anxiety, .38; with Low Anger-Aggr, .59; with good Relationships, .49; with Health, .40; and with Income, .21. Interpersonal skills are discussed in greater depth in Chapter 6 and Appendix E.

Learning skills and academic motivation. Since I was very concerned about college student success, I designed 14 special SHAQ scales to assess learning skills and academic motivation. Combined, they correlated with Happiness, .67; with Low Depression, .49; with Low Anxiety, .46; with Low Anger-Aggression, .42; with good Relationships, .46; with Health, .43; with Income, .37; with Education level, .36; and with college GPA, .45; and with happy work relationships, .60. (For income, education level, and college GPA, only ages over 25 or 30 included.) Most of the rest were college students. Learning skills are discussed in more depth in Chapter 7.

KEY LIFE SKILLS:
Cognitive, Self-Management, and Interpersonal Skills

What are key life skills? Following are some of the key life skills identified by the LSQ and in psychological literature that seem important in many life areas. Assess your own life skills.

COGNITIVE:
_____Learning and study skills
_____Critical-thinking and logic
_____Research and methodology
_____Analysis
_____Synthesis
_____Creative thinking
_____Mathematics and quantitative thinking
_____Reading and comprehension
_____Writing and communication skills
_____Computer skills
_____Disciplines (Science, history, psychology,
          health, business, literature, music, art, philosophy,
          etc.) _List content areas of strength and weakness:_

SELF-MANAGEMENT:
_____Decision-making
_____Life and career planning
_____Time-management
_____Emotional coping skills
_____Self-development
_____Self-motivation, achievement, motivation, and work habits
_____Changing habits
_____Managing money

INTERPERSONAL:
_____Meeting people and talking to strangers
_____Empathetic listening skills
_____Self-disclosure of feelings & intimate information
_____Other intimacy skills
_____Conflict resolution skills
_____Persuasion
_____Managing others
_____Helping and teaching skills
_____Public speaking skills
_____Job search and interviewing

OTHER:
_____Skills in home maintenance, car repair, sports,
          music,, art, hosting, or other activities (list)
_____ Other: list other areas important in your life

OVERALL:
_____Overall Happiness Quotient (HQ) or "Happiness IQ" On a scale of 0 to 100, how confident are you that you can lead _a happy life in the future?_ (This is the _most important question._) You may find your HQ by taking SHAQ.

142 / Dr. Tom G. Stevens

PRACTICE 1: Self-Assessment: Estimate your level of self-confidence and skill levels in each life area. Estimate your own level of confidence and skill in each of the areas in the Key Life Skills table. For a more thorough assessment, try listing more specific, import ant goals or situations within each area. Use whatever standards or goals that you would naturally set for yourself. Relate confidence to your personal reference group or internal standard. *How confident on a scale of 0 to 100 are you that you can reach your own goals in each of these areas?*

PRACTICE 2: Self-Development: Plan your own life skills self-development program. *Make a plan for developing key life skill areas. Try the following:*
(1) List important life areas where you do not feel as confident or skilled as you would like for success and happiness in your career, relationships, or personal life.
(2) For each important life skill area, list potential learning opportunities--such as books, classes, counseling, workshops, observing people who can serve as "models," practice, feedback, or other life experiences that can help you develop your skills.
(3) Develop definite goals and plans for improving skills. Build them into your personal goals and time-management system (see self-management Chapter 9). (4) Seek feedback and do regular self-assessment of overall progress. Integrate into an overall self-management system like O-PATSM (Chapter 9).

THE DIFFERENCE BETWEEN LIFE SKILLS AND CONFIDENCE IN LIFE SKILLS

There is an important difference between *actual* life skills and *self-confidence* in life skills. *Skills* reflect complex, learned beliefs and habits, whereas *confidence* reflects one's assessment of their skills. Self-confidence is based upon actual skills, but includes other factors such as people's feedback or the group you compare yourself to. I may be a good tennis player compared to my friends, but not compared to professionals. So am I "good" or not?

In the practice above, you were asked to estimate your own life skills. SHAQ contains a scale based upon this life skill list to assess users' *ratings of their own skills.* What is actually being measured—life skills or self-confidence?

In the above sections on self-management, emotional coping, interpersonal, and learning *skills*, the LSQ, SRQ, and SHAQ life skill scale scores were measuring a sum of many detailed items describing different aspects of skills. In this section on life skill *self-confidence*, the score is an overall, global rating on one item of a skill area. To the degree that users can accurately rate their own skills, their life skills are being assessed. However, what is more certain is that the *self-confidence* in their life skills is being assessed. Actual skill and confidence are partially independent factors, but both are important.

SELF-CONFIDENCE AND LIFE SKILLS RESEARCH—AREA BY AREA

We have seen how SHAQ users' *actual* life skills relate to their happiness and other positive outcomes. Let's look at how SHAQ users' *self-confidence* in their life skills relates to their happiness and other important life outcomes.

SHAQ Research Results: Self-Confidence

The Self-Confidence Scale correlated with Happiness, .69; with Low Depression, .46; with Low Anxiety, .43; with Low Anger-Aggr, .38; with good Relationships, .50; with Health, .39; with Income, .17; with Education, .15; and with college GPA, .19.

The seven Self-Confidence/Life Skills subscales follow.
1. **Self-development, self-control, self-discipline.** This subscale correlated with Happiness, .67; with Low Depression, .47; with Low Anxiety, .37; with Low Anger-Aggr, .32; with Relationships, .41; and with Health, .42; with Income, .17; with Education, .14; and with college GPA, .21.
2. **Positive achievement and coping.** This subscale correlated with Happiness, .74; with Low Depression, .50; with Low Anxiety, .38; with Low Anger-Aggr, .35; with Relationships, .54; with Health, .30; with Income, .06; with Education, .05; and with college GPA, .08.
3. **Learning.** This subscale correlated with Happiness, .41; with Low Depression, .32; with Low Anxiety, .36; with Low Anger-Aggr, .33; with Relationships, .24; with Health, .31; with Income, .22; with Education, .25; and with college GPA, .25.
4. **Interpersonal skills—focus management/marketing.** This subscale correlated with Happiness, .58; with Low Depression, .38; with Low Anxiety, .40; with Low Anger-Aggr, .23; with Relationships, .45; with Health, .25; with Income, .19; with Education, .09; and with college GPA, .07.
5. **Helping (interpersonal) skills.** This subscale correlated with Happiness, .48; with Low Depression, .27; with Low Anxiety, .28; with Low Anger-Aggr, .34; with Relationships, .41; with Health, .27; with Education, .14; and with college GPA, .14.
6. **Natural science.** This subscale correlated with Happiness, .32; with Low Depression, .23; with Low Anxiety, .22; with Low Anger-Aggr, .22; with Relationships, .20; with Health, .29; with Income, .16; with Education, .06; and with college GPA, .10.
7. **Creativity and art.** This subscale correlated with Happiness, .35; with Low Depression, .20; with Low Anxiety, .18; with Low Anger-Aggr, .22; with Relationships, .31; and with Health, .18.

It should be clear from these results that *self-confidence* and/or actual life skills in these life areas are important factors associated with happiness, low negative emotions, and some life success outcomes. Developing these life skills at higher levels can take many years of education and/or study. However, any progress you make may help. It may be especially important to make an honest self-assessment and begin working on areas that are either low or more central to your personal goals. Reading, taking courses, and learning through experience and role-models are all important ways of improving life skills.

Note: For all correlations, p < .0001 and Ns ranged from 2531 to 3196.

ADDITIONAL FACTORS THAT INCREASE SELF-CONFIDENCE

Following are some important factors that have been shown by research to increase self-confidence and performance.

Past success in similar situations. The more experience and success we have achieved in similar situations, the more confident we will tend to feel. If we have a poor track record or lack experience, then we will feel less confident.

Challenging standards or criteria for success. Our standards or expectations may be too high considering factors such as the *difficulty of the task, our level of experience, our relevant skills, our mental state, or the level of our competition*. Standards that are too high will undermine our confidence.

On the other hand, standards that are too low can make the task unchallenging and cause us to be overconfident. Sometimes we can set ourselves up for an unexpected failure by setting goals that are too low. Setting goals that are optimally challenging (considering all of these factors) is most motivating.

Following are some factors that can affect our standards.

• **Level of goal difficulty**. The easier the task, the more confidence you will feel that you can perform well; the harder it is, the less confidence you will have. If your expectations and goals are too high, it will cause you to feel less confidence and more self-doubt.

• **Reference group.** Who will be evaluating your performance? Who will you be comparing yourself to? The higher the standards of external judges, internalized judges, or your own standards, the less confidence you will feel.

Positive philosophy and positive self-talk. We have seen how the way we talk to ourselves gives us important messages that affect our confidence level. This self-talk comes from underlying belief systems--including our internalized parents or peers, our self-images, our world views, and our Higher Selves. As we confront, convert, or replace old negative beliefs with positive ones, our self-confidence will be improved as well. (See Higher Self Chapter 3.)

Visualizing success. Visualizing success not only implements the positive self-fulfilling prophesy motivation, but it also helps us develop road maps to success. Visualizing ourselves successfully performing some task and reaching a successful outcome can help us overcome mental barriers to success. It might be that we, literally, cannot imagine being successful. Perhaps it is because we have not actually tried getting a clear mental image of either (1) doing the task successfully or (2) being in the successful goal state.

• **Mental practice increases success.** A college student in one of my classes was an Olympic marksman. In the past he had been practicing daily; but now he no longer had time to practice daily, because the practice site was so far away. Instead, he learned to use mental imagery to practice. Six times a week, he imagined--in great detail--shooting at targets as if he were at the target range. Once a week he shot at the range. His shooting scores continued to rise *at the same rate* as when he had practiced seven days a week shooting real bullets at the real target range.

In a controlled experiment, students in Australia who had never shot a basketball used mental imagery to learn how to shoot baskets. During later tests, those only using imagery shot as accurately as students who practiced shooting real basketballs. In other controlled experiments, people learned to increase communication skills by mental role-playing.

• **Visualizing the goal state can help create it.** If you haven't pictured reaching an important goal or imagining what it would be like, develop a mental image of it. Start fantasizing about the goal state just for fun.

In the fifth grade, when we studied all the U.S. states in our geography lessons, I decided that I wanted to live in California. Later, as a teenager, I developed a fear that I might never leave Oklahoma City, because I (literally) hadn't imagined living any place else. So, I started imagining myself living in Southern California--the ocean, the palm trees, the weather, etc. I became fascinated with the Hollywood Bowl because I loved music and had seen it in several movies. I moved to Southern California as soon as I graduated from college.

• **Visualizing increases motivation.** Visualizing something clearly and often helps it seem more possible and increases our motivation to get it. It can also make achieving the goal more rewarding. Many of my dreams and fantasies have been fulfilled. Actually attending my first performance at the Bowl was a thrill. I have had season tickets for many years, and I still sometimes feel like I am living in a dream.

When I am actually participating in something that I have fantasized about, it seems to enhance my emotional experience of it. I get a wonderful feeling of great fulfillment and gratitude when I feel that I am living out a dream.

Others' Expectations and Input. What others say can also affect our confidence, especially if we are young, inexperienced in the area, or more externally controlled. It is also important to observe how we let other people affect us.

Do you feel more or less self-worth or self-confidence after talking with a certain person or being in a certain group? One simple way to learn to become more confident is *to spend more time with people who help you feel better about yourself and less time with those who don't.*

==> *Chapter 6 on internal control can also help with self-confidence.*

Being focused--lack of interfering or distracting factors. To the extent that other concerns compete with the task at hand for your attention, your motivation and confidence will be undermined. The "rise above" Chapter 8 will show you how to keep your focus "on the ball."

Self-esteem is like a mountain stream that begins with a small spring
and ends in a mighty river.
The small spring begins in our Higher Self with empathy
for our own and other's feelings.
Empathy forms a basis for unconditional self-love and
unconditional love of others.
Empathy and love are constant sources of positive thoughts and feelings.

Unconditional self-worth is not dependent upon who we are,
what we do, what we have, or what anyone thinks about us.
If we have self-worth, then self-confidence is a bonus.
Self-confidence is based upon our belief that we have the right motivation,
knowledge, and skills to reach our goals.
The best kind of self-confidence is knowing that
we have the *basic motivation and ability to learn* in any situation.

What began as empathy and unconditional self-love
forms the basis for self-confidence in all areas of life.
That self-caring and self-confidence provides the power of a mighty river
for overcoming life's logjams.

THE TRANSITION FROM EXTERNAL TO INTERNAL CONTROL OF YOUR LIFE

\\

DIFFERENCES BETWEEN EXTERNAL AND INTERNAL CONTROL

Abraham Maslow found autonomy and "independence of culture and environment" to be primary characteristics of self-actualizing people.

> **. . .self-actualizing people are not so dependent for their main satisfactions on the real world, or other people or culture or means to ends or, in general, on extrinsic satisfaction. . .**
> **They would maintain relative serenity in the midst of circumstances that would lead other people to suicide. . .**
> **The determinants of their motivation and the good life are for them now inner-individual and not social. . .The honors, the status, the rewards, the popularity, the prestige, and the love they can bestow have become less important than self-development and inner growth.**
> (Abraham Maslow, 1954, p. 162)

Research has consistently associated autonomy, internal locus of control, independence, and similar personality dimensions with mental health and many types of success. Too much external control is one of the most common problems I see among clients. It is a major underlying problem contributing to such diverse problems as chronic anxiety and depression, nonassertiveness, performance anxiety, addictive behavior patterns, phobias, intimacy and relationship problems, and dysfunctional family problems.

What is this pervasive problem that seems to interfere with the lives of so many people? Why do so many of us have it? The underlying issue about internal versus external control concerns *the relative importance of self-developed, internal guides versus externally-developed guides to decision-making.* When we are about to make a decision, are we being more influenced by our own well-thought out beliefs, values, standards, and goals? Or are we more influenced by what we think others expect or want us to do? Examine yourself with the following ten questions.

1. Do you use external OR internal expectations to evaluate yourself?
2. Do you do what others want to do most of the time?
3. Do you seek approval so much that it is a "must," OR is it a pleasant "bonus"?
4. Do you try to impress others, or are you comfortable about yourself?

5. Do you worry about being "popular" and pleasing everyone OR focus more on taking good care of yourself and those closest to you?
6. Do you frequently want to do the opposite of what others want you to do--no matter what they want?
7. Do you often let others make decisions for you?
8. Do you let others take care of you (emotionally, financially, socially, etc.)?
9. Do you worry about taking care of others' needs or feelings more than you take care of your own?
10. Do you constantly "should" all over yourself OR do what you "want" to do?

The external control answer for all of the above questions was the first alternative or a "yes" answer. If you answered the external control answer to *any* of these questions, then external control is almost certainly a significant cause of unhappiness in your life! A section below will be devoted to each question. If you scored a perfect "internal control," then perhaps you do not need to read this chapter.

PRACTICE: Think of a situation or person where you are under more external control. Think of some areas of your life where you feel more secure and confident and are more internally controlled. Think of at least one area of your life where you feel less secure and think that you are more externally controlled. Or think of a person (or type of person) with whom you tend to be more externally controlled (authorities, strangers, spouse, friends, etc.). Then focus on that person when I describe external control dynamics in the sections below.

USING EXTERNAL VERSUS INTERNAL EXPECTATIONS TO EVALUATE YOURSELF

We may not see ourselves as being externally controlled at all. For example, people who are rebellious usually see themselves as "free" and "independent." However, true rebels are externally controlled people. The word "rebel" implies that they are rebelling *against* something. True rebels do the *opposite* of what others want or expect. They are motivated by getting disapproval, surprise, or some other negative reaction from others. Consequently, they are externally controlled by the expectations of others.

Conformists do exactly what others expect.
Rebels do exactly the *opposite* of what others expect.
Internally controlled people make their decisions based upon
their *own* values and expectations--*independent* of what others expect.
Who is to be the *final judge* of what you do in a particular situation?

Who are you really trying to please? Whose standards are you using to evaluate your behavior? Who are your judges and how important are they? The more you judge yourself by your Higher Self and what is beneficial to yourself and others, the more you are internally controlled. The more you allow yourself to be judged by others--especially those who are not contributing to your wellbeing and the wellbeing of others--the more you are externally controlled.

External control is often related to lack of self-worth, self-esteem, and self-confidence. If you do not love yourself enough, do not respect yourself, and do not trust your own intelligence and judgment, then why would you trust yourself to judge or to decide?

I once read a card that said, "You don't have an inferiority complex, you're just inferior." Down deep many people with low self-esteem believe that about themselves. They may believe that they have some basic defect (such as an "emotional disorder" or "low IQ") that means they cannot trust their own opinions or judgments. Therefore, they always defer to others' reasoning and opinions.

Your own needs, expectations, and opinions are important. The U.S. Constitution does not require that people have an IQ of 120 or pass a battery of psychological tests to vote. It presumes that no matter what a citizen's IQ or emotional health status (except extreme cases), they should be allowed to vote; because *each person's needs are important and each person can best speak for his or herself.*

It doesn't matter whether or not you are the most important, intelligent, or emotionally mature person in the room, your needs and views are as important as anyone else's! Remind yourself of the U. S. Constitution when your old messages tell you that your point of view may not be important.

When it comes to judging yourself, *your expectations are the most important ones,* because you are the one who *is most affected* most by those expectations.

We will only learn to make good judgments and decisions by judging and deciding. We will never learn if we do not practice. To learn to make good judgments or decisions, it is necessary to practice making judgments and decisions. Remind yourself of that when you are tempted to defer to others. Listen to others, but make the final judgments and decisions yourself!

WHAT DO *THEY* WANT VERSUS WHAT DO *YOU* WANT

How do you balance your own wants and needs with the wants and needs of others? Do you tend to constantly focus on others' needs and wants at the expense of your own? When you disagree, do you always end up losing? Is the overall balance of control (who gets their way?) with each person in your life about 50-50%? Or is it disproportionate in some cases (such as 70-30%)? How often are decisions and disagreements settled by "I win--you win" outcomes--in which both people are happy? How often are the outcomes "I lose--you win" or "I win--you lose" types?

The United States constitution asserts that you each have the right to life, liberty, and the pursuit of happiness so long as it does not interfere with the rights of others to do the same. I like that principle. This assertion is basically permissive and says *we can do anything we want to pursue happiness so long as it does not hurt others.*

Jesus, in the New Testament, asserted that we should love others as we love ourselves. He seemed to assume that we love ourselves (and therefore will take good care of ourselves) and will ideally love others as much as we love ourselves and care for their needs almost as if they were your own. This is a great contrast to the belief of many churchgoers--"always put others first."

Your Higher Self automatically cares about you and other people. You cannot be maximally happy without making contributions to others' happiness in addition to your own--not "in place of" your own.

If you are in the habit of focusing on other people's needs and worrying about their feelings before your own, then you need to *reverse* this trend. Start focusing on your own goals first. Remember, you are most responsible for your needs and feelings, and they are most responsible for theirs.

APPROVAL AS A "MUST" VERSUS APPROVAL AS A "BONUS"

Are you constantly seeking others' approval? Are you worried about being popular? Does it seem important that everyone like you, agree with you, or approve of what you do? If you don't get approval and respect from nearly everyone, can you accept yourself? Are you afraid that if others don't approve, some "disaster" will occur--such as total rejection, a terrible conflict, or worse?

These are all signs of external control. They are based on assumptions that *you must have other people's approval to be an ok person or get your basic needs met.* People with more internal control are not so concerned about approval. They do not believe that they must have others' approval. Instead they are concerned primarily about their own internal standards and their approval of themselves. They may enjoy other people's attention, respect, liking, and approval; but they view these external signs of approval as *bonuses-- unnecessary* additions to their own self-approval. Following are some possible underlying causes of a high need for approval.

A powerful fear of *being alone* **(that makes approval a "must").** Do you fear being alone for extended periods of time? Do you fear living alone indefinitely or never having your own family? Those types of fears may underlie a high need for approval.

It is important to remember that many people are happy alone. I have met many people who overcame overwhelming fears of living alone. They thought they would never be happy alone or get over their fear of living alone. I have had many clients who have successfully made this transition. Many of them had previously stayed in bad, unhappy relationships due to this fear.

Overcoming a fear of being alone by learning "to take care of myself." These clients overcame their fears of being alone by gradually learning how *to take care of their own needs and feelings--without depending upon a partner.*

They learned to do everything for themselves--pay bills, cook, do the laundry, get the car fixed, entertain themselves, find new friends, get a job and support themselves, make a cozy home for themselves, and take care of their own sexual and emotional needs. They learned to overcome their fears of going places alone (and their fears of what others would think of their "being alone" or "a loser"). They learned to really enjoy taking themselves out to dinner or a movie--alone.

A key to overcoming this fear is to develop mentally stimulating activities *alone*--to overcome the boredom (and depression). People who learned to feel comfortable alone have usually learned how to entertain themselves without spending much money. Music, reading, TV, computer-related activities, do-it-yourself projects, and art are only a few examples.

People living alone often complain about feeling "lonely" and want emotional support from others. Some people who are happy alone have friends or family to whom they go to for emotional support. However, many people do not have any close friends or family available. What can they do for support? They can learn how to *give themselves support.* They can support themselves in many ways. Following are a few suggestions that have worked for others:

•Get in touch with your Higher Self and related beliefs. Reassure yourself that you and your happiness are important--unconditionally. Remind yourself that there are many routes to happiness in any situation. If you face failure or loss, these reminders can crucial.

•If you believe in a higher power or God, then use prayer or talk with that higher power to get comfort. Develop your relationship. Don't just talk, but also take time to listen.

•Imagine getting a big hug. Imagine giving yourself a big hug--or do it--when you need one. Or imagine getting a hug from someone you love or an image of someone you ideally want to meet in the future. One client imagined God putting His arms around her and giving her a big hug.

• Read comforting passages from books that get you in touch with your basic beliefs, such as the *Bible* or your favorite self-help book. Poetry and music lyrics can be especially helpful.
• Recall times when you have received positive attention, support, or affection from others who really cared about you. Really "get into" the memory so that you can feel the support and warmth. Positive visualizations can be very helpful.

PRACTICE: Use your own ideas to make a list of comforting activities now.

Once my clients became more self-sufficient, they no longer "had" to be in a relationship. One client said that in years past she had lost two men that she really loved; her "neediness" had driven them away. Then she spent three years learning how to take care of herself and her own happiness. She went back to school, got her career going, made friends, learned new hobbies, and learned how to entertain and support herself emotionally.

The irony is that since she has been happy alone and stopped "needing" anyone to make her a whole person, she has had many more opportunities to get involved with *desirable* men. She can now be in a beautiful, intimate, equal relationship with someone she really loves. She had to wait until now, because only now is she the person she wants to be (and the person a man desiring equality and independence wants to find). She no longer has to settle for men who want to dominate her or own her. Domination had been the price for finding someone to take care of her.

TRYING TO IMPRESS OTHERS VERSUS FEELING GOOD ABOUT WHO YOU ARE

Seeking a high degree of approval from others may mean that inside we do not feel secure enough about ourselves (in at least one life area). We may lack self-confidence and not trust our own competence--possibly because we are *too inexperienced* in that area.

Or, we may lack self-confidence because of deeper doubts about our overall competence or value as a person. Inside we may fear something is seriously wrong with our personality or intelligence. Or we may fear that we have a moral or character defect--that we are weak, bad, stupid, a loser, lazy, damaged, dirty, or have low self-esteem.

These fears may have originated from other people's comments (parents, peers, or authorities). These negative comments may have some element of truth, but our critics may exaggerate the negative aspect. In the process they may teach us their *negative cognitive bias styles* (overgeneralization, exaggerations, selective abstraction, or negative bias). Thus, we may learn to exaggerate our own deficiencies whenever we make any kind of mistake or anyone criticizes us. The result of this biased input from others and ourselves is a strong belief--"*deep inside something is terribly wrong with me.*"

Taking a public-opinion poll on our worth doesn't work. Every encounter with another person may represent a battle between the positive and negative parts of ourselves. Each part seeks victory. If we get approval, respect, love, attention, or whatever feedback we seek that validates our belief that we are ok, then it is a victory for the *positive* side. That inner part may generate all sorts of positive thoughts about how great we are.

If on the other hand, if we get disapproval, rejection, or criticism, then the *negative* part feels validated and takes temporary control. Focusing on this negative input generates feelings such as hurt, anger, anxiety, guilt, or depression. It generates negative thoughts such as "I'm a failure," "I'm stupid," "I'm no good," or "nobody would want me."

I have seen many clients whose mental and emotional life consists of playing out this war between their positive and negative parts for years. They will never get an answer to whether they are worthy or not by taking a public opinion poll--which is what they have been doing. If a person "votes" that they are ok, they feel good. If someone "votes" that they aren't-ok, they feel terrible.

Become more dependent upon *internal validation*. Part of the answer to overcoming this conflict is to develop a stronger Higher Self. Recall how the Higher Self gains power as we choose to unconditionally love ourselves and value our own and others' happiness. Our final judge is the Higher Self. As long as we believe that our happiness or opinion of ourselves is dependent upon something *only others* can give us, we are at their mercy.

If they are negative or controlling persons, they have us by the throat, because they can control us by giving or withholding approval. Therefore, to be internally controlled, we must consistently choose to value our own happiness and other mental or spiritual values above money, above other people's opinions, above being loved, above respect, and above any other value that is external or in the control of other people.

Seek healthy inputs and reprogram cognitive biases. Instead of exposing ourselves to negative inputs and negative people or media, we can expose ourselves to healthier, more positive inputs. Spend more time with happier, healthier people. Spend more time with media providing constructive, positive points of view.

To get control over inner subparts that say we are bad, we can choose *to listen and to do* what our healthier parts say. We can validate Higher Self empathy and love. Just keep choosing the alternative that will make you the happiest and contribute most to other people's happiness. Choosing it increases its power. Choosing the way of the negative part increases its power. Almost every choice you make empowers one or the other!

Choosing internal control often means getting far away from family or other people who have dysfunctional needs to "hold on to" and control their adult children or loved ones. It means being assertive about both *how often* you see them and the nature of your interactions when you are together. Structuring time together so that there is minimal opportunity for the negative interactions can help. Examples include small talk, TV, going to public places, and keeping busy.

I have seen many clients who literally had to escape the powerful family system forces in order to choose mental health over severe psychological dysfunction and unhappiness. For many people the choice is to be in this relationship and continue to be dysfunctional and miserable or to leave it to eventually find health and happiness.

Do you seek approval because you do not trust in your own perception, competence, or judgment? Perhaps you do not trust your own intelligence, judgment, or competence. Therefore, you may trust someone else's more. Sometimes, trusting another's judgment more than our own makes sense. If I were going to receive heart surgery, I would certainly trust my surgeon's knowledge about the heart more than my own. However, that trust does not mean that I would automatically take his advice about whether to have surgery or not. I would probably get at least one additional opinion, learn all I could about my heart, and make the *final decision* myself.

I see many people who do not even trust their own senses, memory, or perceptions as much as they trust someone else's statements. Statements like "you can't be upset over that," "how could you possibly feel . . .," or "you can't possibly feel . . ." to someone about how they are feeling may mean that the outside observer either *misunderstands* how the person feels or *wants to change* how the person is feeling. They may not like or want to accept that this is how the person really *is* feeling.

The person experiencing the feeling almost always knows what they are feeling better than the outside observer. Yet many people ignore, deny, or describe their own feelings in such a way as to *agree with the outside observer* instead of *trusting their own senses*. They might even *really become persuaded* that they couldn't possibly feel that way.

If any of these are problems for you, then it is important that you practice tuning into your own senses and perceptions. If you are unsure about what your perception is, then you can at least say something like, "I think that I am feeling resentment" and stick to it.

Do you seek approval because you are afraid people only tolerate you? Do you believe deep inside that people would not like you if they really knew all about you? Therefore, you try to present yourself in a way that *you think they would like--you present a facade.* How much do you distort the truth because you think they would not respect or like you if they knew the truth?

One of my solutions is that *if they do not like me the way that I am, then I would not want to get close to them.* Why would I want to get too close to anyone who can't accept me the way I am?

Perhaps you believe that *no one* could accept or like you the way you really are. In one of his roles Groucho Marx once said that he wouldn't want anyone as a friend who would want someone like him as a friend.

Who do you want to be closest to? Who is *most important* that you be accepted by? If you are concerned about your ability to make friends or be liked, then focus most on the people who you want to be friends with. So what if the others don't like you!

Do you feel that the people *most important to you would accept you?* If so, then remember this at times when you are starting to worry about seeking others' approval-- especially people who are not so important. If you do *not* think that the people who are most important to you would accept you the way you really are, then perhaps you need to begin a self-improvement program or change your reference group.

What if you are afraid to accept some awful truth about yourself? Another possible reason that you might seek approval so much is that *you do not accept some truth about yourself.* Maybe your fear of this awful truth causes you to be more externally controlled.

There are two general solutions to a problem--fix it or accept it. The philosopher Reinhold Niebuhr initiated the famous serenity prayer,

> **God, give me the power to change that which I can change,**
> **the power to accept that which I cannot change,**
> **and the wisdom to know the difference.**

If we love ourselves unconditionally, we can accept any truth about ourselves. The first step in 12-step programs for people addicted to alcohol or drugs is to privately and publicly accept the truth that they are alcoholic.

However, once you really allow yourself to explore some awful truth fear about yourself, you may find that it is not true after all. Other people (such as parents or peers) may have convinced you that something is basically wrong with you--even though it is really not true! If self-acceptance or facing some negative self-label is part of your problem, read the self-acceptance section in Chapter 5.

TRYING TO BE POPULAR VERSUS
TAKING GOOD CARE OF YOURSELF AND THOSE YOU LOVE

One of the sad things about trying to get everyone to like us is that we can end up hurting those we care most for. We may take our own needs and the needs of those we love most for granted, while we are spending our energy trying to please those for whom we care less (and who care less for us).

The more internally directed person has little need for being popular. Maslow's self-actualized people were often famous leaders, but the goal of being popular was unimportant to them. They were much more concerned about their own happiness and goals for making the world a better place. They usually only had a small number of close friends, and other people's opinions of them mattered relatively little.

Internally controlled people realize that their time and energy are limited. They tend to focus their time and energy more on their own and their loved ones' needs. Even when turning their attention to other people outside their inner circle, they focus on other people's *real needs and values*--not on being liked or popular.

An outstanding leader is one who wants to provide *real benefits* to those they are leading--not just get their short-term approval so that they can continue leading. Too many political and organizational leaders do not seem to understand this important principle of good leadership.

BEING TERRIFIED OF DISAPPROVAL VERSUS ACCEPTING DISAPPROVAL

To his friends and supporters a male leader might be viewed as strong and decisive. To his enemies, the same quality might be viewed as stubborn and domineering. His friends see him as progressive, farsighted, and a man of change. His enemies describe the same behaviors as too idealistic, foolish, reckless, and impulsive.

Everyone makes different impressions on different people. Even when the observers agree on the behaviors of the person, they will have *different interpretations--and some will disapprove. No matter what we do, some people will disapprove!* It is impossible to avoid disapproval. We may not always be aware of it, but we each have had lots of disapproval and will continue to have it the rest of our lives.

Therefore, if we want to be maximally happy, we must learn to accept disapproval as a natural event that is ok. Even great leaders have experienced extreme rejection and persecution. Sometimes the more advanced a person is, the greater his or her rejection. Galileo spoke of the earth being round--not flat like everyone believed. His radical idea led to condemnation by the Catholic Church and social ostracism.

Get better acquainted with disapproval so that you can learn to be comfortable with it. Start looking at disapproval as a good friend--at least by those who least understand you. Their disapproval might be *positive feedback that you are becoming more internally controlled and standing up for your beliefs.* If you are in a manipulative or codependent relationship, strong disapproval may mean that you are confronting core aspects of your partner's dysfunctional beliefs.

Being overly apologetic versus apologizing only if you internally validate your mistake. If you receive disapproval, do you apologize automatically? Do you apologize without even thinking about whether you might be right? Do you usually assume that you are to blame for something that goes wrong? Do you automatically focus inward when a problem arises--as if you *assume you caused it or have to fix it?* Does it seem strange to focus on what the other person has done? Do you tend to assume that they are smarter, know more, are more competent, or are better in some way than you are?

These are signs of giving others external control. Are you giving them the benefit of the doubt because of low self-confidence or because you want them to guide you? Or, maybe you would rather take the blame than have a conflict with the other person. Are you afraid of dealing with conflict? Are you afraid of being rejected or hurt by the person if you stand up to them? What can you do instead?

Use your inner observer to rise above the situation and be more objective. Pretend that a part of you is an outside observer who is not involved. Let it look *carefully* to see what *each* party has thought, felt, and done leading up to the problem. Avoid the concept of blame entirely and avoid blaming language. Focus on events 1, 2, and 3 that preceded the problem. And focus on constructive solutions to the problem. Additionally, try some of the following.

   • Notice when you automatically assume the other is right. Talk to yourself when you catch yourself starting to apologize. Stop looking only at yourself for the source of the problem.
   • Stop assuming that questioning them will lead to conflict or rejection. Instead, find a way to speak to them in an understanding, kind--but firm--way. Use diplomacy!
   • Learn what your underlying motives and assumptions are.
   • Seek appropriate alternative beliefs based on your Higher Self beliefs.

LETTING OTHERS MAKE DECISIONS FOR YOU VERSUS MAKING THEM YOURSELF

How often do you let others make decisions for you? How often do you seek help without making a determined effort to make your own decision? How often do you let others just assume what you want--even though it is not what you *most* want? How often do others make decisions with significant effects on you--yet you never tell them that you want something else?

Many of the same underlying causes for seeking approval also cause us to let others make decisions for us. We want approval, acceptance, conflict avoidance, or some reward from them. So, we don't speak up, we let them make the decisions and get their way most of the time.

Perhaps we give in because we are dealing with an exceptionally dominating and controlling person, or perhaps we give in because we feel more comfortable *not making the decisions ourselves.*

If you have a problem making decisions--either with other people or alone, then any of the following factors could be a cause. Following are suggestions for improvement.

   • **Lack of practice.** You have not had much practice making important decisions alone. **To improve**, start making decisions--right or wrong--to get practice. You'll never learn to do it, unless you start!
   • **Fear of decision-making incompetence.** You do not have much knowledge about the decision-area or about decision-making in general.
   To improve, learn how to make better decisions! Read, consult good decision-makers, think the problem through, get counseling, and *practice*. Learn a step-by-step decision-making process such as the one below:

STEP-BY-STEP DECISION-MAKING PROCESS

1-Gather INFORMATION–the best available!
2-Generate and explore ALTERNATIVES.
3-List your CRITERIA and weigh pluses and minuses on each alternative (for each criterion).
4-DECIDE–choose the alternative leading to the greatest happiness for self and others.
5-PLAN *how* to do it.
6-ACTION--Just do it.
7-FEEDBACK--gather feedback about results, and revise your plan as needed.

•**Fear of failure or consequences**. Do you fear making bad decisions or fear the consequences of bad decisions? Do you focus too much on possible negative consequences or feel *too responsible?* **To improve**, *practice, and make mistakes.* Doctors make life or death decisions every day; what if they refused out of fear? Explore the underlying negative outcomes you are so afraid of. Then find a new way of looking at the situation. For example if you fear being a failure, self-acceptance may be the problem (see self-esteem Chapter 5).

•**Fear of criticism**. Do you fear making decisions because of what *others* will think of you or what *you* will think of yourself? **To improve**, if you are primarily afraid of what *others* will think, explore your underlying worst fears. For example, are you afraid they will fire you or leave you? *Develop a plan* for coping with the worst possible outcomes.

•**Self-acceptance.** If you are more afraid of what *you* will think, you have a self-acceptance problem. Do you unconditionally love yourself? Are you making happiness your ultimate concern? Or are you making status on some social ranking scale (such as income, education, position, or class) your number one concern in life? Making social ranking, a high priority creates vulnerability to other people's views of you. **To Improve** go to the section on the self-acceptance process.

•**Fear of conflict.** Perhaps you have a history of unpleasant memories associated with conflict or perhaps you have little experience dealing with conflict. => In either case, you may fear shouting, name-calling, physical or psychological abuse, or rejection. **To Improve:** Learning assertive conflict resolution skills will allow you to diplomatically stand up for your point of view. This assertive style minimizes the potential of aggression or manipulation. If the other person uses an aggressive style, assertiveness skills will help you deal with that style more effectively (see appendix E).

•**Seeking sympathy or passive control**. Giving in or appearing weak, dependent, or incompetent can be rewarding. Perhaps other people feel sorry for you, feel guilty, feel protective, or feel responsible for you when you give in. Consequently, they ultimately give you what you want. **To improve**, try being honest with yourself and others. Remind yourself that when you act weak, you lower your self-esteem by giving yourself subtle messages that you really *are* weak. You also keep yourself in a *submissive role* with other people and *reinforce their domination.*

Often, nonassertiveness is caused by a lack of confidence in our own competence, a nonassertive belief system, or a lack of control by the Higher Self. Assertion training (or other types of interpersonal conflict-resolution skills training) can help you become more confident and effective dealing with interpersonal problems, decisions, and conflicts.

Not consulting others can result from a high need for approval or insecurity. Often someone who is too externally controlled will go to the other extreme--making decisions without ever consulting other people--even when it would be wise. I used to be afraid that if I went to others for help making a decision, that I would be too influenced by them or that I was being weak by not making my own decisions.

I learned that the wisest decision-makers *effectively seek other people's opinions.* They consult with people who will be affected by their decisions to see what reactions those people will have. Otherwise, their decisions may have unintended consequences and are not really democratic in style. They also consult with experts or people who have been successful at the task at hand.

One of the most important lessons I learned was that getting information and advice from others is *different* than letting them make the decision. Other people have valuable information. When making an important decision, I seek input from others. Yet, I am the one in charge of the decision-making process, and I am the *one who makes the final decision.* I look at all of the alternatives and compare them on all of the relevant criteria myself. I calculate to find which alternative I think will contribute most to my own and other people's happiness. Then, *I* make the decision.

LETTING NEEDY OTHERS DOMINATE YOU--
BELIEVING YOU ARE RESPONSIBLE FOR OTHERS' NEEDS AND FEELINGS

Many people who think of themselves as independent are actually being dominated without knowing it. They are being dominated by people they think are too needy to take care of themselves. Others may try to tell them that they are sacrificing too much for the needy people, but they will not listen.

They have some underlying belief or need that is too strong to allow them to let go of being responsible for these needy others. They may be convinced that they have a powerful duty to take care of them. They may base this duty on religious beliefs, on being a close relative, or on being the only person that can be depended upon. Or, they may get some hidden reinforcement for taking care of the other person--such as companionship or approval. Occasionally, they may foster dependence so that the needy person will become so dependent on them that he or she will *never leave them.* Are you being dominated by a dependent person--in at least one relationship?

The Codependence Trap--"I take care of your feelings and you take care of mine." Melodie Beattie, in her book *Codependent No More,* describes the dynamics of codependent relationships and their relationship to addictive behaviors. In most cases there is a "responsible" party who takes care of family needs such as work, finances, and relationships, and there is an "irresponsible" party, who has a serious addiction or other problem. These addictions can be to alcohol, drugs, food, sex, or even work.

One of the hallmarks of codependent relationships is a shared belief system that people *should take care of each other's needs and feelings.* However, if we are responsible for *each other's* needs and feelings, then the implication is that we are *not responsible for our own needs and feelings.* This is the codependent script, "I take care of your feelings and you take care of mine (because we cannot--or should not--take care of our own)."

No wonder that both parties in a codependent relationship tend to be irresponsible for some of their own needs and feelings. It is usually obvious that the irresponsible party is not responsible in areas such as substance abuse, work, finances, honesty, or abusive behavior. What may not be so obvious is that the responsible parties may *not be responsible* for taking care of their own happiness. They make their happiness dependent upon reforming the irresponsible party.

For example, consider a woman I met whose son had had a serious drug problem. He also could not keep a job and was failing in college. She was more *worried about his drugs, school, and finances than he was.* This is another symptom of codependence. *She* was the one who was taking responsibility for *his* drugs, school, and money--not him. Since she was taking responsibility for his drinking--why should he?

She repeatedly threatened to make him move out unless he stopped using drugs and started making progress in college or got a job. However, she never fulfilled her threats. She loved him and was *terrified that he might end up in prison, dead of a drug overdose, or homeless* if she did not keep supplying him with money, food, and a home. He knew that *he* didn't have to worry about these terrible consequences, because his *mom* was so worried about them.

She believed that it was her responsibility to make sure none of these consequences happened. She did not understand that most addicts have to hit bottom before they really begin to take responsibility for their behavior and begin the road to recovery.

She worried about keeping his stress low so that he would not get too upset and take drugs. By taking this responsibility for his feelings, she protected him from the natural consequences of his behavior. In that way, she actually encouraged him to keep taking drugs and to keep failing in his career.

Eventually, she was given an outstanding job offer, which meant moving to the Netherlands. It was also an opportunity to escape this mess. Her son was 20 years old and she decided to give up and let him be responsible for himself. She informed him of her decision, left him with some money, and moved to Holland.

She did not hear from him for three years. She came back to visit and found him. He was off drugs, was supporting himself, and was succeeding in college. He told her that the best thing she ever did for him was to go to the Netherlands. He said that at first he was in a state of shock. He realized that she was no longer there to take care of him. He knew that he had to start taking care of himself or he would be on the streets--or dead. He joined Alcoholics Anonymous and Narcotics Anonymous and began his recovery.

An interesting addition to this story is that through the entire relationship, the mother had also been *depending upon her son to take care of her social needs*. She was shy and hadn't had much social life since her divorce. She had become socially dependent upon her son's companionship. She hated to admit it, but she was allowing him to be responsible for her social needs in ways that were similar to how she was being responsible for his drugs and career.

She covered up her loneliness and rather dull existence by a work addiction that helped her avoid feelings of loneliness and depression in her personal life. Once she went to Europe and lived alone, she couldn't depend on her son for companionship. She took responsibility for her own social and personal life.

To summarize, both mother and son were living by the *same life script* that included taking responsibility for the other--while avoiding responsibility for themselves. Each used addictive behaviors to cover up the resultant bad feelings. The solution was for *each* to take primary responsibility for their own needs and feelings.

Do you give others the CONTROL BOX to your EMOTIONS?
YES, if you assume you are responsible for their feelings--
or if you assume they are responsible for yours.

How do you know if you are in a codependent relationship? Be alert for manipulation or domination by the needy whenever you habitually sacrifice your own happiness for another person's. Ask yourself whether you or the other person is doing any of the following.

- Being dishonest, giving double messages, or hiding the truth?
- Protecting some addiction, weakness, or other bad habit?
- Protecting the other person from facing natural consequences of their bad habits? Are you (or the other) in effect *contributing* to the maintenance of their bad habits?
- Not finding some other way to meet their needs because the bad habit (or your help) is easier? Consider this question carefully, since they may have fooled you into believing they are *incapable of caring for their own basic needs.*
- *Are you more worried about them than they are worried about themselves?* This is the ultimate test of *who* is taking the most responsibility for their welfare. If it is you, then it is time for a change!

A "Yes" answer to any of the questions above is a sign of manipulation or codependence--whether either party intends codependency or not.

Good parenting teaches children to be independent--not codependent. A client came in very upset about her relationship with her mother. Her mother was alone and lonely. My client believed that "Mom is miserable if I don't visit her." Her mom wanted her to visit her many hours each week. Yet my client was working half-time, was a full-time student, and was in a relationship. She felt extremely guilty about not spending more time with her mom and felt she owed it to her because mom had done so much for her. Out of guilt, she spent much more time than she could afford with her mother.

Yet, still, her mom would say, "Do you care about what happens to me?" "I'm so lonely when you're not here." "I'm too old to try to make new friends." "I want to be with my family, and you're the only family I have."

How would you feel, if your mother said that to you? My client felt guilty and responsible for her mother's happiness. Yet, her mother's requests for attention seemed like a bottomless pit. She could never satisfy mom. What could she do to quit feeling so guilty?

The problem was in the beliefs--or *script*--shared by mother and daughter. The codependent script was, "Parents raise their children, then the children are obligated to take care of their parents--at least socially." On the other hand, an independence script says, "Good parents facilitate their children's development into healthy adulthood. They facilitate their children's journey toward self-actualization and toward a happy, independent life. The children owe their parents little but to pass this freedom to the next generation."

Dysfunctional parents train their children to be dependent and enmeshed in family matters indefinitely. Family life becomes a quagmire of quicksand from which children can never escape and lead independent lives. These parents train their children to take care of the parents' needs--not their children's own needs. Ironically, these parents often call their children selfish when their children want to become independent. Yet, it is the parents who constantly *use* their children to take care of their own needs--at the expense of the children--who are being selfish.

More functional parents give the gift of independence and happiness to their children. My client's mother believed that *children have an obligation to take care of their parents* and passed that codependence script to my client. Belief in that obligation was the underlying cause of my client's guilt feelings. It was her own belief--not her mother's-- that was now *her* problem.

According to my client's new independence script, her mom was unhappy and it was primarily her mom's responsibility to take care of her own happiness. In fact, mom had many options for developing new interests and friends so that she wouldn't be so bored and lonely. That was her responsibility--not her daughters. Yet, she chose not to do any of those things, because it was *more comfortable* to call her daughter. Why should her daughter suffer for her mother's choices by constantly feeling guilty and being at her beck and call?

Once she strengthened her new beliefs and discussed her beliefs with her mother, she felt less guilty. She quit responding to her mother's needy, controlling comments. She spent time with her mother when she *really wanted to.* Her mother also began to understand my client's point of view better and became less demanding. She began to feel *closer and more loving* toward her mother, because she was less plagued by guilt and manipulation.

Do not take primary responsibility for anyone but yourself. Saying, "Everyone is primarily responsible for their own self and own feelings" does not mean that we are not responsible for caring about others or for helping them. It means giving them *primary* responsibility for their own happiness and *not sacrificing too much* of our own happiness to protect them from the consequences of their choices.

PRACTICE: Examine possible codependent relationships.

1-Identify any relationships you have that might be codependent. If you feel guilt or responsibility for another, protect them, or take care of them, compare the dynamics to those you have just read about.

2-Underlying Beliefs and Scripts. What is the underlying script and your underlying beliefs related to your duty or responsibility? What dependencies, weaknesses, or inadequacies do they have which seem to keep you hooked? What would happen if you gave them responsibility and let them take the consequences? Think it through, consult with an expert, read *Codependent No More*, devise a plan, and try it!

3-Make two lists--"What I can think and do to give them more freedom to be responsible for selves and take consequences for own choices" and "What I can do to take more responsibility for my own happiness (especially where I have been dependent on them)."

LETTING OTHERS TAKE CARE OF YOU VERSUS TAKING CARE OF YOURSELF

We have just examined cases where the focus was on our taking care of others. Now I will reverse the focus. What are ways that you are not taking care of yourself and are depending upon others to do it for you? In both cases, the underlying script supports **external control**--one person takes primary responsibility for another.

Take charge of life areas where you are too dependent upon others. We may feel *low self-confidence* or feel helpless to provide for ourselves in certain life areas. We may depend almost totally on one or more people to take over that area of our lives.

In return, we may covertly agree to give them control over that area; we let them do all of the thinking, decision-making, and planning. One problem is that if they take control, we may never get involved, motivated, or competent in that area. Continued low knowledge of an area can increase our dependence and external control and keep us under their thumb indefinitely.

People can become too dependent upon another to meet any kind of need. Check each of the following to see if you have become too dependent in any area.

•love	•attention	•play	•comfort	•emotional support
•sex	•money	•household chores		•planning social events
•career guidance	•paying bills			•car repair or fixing things
•place to live	•social contacts			•transportation

Taking care of yourself in each area means questioning your expectation that others should provide you with what you need. In the future, you will expect *primarily yourself* to take care of that need area. Taking care of at least your minimal needs yourself will increase your self-confidence and independence. You will quit being so needy, dependent, and demanding in that need area. You will have no need to get hooked into unhappy relationships just because that person takes responsibility for some area (where you feel helpless and dependent). One client said, "I can't believe how long I stayed in that miserable marriage just because I was afraid to support myself and to get the car fixed. If I'd known how happy I'd be, I'd left years ago."

Spreading your dependencies. One additional way to prevent being *too dependent on any one particular person* is to make sure that we have a *network of people*. This network can assist us as we provide for ourselves. George Kelly called this strategy "spreading our dependencies." If we are dependent upon a variety of people, then we are unlikely to let any *one person* get too much control.

If dependence is a problem, break the pattern of dependence to get more internal control. Spending more time away from the family, getting involved in activities outside the family, making new friends, and advancing your education and career can help.

Becoming more independent of those who overly influence your thinking and important beliefs is especially important to gain more internal control. Expose yourself to points of view and ideas that are different. Identify beliefs that you suspect are dysfunctional and foster dependence. Find healthier ways of thinking from good role models, counseling, groups, and self-help books.

> **PRACTICE: Check your dependencies in each life area.** 1-*Self-test:* How dependent are you on other people for meeting your needs? How much do you expect other people to make you feel good? Check each life area and each important relationship--especially with family members.
> 2-*Alternatives:* Think of new ways that you can start taking responsibility for yourself in those areas. What would be the costs to you (such as rejection, financial, extra effort, social risks, or career)? What would be the gains for increased independence (such as self-esteem, growth, freedom, new opportunities)?
> 3-*Plan:* List (and display) new self-commitments to increase independence.

"I SHOULD" VERSUS "I WANT"

Do you keep "musterbating" or "shoulding" all over yourself? Normally, we use the words "should" and "must" to mean that some part of us is committed to following some rule or set of rules. If we follow the rule, we feel good and if we break it, we feel guilty. Rules in themselves are neither good nor bad. We all have rules we live by. However, problems occur when two rules conflict and we obey a less important rule over a more important one.

Two sisters--Suzy and Eileen--illustrate this dynamic well. Their father was a minister who lived by an extensive set of narrow rules (like the apostle Paul when he was a Pharisee) instead of living by empathy and love. The mother shared these rules and was as rule-bound as her husband. The parents taught both daughters this intricate set of rules about how to be a good Christian.

In fact, neither daughter really strongly *believed* in the rules, or strongly felt that they were beneficial for their own happiness. As adults, both sisters thought many of the rules made no sense. However, their parents' love, acceptance, financial help, and praise depended upon how well they obeyed these rules.

Eileen chose to conform to her parents' expectations and to her internal parent that represented those rules. As a result, her parents were moderately happy with her. Her parents gave her lots of financial assistance and were usually pleasant to her. However, she still felt guilty, because she still fell short of meeting their expectations perfectly, and sometimes the rubbed it in.

While Eileen was glad to receive parental benefits, inside she felt a great conflict and was often depressed. She felt that she could never live the life that she wanted. She felt trapped and helpless. She felt extremely dependent upon her parents and her self-esteem was low.

On the other hand, Suzy chose to rebel from the parental rules. As a teenager, she went wild--drinking, partying, and breaking her parents' rules. As a result, her parents practically disowned her. They openly ridiculed her, cut off financial help, and told her she was "evil" and "going to hell." Inside, part of Suzy felt happy that she could go her own way in life. She didn't feel trapped like her sister, and developed a lot of self-reliance from supporting herself and surviving on her own. However, another part felt tremendous guilt, because it still believed her parents' rules. Also, Suzy still wanted to receive her parents' acceptance, praise, and respect. She was torn by inner conflict.

Both sisters shoulded all over themselves constantly. Eileen obeyed the shoulds and felt little guilt. However, she denied other parts of herself begging for expression. Her playful, sexual, creative, and even professional interests were blocked, because they collided with parental rules. Repressing these playful parts of herself caused her depression and feelings of helplessness. On the other hand, Suzy didn't follow the rules, and felt guilty as a result--constantly being haunted by messages from her internalized parents, "I'm a bad person, and I'm going to go to hell."

What is the solution for these two sisters? Neither following the rules nor breaking them worked. They are "damned if they do and damned if they don't." First, they can commit themselves to some new higher rules--the *ultimate concerns of happiness and love*. Second, *reexamine the old rules* from the perspective of the new ultimate concern. Each time an old rule or should pops into mind, they could ask themselves, "What will maximize happiness for self and others--following this rule or some new action?" Ask yourself, **"What do I really want to do?"** given my new philosophy.

Your Higher Self produces "wants" not "shoulds." When we feel shoulds, the rule-source parts are demanding we follow the rules. On the other hand, if the *executive self* becomes convinced that the *should* is important to our happiness, then we suddenly feel like we *want* to do it. The inner conflict disappears. Our shoulds usually come from *internalized parents* or other belief systems that we have not integrated into our Higher Self.

To the degree that these internalized belief systems are *not integrated* with higher parts of ourselves, we may experience painful conflicts between shoulds and wants. These conflicts can become so awful that we rarely enjoy anything. Like Suzy, if we choose a want activity, our guilt undermines our fun; or like Eileen, if we choose a should, resentment or depression take over.

Converting a "should" into a "want." Learning how to convert a should into something meaningful, interesting, or fun is a skill that can help reduce conflicts between shoulds and wants. An important part of converting a should into a want is focusing on the subpart that *really wants to do it*. Just ask yourself, "Does some part of me really want this?" If so, get in touch with its beliefs, goals, and desires. Let it talk to your executive self and try to *persuade* it--not coerce it with shoulds. The best arguments are (1) that it will eventually be satisfied and (2) that it can contribute to your overall happiness and the happiness of others.

> **As soon as you see a direct connection between an action and becoming happier, you automatically *want* to do it.**

One way to convert a should into a want is to make it more interesting and fun. If it is boring, make it more challenging. Make a game of it or set higher goals. Get more personally involved. If it is too difficult or stressful, try simplifying it. The harmonious functioning chapters explain many ways to get into the zone and to turn unpleasant situations into interesting ones. Again, we can find many routes to happiness even in the most boring or stressful situations.

SOURCES OF DEPENDENCY AND EXTERNAL CONTROL

Why do some people become independent and internally controlled while others become overly dependent and externally controlled? A newborn baby is *dependent* upon its parents for almost everything--food, shelter, love, and all types of care. Its parents have a great deal of *control over the newborn's world*. It doesn't take long for the child to realize how important its parents are. The child's *belief* in external control is rooted in its *actual dependence* upon others to meet its basic needs and values.

Even as adults we are dependent upon many others to satisfy our values. We are partly dependent upon hundreds of people just to supply our groceries. Yet, if adults are left alone, most have adequate resources to get food. On the other hand, if infants were left alone, they would starve. Beliefs in dependence are often *reality based*.

However, beliefs in dependence may be exaggerated. For example, many teenagers (or even adults) *believe* they are still dependent upon their parents for food and money.

External control *beliefs* undermine self-confidence and independence. There is an important difference between teenagers and infants. Teenagers could obtain food if they were suddenly forced to be independent. Teenagers can get jobs or even get food from trash cans if necessary. Quite a few of my clients left home as teenagers, successfully supported themselves, and consequently become wise beyond their years. Therefore, in fact, teenagers *choose to depend* upon their parents.

In most cases, getting food is not really what dependent teenagers or dependent adults are worried about. They are worried about their *standard of living*. They want to live as they are accustomed--that is natural. However, it makes the choice for independence difficult. Consequently, many *choose* to remain dependent, because they would rather have a high standard of living than independence. They don't realize they can learn to be happy with less money. They don't appreciate the value of independence and self-sufficiency--yet. One client said, "I'm much happier being *free*--even working so hard. The stuff my parents bought for me wasn't worth being under their thumb."

If people do not realize that they have the *power to take care of themselves*, but are *choosing* to remain dependent upon others, then they will feel weak and dependent. Parents often reinforce dependency by being overprotective, by being too critical, or by undermining their children's self-confidence. Stressing obedience, authority, and conformity also reinforce external control and dependence.

Believing we can take care of ourselves creates independence. Parents who stress internal control and independence give their children more responsibility. They let their children take the positive and negative consequences of their actions with less interference.

Their children learn how to control their own lives *without going to their parents*. They know that they are not dependent upon their parents; they can take care of themselves.

Getting more responsibility also helps children learn important *life skills*. Hence, they become more competent making decisions, planning, managing time, working, managing money, and relating to others. These life skills not only boost their confidence, but give them more *internal resources* that will help them stay independent.

If you want to increase your internal control, then it is also important to take more responsibility for your own life and emotions. It means you have to do for yourself what you have been hoping others would do for you.

> **If your parents have taught you to be externally controlled and dependent,**
> **be your own good parent--**
> **give yourself independence, responsibility, the opportunities**
> **to learn new skills, and the encouragement to keep trying!**

THREE-WAY CONFLICTS: EXTERNAL PEOPLE, INTERNALIZED PEOPLE, AND ME

One of my clients in her late 40's was having intense conflicts and felt guilty because she knew her mother would disapprove of her lifestyle. The interesting fact is that her mother had been dead for more than10 years.

It was not her real mother that kept haunting her, but her internalized mother. An image of her mother waiving her finger and yelling at her often popped into her head. She said, "Mom may be dead, but she's alive and well in my head."

> We often confuse our *thoughts* about what people will think or do
> with what they *actually* think or do.
> Our thoughts about what others will think or do
> have a much greater effect on our emotions
> than what others actually think or do.
> Therefore, solving problems or conflicts with others
> is often more an internal problem than an external problem.

SOCIETY AND THE MEDIA

If you drive the right car, wear the right jeans and tennis shoes, use the right perfume, keep yourself slim, and maintain the right image, then you have "it." "It" means that everyone will like you, members from the opposite sex will fight over you, and you will probably become rich and famous. This in turn must be the ultimate route to happiness. That message is pounded into us every time we read the morning paper, look at a billboard, turn on the TV, or pick up a magazine.

How many of your peers' beliefs--and yours--have been conditioned by advertising executives trying to sell their products? How often do you notice the dysfunctional contents of their messages and challenge them? Mentally challenging these messages establishes internal control over your tastes and beliefs.

Social rules such as laws and etiquette. We are taught to obey rules about what to eat and what to eat with, about when to get up and when to go to bed, about how to look at a member of the opposite sex and how not to, about how to drive and what is "in" to drive. These rules include the law and rules of etiquette. They come from the government, our families, and our peer groups. We may conform to these social norms or not. If we do not, these groups may punish us. Their punishment can range from mild rebukes and sarcasm to physical harm, imprisonment, and ostracism.

We have seen how people can become rule-bound--by making these rules *ends* in themselves and interpreting them rigidly. The alternative is to view social rules as having value only to the degree that they *contribute to people's happiness.*

Emily Post, the original guru of American etiquette, once said that the ultimate rule of etiquette was whatever best met human needs; any other rule should be broken if it conflicted with that higher rule. Whenever we use our ultimate concern of overall happiness as our guiding principle, then we are being internally controlled–not rule-bound.

REFERENCE GROUPS

Reference group is a useful concept for understanding external sources of control (Sherif & Sherif, 1964). Our reference groups are *any groups that we identify with* or see as important for meeting our values and needs. The group can be as small as two people or it can be as large as all humanity. It can be an **informal group** such as our family or friends or it can be a **formal group** such as a club or place of employment.

We become dependent upon our reference groups to meet important values--social values for acceptance, companionship, and social activities; career and financial values; and even personal values for guidance and feedback relevant to our self-image. Social psychologists have found that our reference groups can have powerful influences upon our beliefs, values, life themes, and self-esteem.

While our reference groups provide many benefits, they also have rules and place demands on us to conform to their values and rules. At times their demands may conflict with the demands of other reference groups. These conflicting demands (between work and family, family and peers, or children and work) can create a great deal of inner conflict. The groups can also conflict with our own personal values such as our values for privacy, play, and even health.

The externally controlled person will be more affected by these demands from their reference groups. They will feel more inner conflict as the varying groups conflict with each other. The internally controlled person will almost *always* take the demands of a reference group less seriously than the externally controlled person. They know that their *internal standards and values* come first--even if that value is to contribute to other people's happiness. Internally controlled people know that *they are the ones who will make the final decisions*. They are not just responding to outside pressures.

COMMON REFERENCE GROUPS

- Family
- Peer group(s)
- Work group
- Church or social organization
- Team or recreational group
- Interest group
- Cultural or ethnic group
- Ideological group or imagined group (e.g. writers, engineers, democrats, spiritualists, etc.)

REFERENCE GROUPS:
(1) have beliefs, rules, and sanctions;
(2) are powerful influences and **sources of identity**;
(3) become **internalized mental models** (e.g. mental model of family);
(4) cause **inner conflict & anxiety** when they conflict with each other or with other important values.

PRACTICE: Identify your reference groups and other sources of external influence. (1) Who are the most important groups in your life? Who are the most important individuals? (2) For each, consider how much they influence you and how positive that influence is. How much do they affect your overall happiness and growth? Do they support or inhibit your becoming more the person you want to be? (3) Make conscious choices to reduce the influence of negative individuals and reference groups and seek out new reference groups that can help you be who you want. List at new reference groups you would like to get more information about.

BELIEFS SWALLOWED WHOLE
(WITHOUT CRITICAL EXAMINATION AND MODIFICATION)

Parents tell their child that this barking, four-legged creature is a "DOG," and the child assumes that this creature is a "dog." This is the truth with a capital "T"--no question about it. The same parents tell their child that people from a particular ethnic group are lazy, and the child believes that statement with the same conviction.

During childhood, we developed elaborate belief systems that we largely swallowed whole. These belief systems may come from our parents, church, or other major influences. Any such belief system can become a powerful subpart of ourselves.

We need to be careful about giving away our own power to these internalized belief systems. I once saw a bumper sticker that said "QUESTION AUTHORITY." Questioning is *not* the same as disagreeing (or agreeing). Questioning means we are trying to understand what is meant and examine the message from a variety of relevant views.

The California State University system--the largest in the world--has decided that critical thinking is such an important mental skill that they require that all students must complete a course in critical thinking as a basic requirement for a bachelor's degree. If we do not learn to critically examine information we receive from the media, authorities, friends, and everyone else, then we will often be duped into believing things that make no sense--or inhibit our happiness.

What do we do when we discover a subpart containing dysfunctional beliefs? We can use the self-exploration method to expose those dysfunctional beliefs. Then we can use our more trusted parts to question those old beliefs--replacing them with more constructive and more accurate beliefs.

EVEN COMPLIMENTS AND SUPPORT CAN FOSTER DEPENDENCE

We have explored several examples where people have used criticism, name-calling, and pressure to foster dependence. Often the recipient of the negative messages is kept off-balance by doubting their own competence or self-esteem. Being uncertain and anxious keeps them feeling weak, and makes them more vulnerable to manipulation. [Suggested responses to negative manipulation are summarized in later in this chapter.]

Has it ever occurred to you that even compliments and supportive statements can sometimes be a source of external control? For example, self-beliefs such as being a nice guy, responsible, caring, committed, or a Christian can be used by other people (or our internalized parent) to get us to do what they want. I once read an introduction to a humorous book that was supposed to have been written by the author's mother. It went something like this,

My son wrote this book and asked me to read it. I am sure that if my son wrote it, it must be a wonderful book. I don't know. I haven't had time to read it because I have been so busy lately without anyone to help me. My son is such a wonderful caring person and loving son. I am sure that since he has finally finished this book he will again have some time for his sick mother who misses him very much and needs whatever help he has time to give around the house. I hope that you will all buy my son's book.

This is a humorous example of manipulation. The mother compliments her son so that he will enjoy the compliments and *increase his dependence* upon them. The subtle threat by the mother is, "if you don't do what I say and spend enough time with me, then I will withdraw the compliments." So the mother uses the compliment as a reward and its *withdrawal* as a punishment. This example of motherly control is a blatant example of what happens to many people. If this ever happens to you try some of the following suggestions:

Dealing with Manipulation by Positive and Negative Labels

**IF SOMEONE TRIES TO MANIPULATE YOU
WITH COMPLIMENTS, FLATTERY, OR INFERS
THAT EARLIER COMPLIMENTS MAY BE WITHDRAWN**

• **Focus on your emotional reaction.** First, notice your ego boost, guilt or other emotions.
• **Self-explore to find the self-image issue.** Self-explore what you are feeling so good or guilty about--such as being a caring person or being selfish. How does this support or conflict with your ideal self-image? Is it more important how others view you or how you view yourself? If so, evaluate yourself using your own standards. Also, seek opinions from those whom you respect more.
• **Work on accepting (potential) negative comments.** Go to the section on self-acceptance in the self-worth chapter.
• **What does the other person really want from you?** *Explore what the other person really wants from you.* Ask yourself, "Is this person complimenting or criticizing me honestly, or doing it *just to persuade me to do what he or she wants?*" The latter is manipulation.
• **Break their game with honesty.** Going along with what they say without acknowledging the manipulative aspect of the compliment is not going to cause them to think more highly of you--on the contrary--they will only think that you are gullible or nonassertive.
    What if a friend gives you a manipulative compliment such as, "You're such a great guy, would you mind doing XX for me?" Try responding with, "Ok, since *I am such a great guy,* I will do XX for you." In that way you are agreeing to do whatever they want--which you would do anyway. However, you are also subtly and humorously telling the person that you know that his or her compliment is for the purpose of getting you to do what he or she wants.
    If you don't want to do what they are asking, you can point out the nature of the manipulation by saying, "Well, I guess you won't think I'm such a great guy after this, but I'd rather *not* do XX for you because . . ."

SOURCES OF INTERNAL CONTROL

Where do we turn to increase our internal control? Using internally controlled people as sources of insight and support can be enlightening. However, the primarily way to get more internal control is by looking inward. Become more aware of internal parts of yourself that will lead you toward happiness and develop them. What are some of these important parts that can help you get more internal control?

YOUR BASIC PSYCHOBIOLOGICAL NEEDS

Our own needs, values, pleasures, and pains are powerful sources of internal control. No matter how passive we may be, if we get hungry enough, sleepy enough, or sick enough we become persistent to get that need met. These internal stimuli give strong internal messages that are hard to ignore.

If we love ourselves, we will listen carefully to these internal signals and give them priority. We will be less vulnerable to external control. Have you ever had to go to the bathroom when someone was talking on and on? Why wait until you are about to have an accident before excusing yourself? Listen to your inner signals while they are still *weak*--don't wait for a crisis to be assertive. Recall that example whenever you are tempted to ignore *any* important internal message.

YOUR HIGHER SELF

To focus inward constantly would cause self-centeredness and unawareness of other people's feelings. If you have been too externally controlled, you may have a big fear of being too selfish or too self-centered. You may worry how you can balance attending to your own desires with attending to the desires of others.

Balancing external and internal needs with a strong Higher Self

One way to resolve the conflict between being too internally focused and too externally focused is to take turns between listening internally and listening externally. By having a strong set of *internal rules* for deciding when to listen internally and when to listen externally, we are actually establishing *strong internal control*.

The Higher Self can act like a filter. More externally controlled people tend to lock on to others' words--which take almost hypnotic control of their thoughts, feelings, and actions. They infrequently question what others said or judge it by their own beliefs.

An empowered Higher Self can control the external versus internal focus, because it is the seat of our strongest love and empathy. The more developed the Higher Self becomes, the more it will exert good judgment about when to focus inward and when to focus outward. Some of the issues you need to consider follow.

- The Higher Self's *ultimate concern* is truth and happiness. Both your own and others' happiness is important, but you can only directly control your own.
- Recognize that you can make yourself happy and do not need other's approval, control, or support. Others' approval and support is a bonus.
- Balance between immediate and long-term happiness
- Balance between different values and subparts of yourself and between different life areas.
- Let the Higher Self act as a mediator to resolve deeper internal conflicts.
- Learn to use gentle persuasion instead of coercion, force, and negative self-talk for self-motivation. Focus on creating "I wants" instead of "I shoulds."

Knowledge and self-confidence increase internal control. One type of dependence on others is *information dependence*. Even the most internally controlled people can't function well without adequate knowledge. More internally controlled people know that *knowledge* helps establish internal control. Externally controlled people may be more concerned about what other people think than becoming competent. Instead, learn all you can, so that you can become more independent and self-sufficient.

YOUR OTHER SUBPARTS (ROLES, INTERESTS, KNOWLEDGE AREAS, ETC.)

We have developed many subparts that represent different activities, roles, and sets of beliefs. The parts of me that love to play tennis, listen to music, watch mysteries, go for nature walks, read, theorize, or converse all love what they do. Each has a strong voice that my Higher Self listens to.

As an inner part grows, its voice gets louder. When I first began to play tennis, my *inner tennis player* was an unskilled and underdeveloped part of myself. It spoke softly and carried a little stick. I didn't care much whether I played or not. However, like all interests, it grew *as I attained more knowledge and positive experiences* until it became a powerful part of me. Now I feel starved if I go an entire week without tennis.

My inner psychologist grew in a similar way. It is no accident that people who have few well-developed interests are more susceptible to external control. Highly-developed interests provide inner power and direction. Someone without interests is left rudderless to be taken by the strongest current.

> **PRACTICE: List your strongest sources of internal control.** What parts of yourself (including Higher Self, values, interests, roles, themes, or other parts) help provide you with strong values, goals, and plans to give you positive inner direction? Be as clear and specific as possible. Which are you the most likely to be assertive about in the face of conflict with others? Which do you want the most to strengthen?

ELIMINATING INTERNAL BARRIERS TO INTERNAL CONTROL

I have addressed many individual factors such as low self-worth and low decision-making experience that trap people in external control. Suggestions were given for increasing internal control for each of these factors.

In the remaining part of the chapter I will suggest additional methods for overcoming external control. The first set of methods focuses on overcoming *internal barriers* to internal control such as belief systems, fears, and thought habits. The second set focuses on *external barriers* to internal control such as other people's manipulation. The first set focuses on *what we tell ourselves* and the second set focuses on *what we tell other people*.

In both cases we are attempting to become more internally controlled in a way that shows empathy and love of self balanced with empathy and love of others. Actively seeking this balance of caring is being **assertive**--seeking win--win solutions to problems. It contrasts first with **nonassertive**–not adequately taking care of one's own needs–I lose, you win. Non-assertion results in passive, dependent behavior. Assertiveness also contrasts with being **aggressive**–seeking one's own goals without adequate consideration of others' needs–I win, you lose. Aggression results in dominating, manipulative behavior.

SUMMARY OF INTERNAL BARRIERS TO INTERNAL CONTROL

Before exploring additional methods of overcoming internal barriers, I will summarize the internal barriers we have discussed so far. I will also describe some of the reinforcers that strengthen these internal barriers to internal control.

Beliefs and other internal states supporting external control. The following list summarizes many of the beliefs, fears, and other internal states (discussed previously) that tend to increase external control and decrease internal control.

- Valuing others opinions, beliefs, approval, expectations, and judgment more than your own.
- Believing that you *must* have others approval and acceptance (for survival, happiness, etc). Making acceptance by your family or others more important than your own happiness.
- Believing that your individual happiness is selfish, immoral, or not important.
- Low self-worth (low unconditional valuing of self)--a weak Higher Self.
- Low self-confidence or low competence in some life area or task.
- Fear of being alone.
- Fear of not being able to take care of yourself adequately (or make yourself happy).
- Choosing to be too dependent (example: financially, emotionally) on someone.
- Allowing your opinion of yourself to be based on a public opinion poll.
- Fearing some awful truth about yourself.
- Being terrified of disapproval or rejection.
- Being in codependent relationships (because you believe people are *primarily* responsible for others--not themselves).
- Letting obedience or rebellion to rules become too important.
- Letting internalized parents, peer groups, or media ideas become too powerful.
- Beliefs in obedience, passivity, and nonassertiveness. We may believe that we should not question authority, should do what we are told, should not have any kind of conflict, or should always put others' desires above our own. Beliefs such as these support external control. We may have swallowed whole entire belief systems supporting external control. These are now important subparts of ourselves.

Advantages (reinforcers) of external control. Underlying beliefs that support external control are not the only factors that promote external control. Another factor is reinforcement. Hundreds of research studies have demonstrated that reinforcement is a powerful motivator. These reinforcers can trap us into external control indefinitely. However, what could be reinforcing about giving up control of our lives to others? Following are some common factors why people get trapped in external control.

- **Avoidance.** We may believe that allowing others to direct us lets us avoid responsibility for decisions, avoid failure, avoid conflict, avoid rejection, avoid doing what we don't like, avoid taking risks, or avoid work.
- **Social rewards.** There can be social rewards of others believing that we are nice, agreeable, weak, or even incompetent. The weaker we are viewed, the more some people will take care of us and do things for us (that we don't want to do for ourselves). However, the cost can be high--giving up our freedom and happiness.
- **Underdeveloped sources of internal control.** Our more positive sources of internal control may be underdeveloped. Developing our competencies may require time, effort, and money. Remaining dependent on others may seem easier or safer.

Disarming dysfunctional reinforcers. These advantages or reinforcers are only reinforcing to those who *believe that they are advantages.* Avoidance behaviors and dysfunctional social rewards usually cause so much long-term damage that they are not worth the short-term benefits. Once someone gains that insight, avoidance stops being so reinforcing. *Insight helps short-circuit dysfunctional reinforcement.*

Similarly, once we understand the long-term benefits of developing competencies and becoming more self-reliant, then we may become more tolerant of the short-term disadvantages. Following are additional methods we can use to get more control over these internal subparts that make us so vulnerable to external control.

COPE WITH INTERNALIZED PARENT CONTROL STATEMENTS

When I feel guilt, it could be that my inner parent is sending a message. When my inner parent says I should or must, my inner child may rebel and feel like doing the opposite. The result is deadlock--no action.

Instead, I let my Higher Self listen to *all inner points of view* including my inner child and any other inner subparts that have something to say. I take the needed time to have a dialogue between the inner parts until some resolution is reached. I won't allow one inner part to bully or name-call (selfish, childish) another inner part and get its way. It's a lot like marriage counseling.

We have already examined ways of responding to internalized parents (or other external control belief systems) by methods such as converting shoulds to wants. However, if this has been a long-term problem, and self-help efforts are not working, then I strongly recommend you seek the help of a competent mental health professional who has a positive philosophy. If you are still not making adequate progress after a few sessions, discuss it with your therapist. If that does not help, then find another therapist.

REPLACE AVOIDANCE, EXCUSES, AND "SHOULDS" WITH CHOICES

Avoidance Behavior--*avoiding negative consequences*--is one of the primary reinforcers of allowing external control. Letting others make decisions and take responsibility for a situation may be *easier than facing the situation and taking responsibility for it ourselves*. The situations we are avoiding could be rejection, conflict, being alone, work, being wrong, failing, being criticized, or any situation which leads to unhappy emotions such as guilt, anxiety, or boredom.

I don't know anyone who really enjoys rejection or anxiety. Nothing is wrong with wanting to avoid unpleasant situations. Avoiding an unpleasant situation is only a problem if *facing the unpleasant situation is necessary to accomplish an important goal*--such as saving a relationship, getting a job, finishing a class, or fighting cancer.

Face fears and unpleasant situations to establish *self-confidence and independence*. We may have built a huge set of avoidance habits that keep us from facing problems we need to solve to be happy. External control beliefs give us a rationale for avoiding unpleasant situations. They provide good excuses for avoiding responsibility and tough situations.

Giving an excuse means that we are being dishonest with ourselves or someone else. It is dishonest because the *real reason* we are making the choice is *not* the reason we are giving.

Many of these excuses are socially acceptable. We tell people that we are too busy to stop by, not that we are bored with talking to them. We don't call in to the office and say, "I won't be in today because I don't feel like going to work and would rather play." Instead we may call in "sick."

These socially acceptable excuses are not so dysfunctional, because they may add more happiness than then they subtract. Nevertheless, we are still paying the internal price of dishonesty and of knowing we are not secure enough to face the consequences of telling our boss the truth. At least--in this case--we are being honest with *ourselves*.

However, in cases when we lie to ourselves, the results are much more dysfunctional. When we avoid job responsibilities, shyness, problems with loved ones, finances, illness, or alcoholism and *give ourselves dishonest reasons*, then these excuses tend to *perpetuate dysftygunctional habits and undermine control by our entire executive self system.* In essence, we become a slave to our habits--operating more like laboratory rats than thoughtful humans.

Blindly following rules (or shoulds') is also dysfunctional. Blindly following rules--just because they are rules--is often similar to making excuses for what we do. Blindly following rules shifts the responsibility *to the rule source* instead of making our conscious decisions by higher values. We do it because we should without ever questioning if it is beneficial to self and others (our ultimate concern).

We may blindly follow the rule to avoid making an independent decision and facing the consequences (of rejection, guilt, or other penalties imposed by the rule-makers).

Eliminate excuses (and shoulds). If you are tired of making excuses (or avoiding independent decisions), use the following steps.

Step 1: Observe and understand your own motives, excuses, and shoulds. Check to see if you are making excuses instead of facing your *real motives*. Or, are you blindly following rules (that might conflict with you highest values and goals).
Most excuses have the following characteristics:
- They *shift responsibility* from internal to external sources.
- They help you avoid a behavior or situation you dread. (A situation with negative consequences or that feels bad when you think about it).
- They protect you from facing the *real reasons* why you are making the choice you are making: they are *dishonest*.
- They give you a *subtle message that you are weak and helpless, and lower your self-esteem.*

Step 2: Take RESPONSIBILITY for your own behavior and HAPPINESS.
- Face the truth and acknowledge excuses and blind rule-following.
- Examine your real motivation. What behaviors, situations, or consequences are you avoiding? What are your underlying fears or anxieties *about*? Use the self-exploration method to find them and deal with them.
- Take control of the situation--make a *conscious choice!* First, seek a *full understanding* of the different values that will be affected by the choice. Weigh the *immediate benefits of avoidance* against the *long-range benefits of facing the situation*. Last, try my final decision test.

**My final decision test (ultimate concern) is,
"Which alternative will maximize my own and other people's happiness?"
Focusing on my own choices and their consequences
gives me more internal control and gives me a positive message,
"I am in control of my own life and happiness."**

When we let difficult situations, sources of external control, or excuses dominate us, we lower self-esteem. When we face difficulties and actively make hard choices that are based on our Higher Selves, we boost self-esteem.

EXAMPLES CONTRASTING AN EXCUSE WITH A CONSCIOUS CHOICE
Following are some common examples of excuses to avoid negative consequences. These examples illustrate how we tend to give external control to others and give ourselves subtle "I am weak" messages--undermining our self-esteem and preventing us

from reaching other goals. If one applies to you, try the internal control option instead.

•**"I'm powerless" versus "I have some power."** "I can't do x..., so I will give up." versus "I may not be able to do x..., but I will...learn to do x, or do the best I can in the situation.

•**"I can't" versus "I don't want to."** You may say, "I can't do this" to yourself or others when you just don't want to do it. ("It" could be math, cooking, a sport, talking to someone, etc.) Yet you may think that you "should" do it, so you say, "I can't" because "I can't" is more acceptable than "I don't want to." Perhaps you would rather the other person think that you "can't" than think that you "don't want to." Or, perhaps you would rather think of yourself as "I can't do it" than think of yourself as lazy, disinterested, or irresponsible.

You don't need to call yourself "lazy" or to hide your real motives from yourself. It is much more productive to explore *why* you honestly don't want to do something. Understanding *why* you don't want to do it gives you a stronger sense of self-control than believing that "I can't motivate myself."

After self-exploration, if you still don't want to do it, then you can assertively state, "I choose not to do it." Inside, you will feel more self-control, because you will understand your *real motives* for making the choice. Outside, people may get upset; but they will eventually respect and trust you more. No more excuses!

If you can't find a positive reason, always remember that the **best reason** is that you and/or others will be happier. Stand up for your beliefs!

•**Blaming others versus "I have choices...no matter what you did to me."** No matter what someone does to you, you have a wide range of responses to choose from. You do not have to be aggressive or nonassertive.

Dr. Wayne Dyer suggests making a BLAME LIST. Include everything that you blame your parents, significant other, friends, teachers, boss, or anyone else for. Then take each blame item and try to look at it from the point of view that *you had/have power to make choices* of how to respond to the situation that you were presented with.

Focus on *your own choices.* Take responsibility for *making yourself happy* for each of these situations. Be creative in finding new ways of making yourself as happy as possible with each situation. For example, spending time with a needy or demanding parent is a choice no matter how strongly you believe that you must do it (or owe it to them). It is not a must over which you have no choice.

REMIND YOURSELF OF EXTERNAL CONTROL CONSEQUENCES

Another way to become more internally controlled is to remind ourselves of the consequences of being too externally controlled. Make a list of negative consequences that affect you. Following are common negative consequences of external control and reminders of key internal control sources. Remind yourself of these consequences--even carry the list with you.

•**Attractiveness.** If you are too dependent, externally controlled, or unhappy, you probably aren't as attractive to others. Do they view you as too needy, insecure, or weak?

•**Dependence--loss of freedom.** If you get trapped in a poor relationship because of your neediness in one area of your life, you will lose freedom and could become miserable and depressed.

•**Victimization.** Have you been in the role of a victim? Say, "I am tired of being nonassertive, tired of being codependent, tired of being too dependent, and tired of being a victim. I can only respect myself if I look to my Higher Self and *persist* to get my inner needs met."

Instead of being a victim, you can remind yourself of the following.

•**Many routes--not one.** You don't need (must have) any one person. You can be happy alone or you can be happy in other relationships. Any good relationship is a gift--a bonus. No one owes you a good relationship; you can create your own happiness. Say, "*There are many routes to happiness and I will find the right ones for me.*"

•**Learning and experimenting.** Sometimes being assertive means *not* knowing what you want and *experimenting*. In practice you will not always know what you will like or what will make you happy. You may require *time for searching* your inner feelings or experimenting to find out what you like and dislike. You can insist other people give you space, allow you to experiment, or even experiment with you.

•**Trusting others versus trusting yourself.** You can never trust others to take care of yourself as much as you can trust yourself. If you depend upon others for stability or direction, then you will constantly be insecure and ultimately anxious. Because, you will be at the mercy of their desires and the possibility that they may let you down or leave you. On the other hand, you know that you will *always be there for yourself and never leave yourself.*

•**Loving yourself.** Say, "I love myself, and I can create a happy life for myself. I am the person most responsible for meeting my own needs. If I am to be happy, I will choose to assertively pursue the values that lead to my happiness."

•**Loving others.** Say, "I can love others and create happy relationship(s) through my own abilities to be happy, and though giving undemanding love to others. I will treat others by what *I believe*--not by what others manipulate me to do."

RESOLVE EXTERNAL BARRIERS TO INTERNAL CONTROL BY BEING MORE ASSERTIVE

We have been focusing on *what we say to ourselves* in order to get more internal control. Now we will focus on *other people* who are influencing us and on *what we say to those other people.*

There will always be people who want to influence us. People who are more externally controlled will automatically tend to do what these people want. People who are more internally controlled will tend to check with their Higher Selves and other internal subparts before responding. Ultimately they will want to know the effects of the request on *both* people's overall happiness before agreeing.

While this chapter is not a course on assertion training, I will provide a few simple tips on what to do when dealing with people who are attempting to persuade, manipulate, or coerce you. Some of these people (especially parents) may truly care about you and have your best interests at heart. Others couldn't care less about you. They may simply be trying to sell you something for their benefit--not yours. Also, see Appendix E: KEY INTERPERSONAL SKILLS.

BECOME AWARE OF AUTOMATIC NONASSERTIVENESS

We may so habitually conform to doing what others expect or want that we are not even aware of it. Becoming aware of automatic conformity is the first step to *consciously choose* what we want. Consciously choosing what we want can greatly enhance our sense of personal freedom and self-esteem. Think of any relationships in which you feel restricted, controlled, or have difficulty being yourself. Become more aware *of any feelings that precede or follow nonassertive behavior.* These feelings may include:

• Feelings of pressure or anxiety
• Feeling weak
• Feeling dependent on the other person
• Fear of being rejected or hurt by the other person
• Feeling afraid of something the other person might do as a punishment or retaliation
• Feelings of guilt or anger at yourself--(often occurring after nonassertiveness)
• Feelings of apathy, loss of motivation, unhappiness, or depression (often occurring after nonassertiveness)

When you get one of these feelings, imagine a big red flag. Then take some of the steps below to become more aware of the consequences of external control and focus more on what you really want.

MONITOR EXTERNAL CONTROL FOCUS VERSUS INTERNAL CONTROL FOCUS

Learning which external and internal messages to focus on is a key determinant of achieving successful internal control and assertiveness. **External control focus** means focusing on what the other person thinks, feels, and wants *without weighing it adequately against our own thoughts, feelings, and wants*.

Internal control focus means *primarily focusing on our own desires, feelings, goals, plans, and thoughts*. An assertive stance is to be sensitive to both your own and the other's values, but normally (1) giving some preference to your own values and (2) attempting to achieve win-win outcomes (so both are happy). Use your Higher Self's genuine empathy and love of self and others as a guide.

For people who are too externally controlled. If you are in the habit of trying to please (or rebel against) others, then it is important to put an *extra emphasis on looking inward* for awhile to see what you really want. Try some of the following suggestions.

• Get away from the influential person (even for five minutes) and focus on your own inner dreams, desires, subparts, values, and goals.
• Talk to other people who are more internally controlled, are on your side, and are more objective.
• Make your decision based primarily upon what you really want. First, decide what you would want or do if the person whom you normally defer to did not even exist. This can help to clarify your own feelings without interruption from your internalized other.
• Role-play in your own mind what the other person might say and what your new, assertive position is. Would they make some valid points that you *honestly want to consider?* Mentally practice how you will deal with any consequences of your new assertiveness.
• Normally, seek the opinion of a dominating person *only if they are directly involved or will be directly affected* by your decision. Make the final decision *alone--without any other person present*.

Focus on internal sources of control to get more *control of emotions.* When we focus on external sources of control, we will often feel weak, helpless, and out of control. The emotions we get will likely either be anxiety, guilt, hurt, or depression. Those emotions may trigger a **nonassertive mode** of thoughts and actions.

On the other hand, emotions of resentment or anger may trigger an **aggressive mode.** Often feeling hurt precedes the anger. We may try to do the opposite of what the other wants (rebel) or try to get even.

When we focus on constructive, internal sources of control (such as our Higher Self or other constructive beliefs, desires, and goals), we feel *more in control, feel more determined, and feel calmer.* This is an **assertive mode**. I ask clients to change focus from external to internal sources of control in my office, and they are amazed at how much more confident they feel within seconds. Try it.

HIDDEN MESSAGES, MANIPULATION, AND GAMES PEOPLE PLAY

A husband (in front of guests at a party) says, "Honey, I'll bet that if you didn't spend all that time watching game shows after work, you'd have time to cook dinner for me now and then." Everyone laughs. His wife responds, "But I'm really tired after working all day and need some time to wind down." Husband, "I know that, I was only teasing."

What has just happened here? On the surface, it appears that the husband is teasing his wife about game shows and cooking. According to the social rules of teasing, everyone laughs at his wife and she is supposed to be a good sport and laugh too. However, the wife heard the (not so) hidden message that her husband really is upset with her for watching TV instead of cooking dinner. He wants to embarrass her in front of their friends and to use group pressure.

She is upset by that hidden message. He did not want their friends to think he would intentionally embarrass his wife in front of them, so he denied that he was playing a game and insisted he was only teasing.

The game is a subtle way of getting her *to feel bad about her behavior and change it.* It is manipulation *because it is dishonest*--he is pretending that he is only teasing. Dr. Eric Berne described *many* such manipulative social games in his classic book, *Games People Play.* Berne calls this game "Sweetheart," because often the manipulator says, "Isn't that true, Sweetheart." If he disguises his attack by smiling and saying sweetheart, she is not supposed to respond negatively.

How could she tell if he were not playing a game--if he were really teasing? If he had been honest and had previously resolved his problem about dinner and if his real goal were to play, then his statement would not be manipulation.

DEVELOP INTERPERSONAL SKILLS TO GET MORE INTERNAL CONTROL

In the above example, the wife could have screamed, yelled, called her husband names, and gone on a tirade. However, such an **aggressive** (or domineering) **response** would probably have made her seem to be the bad guy and alienated her friends as well as driving a wedge further between her and her husband.

She also could have smiled and pretended that she believed he was only teasing. However, this **nonassertive** (or passive) **response** will only encourage him to keep manipulating her and will increase his control of her life.

A more skilled, understanding, and **assertive response** would be to say something like, "Honey, it sounds like you are really bothered by my watching TV after work, perhaps we should talk about it later?" By this assertive response, she shows understanding and concern for him and simultaneously cuts through the dishonest game to the heart of the issue. If he persisted, she could add, "You don't want to discuss it here and now in front of our friends do you?" Recall that in our studies on the SRQ we found that assertiveness and intimacy each correlated over .70 with relationship happiness. SHAQ incorporates the SRQ scales. See the box below for more information.

Most people do not have good assertive communication skills. Assertive skills take time, study, and practice to learn. Following are a few characteristics of assertive (nonaggressive, non-passive) interpersonal communications. Try these tips to become more assertive and to resolve disagreements more constructively.

- **Empathy.** Attempt to understand the other person's point of view thoroughly.
- **Care for other.** Express respect and concern for others and their feelings. Tell them and show them you care--even if you are angry.
- **Care for self.** Focus on own values, goals, feelings--clarify them to yourself and to others.
- **Seek win--win solutions**. Avoid win--lose solutions (even if you will be the winner). What do you win in the long run when you hurt someone you care for or conduct business with?
- **No name-calling, attacking, or blaming.** Use neutral, descriptive language--avoid name calling, negative labels, or personal attacks of any type. Don't blame other or self. Focus on causes and solutions--not on assessing blame and problems.
- **Issue-oriented.** Keep your focus on one important issue at a time and be willing to take whatever time is necessary to reach an eventual solution for important problems. Be flexible about *when* to talk. Make sure there is balanced turn-taking of *whose* main issue is being addressed.
- **Calm.** Attempt to keep an atmosphere of calm concern and understanding by both parties. If emotions get too intense, take a "time-out" (time and space necessary to regain calmness by either party).
- **Listen empathetically.** Listen to others *first.* Let the other thoroughly explore his or her point-of-view. *Frequently summarize* the essence of the other's *emotions* and content.
- **Ask the other to elaborate his or her point of view**, so you can understand it in more detail--even if it is critical of you. Ask them questions like, "Can you give me examples?", "Can you tell me more?", or "What else bothers you?"
- **Get to heart of problem.** Encourage clarification and exploration of underlying issues. (See self-exploration method in Chapter 2 and apply method to both parties.) Help both parties discover the underlying, bigger themes behind the feelings.
- **Be caring, but firmly respond to manipulation.** Respond to emotional outbursts with empathy, but do *not be manipulated by them*. (Example, "I can see you are angry about XX. I care about your feelings and want to understand *why* you are so upset.") Often, the best alternative is to take a TIME-OUT if either party gets too out of control.
- **Bargain.** Be willing (and learn how) to escalate carefully and bargain with rewards and punishments if the other person becomes too manipulative or if simple agreements do not work. Use a calm, but firm approach to *de-escalate* anger or attacks. If you believe that, you are being treated badly by the other person and they refuse to bargain, then consider taking action yourself to better take care of your own needs--even if it upsets them. It might bring them back to the bargaining table!
- **Focus on changing self--not other.** You can only control your own thoughts, feelings, and behavior--not the other person's. Offer suggestions of actions *you* can take to improve matters--especially those that also take better care of *your* needs.
- **Actions consistent with words.** Follow up with actions matching words--persistently. No deceit. If the other does not keep an agreement, examine the problem alone. Discuss the broken agreement.

➔ **See Appendix E: HARMONIOUS ASSERTIVE COMMUNICATION SKILLS TO CREATE UNDERSTANDING AND INTIMACY for more help.**

SPEND YOUR TIME IN HEALTHY SOCIAL ENVIRONMENTS

Moving on to healthier relationships. We can learn to get more internal control in a variety of ways. One important way to get more internal control is to (1) accept that any reference group or close relationship is going to exert *some influence* on your beliefs, thoughts, and behavior and (2) adjust the time you spend with others according to how *positive* you believe their overall influence is on you.

If you feel more unhappy, worse about yourself, and less growth because you are with certain people, take control. You have a choice! I have seen many clients who were much happier after they completely separated themselves from dysfunctional families. Some have not seen *anyone* in their family for many years. Generally, they learned to overcome guilt and loneliness. Most thought it was one of the healthiest things they ever did. As one said, "I quit letting them drag me back into the quicksand."

People leaving unhealthy relationships are often afraid that they will never find someone else who will love them and be with them. Yet, most people go on to healthier relationships. Those who don't get into relationships almost always learn to be happier alone than in that unhealthy relationship.

SHAQ Research Results: Interpersonal Skills

The Interpersonal Skills scales focused upon intimate relationship skills. Combined, they correlated with Happiness, .59; with Low Depression, .39; with Low Anxiety, .38; with Low Anger-Aggr, .59; with good Relationships, .40; with Health, .49; with Income, .21; with Education, .15; and with college GPA, .19.

The eight Interpersonal Skills subscales follow.
1. Assertive conflict resolution. This subscale correlated with Happiness, .46; with Low Depression, .24; with Low Anxiety, .20; with Low Anger-Aggr, .36; with Relationship Outcomes, .37; and with Health, .31; and with college GPA, .08.
2. Open, honest communication. This subscale correlated with Happiness, .50; with Low Depression, .29; with Low Anxiety, .23; with Low Anger-Aggr, .30; with Relationship Outcomes, and .44; with Health, .29.
3. Love and respect for other. This subscale correlated with Happiness, .48; with Low Depression, .29; with Low Anxiety, .27; with Low Anger-Aggr, .43; with Relationship Outcomes, .43; and with Health, .30.
4. Positive and supportive statements. This subscale correlated with Happiness, .42; with Low Depression, .28; with Low Anxiety, .27; with Low Anger-Aggr, .54; with Relationship Outcomes, .27; and with Health, .31.
5. Collaborative behavior. This subscale correlated with Happiness, .41; with Low Depression, .27; with Low Anxiety, .24; with Low Anger-Aggr, .33; with Relationship Outcomes, .27; and with Health, .32.
6. Supportive relationship independence. Support to pursue own interests, goals, time alone, etc. This subscale correlated with Happiness, .38; with Low Depression, .29; with Low Anxiety, .31; with Low Anger-Aggr, .39; with Relationship Outcomes, .14; with Health, .30; with Income, .06; with Education, .08.; and with college GPA, .06.
7. Romantic. This subscale correlated with Happiness, .39; with Low Depression, .17; with Low Anxiety, .12; with Low Anger-Aggr, .24; with Relationship Outcomes, .27; and with Health, .18.
8. Liberated roles. This subscale correlated with Happiness, .17; with Low Depression, .11; with Low Anxiety, .18; with Low Anger-Aggr, .29; with Relationship Outcomes, .14; and with Health, .13.

The assertive, interpersonal skills guidelines in this chapter correspond closely to items on subscales 1-6 above. Follow them to improve relationships and happiness. Go to Appendix E and my website for more free self-help interpersonal and assertive skills training manuals.

Note: For all correlations, p < .0001 and Ns ranged from 2336 to 2906.

SET BOUNDARIES OF RESPONSIBILITY AND CONTROL

One of the key issues in any relationship is the balance of control. Is it 50%-50%, 80%-20%, or what? Who makes more of the decisions in each life area? Who gets their way most often during conflicts? Who gives the most? These questions raise the underlying *control issue* of "How much do I give to my own happiness versus how much do I give to the happiness of others?" Does a sister give up a kidney to save the life of her sister--thus increasing her own chances of death? How much do we each give?

I cannot answer those questions for you. We each need to draw our own boundaries about who we will give to and how much we will give. However, in my experience with hundreds of clients, *balance issues, control issues,* and people's *communication about them* are usually the most important determinates of the relationship's success.

Overcoming conflicts about balance and control can only happen through good communication and a willingness by *all involved* to change.

PRACTICE: Examine current balance and boundaries of control in important relationships. Think of an important relationship you are not satisfied with. Examine the *balance* of control overall and balance in important areas of the relationship. Also, are there problems with dependence, codependence, or other control boundaries--see earlier sections? How can you more assertively communicate and act toward the other? What fears, underlying beliefs, and other internal barriers must you cope with to act more assertively with this person? Develop a plan to overcome them using ideas from this and earlier chapters.

SHAQ Research Results: Internal versus External Control

The Internal vs. External (I-E) Control Beliefs scale correlated with Happiness, .49; with Low Depression, .42; with Low Anxiety, .46; with Low Anger-Aggression, .42; with good Relationships, .29; with Health, .38; with Income, .24; with Education, .14; and with college GPA, .13.

The three Internal-External Control subscales follow.
1. Autonomy, independence. This subscale correlated with Happiness, .55; with Low Depression, .44; with Low Anxiety, .43; with Low Anger-Aggr, .37; with Relationship Outcomes, .33; and with Health, .33; with income, .29; with Education, .15, and with college GPA, .13.
2. Not codependent. This subscale correlated with Happiness, .21; with Low Depression, .23; with Low Anxiety, .28; with Low Anger-Aggr, .24; with Relationship Outcomes, .09; and with Health, .25; with income, .09; and with Education, .11.
3. Not (adult) care provider. This subscale correlated with Happiness, .25; with Low Depression, .21; with Low Anxiety, .27; with Low Anger-Aggr, .31; with Relationship Outcomes, .18; and with Health, .23; with income, .10; and with college GPA, .06.

Internal control can help people achieve integrity—living by what they value and believe. The opposite is external control—letting others determine what you will do or even think. No wonder I-E Control is so large a factor in happiness and success. The autonomy subscale had one of the highest correlations with income of any SHAQ scale (.29). This chapter gives detailed help how you can achieve more internal control of your life.

Note: For all correlations, p < .0001 and Ns ranged from 2001 to 2646.

Many external forces try to influence our decisions--
including many people we love and respect.
Many internal forces try to influence our decisions--
including many lower and higher desires.
If we are too influenced by external forces,
we risk lack of inner satisfaction and depression.
If we are too influenced by our own self-directed desires,
we risk social consequences and guilt.
Allowing the Higher Self to balance empathetic listening
to both internal with external messages, and
to give primary responsibility for meeting desires to each individual
can resolve the internal--external control conflict.
We can attain internal control and win-win solutions.

CHAPTER 7

HARMONIOUS FUNCTIONING CREATES PEAK LEARNING, PERFORMANCE, AND HAPPINESS:

IT IS THE ROOT OF ALL EMOTIONS

\\\

More than 2,000 years ago Aristotle achieved this powerful insight about the relationship between excellent performance and happiness.

> **The function of man, then, is exercise of his vital facilities. . .**
> **in obedience to reason. . .a harpist's function is to harp,**
> **and a good harpist's function is to harp well. . .**
> **the good of man is exercise of his faculties in accordance with excellence. . .**
> **the manifestations of excellence will be pleasant in themselves. . .**
> **the life of these men is in itself pleasant. . .**
> **Happiness is, then, at once the best and noblest and pleasantest thing**
> **in the world, and these are not separated. . .**
> **For all these characteristics are united**
> **in the best exercises of our faculties. . .**(Aristotle, *Ethics*)

PEAK FUNCTIONING OF OUR MIND AND BODY

Occasionally--for brief periods of time--everything in my mind and body is functioning harmoniously. I might be playing tennis and seem to be at one with the court, the ball, and the movement. I feel confident of hitting the ball where I want. My mind and body are highly energized, but not overly so. I am especially alert and able to focus on the ball and where I want to hit it. When I am in this state, I am totally involved in what I am doing and loving it. I am performing at my best.

This harmonious state occurs not only during tennis, but also during other activities such as dancing, conversing, solving an interesting problem, having a special sexual experience, or appreciating a beautiful sunset. During these experiences, I feel as if every cell in my mind and body is functioning at some optimal level doing what it was intended to do. This type of functioning is extremely healthy for both our psychological and our physical health. Whereas its opposites--prolonged anxiety, anger, or depression--are unhealthy states. Evidence is increasing that too much time spent in these negative emotional states is detrimental to both our mental and physical health.

These harmonious experiences may be similar to what Maslow referred to as "peak experiences." He found that self-actualizing people--especially those who focused more on mental activities--tended to have many more peak experiences than most people. He characterized these peak experiences as a feeling of inner harmony and oneness with themselves and the universe.

> **The person in the peak experience feels more integrated**
> **(unified, whole, all-of-a-piece), than at other times.**
> **He also looks (to the observer) more integrated in various ways. . .,**
> **e.g., less split or dissociated, less fighting against himself,**
> **more at peace with himself,**
> **less split between an experiencing self and an observing self,**
> **more one-pointed, more harmoniously organized,**
> **more efficiently organized**
> **with all his parts functioning very nicely with each other . .**
> (A. Maslow, 1960, p.98)

Wouldn't it be wonderful if all humans could function at this higher level most of the time? We could create a much more harmonious and productive society from which we would all benefit.

Wouldn't it be wonderful if *you* could spend most of your time functioning at this higher level; and spend less time feeling bored, under stress, or unhappy? What if you were continually fascinated and performing at your best? What if instead of feeling bored or stressed about a task--avoiding it or doing it halfway--you could become fascinated with it? What if instead of dreading a task, you could create positive anticipation?

Wouldn't it be great if you had buttons in your head that you could push to feel more excited or more calm? The harmonious functioning model can help you understand the root causes of motivation and emotion--and suggest basic strategies for supercharging yourself.

HARMONIOUS FUNCTIONING CREATES
PEAK LEARNING, PERFORMANCE, AND HAPPINESS

A state of harmonious functioning leads to the **big three outcomes**—peak learning, peak performance, and peak happiness.[19] We can create harmonious functioning in almost any situation. This state is not mystical or magical, but it may be what the mystic feels when he or she has a mystical experience.

Harmonious functioning is a special mind-body state in which all activated brain and body systems are operating in the maximum harmony possible for that particular situation. The most central of these systems are cognitive systems and conscious processes. We may experience this mind-body state as euphoria, nirvana, a peak experience, a flow experience.

---

[19] A diverse set of research findings support some of the main ideas of the harmonious functioning model. For example, research supports the famous Yerkes-Dobson Law that maximum performance of (especially complex) tasks occurs at an optimal level of motivational arousal--too low arousal leads to apathy, low energy, slowed performance and too high arousal leads to confusion, increased errors, distractions, or overshooting. (See Brehm, J. W. and Self, E. A. 1989)

Another supportive line of theory and research concerns the Behavioral Facilitation (or activation) System BFS hypothesized by Schneirla (1959). There is some evidence of a general motivational and arousal system that controls a range of reactions from mania at one extreme to depression at the other. Moderate states may be consistent with harmonious functioning. (See Depue, Richard A. and Iacono, William G.,1989) Other theories will be discussed next.

Whatever we call it, it feels wonderful!

Peak learning, performance, and happiness are interwoven aspects of the same underlying phenomenon. This phenomenon is the basis of all higher learning and motivation. It is rooted in brain physiology, but its branches extend into the higher informational/spiritual levels of existence.

What is this underlying phenomenon? Presently, no one can describe its exact nature--though many have tried. I propose that this phenomenon has to do with how we process information. Harmonious functioning has to do with the relationship between the inputs to the mind and its ability to cope with them. It is a complex relationship, but one I will try to describe in this chapter. Understanding how harmonious functioning works will change your life! Let's start with the following example.

A client came in for counseling. An intelligent and mature person, she normally functioned at a high level and was quite happy. However, she was undecided about her career direction, about where she wanted to live, and about her relationship. In addition she had financial and health problems that were potentially serious. She was from another state and had few friends in the area. If she had had problems in only one or two of these areas, she could have solved them herself without so much anxiety.

OVERSTIMULATION—
TOO MUCH CHALLENGE CAUSES CONFUSION AND ANXIETY[20]

Whenever she focused on her problems, she got lost in their complexity. The complexity was too great for her mental organization powers to handle all at once. Feeling overwhelmed, she usually avoided her problems by doing compulsive busywork such as organizing her closet. But organizing her closet didn't solve the real problems. Therefore, she experienced the *big three negative outcomes* from *too much input* for her coping ability. These outcomes were high anxiety, low learning, and low performance.

UNDERSTIMULATION—
TOO LITTLE CHALLENGE CAUSES BOREDOM AND DEPRESSION

At other times--in the face of too much challenge--my client would mentally give up and tune out. When she tuned out, she narrowed her focus so much that she mentally shut down and became passive. That mental shut down created a low arousal state of depression or boredom. When she was in this state, she withdrew from others and became immobilized by her depression. Therefore, she was now experiencing the *big three negative outcomes* from *too little input* for her mental abilities--underarousal, low learning, and low performance.

Boredom or depression produce lowered arousal or apathy. We often confuse these lowered energy states with being tired or sick. These low energy states can further interfere with performance.

Cognitive *overstimulation* or cognitive *understimulation* was the underlying cause for her negative big three outcomes of negative emotions, low learning, and low performance. On the other hand, when there is *optimal match* between the complexity of a situation and our abilities, then we will experience the big three positive outcomes--peak learning, peak performance, and peak happiness.[21]

---

[20] Many people think that the word anxiety refers only to intense degrees of anxiety. However, I am using the term to include nervousness, stress, fear, guilt, and other similar emotional states.
[21] Many people confuse the emotion depression with clinical depression. The emotion depression ranges from mild forms such as slight sadness or unhappiness to intense grief or severe depression. Almost every day we all probably feel some degree of depression for at least a short time. Clinical depression is a label used for a psychological disorder-prime features of which include prolonged,

HARMONIOUS FUNCTIONING IS OUR MOST BASIC DRIVING FORCE

What is the most basic human motive? Many have attempted to answer that question. Freud thought that we had two basic motives--sex and aggression. Maslow thought that we began focusing on the biological lower needs--such as needs for food and sex, and gradually moved on to the higher needs--such as love, creativity, and ultimately self-actualization. I agree with Maslow's idea about the progression of needs to some extent, but think that there is a more basic human motive.

Growth **is our strongest motivator.** Does it seem strange to think that the most basic human motive might not be sex or aggression as Freud believed, but knowledge? After all, the brain is primarily a giant information processor. Estimates are that we have between 10 and 100 billion neurons with perhaps 20 quadrillion connections. Each of these connections is a potential storage unit of knowledge, and each cell is striving to be active and learn.

Why have our brains evolved so far beyond the lower animals? Clearly, there is evolutionary value to intelligence that gives humans advantages. Social evolutionary value also gives individuals, groups, and nations with greater knowledge advantages over those with less knowledge.

Our brains automatically strive to develop more and better organized knowledge--to develop more elaborate cognitive systems. Our cognitive system tries to keep from being overwhelmed by too much information, on the one hand, and to keep from being deprived by too little on the other. Our cognitive system is functioning harmoniously during maximum learning and growth. Evolution has made this mental harmonious functioning state the most pleasant and desired state attainable, because knowledge has so much survival value. Harmonious functioning (happiness) is also the most rewarding and motivating force affecting our daily lives.

Several psychologists have made important contributions to understanding the importance of growth as a primary motive. The following four each began from very different points of view and methods, yet each arrived at similar conclusions. [22]

1. OPTIMAL LEARNING AS THE BASIS OF HAPPINESS--DR. GEORGE KELLY

Dr. George Kelly wrote his 1,218 page *The Psychology of Personal Constructs* in 1955. I first read it in graduate school. He was a man whose ideas were far beyond his time. Though always influential, his principles have gained acceptance over the years. Today, his principles provide a foundation for many of the latest approaches to cognitive therapy. Every major book on theories of personality includes Kelly's theory as one of a handful presented.

Dr. Kelly viewed our basic nature as attempting to understand the world around us-- so that we may best adapt to it. He quotes the poet Shelly; "*The mind becomes that which it contemplates*" (p.6) to reflect his belief that we develop what I have called mental models of the world.[23] Dr. Kelly also states,

---

intense depression and suicidal thinking. Experiencing even intense depression does not necessarily indicate clinical depression. If concerned see a professional.
[22] The first three theorists made important contributions to my understanding. I had not heard of Dr. Csikszentmihalyi's theory until after most of my ideas were developed. Their different points of view can help you understand different aspects of harmonious functioning.
[23] Kelly uses the term *construction system* which I consider roughly equivalent to the term mental model as I am using it in this book. He also uses the term *personal construct*, which is similar to the term category--except that it is a dichotomous category.

**Man looks at his world through transparent patterns or templates which he creates
and then attempts to fit over the realities of which the world is composed.
The fit is not always very good. Yet without such patterns the world appears to be
[so confusing] that man is unable to make any sense out of it.
Even a poor fit is more helpful to him than nothing at all.**

Dr. Kelly believed that every aspect of the universe could be viewed in a variety of ways. In other words, one person can hold several models or theories that explain the same phenomenon. Each of these models or theories can be partially correct. Our brain automatically chooses the view [model or theory] that seems to best predict future events.

What happens when our "pet theory" doesn't adequately predict events? Or even worse--what happens if none of our theories predict the events? According to Dr. Kelly the result is *anxiety*. To the degree that our beliefs are not able to cope with inputs-- especially higher level beliefs--we will feel anxiety.

Thus, it is as if we each have a head full of little scientists--each trying to build better theories to predict the future. These inner experts each have their own area of expertise (*range of convenience*). Each inner expert is most interested in events that will affect it. For example, the part responsible for eating and hunger is constantly trying to predict and understand the meal schedule. The schedule may be routine unless the supply of food is suddenly cut off. Then, that inner food expert becomes active. The increased uncertainty that the food expert feels creates anxiety for the entire cognitive system.

What if these little experts are all confused at once or are in disharmony among themselves? According to Kelly, cognitive confusion is the basic cause of anxiety. The most happy state is one in which the currently active experts find an optimal degree of *match* [or validation] between their theories and the events they are trying to anticipate. *Too little match* (too little cognitive control) is confusing and little is learned--it is overchallenging and anxiety producing. *Too much match* (cognitive overcontrol) is boring and little is learned--it is underchallenging and depressing. Kelly's theory has produced many supportive research studies (B. Walker and D. Winter, 2007).

2. OPTIMAL STIMULATION AS A BASIC HUMAN MOTIVE—DR. DONALD BERLYNE

Psychologists know that if a biological subsystem is either overstimulated or understimulated, we experience these states as unpleasant. If it is stimulated at a moderate degree, then we tend to experience that state as pleasant. This general principle of optimal stimulation or optimal arousal seems to work for almost every cell and system in our mind and body. For example, if our blood sugar is too low, our blood sugar detection system gives us the sensation of being hungry. The taste of food--especially something sweet seems very good. If our blood sugar level is too high--such as after having eaten a lot of sweets--then we may get sensations that cause us to feel sick if we taste something sweet. Our blood-sugar-regulation system is a basic biological system that produces pleasant feelings when the sugar level is within the optimal range and unpleasant feelings when either too high or too low.

The optimal stimulation principle also applies to our emotions. Dr. Berlyne (1960, 1967) believed that our brains seek to maintain an optimal level of stimulation. He believed that curiosity, the desire for knowledge, is perhaps our most powerful motivational force.

3. OPTIMAL CHALLENGE CAUSES THE FLOW EXPERIENCE--
DR. MIHALY CSIKSZENTMIHALYI

Dr. Mihaly Csikszentmihalyi has taken Maslow's concept of peak experience and led research efforts to understand optimal experience and its relationship to happiness for over two decades. His book is *Flow--The Psychology of Optimal Experience.* Dr. Csikszentmihalyi believes that happiness is of primary importance to people and that it is achieved primarily through controlling our thoughts. He states (page 6):

> **The optimal state of experience is one**
> **in which there is *order in consciousness*.**
> **This happens when psychic energy--or attention--is invested**
> **in realistic goals, and when skills match the opportunities for action.**
> **The pursuit of the goal brings order in awareness**
> **because a person must concentrate attention on the task at hand and**
> **momentarily forget everything else.**
> **These periods of struggling to overcome challenges are what people**
> **find to be the most enjoyable times in their lives . . .**
> **By stretching skills, by reaching toward higher challenges,**
> **such a person becomes an increasingly extraordinary individual. . . .**
> **"Flow" is the way people describe their state of mind**
> **when consciousness is harmoniously ordered, and**
> **they want to pursue what they are doing for its own sake.**

Notice the similarity between Dr. Csikszentmihalyi's theory and Dr. Kelly's. Both focus on optimal levels of matching between inputs and cognitive abilities. Also, notice the similarity to Aristotle's observation.

Dr. Csikszentmihalyi describes many cases of individuals who have experienced the flow experience more frequently and intensely than most of us. Some, such as a dancer who frequently experiences flow while dancing, are not so surprising. Others, such as a homeless man who achieved frequent flow experiences, are more surprising. He had developed a highly active mental life and oneness with his environment. Does it seem incredible that someone we so often pity could be happier than we are? It appears that flow is more a result of mental conditions than external conditions.

Dr. Csikszentmihalyi has discovered that certain situations and activities seem to make the flow experience easier to obtain. Examples include sports, games, artistic and creative activities, social activities, religious activities, and more challenging work activities. Some flow experiences seem to involve more sensory and physical activities such as sex, athletics, or listening to music, while other flow experiences seem to involve higher mental processes and symbolic skills more. These include activities such as poetry, mathematics, philosophy, or solving an everyday problem.

Yet, Dr. Csikszentmihalyi recognizes that even the most sensory or physical activity must have some higher mental counterpart which is in tune with it or at least allows it to happen. In other words, each *cognitive* system must actively or passively support the activity to achieve flow [harmonious functioning].

Dr. Csikszentmihalyi provides some general guidelines for achieving the flow experience, but he is not a clinical psychologist. He suggests that more specific guidelines (like those in this book) are needed from someone who has more experience working with clients.

Several research studies have provided evidence that Dr. Csikszentmihalyi's main ideas are not only valid, but seem to be valid across many diverse cultures (Csikszentmihalyi,1988). These studies support the idea that the basic causes of the flow experience are part of human nature, not cultural. They are not dependent upon Western or Eastern cultural factors or religions.

4. ADAPTIVE RESONANCE IN NEURAL NETWORKS UNDERLIES LEARNING, MOTIVATION, AND AROUSAL--DR. STEPHEN GROSSBERG

A major theoretical approach in psychology, artificial intelligence, and neuroscience views our brain as consisting of neural networks. These neural networks are synonymous with what I have been calling cognitive systems. Dr. Stephan Grossberg is one of the leading scholars in this field and proposes that when we learn something significant, some neural network [cognitive subsystem] resonates (harmoniously) and reinforces the new learning—stamping it into memory.

The primary activity of each neural network is trying to **match** current knowledge (in the form of **expectations**) with **inputs**. When there is too much **mismatch**, the network searches for other expectations to match the input. This search process produces arousal.

Trying to match inputs with expectations is like a bee-catcher trying to catch a swarm of bees with a net. If his net has big holes (like a theory with big holes), he can catch only a few bees and the rest can swarm over him. Inadequate expectations [or hypotheses] are like the net with big holes--too much input escapes the expectations [abilities to process the input]. The input which cannot be processed (the escaping bees) produces too much search (to capture the bees) resulting in too much bee-keeper arousal, confusion, and anxiety.

If his net catches all the bees (like a very proven theory), then there will be no escaping bees resulting in too little search and arousal to be interesting. If the expectations **match the input too well**, then nothing is learned and the result is too little search for new hypotheses, low arousal, and boredom.

If his net can catch an optimal number of bees (like a developing theory), then just enough bees escape to make the catch challenging and fun. Harmonious functioning is like using a net with a few holes. The few escaping bees produce optimal search, learning, and arousal. The bee-catcher loves optimal challenge. He likes to have just enough bees escape so that he can prevent boredom from understimulation and prevent anxiety from overstimulation.

Grossberg says that an **optimal degree of matching** between input and expectations causes adaptive resonance. **Adaptive resonance** causes optimal stimulation and arousal. It may be the *root cause of the emotion of happiness*. It may be the major cause of what learning psychologists call reinforcement [at least at a cognitive level].

This resonance between brain cells is similar to members of an orchestra playing together in harmony. The result is a feeling of exhilaration---the "ah ha" type experience. An optimal degree of matching between inputs and predictions is the state that causes optimal learning and optimal stimulation. It is like fitting a key piece of a puzzle together.

I believe that this type of resonance within our cognitive systems is the neural basis for our experience of optimal stimulation, peak experience, or flow. What causes this experience is an *optimal rate of new learning*. The cognitive system is neither underchallenged and bored or overwhelmed and anxious. From an entirely different theoretical approach, Dr. Grossberg seems to have found a concept of resonance that is quite similar to the concepts of peak experience, optimal stimulation, and flow[24].

---

[24] Davidson, Pizzagalli, Nitschke, & Putnam, 2002, have presented neurophysilogical evidence

Harmonious functioning stamps in memories. According to Dr. Grossberg's theory, adaptive resonance is the mental arousal process that actually causes information to be stamped into long-term memory from its current state in short-term memory. He presents a great deal of evidence which seems to support his theory. Thus, when we are most involved and fascinated with something, we are actually stamping it into long-term memory.

Think about your mental state when you are learning the most and when you are most likely to remember something a long time. If you are listening to a close friend talk about an important problem, you do not have to take notes or repeat over and over again what they said in your mind to remember it--you just remember it. You remember it because you were interested in it and your brain automatically stored it away in long-term memory.

Think of other times when you remember well automatically--without studying-- watching a good movie, listening to a song you like, visiting a new city, or learning to ride a bike. To learn, get mentally involved in understanding the content of what you are learning and *integrate* it into what you already know, and then you do not need to study.

You can measure your learning and study efficiency by observing your emotions. When you are fascinated, you are in the zone of harmonious functioning and learning at a maximum rate. When you are too confused or anxious, you can't understand the content and therefore will not remember it well. When you are too bored or depressed, you will not remember the material

- It may be so old to you that no new learning takes place.
- Or, your learning rate may be so slow that you become bored. Most rote learning techniques are boring. Your boredom tells you what researchers in memory already have discovered--that most rote learning methods such as pure repetition are inefficient.
- A third cause of boredom is tuning out. If the material is confusing, you may tune-out-- leaving a vacuum of boredom.

Any strong emotional experiences may be remembered. Even when we may be having negative emotional reactions, some *other part* of our brain may be interested in understanding why we are having that negative experience (so we can avoid it in the future) and stamp it into long-term memory.

Can harmonious functioning occur when we are not learning or involved in a challenging task? Try to think of times that you feel happiest. What activities do you enjoy the most? According to the harmonious functioning theory, all these experiences involve some degree of harmonious functioning in neural networks (cognitive subsystems).

Activities I experience harmonious functioning in most often include tennis, skiing, sex, good conversations, reading, writing, listening to music, seeing a good movie, or appreciating a sunset. I am also happy when I observe that I have accomplished a goal, see that someone else is happy, or read that something good has happened in the world. I can see how each of these situations involves optimal matching between my cognitions (expectations, goals, knowledge, or skills) and some input situation.

Consider any of these activities. How can we apply the idea of harmonious functioning to listening to music? Think of times when you have enjoyed a piece of music the most. Remember when your emotions soared and your mind was filled with visions inspired by the music. It could be any type of music from rock to classical. Examine the actual mental associations, images, and thoughts which were elicited by the music. Note the amount of mental activity, cognitive processing, and *learning*. It was not textbook or

---

that may show the Anterior Cingulate Cortex (ACC) brain center has functions similar to those proposed by the Harmonious Functioning Model.

academic learning. Perhaps you never thought of listening to music as a form of learning, but from your brain's point of view--there is a whole orchestra of cells which are, indeed, processing information and learning.

However, the learning is often not just about music, we may associate the music with underlying life themes or other aspects of our life--giving the music important *meaning*. I still recall a night when I was 22 years old listening to a piece by Ravel. The next day I was leaving Oklahoma City, where I had spent my kindergarten through college years. I was moving to Claremont, California to begin attending the School of Theology. I realized that I was beginning a new phase of my life, and had many visions of the future which I associated with the music. The total experience of listening to that music, my visions, and looking up at the stars elicited a peak experience.

Compare the times when you reached your highest emotional levels with music to the times when you were either overstimulated or understimulated by it. During periods of *overstimulation*, the music may have sounded like noise. Just the way rock music or classical music sounds to the uninitiated. There is too much new input: the patterns are too unfamiliar for the cognitive system's ability to process it.

During periods of *understimulation*, the music is too repetitive or you've heard it too many times before. It provides too little new input; the patterns are too familiar to your cognitive system to generate learning. You feel bored.

If you are like me, you avoid listening to favorites too often, so that you won't get too saturated hearing them. Then the music can keep its freshness each time you hear it. That is a necessary condition for harmonious functioning. Listening to a song from a *new perspective* is another way to rekindle interest. It is our *cognitions* that must be fresh, not the just the input.

> **PRACTICE: Accept my challenge.** Take *any* activity or experience in which you felt peak happiness or involvement. Try to apply the harmonious functioning model to your experience. Think of how the input-cognitive processing match was within some optimal range. Compare it to similar, but overstimulating, experiences in which there was too much complexity, challenge, or newness. Then compare it to similar, but understimulating, experiences consisting of too little challenge, complexity, or newness.

INTRINSIC MOTIVATION, SELF-ESTEEM, AND PHYSICAL HEALTH ARE DELAYED OUTCOMES OF HARMONIOUS FUNCTIONING

The three *immediate* outcomes of harmonious functioning--peak learning, peak performance, and peak happiness--are usually followed by three *delayed* outcomes. These delayed outcomes are less certain, but can have powerful effects over time. These delayed outcomes include increased liking for the activity, increased self-esteem, and increased physical health. Increased liking for the activity *per se* causes us to want to do it more. [This increased liking for the activity *per se* is called intrinsic motivation).

HARMONIOUS FUNCTIONING DRIVES LIKING *UP*-- OVERSTIMULATION AND UNDERSTIMULATION DRIVE LIKING *DOWN*

For any activity, experience, object, or person, harmonious functioning increases our liking and overstimulation or understimulation decreases our liking. This is one of the most important principles of motivation and is at the bottom of most of our likes and dislikes.

Harmonious functioning increases our *liking* and intrinsic motivation. When we enjoy doing something, we will probably want to do it again. If we don't enjoy it, we probably won't. Enjoyable and meaningful activities become self-reinforcing or intrinsically motivated. We do them because we enjoy doing them. Research evidence from many types sources support this general hypothesis (Staats, 1968; Brehm, J. W. and Self, E. A.,1989).

> **PRACTICE: Compare activities you like to those you dislike.** Think about something with which you are fascinated. It could be watching a TV show or movie, listening to music, solving a puzzle, participating in a sport or interesting conversation, or it could be almost anything. Compare your motivation for doing one of those activities where you have functioned more in the zone to an activity that has been too confusing or too boring in the past.

Harmonious functioning and love. Harmonious functioning causes us to love its perceived causes. What activities do you love? What activities do you dislike? Compare the relative amount of time spent "in the zone" between those you love and those you dislike.

Sometimes the activity is more *exclusively mental*. We may be appreciating a sunset or be in tune with it. It may seem that we are being passive, but actually our mind is active and functioning harmoniously. Many passive activities we enjoy are like that-- music, reading, TV, concerts, absorbing nature, or people watching. We can come to love nature, art, music, or any of these events or activities associated with this mental activity of appreciating, learning, or absorbing.

Our feelings for another person can also be caused by our harmonious functioning when we are with them or thinking about them. When we are in harmony with the other person--having fun together, appreciating something about the other, communicating harmoniously, or having harmonious sex--then our feelings of closeness and attachment grow. These short-term feelings of closeness contribute to an *overall* feeling of love.

Why do people fall out of love? Clients often wonder why they no longer love someone they once adored. The cumulative effects of many small disharmonies can undermine a feeling of love--especially when they are not offset by positives. When we are in disharmony--feeling controlled, arguing, getting in a rut, being frustrated, feeling hurt, or feeling guilty--our feelings of distance grow. ("Distance" is another word for resentment.) Our overall feelings of love decrease.

Sherry and I have learned to pay careful attention to these little weak, daily feelings of closeness and distance. We know that over the long run they have a powerful effect on our overall feelings of love that we feel for each other. Whenever we feel distance (resentment), we usually take immediate steps to resolve the problem and get the closeness back. These daily feelings of closeness nurture our love and marriage. It really works! We have a marriage that is so special and feels so good, that we are both willing to be cooperative in order to keep that feeling alive.

We also teach our clients how to monitor and correct this emotional distance. Clients with relationship problems have often found this lesson to be one of the most valuable insights they have obtained from therapy.

TAKE RESPONSIBILITY FOR YOUR OWN INTEREST, LEARNING, AND MEMORY

Many of us believe that people are born to like or dislike math. Yet, math interest-- like all interests--is essentially learned. How? Look at your own experience. Do you like or dislike math? What experiences have you had that caused you to like or dislike math? I have often asked my classes these questions. Typically, half my students say they dislike math. They almost always tell of many bad experiences with it. Often the original cause was being in math situations which were too challenging for their current knowledge. Often the cause was never giving math a chance because they had heard others make negative comments about math or about their math abilities. By never getting involved, they remained bored and unskilled at math. Disharmonious functioning can produce a strong dislike of math even though it was not the math itself which caused the bad experiences. It was the lack of optimal learning conditions and optimal challenge.

I have often asked my classes how many people had radically changed their degree of interest in math. Many students had formerly disliked math and now love it. Usually, these students tell me that they began liking math as a result of *one* class in which they started doing well in math. In that class the challenge was more optimal than in the past.

One person told me that he had hated math all his life. He had been told by a high school teacher that he would never do well in math. Later, he took a college math class with an instructor who helped him understand math. He liked it so well he took a second math class. Today that person has a PhD in engineering and is an engineering professor. He loves math and is an expert!

Once we learn the harmonious functioning principles, we can function harmoniously doing almost anything (we believe in) that we formerly disliked. We can give up the old belief that the activity is inherently too negative, too difficult, or too boring. For example, we can give up the belief that our genetic math ability or intelligence is too deficient to like the math. Math interests and math skills are learned; maximum performance, learning, and interest result from reaching a state of harmonious functioning while learning math. We can learn to like and do almost any (constructive) activity well--if we create the proper learning conditions. I may say that I *don't* like something or *don't* do it well, but I never say that I *can't* like it or *can't* ever do it well. That belief needlessly lowers my self-confidence.

Examine activities where you lack motivation. Consider the example of students who lack motivation to study. Some students are confused and overwhelmed by the material and do not know how to overcome this confusion. They experience the big three negative outcomes of *overstimulation*--anxiety, low learning, and low performance. Other students mentally shut down either because they reject the material as too difficult or because they already know it too well. They experience the big three negative outcomes of *understimulation*--boredom, low learning, and low performance.

In either case, the student experiences a negative emotional reaction which becomes associated with studying that subject. This negative attitude may even undermine the student's enjoyment and motivation for studying *all* subjects. Ultimately the student may come to dread studying and become unmotivated. We often call this state, **burnout**. Has this happened to you in some activity? We can reverse burnout by getting back into the zone.

> **Instead of the word "burnout," use the word "unplugged."**
> **If you become unplugged, plug yourself back in**
> **by making the activity challenging again.**

If you are too CONFUSED studying or trying to learn new ideas:

• **Create a simple overview of the subparts**--such as a diagram or outline. Try making a diagram showing the major parts.
• **Break a complex problem into smaller, simpler parts.** Then cope with each part, one at a time.
• **Look up terms or concepts you are confused about.** Often a book uses terms that the author assumes we understand--and we don't. It may be from a previous chapter or course. If that happens, look it up--it is time well spent! Or as a last resort, get help from someone who is an expert or has done it successfully already.
• **If the input is too abstract, invent an example.** The more concrete and sensory-related the example, the easier it is to understand. Sensory, concrete data is the root of all knowledge and understanding.
• **Create a visual representation of an abstract or complex set of relationships.** For example, draw a diagram or try to map relationships. Or find an analogous real life working model. A teacher trying to show students how electricity works may use a plumbing analogy of water running through pipes. Mathematical symbols are understood better when graphed–graphing is a key to intuitively understanding math.
• **Use or create a story with meaning to organize and remember events occurring over time.** For example, make a mental movie of historical events in which you picture yourself as the star.
• **Use comparison and contrast to find the similarities and differences** between two ideas you are confused about. List all of the main features of each idea and compare the two ideas on each feature or dimension.
• **Relate to other theories or knowledge from other fields** that you know better. Often the same principles will apply and you cannot only understand the new area better, but you will be broadening and strengthening your own general theories.
• **Keep relating new information to both more concrete data *and* a more abstract overview.**

Use these tools to take responsibility for your own interest and learning. What do you do if something you are trying to learn is too difficult or boring? Do you take responsibility for your own interest and learning--or blame it on the teacher or book? People who have successful mental strategies for coping with too complex an input can get a more optimal match between the input and their mental abilities. Following are some methods *to simplify inputs that are too complex.*

We are building a **cognitive tree of knowledge** in our minds. The main branches are the more abstract concepts and the small branches are the more concrete concepts and sensory images. An example I often use is the biological tree of animals. The concept "animal" is at the top. At the next level are "mammals," "fish," "reptiles," etc., until we get to the more concrete levels of "dog," "cat," "snake," "trout," etc. Our brain contains many knowledge hierarchies such as this; because, it is such an efficient way to learn, remember, and use knowledge. That hierarchical knowledge tree is what understanding *is*. Building our own knowledge trees and building our own theories at a fun rate will keep us in a state of harmonious functioning much of the time.

We can also develop strategies to *generate stimulation and interest when the input is too slow, simple, or boring.* These strategies often depend upon our *adding* internally generated input to the situation. We can create our own thoughts or activities, which fill the gaps left by the understimulating activities or inputs. Choose how you feel by using one of these strategies.

If I am in a boring meeting, but cannot afford to mentally or physically leave, I follow the discussion and mentally associate it with related topics to increase my interest. I will think about the people involved, their communication styles, other approaches to solving the problems, or related topics. Viewing the situation from these other points of view not only makes the meetings more tolerable for me, but it also allows me to make contributions from these unique perspectives. When I start to get bored, I remind myself that *I will stay bored only if I choose to allow my mind to remain understimulated.*

If you are TOO BORED or UNINVOLVED in learning or doing a task,

• **Did you tune-out because the input was too complex, new, or confusing?** If so, admit it to yourself, and use methods such as those above to get yourself re-engaged with the input.
• **Focus on how unpleasant and unproductive the situation is to change it.** Would you rather be bored or use your mind to think of related topics?
• **Think about an unrelated interesting topic.** You can mentally escape by focusing on some unrelated, but mentally stimulating topic. However, you will not learn the topic at hand.
• **Generate your own associations with the topic.** Look at an old idea from a new perspective to immediately engage your interest or even humor. Think of a new way to use the information in your life. Or think of an interesting topic you can associate the current input with. Use the learning techniques suggested for difficult topics such as compare and contrast or generating your own examples.

Through mental skills such as these, we can create an optimal level of challenge for each task we are engaged in. This is how we can choose to be happy and effective in almost any learning situation. Once we experience these positive outcomes, we start looking forward to the activity that was formerly too stressful or too boring.

**Stress and boredom are not inherent to any input,
they occur in our minds and can be corrected in our minds.**

HARMONIOUS FUNCTIONING CAN INCREASE OUR SELF-ESTEEM—
PROLONGED NEGATIVE EMOTIONS CAN DECREASE IT

How do you feel after a state of harmonious functioning? Don't you notice that you feel mentally and even physically stronger? After being in the zone during any activity, we usually feel an increased sense of mastery over the activity or task. We feel stronger after we have struggled and made progress just to know that we have met the challenge.

When we are in a state of anxiety or boredom, we tend to feel less competent. Suppose Scott spends 80 percent of his life being in (or near) the zone versus 10 percent feeling bored and 10 percent anxious. On the other hand, suppose Jason spends 30 percent of his time in (or near) the zone, 30 percent anxious, and 40 percent bored. Think of the cumulative effects on their self-esteem and their overall happiness in life.

How much time are you spending in these three different states of being more in the zone versus overaroused or underaroused? What effects is it having on your self-esteem and happiness?

SHAQ Research Results: Learning Skills

Three of the 14 Academic Success scales were based upon the ideas in the Harmonious Functioning (HF) model of learning (listed below). The combined scales correlated with college GPA, .29. All 14 scales together correlated with college GPA, .46.

The three Harmonious Functioning-related learning scales follow:
1. **Build mental structures (theories, models,etc.).** This scale correlated with Happiness, .30; with Low Depression, .13; with Low Anxiety, .20; with Low Anger-Aggr, .13; with Relationships, .19; and with Health, .12; with Income, .17; with Education, .17; and with college GPA, .25.
2. **Underlying, review, mental mapping.** This scale correlated with Happiness, .36; with Low Depression, .16; with Low Anxiety, .27; with Low Anger-Aggr, .22; with Relationships, .25; and with Health, .21; with Income, .20; with Education, .27; and with college GPA, .27.
3. **Math, science interest underlying principles.** This scale correlated with Happiness, .22; with Low Depression, .18; with Low Anxiety, .09; with Low Anger-Aggr, .16; with Relationships, .10; and with Health, .12. with Income, .09; with Education, .10; and with college GPA, .18.

Though most people think of academic learning and emotions as being very separate phenomena, the HF model posits that we have one brain that doesn't radically separate academic situations from situations that people associate more with emotions. So it is no surprise that cognitive learning skills are also related to emotional well-being. Thinking well helps solve problems and improve learning of all types—including personal ones.

Note: For all correlations, p < .0001 and Ns ranged from 270 to 540.

PROLONGED HARMONIOUS FUNCTIONING IMPROVES PHYSICAL HEALTH-- PROLONGED NEGATIVE EMOTIONS DETERIORATE IT

Many studies have shown that prolonged negative emotions increase health risks for heart problems, cancer, and many other diseases. On the other hand, time spent in activities, which increase harmonious functioning in physical systems increase health. The epidemiologist Ralph Paffenbarger Jr. has studied the health of several thousand Harvard graduates for over 30 years. He has concluded that people who participated weekly in three hours of vigorous sports activities such as tennis cut their risk of death from all causes in half. Dr. James Blumenthal conducted a five-year study on 107 heart patients. He found that those who participated in weekly stress-management/group therapy meetings to reduce sadness, hostility, and anxiety had only a 9% heart attack rate compared to 21% who had daily exercise and 30% who had normal care. Being happy helps us to be healthy.

Anger, anxiety, and depression have negative effects on our immune system. We are only beginning to learn the beneficial effects of prolonged positive emotions. I believe that we will find many more. When our mind and body systems are functioning in harmony (the way they were "designed" to), then they tend to last. But when a system functions in disharmony or gets too little use, it deteriorates. "**Use it (right) or lose it**" seems to be an accurate summary of how every system in our mind and body works[25].

---

[25]   See Cohen, Sheldon and Herbert, Tracy (1996); Ader, Robert and Cohen, Nicholas (1993) for reviews of psychological factors effects on health.

HARMONIOUS FUNCTIONING (or not)
IS THE ROOT CAUSE OF ALL EMOTIONS

Learning how to maximize our time spent in harmonious functioning is one of the most important keys to happiness. Maslow's self-actualized people spent most of their time highly involved in what they were doing. Their ability to regulate their own harmonious functioning (emotions) may be one of the main reasons why they were so happy and successful.

THE HARMONIOUS FUNCTIONING MODEL EXPLAINS OUR EMOTIONS

A good example of the harmonious functioning principle is regulation of body temperature. The human body functions most harmoniously in the comfort zone of about 98.6 degrees Fahrenheit. If the body temperature gets too high or too low, all cells will die. The brain regulates our body temperature. It monitors body temperature and controls various body mechanisms--such as perspiration or metabolism rate--to lower or raise our body temperature.

For example, when the outdoor temperature rises to 110 degrees, lower brain centers cause us to feel too hot and to perspire. If the outdoor temperature lowers to 10 degrees, these brain centers cause us to shiver and feel too cold. They redistribute our blood away from our extremities so that our vital organs will stay warm enough to survive.

Higher brain centers (the cognitive brain) also help control body temperature. The conscious temperature discomfort is very functional, it causes the conscious part of our brains to pay attention to our body temperature and take actions to fix it. If we feel too hot, we can remove clothes or enter an air-conditioned building. If we feel too cold, we can put on a coat or stay indoors.

Our brains attempt to keep us in the comfort zone. The brain attempts to get mental control over the outdoor temperature. It has one bag of tricks to cope with temperatures that are too high and another bag of tricks to cope with temperatures that are too low.

The brain needs optimal stimulation and learning to be healthy. The brain has special needs of its own. Like the cells in our muscles, our brain cells need stimulation and exercise. Just as the body has an optimal temperature for optimal functioning, each part of the brain has an *optimal level of stimulation* for optimal functioning. In other words, each cognitive part of the brain has an *optimal level of learning or processing input* that keeps it maximally healthy and happy.

If it gets too hot--overwhelmed with too much input it cannot adequately process, it gets overstimulated and produces negative overarousal emotions such as anxiety or anger. If it gets too cold--too little input for its processing ability, then it produces negative underarousal emotions such as boredom or depression. To be happy we must keep an optimal level of *matching* between our *inputs* and our *abilities to process* them. Too little or too much matching is the brain mechanism at the root of unhappy emotions.

The harmonious functioning model provides a unifying explanation of all emotions. Being in the zone of harmonious functioning produces varying states of happiness--such as enthusiasm, love, joy, or peace. Being above the zone produces overarousal emotions such as anger, anxiety, guilt, or fear. Being below the zone produces underarousal emotions such as apathy, boredom, grief, or depression.

The zone of happiness ranges from peace and tranquility to exhilaration and ecstasy. When we are fresh, at peak energy levels, and have a highly challenging task such as a big tennis match or speech to give, being in the zone of harmonious functioning is at a much higher level of stimulation and arousal than being in the zone is at the end of the day.

At the end of the day lying on the couch with my head in Sherry's lap, a fire in the fireplace, and watching a good mystery on TV is being in the zone. "Being in the zone" covers a range of stimulation and arousal levels. It also depends upon a variety of conditions--such as my expectations, energy level, and the external situation.

EMOTIONS MAY HAVE BRIEF OR PROLONGED TIME SPANS

During any single hour or day, it is likely that all basic emotions will be felt at least briefly. These emotional variations are caused by variations in cognitive states. It is also theoretically possible to measure an emotion occurring at any instant or to mathematically sum the intensity and duration of any particular emotion over a specified time period. That summative or average measure for the hour, day, or even year would be an overall measure. Thus, it is possible to have brief moment-to-moment or long-term overall measures of any emotion. For example SHAQ's *Overall Happiness Scale* is designed to be a long-term average measure of huge numbers of actual happiness emotional responses over a long time period.

HARMONIOUS FUNCTIONING INCREASES VALUING
OF OBJECTS, ACTIVITIES, PEOPLE

The more we understand about *values*, the more we gain a tool for getting control of our happiness. The next few sections will show how closely the key concept of *values* is connected to the concept of *harmonious functioning*.

Happiness is caused by satisfaction of underlying values. In earlier chapters I stated that our happiness depends upon satisfying underlying values, and I gave examples of common values--such as desires for achievement, intimacy, money, independence, and security. However, I didn't say what I think causes us to learn these values in the first place.

The harmonious functioning model explains how values are learned. When I was in the second grade, I didn't know anything about baseball and didn't like or dislike baseball. I had little knowledge of it and did not *value* it. But Mom literally pushed me out the door and forced me to try out for the little league team. The coach taught me the rules and taught me how to play. At first, I didn't like it too well.

However, as I improved and began to function more harmoniously with the ball (I learned to throw, catch, and hit it), I began to enjoy playing with it. I also began to enjoy the social aspects as I functioned harmoniously with other team members. Within a year or so, baseball seemed like the most important value in my life. I wanted to be a big-league baseball player when I grew up. I kept that dream until the eleventh grade.

This story illustrates how baseball became an important value for me. My brain had associated baseball with harmonious functioning. There wasn't anything in my life where I felt as much in the zone as I did playing ball. Baseball--and nearly everything associated with it-- became a positive value. I loved playing baseball, I loved thinking about baseball, I even loved the smell of the grass.

Those stimuli all gave me happy feelings. The *underlying cause* of loving baseball was that my brain had learned that playing ball *meant* harmonious functioning. Harmonious functioning made me love baseball.

Each subpart has its own values and potential for harmonious functioning. As a boy, my inner baseball player had grown to be a big part of me. It developed a lot of expertise at baseball and its own set of values and goals. I no longer play ball. However, whenever I see a movie about baseball, the smell of the leather gloves, the sensations of pitching, and the excitement of the game all rush back. That role of baseball player is etched in my brain and still loves baseball, playing on a team, and the excitement of everyone focused on whether my next pitch will be a ball or a strike.

We consist of many subparts. Our **values** reflect our various subparts' desires. Happiness is the emotion we feel when these values are being met (i.e. when that subpart is in harmony). When *all* of our *active* cognitive subsystems [little people in our heads] are functioning in harmony at any one moment, then we feel happy for that moment. When these values are *not* being fulfilled, the feelings they cause are the feelings of unhappiness such as anxiety, anger, and depression.

MONITOR EMOTIONS TO GET BACK IN THE ZONE AND FEEL HAPPY

Emotions--even the negative ones like anxiety, anger, and depression--are *useful and normal*. They tell us about the states of our values, goals, and expectations. We each feel some degree of anxiety, anger, and depression *every day*.

Our emotions vary moment to moment. We all have periods in our lives--especially during transitions--when we feel prolonged, intense amounts of these emotions. That is also normal. Frequently, these intense emotional transition periods are periods that help produce our *greatest growth*. Therefore, they are periods of great opportunity.

Emotions serve as warning signals about underlying issues. The main positive function of the negative emotions is that they tell us that something is wrong. There is a mismatch or conflict going on in our cognitive system. Our goals, expectations, plans, perceptions of reality, or other thoughts aren't in harmony.

Some part of ourselves is *not getting its values met at the level it expects*. For example, if you are about to be laid off from your job, your inner financial manager (valuing money and your job), might feel threatened. Similarly, if someone you love starts giving subtle messages that he or she is tiring of the relationship; your inner lover might get upset. You may feel the negative emotions *before* becoming conscious of those subtle messages.

LEVEL of CHALLENGE:

EFFECTS:

"ABOVE THE ZONE" --

OVERSTIMULATION:
(Too Challenging, Complex, or Difficult--Overwhelms ability to understand or cope with input.)

* The IMPORTANCE of the underlying VALUES or biological NEEDS "raises the stakes" & increases arousal.

CONFUSION, SEARCH
1. Poor Learning
2. Poor Performance
3. **OVERAROUSAL EMOTIONS:**
   Anxiety, Confusion, Anger, etc
* Overwhelmed, confused, frantic. (negative) interfering thoughts.
* Runaway emotions cycle? (panic attacks, temper tantrums, etc.)

DELAYED EFFECTS:
* Dislike, Avoid, or Fear Activity
* Lower Confidence & Self-Esteem
* Lower Immune System & Health

"IN THE ZONE" of
HARMONIOUS FUNCTIONING:
(Optimally Challenging, System functioning "as it was designed" for maximum health)

Optimal MATCH between:
(1) **INPUT** Complexity, Difficulty, Newness, Danger, Ambiguity, etc

(2) **COPING ABILITY--**Skills, Knowledge, Understanding, Expectations, Goals, Beliefs, Ability to structure or cope with experience.

"BIG 3" OUTCOMES:
1. **Peak Learning**
2. **Peak Performance**
3. **Peak Interest & Happiness**
* Optimal Arousal & Energy
(Happiness zone varies from tranquil to highly excited states)

DELAYED EFFECTS:
* Value Activity (Intrinsic Interest)
* Confidence & Self-Esteem
* Physical Health (brain & body)

"BELOW THE ZONE"--
UNDERSTIMULATION:
(Too Little Challenge--Too simple, easy, redundant, limited growth potential)
* Often caused by:
  1-Loss & goallessness
  2-Avoidance of situations which are "above the zone" &produce too much anxiety.
  3-Too much structure or overcontrol of input.

TUNED-OUT, "NUMB"
1. Poor Learning
2. Poor Performance
3. **UNDERAROUSAL EMOTIONS:**
   Bored, depressed, grief, lonely
* Low energy, feel tired.
* Nothing seems interesting
* Runaway Emotions Cycle? (Deep depression, etc)

DELAYED EFFECTS:
* Dislike Activity, General Apathy
* Lower Confidence & Self-Esteem
* Lowered Immunity & Health

HARMONIOUS FUNCTIONING MODEL
of LEARNING, PERFORMANCE, and EMOTIONS
Tom G. Stevens PhD

FACTORS AFFECTING EMOTIONAL *INTENSITY*

Do you ever wonder why you feel an emotion so *intensely*? A client came into my office because he was feeling a great deal of anxiety and depression. His partner had just broken up with him, his college work had deteriorated, he had lost his job, his finances were a mess, and he couldn't sleep. The importance of the value, the number of values affected, and the immediacy of the value all can have *major effects* upon our emotions. In his case his career, relationship, finances, and sleep are all important values and the threats to them were current- -not sometime in the future.

KEY FACTORS AFFECTING EMOTIONAL INTENSITY

1. Importance of the values affected. How important is this one value to your overall happiness? The more important the value, the higher the emotional intensity.

2. Expectation and adaption levels of values affected. The higher your expectations and standards, the harder it is to meet them. Values, expectations, and goals are key aspects of the HF model and directly cause mental search, stimulation, and reinforcement. Adaption levels and novelty also cause varying degrees of search, stimulation, and reinforcement. For example a child used to poverty may feel very happy about receiving a used toy that a wealthy child would feel upset receiving.

3. Number of values affected. The greater the number of values, the greater the emotional intensity.

4. Immediacy (versus delay) of the values affected. The closer the deadline or event, the greater the emotional intensity.

5. Certainty of value satisfaction. The greater the certainty that it will be met, the happier we will be. The greater the certainty that we will *not* get the value met, the more depression or anger we may feel about it. The greater the uncertainty, the greater the anxiety. Certainty affects the type of emotion as well as the degree of emotional intensity (see Chapter 8).

6. Length of time value will be satisfied (or not). The longer the expected period of satisfaction or dissatisfaction, the greater the intensity.

7. Amount of understanding and planning related to getting the values met. The more we understand important aspects of the situation and the more confident we are in a clear plan to meet the value, the more confident and happier we will feel.

The less cognitive structure we have for coping with an important value situation, the greater the negative emotions--especially anxiety. In the next chapter, you will learn a variety of specific methods for gaining increased understanding and planning to get mental control of your emotions.

8. Classical conditioning (mental association). Cognitive responses can also become classically conditioned (associated) with emotional responses. An image of the ocean can lead to very different emotions for a surfer versus a person whose sister drowned there. Mental associations are powerful stimuli.

Mental associations may work in either direction. For example, research shows that people who become happy tend to generate more positive and less negative thoughts; while those who become depressed tend to do the opposite.

It is no wonder that he felt so much anxiety and depression, since he had little mental control over any of these important values when he first sat down. However, after looking at these situations and gaining more mental control, he felt much better. He achieved that mental control through increased understanding, making some decisions, changing some expectations, and developing some alternative plans. Within one hour he had increased mental control in all four areas and felt much more in control. To understand why you get so upset, it is important to consider each of the following seven factors which influence the intensity of your emotions. It is useful to memorize them (See box.)

UNDERSTAND YOUR KEY VALUES TO UNDERSTAND YOUR EMOTIONS

We have seen how functioning in the zone and satisfying values are essentially the same phenomena. We have seen how the seven factors listed below affect the intensity of our emotions. If you have not already done so, now would be a good time to begin exploring your own key values so that you can understand *why* you feel the emotions you feel, and so that you can get more conscious control over your values and therefore your emotions.

PRACTICE 1: Make your values checklist. If you have not done so already, (1) make a Values checklist of all your important values/needs for each area of your life--such as career/school, people, recreation, safety/health/physical activity, self-development, spiritual, and financial. (2) Include important activities, types of activities, and underlying, more general needs/values on your checklist. (3) Assess the relative importance of each value/need. (4) Assess how well each value is currently being met (relative to your own standards). (5) Begin problem-solving on needs/values that are not up to expectations. You can either modify expectations or modify what you are doing to meet that value.

PRACTICE 2: Understanding why you feel so bad--identify the factors that increase the emotion's intensity. Think of a problem that is upsetting you (perhaps more than you expect or think it should). Try the self-exploration method (Chapter 2) to identify the underlying issues that are bothering you. List which important values are being affected, denied, or threatened by the situation. Then consider the seven factors described above to understand why you are experiencing the emotion with such intensity. What are the important values? How many are being affected? What conflicts between values (and subparts) are occurring? How immediate and certain is the threat or problem? How long can the effect last?

WE CAN GET MENTAL CONTROL
OF HARMONIOUS FUNCTIONING AND EMOTIONS

The harmonious functioning model is a powerful idea for understanding how our mind processes inputs and how our emotions monitor that processing to reinforce us when we are in the zone and warn us when we are not. It unifies ideas from many areas of psychology. You can use it to gain control over your emotions (and life) in any area-- such as your career, academic life, relationships, self-development, health, or spiritual life.

In the next chapter I will present some powerful methods for getting mental control over your emotions. I use them almost every day with my own emotions or with my clients.

**We were designed to maximize learning and growth.
When the mind has optimal challenge and inner harmony,
it produces maximum learning, performance, and happiness.
Over time it produces maximum motivation, self-esteem, and health.
It is as if all the members of a great orchestra played in perfect harmony
to produce one great crescendo at the climax of a magnificent concerto.
Our Higher Selves can conduct our subparts
to focus our knowledge and energy
toward our best performance and keep us in the zone
of harmonious functioning--benefiting ourselves and others.**

CHAPTER 8

"RISE ABOVE" ANXIETY, ANGER, AND DEPRESSION:

ADJUST YOUR EMOTIONS LIKE A THERMOSTAT

\\\

MENTAL CONTROL INCREASES HOPE AND HAPPINESS

**Our thoughts can control our emotions
through external routes and internal routes.
The external route to happiness requires skilled actions and
cooperative forces in the external world.
The internal route to happiness is much more direct.
For those who believe their happiness
totally depends on conditions in the external world,
direct mental control over emotions seems magical.**

THE MAGIC OF MENTAL CONTROL

Clients come into my office with many types of problems. Many of these problems are about concerns over which they have no immediate external control. People worry about their relationships, careers, finances, addictions, health, and everything imaginable.

Some have almost given up hope and are seriously considering suicide. We can do nothing in one hour that will actually eliminate any of these external problems. We cannot reform partners, find a new job, or find sudden wealth. All we can do is think and talk.

Yet, amazingly, almost all of my clients leave my office feeling much better than when they came in. If they cannot immediately change the external causes which they believe cause their misery, then how can they immediately feel better? They can achieve more mental control of the situation and increase hope. Since mental control is the *most important* factor regulating emotions, clients can feel much better in less than an hour.

External conditions are important to our happiness; but most of the external conditions we assume to be essential, are not. When we *believe* that we cannot be happy unless the external world matches our desires, then we lose mental control.

The beliefs
(1) that *no particular external conditions* are essential for happiness and
(2) that we *can mentally control our emotions*
are foundations for mental control of emotions.

There are limits on external events, but no limits on thoughts. Real world events must stay planted in the ground, but our thoughts can soar. If we achieve *mental control over these thoughts and emotions,* then achieving control over the external events is not so important.

Two different clients faced two different tragic situations. These situations dramatically changed their lives. One--I will call Mary--developed an illness at age 19, which left her with no vision. Mary had loved visual beauty, reading, driving a car, going to movies and plays, and participating in many activities with her friends. She also loved her independence. After losing her sight, she could not even go for a walk by herself if it meant being in traffic; and her social contacts became much more limited.

There was no way that Mary could get her sight back--that was out of her control. She also had new limits in many life areas. She could never again drive a car, watch TV, or see a sunset. Although she had new limits to the real control she had over the external world, she discovered how to get *mental control over the situation and her emotions.*

Once Mary *believed* that she could find different routes to happiness, she began finding them. She found *new routes to happiness* in *old* activities she loved. She even learned how to "watch" TV and movies by listening and using her imagination. When she wanted to go for a scenic drive, she would ask people to describe the scenery and she would create mental images of what she saw. She continued to go with her friends to the same places. She even went to singles bars and danced.

She also found many *new routes* to happiness through a *new view of life, new activities, and an inner world* that she learned to love. She told me that her loss of sight had opened doors and created a world of opportunities previously unknown to her. It is ironic that she is so much happier than most people with normal vision. She brought light into my life and I will never forget her. She was so happy and radiant that she helped me see how even loss of sight can be overcome by living in harmony with our outer and inner worlds.

Too much *dependence upon others* means loss of mental control over our happiness. The other client, Nancy, also had a tragic loss. Her husband suddenly died. She had been extremely close to him; and had depended upon him as her main source of happiness in many life areas.

Nancy had feelings of helplessness, anxiety, and depression because she had *lost* control over much of her life. She had been so dependent upon her husband for taking care of her that she had little confidence she could take care of herself. She had developed a strong belief that he made her happy and had little confidence that she could make herself happy. Nancy believed that the center of control over her happiness was *external*--her husband--and not *internal.*

Deciding to take *responsibility for our own happiness* increases our mental control. To get mental control over her life she had to learn that she could make herself happy and develop realistic plans for getting her values satisfied. She learned how to do the scary things her husband had done for her such as pay the bills or get the car fixed.

She was feeling especially lonely and out of control when alone at home. Therefore, it became especially important for her to learn ways that she could make herself happy when she was at home alone. She found ways to entertain herself during times of the week when she had been used to doing things with her husband--such as Saturday night. Nancy changed expectations that she shouldn't be alone and thoughts that she was weird if she went out alone.

Understanding and planning establish mental control. *The essence of mental control is understanding and planning.* These are means of cognitively processing the input at an optimal level. Nancy worked on understanding the situation and its causes and on developing realistic plans for getting her values satisfied. Her *increased understanding and planning* gave her the mental control and relief she sought.

It was not necessary that she had not yet carried out those plans. Of course, once she did successfully complete her plans and get her values satisfied, then her confidence was strengthened even more.

Knowing the *limits* of mental control gives us more mental control. After reading this or other books about feeling happier, do you ever feel guilty because you aren't happier? You may have turned the ultimate concern of maximizing happiness into an expectation that you should feel happy all the time--or there is something wrong with you. That only leads to unproductive guilt. Aim for gradual improvement (with some backsliding) instead.

Mental control and hope. Does it seem like magic that--without any real world changes-- we can feel a lot better and still be honest with ourselves? It isn't magic, but it *is* powerful medicine! What is the essence of this magic? Perhaps it is realistic *hope.*

SIX HARMONIOUS THINKING MENTAL CONTROL STRATEGIES
TO "RISE ABOVE" ANXIETY, ANGER, AND DEPRESSION

**If one man conquer in battle a thousand times a thousand men,
and if another man conquer himself, he is the greatest of conquerors.**
(Gautama, the Buddha, *Dhammapada*)

Recall one of Victor Frankl's most miserable experiences in the Nazi concentration camp when he was able to psychologically remove himself from the situation and imagine himself lecturing about the experience. Suddenly, he felt much better.

One summer, Sherry and I were trying to summarize the essence of overcoming negative emotions, and we first created our "rising above" mental image. We decided that whenever we started feeling an unpleasant emotion, we would create a visual image of our bodies immersed in the muck of the difficult situation. Then we imagined our Higher Selves rising above the muck to a safe place. From this vantage point we could look down upon life's problems from the enlightened perspective of our Higher Selves. That image had a very calming effect. We have often used this image to bring calm to an otherwise stressful situation and get centered in our Higher Selves. This is just one example of a simple mental control technique that works for us.

Dr. Wayne Dyer tells the story of an airline flight attendant who felt constant stress from people making negative comments about the airline or service as they left the plane. The flight attendant felt personally attacked by their comments--even though the comments were not directed at her personally. She didn't know what to do.

Dr. Dyer told her that the people were really addressing her uniform and not her. He suggested that she imagine her uniform was like a suit of armor. Whenever anyone made a negative comment, she imagined the words bouncing off the armor. This image helped her keep a more positive attitude and control her stressful feelings.

There are many specific techniques that can help us get more mental control over our emotions. I have tried to refine them into their basic elements. The result is the following set of six Harmonious Thinking mental control strategies. Learn and use these six to lower your emotional temperature when it is too hot or raise it when it is too cold.

**The SIX HARMONIOUS THINKING mental control strategies
to RISE ABOVE negative emotions:[26]**

1. **C** HOICE--replace or accept and convert the situation?
2. **H** ARMONY of motives--resolve inner conflicts.
3. **U** NDERSTANDING--create a road map to success.
4. **G** OALS and EXPECTATIONS--adjust to keep the task *optimally challenging.*
5. **O** PTIMISM that you can be happy *no matter what happens.*
6. **F** OCUS--keep your eye on the ball.
Think of **CHUG-OF** to remember these six strategies.

We will now look at each of these six harmonious thinking strategies to rise above anxiety, anger, and depression and get into the zone of harmonious functioning. Get in touch with a real, complex emotional situation and relate these techniques to that problem as you study each.

Mental Control Strategy 1:
CHOICE of Episode: *Replace* it or *Convert* it?

When you feel negative emotions, examine your choices. *Do you have a choice of whether or not to be in this situation? What are your alternatives?*

TO CREATE HARMONIOUS FUNCTIONING *REPLACE OR CONVERT* ACTIVITIES

Let's revisit the question I asked on the first page of this book. How much of your time during a typical week is spent in a state of arousal that is too high--feeling anxiety, stress, resentment, frustration, guilt, or other emotions of overarousal? Is it 20%, 40%, 60%, 80%--or even more? Some people tell me that they are in this state over 80% of the time. How much of your time during a typical week is spent in a state of arousal that is too low--feeling bored, lonely, depressed, apathetic, tuned out, or unmotivated? Some people tell me they feel this way over 80% of the time.

In comparison, what percentage of your time is spent where your arousal level is in the zone of harmonious functioning–from peaceful and calm to joyous and jubilant? Do you feel confident and look forward to your activities?

Many people spend most of their time doing what they don't like and little time

---

[26] The Buddha's (Gautama's) eightfold path and my six Harmonious Thinking mental control methods have vague similarities, which those familiar with his teachings may notice. My six were not derived from or based upon his, but both stress mental control of emotions through some similar thought devices.

doing what they do like. How sad! What if we could transform our lives into more time spent doing what we really enjoy? What if we could spend 80 or 90% of our time in the harmonious functioning zone?

It may not sound possible, but it is! Sherry and I have greatly increased our own percentage of time in the zone by *replacing* or *converting* activities. We each are interested or happy in what we are doing at least 80% of our time. During the past few years, the biggest changes have occurred not so much from replacing activities as from *converting* them from stressful or boring ones into interesting ones. What have changed most are our thoughts--our mental control, involvement, and interest.

REPLACE ACTIVITIES TO GET MORE IN THE ZONE

You may assume that you have no choice but to do certain unpleasant activities, because they are necessary to accomplish important goals. One alternative to spending your time in unpleasant activities is to replace as many of these with *more enjoyable ways of accomplishing similar goals.*

When you question your assumptions, you may find that an unpleasant activity *serves no current high priority goals.* If so, consider eliminating it or consider spending less time doing it. When you begin to question your assumptions behind the "I have no choice" statement, you will find that you almost always have other choices.

Many people have eliminated or reduced time spent on unpleasant tasks. They minimize chores by moving from high-maintenance to low-maintenance homes, by planting low-maintenance plants, and by shopping infrequently. They minimize housework and teach children to do more for themselves.

ACTIVITIES TO HELP YOU GET EMOTIONAL CONTROL:

Many will work for both OVERAROUSAL or UNDERAROUSAL emotions!

- Talk with a person you feel good with
- Reading, TV, music, games, tapes
- Problem-solving, planning
- Help someone, acts of kindness caring for something
- *Plan* fun or interesting activities
- Relaxation techniques (such as progressive muscle relaxation)
- Growth or learning activities
- Explore a new place, idea, activity

- Physical exercise, dance, sports, walk, bike, swim
- Appreciating beauty or nature
- Massage, sexual activity (together or alone)
- Hobbies, plants, building, creating,

- Fantasizing, dreaming, playing with ideas
- Visualization of relaxing or positive scenes

- Making progress (1-step) on a big project
- Inspirational books or tapes

Good time-managers do the highest priority tasks (those with the most happiness and productivity payoffs) first, forcing themselves to do the low payoff activities in what little time is left. Sherry and I find that these methods give us much more time for activities like writing, tennis, going out, travel, and other things we love to do. (See O-PATSM self-management Chapter 9.)

Involving and enjoyable activities can help cope with negative emotions. One way to get control of your emotions is to get *more control over how you spend your time*. You can choose your environments and activities.

Evaluate every situation or activity you are in for its emotional effects on you. How do you feel afterward? Anxious? Resentful? Frustrated? Or another *overarousal* emotion? Do you feel depressed? Bored? Apathetic? Tired? Lonely? Sad? Or another underarousal emotion?

You have a lot of control over your schedule--no matter what you think. You have choices. Sprinkle in more activities that get you into the zone and add variety to your schedule. Try to achieve some balance in meeting different values, interests, and parts of yourself. You are unique and must find the combination of activities that works best for you.

> **PRACTICE: Make your own lists of emotional coping activities.**
> **A. Evaluate emotional effects of regular activities:** List every activity that you do regularly or spend a significant amount of time doing. On a scale of 0-100, rate how happy you are when you do it. Is the negative emotion an *overarousal* or *underarousal* emotion?
> **B. Make four lists:**
> (1) a list of stress-reducers to calm you when you are feeling overstimulated, overaroused emotions like anxiety, anger, or confusion;
> (2) a list of stimulators to get you mentally and physically more energetic, when you are feeling down, depressed, apathetic, tired, or lethargic; and
> (3) a list of activities that get you in the zone at almost any time. Make sure that you include items that you can do quickly, inexpensively, and alone.
> (4) List activities, thoughts, and/or people to *avoid* when you want to feel better.

CONVERT ACTIVITIES TO GET MORE IN THE ZONE

If you do not choose to get out of the situation (or replace the activity) to feel better, you can accept the situation and change how you *view* it or *cope* with it. In other words, you can *convert* the activity into an interesting one. Does that seem impossible with many tasks you hate?

Let's return to Victor Frankl's life in the Nazi concentration camps to see how he coped with the boredom and pain of minimal human existence. He wrote,

> **Almost in tears from pain (I had terrible sores on my feet from wearing torn shoes),**
> **I limped a few kilometers. . .to our work site. Very cold, bitter winds struck us.**
> **I kept thinking of the endless little problems of our miserable life.**
> **What would there be to eat tonight? If a piece of sausage came as an extra ration,**
> **should I exchange it for a piece of bread? . . .**
> **How could I get a piece of wire to replace . . .my shoelaces?**
> **I became disgusted with the state of affairs which compelled me, daily and hourly,**
> **to think of only such trivial things. I forced my thoughts to turn to another subject.**
> **Suddenly, I saw myself standing on the platform of a well-lit, warm and**
> **pleasant lecture room. In front of me I saw an attentive audience**
> **on comfortable upholstered seats. I was giving a lecture on the psychology**
> **of the concentration camp! All that oppressed me at that moment became objective,**
> **seen and described from the remote viewpoint of science.**
> ***By this method I succeeded somehow***
> ***in rising above the situation,*** **above the sufferings of the moment,**
> **and I observed them as if they were already of the past.**
> **Both I and my troubles became the object of an interesting psychoscientific study. . .**
> **Emotion, which is suffering, ceases to be suffering as soon as**
> **we form a clear and precise picture of it.**

It was how Dr. Frankl *thought* about the situation that was the critical difference. He switched from thoughts that *focused on the details of his misery*--trapped in its midst--to thoughts that came from *higher parts of himself*--such as his inner psychologist. When he switched into the role of thinking about the situation as a psychologist, it became *interesting*.

Dr. Frankl also found that to have positive emotions--such as hope--people must not only find their lives *interesting*, but also *meaningful or purposeful* in some higher sense. Thoughts that reflect *higher meaning* are therefore more helpful for overcoming negative life events.

> **The prisoner who had lost faith in the future--his future--was doomed.**
> **With his loss of belief in the future, he also lost his spiritual hold;**
> **he let himself decline and became the subject to mental and physical decay. . .**
> **Regarding our "provisional existence" as unreal was in itself an important factor**
> **in causing the prisoners to lose their hold on life; everything in a way**
> **became pointless. Such people forgot that**
> **often it is just such an exceptionally difficult external situation**
> **which gives man the opportunity to grow spiritually beyond himself. Instead**
> **of taking the camp's difficulties as a test of their inner strength,**
> **they did not take their life seriously and despised it as something**
> **of no consequence. . .Yet in reality, there was an opportunity and a challenge.**
> **One could make a victory of those experiences,**
> **turning life into an inner triumph, or one could ignore the challenge**
> **and simply vegetate, as did a majority of the prisoners.**
> **Any attempt at fighting the camp's psychopathological influence on the prisoner. . .**
> **had to aim at giving him a future goal to which he could look forward.**

Dr. Frankl's keen observations of hundreds of concentration camp prisoners can be a lesson for us all. Their external situations were similar. The factor that made the difference in their emotions was their thinking--finding positive meaning in a hostile environment.

Much time may be spent in unpleasant activities pursuing *important goals*. What activities do you dread? Going to work on Mondays? Doing household chores? Being with certain people? Doing some important project that can make a difference in your career? Looking for a better job? Facing a major decision? How much of your time is wasted dreading the future?

You may spend most of your unpleasant time pursuing important goals such as working, doing chores, commuting, caring for children, or obtaining a college degree. You may assume that these tasks *must remain unpleasant*. You may believe that you have an innate dislike of paperwork, doing the dishes, confronting people, studying math, going to meetings, or commuting. All of these activities may be important in order to meet important goals, but you *do not need to feel unhappy while you are doing them*.

The first step to convert these unpleasant activities into more pleasant ones is to realize that these feelings are *not innate or unchangeable*. Being closer to harmonious functioning immediately increases our enjoyment of the activity.

We can get into the zone for any activity. At one time, I didn't look forward to seeing certain clients, because I was not feeling as interested or challenged by what they were saying. I used to think that it was because I had seen too many clients with that type of problem. Now I realize that it is my responsibility to maintain my own interest, and that my own interest is a good predictor of progress in therapy.

My boredom is a *red flag* that something is wrong with what is happening in the counseling session. For example, I had a client who talked about her problems with her family one week, her problems with school the next, and something else the next. Yet it didn't seem that any of these problems were very upsetting to her. She was handling them all fairly well, and the sessions were ho- hum. I was not looking forward to seeing her, because it seemed our time was not productive.

In the past I probably would have continued focusing on these minor problems. However, I no longer do that. Now I look for a fresh approach. I told her I was feeling that something was wrong. I asked if she was really upset about these problems. She said that these problems weren't bothering her much, but that *something* was bothering her and she didn't know what it was.

She had only been talking about these more minor problems, because she had assumed they were the source of her unhappiness. Therefore, it was her *unhappiness with her life* that had brought her into therapy, not any of these minor problems.

That insight may seem small, but it was important and led to an entirely new direction in therapy, which we both suddenly became fascinated with. Her life lacked direction and meaning. She was having a great deal of inner conflict between wanting a life focused upon inner peace and happiness versus a life focused upon success, money, getting married, and having a family. Progress resolving that underlying conflict helped her feel more inner peace and confidence in all of the situations she had formerly been discussing.

This breakthrough happened when I took responsibility to convert my own feelings of boredom into interest (and not blame the client for my feelings).

Adjusting involvement, challenge, and complexity adjusts emotions. I first learned several mental control methods while working with students who were trying to improve their academic performance. Their main goal was to improve *their motivation, memory, and grades.* We learned that the best way to improve all three was getting out of the zones of confusion or boredom and into the zone of harmonious functioning.

As a by-product of using techniques to get *more mentally involved in the content and understand it at a deeper level*, I witnessed many students who had hated a class become genuinely interested in it. The class didn't change, the students did. They became much more mentally involved in the class.

These students learned to use their inner observer to monitor their emotions. If they felt highly interested, they were in the zone of harmonious functioning and maximizing their learning. If they felt too confused or anxious, they would use methods to get more understanding.

If they felt too bored, they would use methods to increase the involvement, challenge, or complexity of the studying. Thus, it is almost as if they were adjusting a thermostat to keep their interest (and therefore their learning) in the zone. We can either replace a situation or we can convert it to a more positive one by changing our thinking. Then you will be able to say,

No longer is the *situation* master of my emotions,
_I_ am master of my emotions.

PRACTICE: Practice *accepting and converting* situations or activities. (1) List at least three very unpleasant, boring, or stressful situations (or activities) that you will probably have to endure in the future. (2) What thoughts have you had in the past *during* those situations? (3) What negative thoughts have you had *about* the situations? (4) List thoughts that will help you *accept* the situations (find meaning in them). (5) List interesting thoughts you can have *during* the situation.

SUMMARY: MENTAL CONTROL STRATEGY 1: CHOICE,

No matter how bad the situation, you always have a choice.

The first choice is to *replace* the situation or to *accept and convert* it.

Consider replacing unpleasant situations.

Make a creative list of alternatives.

Otherwise, accept and convert the situation. Even if you cannot change the situation (or don't choose to),

you still have choices. You can choose to look at the situation negatively and keep thinking boring or stressful thoughts--like most people would.

Or, you can be like Victor Frankl,

and choose to find meaning and interesting thoughts.

Strategies 2-6 tell how to convert it. In short,

do what you enjoy or enjoy what you do!

Mental Control Strategy 2:
HARMONY of Motives: Resolve conflicts to increase motivation

"A house divided against itself cannot stand."--Abraham Lincoln

Have you ever noticed that after work on Monday you feel too tired to cook dinner or wash the laundry? Yet after work on Friday, you may have plenty of energy to go out for a fun evening and have fun until midnight. Where did all of this energy come from Friday that was not there Monday?

It came from your *natural motivation and enthusiasm*. It came from a harmony of motives that was present when you wholeheartedly wanted to go out and have fun Friday night. That energy was missing for doing the chores because you only *partly* wanted to do them. Another part of you was rebelling and refusing to cooperate. The result was a tired feeling based on *emotional underarousal*--not physical tiredness. When you feel tired--but have not performed hard work--don't think, "I'm too tired" think, "I'm feeling underaroused or mildly depressed."

To function in the zone of harmonious functioning, we must have *harmony of motives*. It is one thing to set a goal or write something on a to-do list, and quite another to actually do it--or to do it well. We may feel too stressed or too apathetic.

You may try to force yourself to do it anyway. However, that little person inside yourself that you are trying to force may resent your dominating methods--and get more stubborn. The only way you can generate wholehearted enthusiasm is to treat that resistant part with empathy and love. Give it a voice in the final decision.

HARMONIOUS POSITIVE ANTICIPATION:
LOOKING FORWARD TO THE ACTIVITY OR OUTCOME

Harmonious positive anticipation means that our inner parts are in harmony looking forward to an activity. If we are dreading the activity because some part anticipates being **understimulated**, we will feel bored or depressed at the thought of doing it. If we are dreading the activity because some part is afraid of being **overstimulated**, overwhelmed, or injured, then we will feel an overarousal emotion like anxiety.

Mental states affect mental and *physical* energy levels. Positive anticipation stimulates our *arousal systems*--bodily systems that increase or decrease mental and physical energy. This is a biological process. Hormones such as adrenaline are released into our blood causing our nervous system to become more energized. We become more mentally alert, our heart and breathing rates increase, and our muscles get more prepared to exert force.

When we are thinking about doing something fun or interesting, then these expectations produce positive emotions that increase mental and physical energy. They increase both our mental alertness and our physical energy. They prepare us for functioning both mentally and physically in the zone. That is why we get more energy after work Friday looking forward to a fun night.

The tiredness we felt when thinking about doing the laundry was actually mild depression or unhappiness. This anticipation of being *understimulated* reduced both our mental and physical energy systems and we felt tired. It is difficult to tell the difference between feelings of tiredness caused by negative expectations about an activity and genuine tiredness due to overexertion. Many people experience tiredness due to lack of interest so often and physical tiredness so infrequently, they completely confuse the two.

Another type of negative anticipation comes from anticipation of *overstimulation*. Anticipation of overwhelming or harmful situations causes emotions like anxiety or fear. This type of anticipation leads to too much arousal. Our heart, breathing, and thoughts may race at such a pace that we cannot relax, concentrate, and think clearly. Or, we may fear the outcome so much that we avoid an important task.

HARMONIOUS MOTIVATION VERSUS *CONFLICTED* MOTIVATION

Conflicted motivation is the waiter presenting me with a desert tray--filled with chocolate goodies-- when I am trying to watch my weight. It is looking at the clock and seeing that it is time to go play tennis when my writing has just begun to flow. It is feeling romantic with Sherry in the morning and seeing that it is time to go to work.

During conflicted motivation, we experience both positive and negative motivational forces toward doing the activity that we are attempting to focus on. We may *attempt* to perform the activity to the extent the positive forces outweigh the negative ones. However, the stronger these negative forces are, the more we will experience mixed motivation and be unable to feel happy and perform at a peak level.

Harmony between our inner subparts increases harmonious functioning. When our internal subparts are in harmony with each other and all agree, then we feel a great deal of positive anticipation. In the examples above, my inner parts did not agree. My inner gourmet was at odds with my inner health-care specialist. My inner writer conflicted with my inner tennis player. And my inner lover was upset with my inner psychologist.

No matter which activity I choose, *if I do not adequately cope with the feelings of the neglected part*, then I will feel less positive anticipation. To the degree that there is *unresolved conflict* between two subparts, then I will not feel harmony and positive anticipation, I will feel loss of mental control and anxiety.

SELF-EXPLORATION--THE FIRST STEP TO RISE ABOVE NEGATIVE EMOTIONS

When you feel a negative emotion and want to get control over it, the first step is to explore the emotion. *Follow the emotion to the underlying issues*--do not avoid it like many people do.

Taking time to self-explore creates more quality time and increases productivity. You may be thinking that you don't have *the extra time* it takes to settle conflicts between your inner parts. However, the *cost of conflicted motivation is not only feeling unhappy, but also significantly reducing performance*. The same underlying issues will keep interfering with your life day after day, unless you put them to rest.

Following our most intense emotions can help us identify important, underlying life problems. Use the self-exploration method for following your most intense emotions to identify underlying issues, conflicts, and problems. You may have learned habits to *avoid emotions and to avoid dealing with painful underlying problems*. Self-explore *now* if you are working though a problem using this chapter as an emotional repair manual.

(1) *Follow the strongest emotions.* The hotter your feeling, the closer to the fire causing it.

(2) *Accept these emotions and thoughts* as natural.

(3) *Accept yourself* as ok for having the feelings and thoughts. (See self-esteem Chapter 5).

(4) **Explore the associated images, thoughts, and underlying conflicts and beliefs, and pay more attention to thoughts that** *generate the most intense emotions*

(5) **Find new ways of resolving any problems.** Use your Higher Self beliefs as your Supreme Court for resolving conflicts (Chapter 3).

→ *Refer to Chapter 2 to review the self-exploration process in depth.*

RESOLVING ONE INNER CONFLICT BRINGS HARMONY TO MANY SITUATIONS

One inner conflict can spread to many situations and interfere with our harmonious functioning in all of them. Resolving one underlying conflict can increase harmony throughout our lives as the following example illustrates.

A common underlying conflict---Work versus Play. When I was in graduate school, one of my greatest conflicts was between work and helping others and play and having fun. Too often, when I worked, I felt resentment; and, too often, when I played, I felt guilty.

I explored the feelings of my inner helper and the feelings of my inner parts conflicting with it. My inner helper expected me to dedicate my whole life to my work. That dedicate all my time expectation was being reinforced by my peers and respected professors.

I explored my own philosophy of life and remembered my ultimate goal of happiness for myself and others. To be happy I knew I must listen to *all* parts of myself, find balance, and set limits on my work goals. My first attempt to resolve the problem was to divide my time between work and play.

My new rule of thumb was that I would work a maximum of about 50 hours per week (as efficiently as possible) to give what I could for others and provide an income for myself. That was all the time my achiever could have for work or impact on the world. The rest of the time I was free to focus on happiness for myself and my immediate family and friends.

I reached that agreement with myself many years ago. It has helped keep my work and personal life in balance, with little conflict, since. Lasting inner peace results from many such agreements between subparts.

REPLACE "SHOULDS" WITH NEW CHOICES

How often do you have a conflict between what you think you should or must do versus what you want to do? Many of us think we **have no choice** about a "should" or "must." Shoulds and musts usually come either from external authority figures or from *internalized* authority figures. Or they may come from commitments we refuse to question.

To replace "shoulds" focus on consequences and maximizing happiness. How do we replace a "should" or "must" with an "I want to?" Examine the *expected consequences* of your decisions and their *effects upon overall happiness for self and others*. Examine each alternate course of action and its possible consequences. Then choose the alternative that you estimate will lead to the greatest overall happiness (over time).

In this way you are always doing what you want. You never a need to refer to the words "should" or "must." [See internal control Chapter 6 to get more internal control of "shoulds."] Choosing the alternative *you believe will make you the happiest* gives you *natural* motivation to do it. You don't need to force yourself to do it or beat yourself up if you don't do it.

Replace "shoulds" by reexamining old commitments. Sometimes a should can result from an old decision or commitment--such as a career choice, marriage, decision to attend college, or commitment to take care of someone. I have had many clients who felt trapped by such old commitments.

Others felt guilty because they couldn't force themselves to do something they no longer believed in or can't see the reason for. When they made the decision, they may have thought it was forever, irrevocable, or 'til death do we part. When we feel a decision is irrevocable, part of us may feel trapped--especially if things turn sour.

A different point of view maintains that *life is a process of continually deciding*. No decision is necessarily permanent for one's *entire* future. Conditions change, and people change. It is impossible to predict the future and know what we will want in the future. Permanent commitments always have exceptions. It is better to honestly state them before the commitment is made. Even the Catholic Church recognizes reasons for ending a marriage.

I know professionals who feel trapped by their jobs. I do not. Almost every year I make a fresh decision whether or not to stay in my current job. Once I consider all the alternatives and decide to stay, then I appreciate my job more. It is almost like having a new job.

Once we make a free choice to remain in our job or marriage after an honest comparison to the alternatives, then we feel a new sense of freedom and appreciation for that situation. We no longer feel we are doing it without a choice and we get a renewed sense of motivation to make the most of it.

We may choose to remain in a situation where there are dire consequences for leaving it--which we find too unacceptable. It may be tempting to say that we have no choice in order to avoid the responsibility for choosing to stay in an unpleasant situation. However, saying that we have no choice subtly gives us a message that *we are weak and powerless*.

We still have many routes to happiness available *within that situation*. People who choose to remain in unhappy marriages or jobs can learn to be happy *even* in those situations. Think of Victor Frankl in the concentration camp when you think it is impossible to be happy in a situation. Instead, think of it as a challenge to your new ability to mentally control over your emotions.

Find the *right balance* to achieve harmony. We need balance between giving to others and giving to self, balance between short-term and long-term values, and balance between our different values and parts of ourselves.

We must each discover our own optimal balance levels. Some will focus more on themselves; and others will focus more on helping other people. Some will focus more on the present; and others, more on the future. Too much imbalance can lead to problems. Aristotle's famous *golden mean* stated that a key to wisdom and ethics was finding the right balance between extremes.

What do you do when there is a direct conflict between what is good for you and what is good for others? Some questions to ask yourself include: Which action would create the greatest happiness in the world? How much happiness do I give up in return for how much happiness others receive? Who is most responsible for taking care of the problem? I assume that each person is primarily responsible for their own happiness.

Conscious and thoughtful attention to these different types of balance contributes to inner harmony, because we cannot forget other people or our future needs. Parts of our mind constantly monitor other people's feelings and the future--whether we choose to focus on these issues or not. We can't hide from them, and we can't have inner peace without dealing with them.

USE POSITIVE CONSEQUENCES TO INCREASE MOTIVATION

How do you motivate yourself to do something you don't like to do? If examining inner motives doesn't give you enough motivation, what can you do next? A great deal of research has shown that making positive consequences dependent upon the desired behavior can increase motivation.

Years ago in college, I made a deal with myself that if I were caught up with my homework by Wednesday nights; I could go to the special 25 cent Wednesday Night Movie. Consequently, I studied furiously on Tuesdays and Wednesday afternoons.

We can use reinforcements such as pleasant activities, money, praise, privileges, tokens or points, freedom, responsibility, free time, or almost anything that we value. We can even make a formal contract with ourselves to change a regular habit. (*Warning:* in some circumstances artificial reinforcement contracts may backfire and reduce our motivation-- especially if we feel we are being controlled by others or some repressive part of ourselves.)[27]

Tharp and Watson's classic book, *Self-Directed Behavior Change* details how to use these techniques. I studied with these authors and they impressed me with the insights of this approach. However, I have discovered that while understanding the principle of reinforcement is very important, I rarely *explicitly* use behavior modification contracts to change behavior. I have found that--for the clients I see--most problems are more effectively overcome by changing knowledge, beliefs, and other cognitive structures using the methods suggested in this book.

Nevertheless, behavior modification methods using reinforcement and punishment can be effective in many situations--especially with young children. Therefore, I will not describe these methods in detail, but refer you to their book if you are more interested.

Use negative consequences to decrease motivation. We can also use negative consequences (or punishments) to get ourselves to reduce or eliminate behaviors. Punishment-oriented behavior modification methods can also be helpful in certain

---

[27] See Eisenberger and Cameron (1996) for a research review of how artificial rewards increase or decrease the intrinsic rewards of an activity.

situations. However, as a rule, negative consequences for undesired behaviors should be combined with positive consequences for alternate desired behaviors.

Use of punishment has several risks including stopping the self-change program or becoming self-abusive. If someone else administers the punishment, then punishment can lead to conflict and even dislike of the administrator.

Imagine **natural consequences.** In high school, Don had never seemed very motivated to work hard, be self-disciplined, or persist long at anything. Yet, suddenly, he began to run cross-country track for hours every day. I couldn't understand what motivated him and where he suddenly got such self-discipline. He said that he had decided he wanted to letter in track. When he got so tired he felt he would drop, he imagined a big letter "O" in front of him. He kept running to catch that letter "O." It worked--he finally caught that "O" when he lettered in track.

We can increase our motivation by imagining consequences. First, list all of the natural positive consequences of doing the desired behavior and all of the natural negative consequences of not doing it.

When you need to motivate yourself, vividly imagine one or more motivating consequences. You can use the same technique in reverse for getting yourself to stop doing something you want to stop. Using or imagining *natural* (positive and negative) consequences has few negative side-effects.

On the other hand, using *artificial* rewards or punishments occasionally has effects *opposite* those intended. Because we usually do not like arbitrary consequences and may feel controlled by them--even if we impose them upon ourselves. We usually feel less controlled knowing that imagined consequences are real world consequences--so they have more punch.

Out of sight, out of mind--overcoming delayed consequences. Many things we want in life are delayed or out of sight. Therefore, they lose their power to motivate us. We are much more motivated to work the day before the deadline than a month before it. Use visualization techniques to clearly imagine positive and negative outcomes that are important to you and raise your emotional levels. Vivid visualization can bring you out of apathy more effectively than just talking to yourself. Use words *and images!*

> **PRACTICE: Recognize negative anticipation and convert it to more positive anticipation.**
> (1) Think of situations in which your arousal is too low. From now on when you say that you are "too tired" to do something, try substituting "too depressed." Then if you still want to do it, think of ways to increase positive anticipation and decrease negative anticipation.
> (2) Explore your reluctant inner parts and give attention to their concerns. Find underlying common themes or issues--such as the work versus play issue. Make new agreements to make win--win solutions between the conflicting parts.
> (3) Visualize natural consequences of potential outcomes. If you are still having trouble, you may want to use reinforcements to increase your incentive.
> (4) Similarly, think of some situations where you think your arousal is too high for optimal motivation. If you are faced with too high arousal from anxiety or anger, use self-exploration and other methods listed here to resolve underlying conflicts.

SUMMARY: MENTAL CONTROL STRATEGY 2: HARMONY OF MOTIVES

If you feel apathetic or dread an important activity,
self-explore to find the source of the inner conflicts
between the parts that want to do it and those that don't.
To resolve these conflicts, refer to your *highest values* (such as overall happiness,
truth, and balance) to strike bargains between your inner parts.
Techniques such as *visualizing or modifying consequences* can also help.
Resolving *one* underlying conflict can make life happier in *many* situations.

Mental Control Strategy 3:
UNDERSTANDING:
Understand the situation and create *a road map to success*

As a child, I would become frightened or angry with my father when he would go into one of his tirades, call me names, or say whatever he could to make me feel as bad as possible. Today, we would call that psychological abuse. However, as a child I just knew it hurt a lot and I either felt guilty, hurt, or angry. Clearly, he was giving me input that was overwhelming to me. I didn't know how to cope with it effectively, so I felt upset.

With all this confusion in my mind, I needed a way to cognitively structure his verbiage (get mental control over it). I could not understand *why* he would get *so upset and abusive*. It was especially hard to understand, since mom never got abusive--no matter what I had done.

Eventually, I learned how to understand him better. I learned four major lessons about my anger toward him that have lasted throughout my life.

• *Boundaries of responsibility.* I may have made a mistake, but his *excessive* criticism and name-calling were due to *his problems* not mine. I wasn't more guilty just because he was more angry. His anger went far beyond my actual misdeeds.

• *He was punished by natural consequences.* Although I suffered from his verbal attacks, *he suffered more* from his temper than I did. It undermined his happiness throughout his life. That helped me lose my need to get even with him for his abuse.

• *He cared about me, but couldn't do any better.* Underneath all of his anger and abuse, he actually loved me a lot. The great irony was that it was partly *because he loved me* that he got so angry.

Part of his problem was that he didn't know how to be a good teacher. He thought that getting angry and making me feel bad would teach me a lesson so that I would grow up being the kind of person he thought would be best for me.

• *If he couldn't control me or important aspects of my life, I needn't fear him.* I never allowed myself to become too dependent upon him. Even though he often told me he wanted me to go into business with him someday, I never wanted to work with him. I set my own career goals independently.

After I **understood** these lessons about my dad and my anger, I could remain calm and effective even when he went into a tirade. His attacks rolled off me like water off a duck's back. I still loved him; however, I felt sorry for him, because he was suffering from his anger far more than I. The key to overcoming dad's abusive behavior was *understanding, empathy, acceptance, and control of my own values.* It came from a deeper understanding of my father--and of my own reactions to him.

A ROAD MAP TO SUCCESS--*HOW* DO WE GET WHAT WE WANT?

Satisfying values leads to happiness. We can think of satisfying each value (or goal) as a destination that we are attempting to reach. However, if we do not know the path to an important goal, then we will feel confused and anxious.

Knowledge, skills, and a plan of *how* to get there increase mental control. Marge's husband suddenly fell over in their living room grasping his chest. She panicked, "He must be having a heart attack, will he die?" She ran in all directions at once and felt helpless. Finally, she called 911. While she was waiting, she ran around in circles feeling her own heart would burst.

Our brains automatically know when *we know how to do something*. When the brain lacks adequate cognitive structure, complex inputs overwhelm it and the brain system becomes overstimulated. That causes overarousal emotions. Marge panicked because she didn't know how to cope with this vital episode.

If we feel overarousal emotions such as anxiety, anger, or confusion, then we need to *increase understanding and planning*. If Marge had had Cardio-Pulmonary-Resuscitation training, she would have been calmer--channeling her energy into CPR instead of running all around the house.

For really important events, greater advance knowledge and planning usually increase chances of success. Any team going into the Superbowl will have an elaborate game-plan and rehearsed different scenarios over and over again--until they feel thoroughly prepared.

Have others found the path? If so, *the path exists* and they can lead us. Do you doubt your ability to reach some important goal in your life? Have you partly given up hope that you can have the kind of job, marriage, or life that you really want? Perhaps you need to accept the reality of your current situation--or perhaps not.

What if that path to happiness exists, and all of this time you have simply not found it! One important question to ask yourself is, "Has anyone else found success and happiness in a similar situation?" No matter what the situation is, someone in the world has probably learned how to enjoy it--even cleaning toilets or doing taxes.

For example, my wife Sherry has a friend who hated washing dishes for many years. Then he tried to overcome his dislike. Her friend began to view dishwashing as an art form--cleaning each dish with care and admiring the result. He created beautiful mental images--such as recalling images of his dinners or friends he shared them with. He was so successful that he now values dishwashing as a special time to relax. Quite a reversal!

Once just one person *finds the road map to success and happiness,* we can potentially learn their secrets and apply them to our own situation. Many self-help organizations such as Alcoholics Anonymous were created by people who found the path to solving a deep problem.

AA has condensed its knowledge into a 12-step program. AA has been successful because people in recovery teach others how they did it. New members feel reassured by working with a sponsor who has already overcome many roadblocks to recovery.

EPISODE ANALYSIS CAN INCREASE OUR UNDERSTANDING AND SKILLS

During the hot summer, when I was seven years old, I loved to go to a local park in Oklahoma City. At the pool, I watched all the other kids swimming around in the deep (3 feet deep) water. I wanted to learn how to swim so badly; but no lessons were available, and I had no one to teach me.

Not knowing what else to do, I watched the other kids. First, I tried to figure out who the best swimmers were. They became my models. Then, I tried to analyze how they swam. I looked at how they moved their arms and legs. I tried to imitate their movements. I swam without breathing in the shallower part of the pool. One step at a time I learned to swim until I became pretty good.

Learning how to teach myself skills by watching expert models became a valuable skill in itself. I have learned golf, tennis, and skiing by watching experts or pictures of experts. As a teenager and young adult, I learned how to become more assertive and diplomatic by observing and analyzing people who had exceptional interpersonal skills.

Graduate students (under my supervision for their theses) made a series of self-instructional, Life Skills Training videotapes to help students learn various self-management and interpersonal skills. The interpersonal skills presented were often based upon careful observation and analysis of experts (with exceptional life skills) compared to average people. Our research showed how these tapes could help people who were shy and unassertive improve their skills and gain confidence.

**Compare the differences between experts and novices
to discover the secrets of how to be successful at any activity.
Do Episode Analysis to understand HOW.**

The EPISODE's three phases are the situation, the causal forces, and the outcome.[28] All activities can be analyzed as an episode consisting of three basic phases--the situation, the causal forces that occur in that situation, and the outcome. The **situation** is the state of the internal and external systems at the beginning of the episode. During the episode, various internal and external **causal forces** interact--producing some outcome. The **outcome** is defined as the state of the internal and external systems at the end of the episode.

Episodes may also include **goals, activities**, and the **outcome** relevant to each goal. The motivation and skill of the performer(s) are major causes of the outcome. However, they are not the only causes--many outside factors (often called luck) also intervene. In the game of tennis, the motivation and skills of the other player, the weather, the referee, and many other factors can affect the outcome of the match. Many of these forces are outside the control of the tennis player. We have seen how important it is to make clear *mental boundaries between what we can control and what we cannot control.*

The **episode** is everything that occurs during that time interval. In practice we are not able to perceive everything that occurs in a particular time interval, and we are not interested in everything that occurs. We can arbitrarily define what an episode consists of. For example the game of tennis consists of one match. A match usually consists of three sets. Sets consist of games and games consist of points. Points consist of strokes. So a tennis episode could be a stroke, point, game, set, or match--depending on the level of detail you want to analyze.

In a match episode, the *situation* is the state of the players and score at the beginning of the tennis match. The players are rested and ready to play and the score is zero (or love) for points, games, and sets. The *outcome* would be the state of the players at the end of the match--probably tired with one being a winner and the other a loser. There

---

[28] Dr. Donald Ford has written the 664-page *Humans as Self-Constructing Living Systems* (1987)--a theory of psychology in which he also makes episodes and their analysis a central idea. Independently, I arrived at similar conclusions and used the term episode in a monograph, Stevens (1986). I recommend his book for professionals desiring to learn more about the psychological systems point of view.

would also be a final score. From the point of view of the game, the final score is the most important outcome.

However, from the point of view of each player, other values are important. These outcomes include the enjoyment from playing tennis *per se,* how well I played, learning, socializing with others, and health benefits.

Causal analysis of the episode. To get a deeper understanding of an episode, look at the **causal forces** involved in the episode. Start with deciding *which outcomes* are most important to you. If you want to maximize your own performance, then focus on the *forces you can directly control--your own behavior and your own internal state.* Just as I learned to swim by watching the older kid experts, I learned to play tennis by watching frame-by-frame pictures of various tennis strokes, and read what the world's top tennis players and coaches said about how to hit the ball and what tactics to use.

I learned to play golf by watching frame-by-frame pictures of golf swings by top golfers. When I learned to ski, I bought a book called *World Cup Ski Techniques* which showed detailed frame-by-frame pictures of the top skiers in the world. It also explained principles of biomechanics, which helped me understand *why* certain movements were important. I have taken only a few lessons but have learned these sports well from self-help books and videotapes.

Good self-help books in any area will give detailed information about how to improve your performance in that area of your life. For example, learning the **CHUG-OF** and **O-PATSM** systems are examples in this book of step-by-step descriptions of key life skills.   You can decide which causal forces you want to look at. You can look at **specific** causal forces or **global** ones. Both are important. The novice will tend to focus more on the global aspects, while the expert will tend to focus on the details. But often the expert also needs to get a new view of the whole.

Analyze both external and internal causes. Use external, **behavioral task analysis** (such as analyzing tennis strokes or interpersonal interactions) to find which actions lead to successful outcomes. Actions are relatively easy to observe. However, other causal forces aren't as easy to observe. The thoughts, expectations, arousal states, and attentional focus of the players may have been important underlying factors that also influenced their level of play.

Use internal state analysis to find how internal conditions such as sensations, cognitive states, thoughts, emotions, and arousal conditions affect the outcomes. In this type of inquiry, we attempt to find out what is in the mind of the tennis player that produced the winning combination.

Use this SKILLS TRAINING PROCESS to improve performance for any skill in life. Whether you want to improve your skills in a sport, interpersonal situations, writing, math, self-management, or any other life area, the following process can help.

   (1) **Find the best proven experts to study.** Use books, videotapes, people you know, classes, individual instruction, or any method you can think of.

   (2) **Do episode analysis as described above.** Ideally, the experts will have done most of this for you and you can read the **key rules** and **step-by-step** analyses of how to do it. If not, do your own step-by-step analysis of what you observe the experts doing. Contrast them to your own behavior. Concentrate on identifying the key differences in behavior that make the biggest differences in outcomes.

   (3) **Experiment and practice, practice, practice.**

(4) Get feedback. Observe yourself, actively seek feedback from experts or others who observe you, try videotaping or audiotaping performances, and get feedback. When you are ready for your next lesson, go back to step one and recycle until you reach your personal goals.

PART OF OUR BRAIN AUTOMATICALLY DOES EPISODE ANALYSIS-- AND IT AUTOMATICALLY PRODUCES POWERFUL EXPECTATIONS!

What I described above was an example of *conscious, purposeful* episode analysis. However, our brain performs a type of *automatic episode analysis*--for which we often have little awareness. For example, when we meet another person for the first time, our mind automatically does a lot of information processing. Our cognitive system observes their dress, physical characteristics, body language, and the content of their speech and actions. It categorizes the person by their sex, ethnic origin, age, and personality characteristics. It gives us an almost instantaneous first impression of the person.

Our cognitive system also classifies the situation. Is it a business meeting with an important customer? Is it a potential situation leading to dating? Is this someone who might try to harm me or rob me? The *internal experts, thoughts, and behaviors* that are activated toward that person will be determined by what type of episode we anticipate this to be. We would not treat a potential robber the way we would a potential date or a potential client.

When automatic episode analysis is inadequate, *use conscious episode analysis.* In most daily life situations, our inner experts function so automatically that we barely notice them. However, when we are faced with an overly complex situation, then our inner experts become confused and we need *to apply conscious episode analysis methods.* Once we *understand* the episode better and develop a plan to deal with it, then we will *immediately feel more confident* and improve our chances for success.

UNDERSTANDING AT A HIGHER LEVEL--A MENTAL SAFETY NET

My client was a caring and warm person who would never harm anyone. Yet one night while walking home, a man of her own ethnic group wearing a hood brutally grabbed her and raped her. She came in for counseling because she was having terrible nightmares about being raped and because she had become afraid of men. She was terrified when men of her own ethnic group came near her--especially if they approached her from behind.

Though normally a nice, quiet woman, she was enraged. She had frequent fantasies about mutilating her assailant. She even thought of mutilating other men. Her rage was out of control and was causing her a great deal of unhappiness. The question she kept asking was, "Why? Why would he do this to me?"

It may seem obvious why she felt so afraid, but how could she get over her nightmares, her terror, and her anger? The key was her understanding of the situation. She could not understand why anyone would grab her, beat her up, and rape her. She had never known anyone who was capable of such deeds.

We had many issues to resolve. First, my client was worried about her own safety as never before. She needed to develop *plans* to get as much control over her own safety as possible. She took a self-defense class. However, her safety plans had only a small effect on her fear or anger.

If we cannot understand at a lower level, we can understand at a higher level. She wished that she could look inside the man who raped her and find out *why* he did it. Yet, she would probably never even find out who this man was. She had not seen him before, or since; and she had no idea who he was. Nevertheless, the question haunted her--"Why would he do that to me?"

She was not so upset about why this particular man would hurt her, but why anyone would hurt her so brutally--with no justification. She had done nothing to hurt him. This act had threatened her underlying core belief that the world is a fair place. Our core beliefs help hold our world together. When these higher level beliefs are threatened, then we experience greater overstimulation (such as anxiety and anger) than when lower level beliefs are threatened. To solve her problem, we looked at four higher level belief issues. We looked more at the issue of why anyone would brutally hurt or rape someone else.

(1) We looked at typical reasons *why men rape*--such as sexual gratification, domination, and hostility against women in general. We discussed scenarios about how someone could become a rapist. These discussions increased her understanding of why someone would rape her. She began to understand that the brutality was probably not directed at her personally, but directed more toward women in general.

(2) We questioned her *assumption that the world is a fair place*. She learned to accept that life often is *not fair*. She chose to view life and all we receive as a gift and replace the goal of fairness with the goals of growth and happiness.

(3) She learned that *psychological justice* can help balance the scales. She was enraged that this man would probably go unpunished by the law. However, she learned that any rapist is probably tormented for years--not by just his misdeeds. He must be a psychologically disturbed person to commit such a brutal act.

(4) Finally, she wanted to find some *higher level positive meaning* in this awful experience. Like Victor Frankl and the other prisoners at Auschwitz, she needed to find some positive meaning in her suffering to help ease her frustration and helpless feelings. She used her Christian perspective to look upon this experience as God's will for her to *learn new lessons about understanding and forgiveness*. She thought she was a wiser, stronger person because of these lessons.

After three sessions, she stopped having the nightmares, felt much more comfortable talking with men, and could even forgive her attacker. She felt sorry for him. Six months later, she was still sleeping well, friendly to men, and much happier.

Having a strong Higher Self and philosophy of life is our safety net. We need a well thought out, understanding, and positive Higher Self to deal with the dark side of life. Our philosophy of life and world view will color the meaning of every event. (See earlier chapters.) If we do not have strong Higher Selves, then we are like the high wire walker with no safety net.

We can inoculate *ourselves*–like taking a tetanus shot. Having already dealt in thought with issues such death, serious illness, poverty, violence, and injustice help us remain calm in the face of specific threats. Looking at these threats from functional higher level beliefs and a broader frame of reference gives us more mental control to process the threatening inputs.

> **In the midst of the night, when all is dark around me,**
> **and I look the monster in the face, it appears overwhelming.**
> **But when I bring it into the light of day,**
> **where I can also see the trees, the flowers, and the sky,**
> **I find that it isn't a monster at all--just my active imagination.**

PRACTICE: Look at a problem from a higher level of understanding and a broader frame of reference. Find an emotional problem that you have repeatedly tried to solve-- such as not being able to understand or forgive someone. Use your Higher Self beliefs to try to develop an empathetic, realistic understanding of the person. If you cannot form a positive, empathetic view from understanding that *particular* person, time, or problem; form a point of view that takes a *broader point of view*. Look at the problem over a broader frame of reference--a longer time frame, a larger number of people, or considers background factors which might have caused the event to happen.

SUMMARY: MENTAL CONTROL STRATEGY 3: UNDERSTANDING

Cognitive structure (such as knowledge and plans) reduces anxiety.
Also, understanding gives us power and control.
Episode analysis can help us build knowledge and skills for success.
If we cannot understand at a lower level of analysis,
then we can still understand at a higher, more philosophical, level.
High level understanding gives us a mental safety net and
is our best road map to success.

Cognitive Therapy of Anxiety and Depression Research Results

In their review of research on treatments of anxiety and depression, Steven D. Hollon, Michael O. Stewart, Daniel Strunk (2006) concluded, "Recent studies suggest that cognitive and behavioral interventions have enduring effects that reduce risk for subsequent symptom return following treatment termination. These enduring effects have been most clearly demonstrated with respect to depression and the anxiety disorders....No such enduring effects have been observed for the psychoactive medications, which appear to be largely palliative in nature. Other psychosocial interventions remain largely untested, although claims that they produce lasting change have long been made." As a therapist, I used primarily cognitive therapy techniques and this book and this chapter teaches you many of these powerful techniques that you can apply to yourself.

Exercise As An Effective Treatment For Depression and Anxiety
Studies have found that exercise alone is an effective treatment for depression. Babyak, *et. al.* (2000) found exercise as effective as medication for treating depression.

Mental Control Strategy 4:
GOALS AND EXPECTATIONS--Keep the activity *optimally challenging*

OPTIMAL EXPECTATIONS INCREASE HARMONIOUS FUNCTIONING

Our receptionist told me that I must see this student as soon as possible because she was crying and very upset. When I took her to my office and asked her what was wrong, she told me that she had made a "C" on a biology exam. I had seen many students who would be delighted at making a "C" on a biology exam. However, she explained that she was a senior and had a 4.0 grade average and she lived in terror that something might spoil her perfect grade average before she graduated next semester.

These fears had caused college to become a nightmare for her. The more she worried about losing her perfect 4.0, the more she dreaded school and studying. These fears and thoughts reduced her concentration and caused her to avoid studying--further increasing her fears. How could she get out of this negative cycle?

I asked her how she felt about her grades during previous semesters. She said that she felt ok about making 4.0 grades, but that it was nothing special. A 4.0 was just what she expected of herself. It was not her parents' expectations--only hers. How sad! There were over 30,000 other students at our university who would have been thrilled at making a 4.0 for even one semester--yet she could only be ok about it.

Her expectations were too high: her *minimum* expectations were to make *perfect* grades--all "A"s. She had boxed herself into a situation where she could never surpass her expectations, she could only barely meet them--or fall short. She had developed *expectations that created a high probability of unhappiness*--not only from grade pressures but from the resultant unbalanced life.

The solution was for her to examine the causes for her extremely high expectations and choose a new set of standards for herself. She decided that her overall happiness was more important than her grades. That decision helped her put her grades into a better perspective. Trading her *minimal expectations* from 4.0 and an *unbalanced life* to a 3.8 overall grade average [easy for her] and a *balanced life* was not lowering her expectations for her overall life. It was a trade off that *increased her overall happiness.* She felt immediate relief and made a number of related decisions about what she could do to start enjoying life more.

Expectations and our Frames of Reference. What causes us to have expectations that are too high or too low? One major factor is our frame of reference. A **frame of reference** is like a ruler. For example, someone growing up in a poor African country would not expect to have a TV, computer, car, and 3-bedroom suburban home as would someone growing up in the United States. Their frame of reference is very different.

A **reference group** is a group of people that we *identify with* (such as family, peer group, church, or team) and that we use as a frame of reference. One way we use reference groups is to measure our performance. For example, a baseball player will probably compare his batting average first to members of his own team, then to members of the league he is in. Let's see how reference groups can cause psychological and emotional problems.

We can *choose* a Frame of Reference that will bring inner harmony and maximize performance. A 37-year-old undergraduate student came in for counseling because he was unhappy with his academic performance and was experiencing too much test anxiety. He had felt pervasive anxiety and guilt for years. A large part of the problem stemmed from his reference group--his father and brothers. All three brothers and his father had received doctorates and were established in their professions by the time they were his age.

He felt under a severe time pressure to catch up with them. He said, "I feel as if I am 15 years behind where I should be." He feared that he would never catch up with them or be where he should be. The result was severe anxiety, depression, and anger at himself--even though he had more than a 3.5 grade average.

How could he overcome all this guilt? First, I challenged his reference group. Why should he compare himself to such an unusually high group of achievers--even if they were his own family? As long as he continued to do so, he would feel guilty, because he might never catch up with their success.

He learned to establish a new time line for events in his life. When he compared himself only to people in general (less than 30% ever get a college degree), he felt much better about himself. A better frame of reference was not *other people at* all--it was his *own realistic goals*. It was realistic for him to do well in college. It was not realistic for him to obtain a doctorate by the time his family members had. Afterwards, he felt as if a great weight had been lifted from him--a weight he had been carrying around for many years. In addition, then he did even better on his exams and enjoyed college more!

The frame of reference influences our emotional states and our performances. Normally, the selection of the frame of references is an automatic process. On the other hand, it is possible to *consciously select* the frame of reference (or reference group). We can confront an old expectation with a new expectation. Each time we choose the new expectation over the old--we reprogram our cognitive system until these *new expectations become fully automatic*.

> **PRACTICE: Examine your reference groups and important minimum expectations**. *How* do you *primarily* measure yourself and your success? Money, career success, number of friends, amount of pleasure and excitement? How much is important? What is their relative importance?
>
> *Who* do you compare yourself to--who are your *reference groups*? What do they expect of you and what pressures do you feel from them? How do you cope with them? If you are feeling too much stress from trying to meet reference group expectations, read the internal control Chapter 6. Developing more internal control by developing your own *conscious internal standards* is an important step in your journey toward self-actualization and happiness.

ADJUST *CHALLENGE* OF THE GOAL TO GET INTO THE ZONE

To be sure you hit the target, make the target that which you hit.

Recall (from Chapter 7) that a primary cause of harmonious functioning--peak learning, performance, and happiness--is an *optimally challenging activity*. *Overchallenge* causes overarousal emotions such as anxiety, guilt, fear, and anger. *Underchallenge* causes underarousal emotions such as boredom, sadness, depression, and apathy. Therefore, to get into the zone of harmonious functioning--and happiness--*optimize goal challenge*.

If you are too anxious and overchallenged, change your goals to make reaching them easier. If you are too bored and underchallenged, change your goals to make them more difficult and challenging. Learn how to set *realistic and optimally challenging goals*--it is a key to happiness. I probably use this mental control strategy more than any other (with myself and with clients).

A powerful source of arousal is *uncertainty about important outcomes.* A client said to me, "I'd rather she just leave me, than leave me dangling on a string." Uncertainty--not knowing about important outcomes--can be a major source of anxiety and arousal. Not knowing whether we will be rich or poor, happily married or alone, or alive or dead can create high stress. How could my client get more certainty and mental control--when the decision to be together seemed to be all hers?

Focus on *more certain and controllable* aspects to *lower* arousal. The client dangling on a string felt that way because he believed that *she had all the control over his life and emotions*. Her acceptance or rejection of him was like life and death--and it was in *her* control. However, his *belief* that his happiness depended on her decision *gave* her that control over his emotions.

224 / Dr. Tom G. Stevens

My goal was to help him take back control of his emotions--by understanding that his happiness was in *his* hands, not *hers*. For example, I asked him to question whether or not *he wanted her!* He realized that he had actually been much happier alone than in the extreme highs and lows of this relationship. He focused more on the negative aspects of the relationship and all the pain it had brought him. He realized that he might eventually *choose* to end the relationship. That insight boosted his mental control. Gradually, as he got more mental control, he felt much better. He said, "My self-esteem is so much better I can't believe it. I wondered if I'd ever feel this good about myself again."

In sports, many athletes get very upset with themselves when they perform poorly, get behind, or lose. Yet berating themselves tends to undermine their concentration, alienate other players, and leave them feeling stressed out. In my tennis, I had to learn that my overall goal is to enjoy playing. I also like to play my best and I like to win. Years ago, I almost quit tennis because my focus on winning interfered with enjoyment. It also eroded my performance. Now, I can adjust my arousal like a thermostat by adjusting my goals and what I say to myself. If I play poorly, or get behind in a match with a player I think I should beat, I may start to get upset. Recently, I was playing the top player in a league we were in. Previously, I had never won even a set from him. He was ahead 4 games to 0 in the first set and was ahead serving 40-love in the fifth game. I was upset with myself because I thought I had blown opportunities to win all four games.

I reminded myself that I needed to focus on enjoying the game and *on the ball*--not on the score or past mistakes. I won that game and the next four. Once ahead, when serving for the set, I started focusing *on the score* again and got anxious that I might blow my lead. Sure enough, I lost that game and he got ahead 3-1 in the tiebreaker. I again reminded myself to love the ball. My performance immediately improved and I won the set!

I could not control the score, only my thoughts and actions. By making the more controllable (and more certain) aspects of the situation my primary goal, I got more mental control. Anytime overarousal interferes with your comfort or performance, *focus on more certain and controllable aspects* of the situation to get more mental control.

Focus on *less certain and less controllable* aspects to *raise* arousal. What do we do if we are feeling bored, apathetic, or overconfident? If our arousal is too low, we can raise it by focusing on more *uncertain* or *uncontrollable* aspects of the situation.

Sometimes my arousal is too low to play tennis well. I might get overconfident or tired. If my arousal gets *too low*, then I can *increase the challenge*. If I get overconfident, I can remind myself that in one match I was ahead 5 games to 0 and lost *7 straight games* to lose the set. Another way to increase challenge is to increase my goal from just winning to winning by a large margin--such as 6-1.

The same principle that works for increasing arousal in tennis also works for increasing arousal in other life areas. A client came in because she had been depressed for several years. Her time each week was filled with work, study, child care, and housework. She had lots to do; but to her, it was all routine--one endless stream of waiting tables, books, diapers, and dishes. Worse, she *viewed her life* as one endless stream of humdrum activities. She wasn't having any fun--and didn't believe fun was even *possible*.

She needed to make her activities more challenging, unique, and creative. For example, instead of seeing every customer as a faceless blob, she began to look for the uniqueness in each one. She set goals to learn something from each customer and to bring a little joy to each customer. She set goals to find meaning in every text chapter, to have more fun with her child, and to make her home a place of beauty and warmth. She also prioritized her activities and *added time* for more fun activities while subtracting time from some routine chores.

Where my client had found a humdrum schedule of chores, she now found stimulation and challenge. Where she had seen only faceless, demanding customers, she now saw unique human beings. For her creative efforts, she received a more joyous life.

ADJUST THE LAPDS GOAL DIMENSIONS TO ADJUST AROUSAL

Following are five methods for adjusting goal challenge to increase or decrease emotional arousal. If you are *overaroused or overchallenged*, try using the methods in the first column. If you are *underaroused or underchallenged*, try using the methods in the second column. (See LAPDS box.)

In the sections below I will describe each of these five methods in more depth. First, we will look at the five methods for *reducing overarousal and increasing calmness*. Then we will examine methods for *increasing arousal*.

FIVE GOAL CHANGE METHODS TO LOWER ANXIETY AND STRESS

What is the most common complaint of clients? Too much stress and anxiety. Think of anxiety as the emotional component of stress. Anxiety is a national problem affecting both mental and physical health.

THE 5 LAPDS GOAL-EXPECTATION DIMENSIONS TO ADJUST CHALLENGE

To DECREASE emotional arousal and reduce stress, anxiety, and anger: (Decrease challenge, uncertainty, and attachment)		To INCREASE emotional arousal and reduce boredom and depression: (Increase challenge, uncertainty, and attachment)
(1) Lower goal and expectation LEVELS	<=>	Raise goal and expectation LEVELS
(2) Develop ALTERNATIVE goals & plans	<=>	Become MORE ATTACHED to one goal or plan
(3) Focus on PROCESS goals	<=>	Focus on OUTCOME goals
(4) Focus on DYNAMIC, growth-oriented goals	<=>	Focus on STATIC, "one-shot" goals
(5) Focus on SIMPLE, SMALL-STEP goals	<=>	Focus on COMPLEX, LARGE-STEP goals

[To remember the five goal dimensions in the left column, think of LAPDS -- the Los Angeles Police DepartmentS to help you remember Levels, Alternatives, Process, Dynamic, and Simple.]

Recall that harmonious functioning is caused by optimal challenge between a situation and the ability to cope with it. The root cause of overarousal emotions like anxiety and anger is that the challenge is *too great*. We feel overwhelmed (or scared) that we will not meet our basic goals or expectations. Therefore, adjusting our goals and expectations in ways that *reduce the challenge* help reduce anxiety.

The methods I am about to present are extremely effective for *immediately reducing stress and anxiety*--even when nothing can be done in your immediate environment. Clients feel much better within the course of an hour--the first session! For these reasons, I am devoting more space to these five powerful methods for controlling stress by changing goals and expectations. *Learn them well and practice them often!*

(1) Lower goal and expectation LEVELS. One way to reduce the challenge and anxiety is to *lower our goals*. The student I described who was crying over her first "C" grade lowered her expectations from, "I always have to make an 'A' in every class and finish college with a perfect 4.0 grade average." This gave her immediate relief.

Make MULTIPLE goal and expectation levels. This student decided that she still *ideally* wanted to make a 4.0 grade average. For her this was a realistic goal, since she was a senior with a perfect 4.0 for all her work so far. It was not necessary to change that goal as a *preferred target* goal.

The problem was more that she felt she had to make a 4.0. That was her *minimal expectation* for which she could be happy with herself. I sometimes call that our bottom-line or minimal expectations goal. It is often this type of goal which causes the most emotional upset.

She worked on setting a new minimal expectation for herself that was much more tolerant. Her bottom-line goal was to learn, get a degree, and get into the occupation she wanted. She also worked on appreciating how much she had already accomplished relative to those goals. Consequently, she was happier and no longer terrified at the thought of making a lower grade.

The link between too high expectations and depression. Overly high expectations are a common problem--especially among people suffering from depression. The reason people with too high expectations often get depressed is that when they perceive that they are failing, they tend to shut down--give up or withdraw. When that happens, they essentially reset their goals or expectations to low levels and go rapidly from anxiety (an overarousal emotion) to depression (an underarousal emotion--often connected with goallessness--see later section).

If you set goals and expectations that are too high, you are setting yourself up for failure and depression. If you also tend to beat yourself up when you do not meet your goals, then that will exacerbate the depression and lower self-esteem even more. (See Chapter 5 self-acceptance section.)

When you are feeling under too much stress or pressure, self-explore to see what your underlying goals and expectations are. Perhaps you need to lower their level-- especially the level of your bottom-line goals.

(2) Make ALTERNATE goals and plans to increase calmness. Developing alternate goals and plans is one of the most useful tools I have found for reducing anxiety. When we have no alternate goals (or plans) to get underlying values met, we face the black hole of the unknown.

A cosmic **black hole** is dead star. It has tremendous energy--affecting everything around it. A cosmic black hole can even suck in neighboring stars larger than our sun. So it is with an emotional black hole. It is a source of great emotional energy--usually anxiety. We work hard to avoid it, to cover it up, and to deal with its negative emotional effects. It is not only a powerful force in itself; it also interferes with many positive activities.

An emotional black hole is a hole in our planning. For example, a pre-med student was suffering from very high anxiety. It was interfering with his studies, his relationship, and his whole life. His dream since childhood had been to be a physician, yet he was scared to death that he wouldn't ever get admitted to medical school.

I asked him what he would do if he didn't get admitted; and he replied, "I can't stand to even think about the possibility of not getting admitted--it's too awful to think about." He also said, "I don't want to think about the possibility of failure, because that kind of negative thinking makes failure more likely."

I believe the opposite was true--he needed to face his black hole, not avoid it. His black hole--no alternative plans or mental structure--was the cause of his anxiety. He needed alternate plans B, C, etc. to cover the real possibility that he might never be accepted into medical school. His black hole created so much anxiety that it not only made him miserable, but it also interfered with his studies and *decreased* his chances of getting into medical school.

To eliminate his black hole, he had to *face the worst possible outcomes* and *develop acceptable alternative plans.* Once he developed alternate career plans to cover almost any possibility, he felt much better and could study effectively again.

> **PRACTICE: Fill your black holes with well-thought-out,** *acceptable alternate plans to* *cover the worst possibilities.* Systematically consider each important life area such as career, relationships, family, being alone, health, finances, and recreation. What are your greatest fears and anxieties? Face the *worst possibilities--your black holes.* Find *acceptable* alternative scenarios or plans that seem to cover all the bases. Develop not only Plan A, but Plan B, and some minimally acceptable Survival plan. What makes an alternative acceptable is believing that it will meet your basic values and create at *least a minimally happy life.*

Being too attached to one alternative causes tunnel vision and magnifies stress. I see many clients who have been rejected by their partner in a marriage or other primary relationship. A common problem is that the client feels as if they will never get over the loss of their partner. These clients often dream and fantasize about their ex-partner for months--even years--after the separation. The underlying problem behind this grief and fear is often that they have become too attached to their partner in several respects.

For example, a 40-year-old woman client had initiated a breakup; but had been extremely anxious over this on-again, off-again relationship for about 2 years. She was addicted to him--constantly thinking and talking about her ex-partner and their relationship. She kept getting fantasies about her ex-partner even when she would date other men. She was desperate--she even moved to a different city just to forget him. What was the problem? Why couldn't she get mental control over her emotions?

She couldn't get mental control because she believed that he was *the only man she could ever be happy with.* In the many years she had dated, he was the only one she had ever felt so in love with. She also believed that she *had to get married to be happy.* In other words she had painted herself into a corner--her beliefs gave her no way out! She believed that her *only route to happiness* was to be in a relationship with this man.

Yet she had left him, because she was so unhappy when she was with him! Clearly, she was miserable with him and miserable without him. I told her that as long as she believed he was her only route to happiness, she would continue to be miserable. The only solution to her problem was to realize that she had many other potential routes to a happy life. She could be happy--even happier--with another man. And even more importantly, she could learn to be a happy person living alone.

What was going on here? Let's look at this from a different perspective. There were many subparts that were in conflict. One part wanted a happy relationship and good sexual relationship. That part kept producing fantasies--including highly sexual ones. Since her most recent and positive sexual experiences had been with her former partner, the mind produced fantasies with him as the male partner. From these persistent fantasies my client concluded that some part of her was so attached to her former partner that she could never let go. She concluded that she could be happy with another man.

We needed to reduce her attachment. We looked at this assumption that she could only be happy and sexually satisfied with him. This fantasizing was normal behavior. Many who end a relationship continue to fantasize about their ex-partners. Our brain will often keep focusing on a past object until it finds a new one that meets the same values and desires. I told her the story of how men in a starvation experiment constantly dreamed, fantasized, thought, and talked of food.

She could find a new alternative goal by fantasizing about other men--even movie stars or an imaginary future partner. She began to realize that she was not so attached to her *former partner* as to her *values* for sex and companionship.

Her new realization was that her general underlying values were more important than any one route to getting them satisfied. Thus, she made her primary goal getting those underlying values satisfied. *Who* the particular man she might be happy with was secondary. She began to consciously say to herself that what she really wanted was "good sex and a good man"--not her former partner.

This insight helped free her of obsessive thoughts and attachment for her ex-partner. Reminding herself of the unpleasant experiences causing her to leave him in the first place also helped her quit thinking about him. She also learned new ways to make herself happy alone or with others.

(3) Focus on *PROCESS goals* to increase calmness. What is the difference between the first and second types of goals in each of the following pairs? Would you feel more *confident* about achieving the first goal or the second in each pair?

•Do my best	vs. Win	•Interview for a job	vs. Get a job
•Be friendly	vs. Be liked	•Work hard	vs. Get promoted
•Study hard	vs. Make high grades	•Focus on the ball	vs. Hit a home run
•Make the pitch	vs. Make the sale	•Competence	vs. Career success

The first items in each pair are process goals and the second items are outcome goals. Notice how much *more control* we have of process goals than outcome goals. **Process goals** are about what we *think or do* as opposed to outcome goals. **Outcome goals** are about what happens outside us or what happens as a result of our actions.[29] External outcome goals are about changes in our environment. Internal outcome goals are about changes in us that we cannot *directly* control such as changes in bodily functions, health, or distant learning goals. Outcome goals are we *hope* will take place as a result of choosing our thoughts and actions.

We have a high degree of control over our thoughts and behavior. However, we do not have total control over the external environment. Each external event is a *multicaused* event. We may control some--but never all--of those causes. We cannot control what other people do, what nature does, what the economy does, or what the government does. We can only take actions that *might* result in the intended outcomes. Whenever we choose a primary goal that is too far out of our control, we *immediately create excess anxiety.* Thus, whenever you choose an outcome goal as a primary goal, you are probably increasing the pressure you put on yourself.

---

[29] Process goals are similar to **behavioral goals**. In many cases they are the same. However, when I use the word process goal here, I mean any thought, action, other process *within the actor's own control.* The process goal can also be an end in itself--in which case it may also become the outcome goal. However, normally the process is the means to some separate outcome.

Choosing process versus outcome goals is another effective method for adjusting our arousal and emotions like adjusting a thermostat. If it's too hot (the pressure is too high), focus on process goals. If it's too cold (you are apathetic), turn up the heat by focusing on outcome goals. For example, I have worked with many students who were shy about meeting new people--especially people of the opposite sex. Many of these students lacked experience and some of the social skills needed to be successful. Initially, the less experienced students' chances of getting negative reactions were high.

However, the type of goals and expectations they set made a critical difference between feeling good about the experience of meeting people--or giving up. If they set an outcome goal such as getting a date, they immediately felt anxious. Their anxiety often caused them to become tongue-tied or overtly nervous--making them appear awkward and unconfident. In addition, they often got discouraged after being rejected. They feel anxious because their goals were outcome goals over which they had *little control* and had *little chance of meeting*. Instead, they can reduce their nervousness (and increase their confidence) by focusing upon process goals--which they *can* control.

I encourage these clients to set goals for their own behavior--such as meeting and talking with a new person, self-disclosing personal information, or using a reflective listening method to get more personal. They focus on goals like enjoying the experience and learning from it--so they will be better in the future. Focusing on process goals increases their calmness and confidence.

Process goals can increase the person's chances of performing in the zone when they are feeling too anxious. Process goals can be especially useful *in situations where the realistic chances of meeting the outcome goals are not high*. Reaching difficult and remote goals usually requires a great deal of motivation, energy, and work and time. Goals like making habit or personality changes, completing a major project, writing a book, starting a business, becoming a professional artist or athlete, or getting a college degree require an enormous amount of work.

To be successful reaching these difficult goals requires positive reinforcement along the path. Few people can persist indefinitely without some feeling of success. Reaching process goals and intermediate outcome goals provide the reinforcement we need to keep persisting. Keeping ourselves in the zone (happier) helps us persist.

Good managers can also use process goals effectively with their team members--especially if team members think outcomes aren't in their control.

I will not take responsibility for any factor over which I do not have control. I will try to let go of a sense of responsibility for those factors or events which I cannot control. Therefore, I will choose as my primary and immediate goals the thoughts and actions I can control. These are process goals. Try using them more--especially when you have less control over the outcomes.

The Process-Outcome Cycle. Although we cannot completely control any external outcomes, we can influence many of them. If we follow the responsibility follows control rule, then we will take responsibility for outcomes *to the degree that we can influence those outcomes*.

Tennis is often a good metaphor for the game of life. As in life, I can only directly control what I think, where I focus my attention, and my actions. I have a lot of control over where the ball goes after I hit it but not total control. I have little control over what my opponent or the wind does to the ball. Therefore, I can only partially control the outcome of the tennis match. My overall *process goal* is to play the best tennis I can. My overall *outcome goal* might be to win the match. I will adjust my outcome goal to the level of my opponent so that it is a challenging goal.

However, my process goals are not completely independent of my outcome goals. I choose the process goals with the greatest chance of obtaining the desired outcomes. If my purpose is to win a tennis match, I will try to choose a winning strategy. I might choose to serve and volley. Once I choose that strategy, I focus on serving and volleying as well as I can and forget the score.

Alternate between focusing on process and outcomes. After trying that strategy for a while, I *stop and evaluate it* to see if it is helping me win. If not, I pick a different strategy--such as staying back and hitting from the baseline. I use feedback from how well I met the outcome goals to help *select* the next process goals.

When I get involved in the process, I focus on the process goal as if I didn't care about the outcome. Focusing on the ball maximizes my chances for getting in the zone and winning. Even if I lose the match, there are still many benefits from being in the zone: I still enjoy playing, I am still learning, I am still doing something healthy, and I am still spending my time feeling happy.

Periodically focusing on the outcomes for *direction*, and focusing on the process the rest of the time maximizes chances of success. When meeting strangers, my clients learned to periodically evaluate which behaviors were most effective in influencing other people to like them--especially people they liked best.

But when they were talking with someone, they only focused on *being the person they wanted to be* in a relationship. If they thought that being empathetic would help produce happy relationships (outcome), then they would focus on being empathetic (process).

(4) Focus on DYNAMIC, GROWTH-ORIENTED goals. Static goals are goals that can be completed. Static goals usually center on brief amounts of time. **Dynamic** goals may never be completed. Dynamic goals usually center on processes occurring over *extended* periods of time. Some examples follow--the first goal is a **dynamic goal** vs. the second is a **static goal**.

•Improve skills	vs.	Win the gold medal
•Improve my income each year	vs.	Make a million dollars
•Have a happy marriage	vs.	Get married
•Spend my life helping others	vs.	Become a physician
•Create beauty where I can	vs.	Get a beautiful new house
•Learn and grow	vs.	Achieve perfection
•Be happy	vs.	Get the job I always wanted

One of my clients was extremely anxious about her success in graduate school and in her later career. Despite having a very high grade average, she felt like a fake who was not intelligent or creative. She said, "I can learn and recall material well for tests, but I can never express my own ideas or do anything creative."

The real problem was not that she didn't have creative ideas, it was that she never expressed them. She feared being thought wrong or stupid. She was terrified of being wrong, because all of her life her family and best friends had overemphasized being right. Being wrong was terrible; no one should ever admit being wrong or at fault.

During counseling, she chose to make the *process* of learning and self-development more important than being right. Then it did not matter much whether she was right or wrong--only *how much she learned*. Once she resolved that underlying issue, she felt much better about expressing her own ideas--even when others might disagree.

Get in tune with the dynamic nature of life and the universe. The entire universe is dynamic--not static. It is in continual evolution. We will never see the universe's end goal, we can only know a dynamic process that makes changes each moment.

Similarly, our bodies and minds are dynamic systems in continual evolution and change so that they can deal successfully with a continually changing environment. By setting goals that emphasize dynamic processes such as learning, growth, and happiness we can be more *in tune with the fundamental nature of the universe.*

We can learn to view negative events as part of the dynamic, interesting process that is life. We can develop a world view that will welcome change. We can find life interesting and fun--instead of being so anxiety-ridden by the world's constant state of change. The hardest times of our lives are often our greatest opportunities for growth.

Once we see life as a dynamic process,
then *individual events do not matter as much.*
What matters most is how we *spend our time* in that dynamic process.
What matters most is our overall growth, productivity, and happiness.

(5) We can set SIMPLER, SMALL-STEP goals to increase calmness. What can you do if you are facing an overwhelming project? Often the most effect strategy is to *break it into smaller steps*. These steps must be small enough so that you feel confident about *how* to perform each step. Consult an expert (or book) who can help teach you the steps, or spend adequate time figuring the steps out yourself.

One simple step at a time can overcome great anxiety and accomplish long-range goals. "One day at a time" is an important motto in 12-step recovery programs like Alcoholics Anonymous. This strategy can help overcome enormous tasks and overwhelming amounts of anxiety or stress.

Systematic desensitization is one of the most successful techniques used by psychologists for overcoming anxiety. Dr. Joseph Wolpe, one of the founders of behavior therapy, invented systematic desensitization. Systematic desensitization consists of having people take small steps toward some more frightening goal--while *feeling calm*. Taking these small steps while actually feeling calm--either in their imagination or in real life--can help reduce their anxiety. If you do not feel calm enough, take a smaller, safer step.

Much of the technique's success is due to *breaking up big, overwhelming goals into step-by-step goals*. For example, a man came to see me who had wanted to meet more women at bars, but was terrified of going into bars and asking someone to dance. His anxiety was so high that he wouldn't go near a bar. Part of his anxiety came from lack of social skills and not knowing what to do in a bar situation. Therefore, he set up a series of small, easy goals to achieve his overall goal of meeting women to date in bars.

The first night he parked outside a bar for about 20 minutes and just watched people go in. He also learned what people were wearing. His next goal was to go into the bar and just look around and learn for five minutes. His next goal was to go in and order a drink, but not to talk to anyone--just watch people. He kept going to bars and learning from watching others. For example, he learned that although many men were better looking than himself, about 90% of them never asked a woman to dance. Realizing that he wasn't the only one with social anxiety comforted him.

He learned to talk to women, dance, and ask women out with confidence. He became so confident about meeting women in bars, he concluded that bars are "a gold mine most men are too scared to take advantage of."

What a change in attitude from the man who was terrified about even entering a bar! It was done *one small step at a time* over a time span of a year, but he was persistent and accomplished his miracle.

MULTIPLE GOALS: *GO FOR THE GOLD*--BE PREPARED FOR THE WORST

What kind of attitudes and goals do people who reach the top have? I listened carefully to the American Gold Medal winners in the Winter Olympics as they described their attitudes and goals before their performances.

They entered their gold medal performances in quite different situations. The downhill skier Tommy Moe had never been in an Olympic contest and was only given an outside chance of medaling. Bonnie Blair had won three gold medals in previous Olympics and was a favorite. On the other hand, Dan Jansen seemed to carry a dark cloud around; he had been the favorite several times, but had never won a medal. People were saying that he froze on the ice. Did the three winners have similar attitudes that helped them win?

Yes, in separate interviews all three athletes expressed similar attitudes and goals that I would summarize as, "My goals are to enjoy what I am doing and to perform at my personal best. I would love to win the Gold Medal, but the bottom-line is that I feel honored for the opportunity to participate, and just want to enjoy the experience."

Note that all of these gold medal winners had *multiple goals*. Their top goal was to go for the gold, but that was an outcome goal they had little control over. For example, they had no control over other competitors' performances. In addition to the high outcome goals, the gold medalists set bottom-line, realistic *process goals* that they *could control* themselves. They set goals to *enjoy* their performance and do their *personal best*.

> PRACTICE: Change high anxiety goals and expectations with LAPDS.
> (1) **Identify anxiety sources.** Think of a life area (or major goal) where you feel too much stress or anxiety--or an area you have given up or avoid. What are the outcome goals you are discouraged or worried about? What are the goal levels? Are they unrealistic? Make MULTIPLE GOALS or goal levels. Write them down, and modify them if needed. Is the problem an unrealistic time line? If so, modify it or go to step 3.
> (2) **Simplify the outcome goals.** Break long-term or complex, large goals into smaller, intermediate goals. What are the big steps necessary to reach those big goals? Get advice if needed.
> (3) **What happens if you don't reach your goals--worst possible outcomes?** Find and write ACCEPTABLE ALTERNATIVE GOALS AND PLANS.
> (4) **Emphasize (or substitute) PROCESS AND DYNAMIC GOALS** instead of outcome and static goals.
> (5) **What more DETAILED STEPS need to be taken?** What little steps need to be taken to accomplish the big steps (above)?

OVERCOME UNDERAROUSAL EMOTIONS—
DEPRESSION, GRIEF, and APATHY

Choose more *challenging* goals to increase interest and excellence

We have looked at the overarousal emotions such as anxiety; now let's consider the *underarousal emotions* such as apathy, boredom, depression, and loneliness. All of these underarousal emotions have in common that our *emotional arousal, energy, and motivation are too low.* You may feel listless, uninterested, unfocused, helpless, or hopeless. Your feeling will be intensified to the degree you believe that your life will continue in this state. (Recall that *understimulation and underchallenge* lower emotional arousal below the zone of harmonious functioning.)

Depression caused by GOALLESSNESS that results from a LOSS. A client's fiancé, Barry, was killed in an automobile accident. Annette experienced a grief reaction in which she felt very depressed. Of course, she also felt varying degrees of anxiety, anger, and guilt at other times, but her most frequent feeling was depression.

It is interesting that her emotions changed as her focus on different expectations and goals changed. She had developed a mental image of what her married life would be like. She had pictured a marriage that would satisfy her values related to intimacy, romance, children, and having someone always there for her. When she focused on any of these expectations, she felt more depressed. These goals and expectations would never be fulfilled *with Barry*. In addition, she had envisioned her marriage fulfilling other goals less related to Barry--such as having a nice house, travel, and financial security.

Barry's death, and the sudden end of her dream caused her temporarily to give up on meeting all of these goals and expectations; it was as if she suddenly had *no goals or expectations at all!* She was in a *goalless state that creates underchallenge and therefore underarousal*--depression.

As long as Annette did not *substitute new, realistic, acceptable goals and expectations*, she would remain in a depressed state. First, I helped her realize that the happiness she had found with Barry could possibly be realized with someone else. After all, she was as responsible for her happiness in the relationship as Barry had been. Second, I helped her build a new image of how she could be happy alone. We focused on the specific values and goals that were not being satisfied such as intimacy, romance, companionship, emotional support, financial security, and having a nice home environment. Currently, her levels of satisfaction were very low for all these values, but she made new goals and plans for *increasing* her satisfaction to acceptable levels. Her new *realistic, challenging* goals gave her a renewed feeling of control over her life and emotions--and a return to her more optimistic, happy self.

What can we learn from Annette's experience? Depression (sadness) can be triggered by a loss, such as loss of a job or loved one. It can be triggered by failure to meet important goals. In any case, we feel a sense of loss and helplessness, because we aren't satisfying important values. We feel we have *lost control of our emotions*.

When many people feel down, they give up, withdraw from people and activities, and constrict their goals and interests. They believe that--because their old goals and expectations appear bleak--they can't be happy or successful in that life area. They create a *goalless state* in which their old goals are suspended, and they have yet to create new, realistic, acceptable goals. That goalless state is the *cause* of the underarousal emotion, depression. Very low goals have a similar effect.

The existentialists, such as Frankl, point out that goallessness creates a vacuum in our lives that we perceive as meaninglessness. They recognize that meaninglessness is a major cause of depression.

When we feel underarousal emotions, we need to both (1) examine *the original goals and expectations* now viewed as unattainable and (2) *create new (or modified) goals and expectations* that are *realistic, optimally challenging, and acceptable* ways to meet important underlying values. We can find new goals, new interests, or new ways of meeting our goals that can fill our time and satisfy our underlying values. That is a primary therapeutic method to convert the depression from grief, loss, or failure to happiness.

Other causes of goallessness. Annette had experienced a loss that was completely outside her control--her fiancé had been killed in an automobile accident unrelated to her actions. Depression such as hers is usually called depression due to grief or loss. What if you are feeling down, and you do not know what the cause of your depression is? What if your depression is caused by a failure? Do you think something is wrong with you–such as low self-esteem, shy, immoral, or dumb? These conditions can also help cause depression. How?

Depression caused by failure, avoidance behavior, or withdrawal. What if your relationship ends partly because your partner was not happy with you? What if your boss didn't feel you were good at your job? What if you didn't get admitted to graduate school or couldn't get the job you wanted? What if your business failed?

If you fail or if you feel overwhelmed by a situation and give-up, then you end up in the same type of goalless vacuum Annette experienced. The only difference is the original cause. In Annette's case, the cause--a car wreck--was out of her control. In this case, you may *perceive* part of the cause as being your own *inadequacies* (and that perception may be accurate).

Therefore, you have an additional factor causing your depression--your own *real or perceived inadequacies.* In either case you need to establish new goals and expectations. If you just had bad luck, then perhaps just trying again will work. If you need to work on improving some knowledge, skill, or other resource to be more successful, then set your goals on getting the needed improvements. Otherwise, give up the original goal and find a new, more realistic one.

FACTORS THAT PREDISPOSE SOMEONE TO DEPRESSION.

Many of us struggle for many years to overcome depression. At one end of the spectrum of prolonged depression are people whose depression is mild--they just consider themselves not happy. At the other end are people who are often severely depressed and frequently consider suicide. Has this been a problem for you or someone you care about? What are some of the factors that predispose someone to feel depressed over a long period of time?

First, remember that these factors work by causing the person frequently to be in a state of *underchallenge and underarousal.* These factors keep them from harmonious functioning. Important values and parts of themselves are not being engaged at a challenging, fun level or they are not being satisfied at all. The person may often be in a goalless, meaningless mental state. These factors are considered in other chapters, but this is the only place that they are summarized as a whole. I will briefly discuss them and their solutions. Carefully study the depression causes table below. It summarizes most basic causes of depression.

Additional comments about factors predisposing one to depression. Following are some brief comments that elaborate on some of the items in the box above.

• **Low internal control, coping skills, or assertiveness.** People who are habitually depressed often lack internal control and assertiveness. Often assertion training can help them not only become more successful with others, but can help them get out of their depression (see internal control Chapter 6). People who are habitually depressed also often lack self-direction, initiative, or self-management skills (see self-management Chapter 9). Emotional coping skills--such as the **CHUG-OF** mental control skills–are commonly deficient in habitually depressed people. Therapies that teach depressed clients these skills can have dramatic effects on depression (for example see Matthews and MacLeod, 1994).

• **Negative world views and self views often cause depression.** Depression may not be so much that you are so inadequate or have too high expectations. It may be caused by how you view yourself or the world. If you view yourself as bad or stupid no matter what you do, then you will feel depression. If you view the world (or other people) as so negative, hostile, or different from you, that you don't have a chance to succeed, then you will feel depressed. For these problems, see Chapters 4, 5--world view and self-esteem.

• **Too much self-denial can cause depression.** A woman I saw was a cardiac nurse. She knew the signs of a heart attack. She started getting those signs--such as excruciating chest pains--three days before her daughter's wedding. Yet she did not tell anyone or see a doctor; because she knew it was so bad, he would hospitalize her. She feared it would disrupt her daughter's wedding. While she was dancing at the reception, her chest pains were so bad; she thought she would probably die right there. That is self-denial--putting her own *life* at risk to make sure her daughter's wedding was undisturbed. What would you do in a similar circumstance?

When we make choices that deny important parts of ourselves (important needs, values, or goals), we can cause those parts to feel depressed and lower our overall motivation and happiness. Even when other parts may feel happy, denying one part can reduce our happiness over time. People may habitually choose self-denial when they put all their energy into meeting long-term goals such as working exceptionally long hours to get a college degree or obtain career success.

Another cause of habitual self-denial is a belief system that puts too high a value on sacrificing one's own values and happiness for others. Many parents teach their children that their children's needs are not important or teach them that they don't deserve to be happy. These children may grow up believing a dark cloud follows them–that they are so bad or incompetent, they don't deserve anything good. Therefore, they automatically feel guilty whenever they think about something fun for themselves--and often choose to not pursue such selfish goals. The result is a life of self-deprivation and depression.

What if you are one of these people? What do you do about it? The solution is to confront the original belief systems that cause the self-denial. Focus on belief systems (such as the Higher Self) that support personal happiness (see codependence section of Chapter 6). Focus on areas of greatest deprivation (sex? fun? play? artistic interests? spending money on yourself? taking time to be alone? etc.) Then make practical goals and plans for leading a more personally rewarding life. Schedule these new activities into your daily, weekly, and monthly plans.

Major Causes and Solutions for Habitual Depression

Do you feel depressed, sad, low motivation, low energy, tired, apathetic,
or helpless? Are you not looking forward to anything?

THE IMMEDIATE DEPRESSION CAUSE IS *A LOW CHALLENGE STATE*
  Being below the zone causes low performance, low learning, and low emotional arousal.

IMMEDIATE CAUSES OF THE *LOW CHALLENGE STATE*:
1. UNDERSTIMULATING SITUATIONS--often an *overly constricted* situation caused by withdrawing from an overwhelming one. Too simple or routine.
2. LOW GOALS and EXPECTATIONS--goallessness. A vacuum--often caused by giving up other goals--or even by accomplishing other goals.
3. POORLY MATCHED ABILITIES--
 • **TOO LOW relevant knowledge, skills, or other resources** (perceived as necessary to accomplish *original goals*). Often fear creating new goals from fear of failing at those too because of low abilities.
 •**TOO HIGH abilities for resultant *goalless state.*** All parts of ourselves need to be used and functioning harmoniously to create optimal arousal and happiness. Disuse causes underarousal, atrophy, and eventual death of part of ourselves (physical organ systems as well as psychological systems).
 • **MENTALLY TUNING OUT** (withdrawing, avoiding) **DUE TO:**
   >> **Anxiety, feeling overwhelmed + Lack ability to deal with situation**
   >> **Lack of involvement, tiredness, depression, etc.**
   >> **Conflict or Attention to higher priority concerns (see this chapter).**

BACKGROUND CAUSES (predisposing one to depression) INCLUDE:
1. TOO HIGH GOALS & EXPECTATIONS--for one's resources & abilities (see above).
2. LOSS--Such as death, abandonment, etc. (See values in Chapter 9).
3. NEGATIVE SELF VIEWS. Lack of general self-worth or self-confidence (Chapter 5).
4. NEGATIVE WORLD VIEWS or views of other people. These can cause us to exaggerate the difficulties involved in meeting our goals (see world view Chapter 4).
5. EXTERNAL CONTROL. Giving control to others undermines control of emotions and lives; shoulds, rule-bound, codependent, etc. (see Chapter 6).
6. NEGATIVE COGNITIVE STYLES--negative bias, overgeneralization, catastrophizing, "always--never" or "black-white" thinking in extremes (Appendix D).
7. LOW ASSERTIVENESS, INTERPERSONAL SKILLS (see internal control Chapter 6).
8. SELF-DEPRIVATION, self-denial (see section in this Chapter).
9. LOW SELF-MANAGEMENT SKILLS--Poor abilities for self-organization, decision-making, time management, etc. (see self-management Chapter 9).
10. LOW EMOTIONAL COPING SKILLS (see this Chapter and much of book).
11. LIFE AREA or TASK-RELATED ABILITIES too low--lack knowledge, skills, or resources.

=> **COMPLETE SHAQ TO GET DETAILED PERSONAL FEEDBACK ABOUT MANY KEY FACTORS RELATED TO DEPRESSION, ANXIETY, ANGER, AND HAPPINESS (on my website).**

• **Underlying fears and habitual avoidance behavior.** A person is lonely because she avoids her fear of rejection. An underemployed worker feels trapped because he avoids the anxiety of looking for a job. A person stays in a controlling, restrictive relationship because she avoids dealing with her fear of being alone or taking care of herself.

A major cause of depression is *avoidance* of situations or avoidance of tasks that are *too challenging* and anxiety producing. Perhaps we have good reasons for avoidance. Perhaps we have experienced pain from those situations. The underlying factors causing the depression are (1) the *inability to cope* with the overchallenging situation, (2) the resultant anxiety, and (3) our choice to avoid the situation.

We may *blame the other person* for our depression, when in fact our emotions are primarily our own responsibility. We *choose* to remain depressed because it seems safer than *replacing or converting* the current situation that is depressing. If you are depressed because you are not facing overwhelming situations, then use the methods described earlier for dealing with overarousal situations.

Alternating between high and low goals. Some people tend to alternate between anxiety and depression--an extreme example is manic-depressive episodes. These people may experience success that causes them to get overly optimistic or idealistic. Then they set unrealistically high goals and expectations. When they try to accomplish these lofty goals, they feel overwhelmed by the size of the task.

To avoid the anxiety, they may begin avoiding responsibilities or quit. Completely giving up their sky-high goals immediately lowers their goals too much. They go from extremely high goals to no goals. Becoming goalless shuts down their arousal. The result is apathy and depression.

Their depression ends when they find new lofty goals, and the cycle from exhilaration to depression starts all over again. To prevent this cycle, first set realistic, *moderately difficult* goals. Then *revise goals* using the LAPDS principles to keep yourself motivated when the going gets tough.

We can feel depressed after accomplishing goals. People are often puzzled about why they feel depressed *after they accomplish goals*. Without new goals, they may be in a goalless state similar to people who have given up. Finding new challenging goals adds meaning to life and re-sparks enthusiasm.

Challenging and involving activities give mental and physical energy. Whatever the *original cause* of depression, while in a state of depression, we are generally *underchallenged and understimulated*. Therefore, if we want to feel more aroused, energetic, motivated, and happier, then we can by *increasing the complexity and challenge* in the immediate situation.

Even if we don't feel like doing something initially, it is likely that any episode that engages a higher level of mental and physical involvement will help reduce our depression. That is why activities like sports, dancing, biking, crossword puzzles, TV, music, talking with friends, or solving a complex problem can have an immediate positive effect upon depression.

These activities may only have temporary effects if they do not cope with the underlying causes of the depression. However, if you are having problems with too much depression, unhappiness, boredom, or tiredness, try building these energy-producing activities into your schedule. Filling your life with these positive, stimulating activities gives you *energy for coping* with the bigger problems. When integrated into your lifestyle, they can have powerful, permanent effects on your happiness.

SUMMARY--INCREASE EMOTIONAL AROUSAL
BY *INCREASING CHALLENGE AND COMPLEXITY*

To *increase emotional arousal*, we must do the opposite of what we would do if we want to *decrease* our arousal. We focus on goals that are more challenging, complex, difficult, and uncertain. Learn and use the following five goal-change methods *to increase emotional arousal*--the opposite ends of the LAPDS dimensions.

(1) Raise goal and expectation LEVELS. This is a simple, but powerful way to increase challenge and arousal. For example, if you are bored with your job, adopt goals for yourself that add to the job and make it more challenging. If you are not challenged by your boss or the people you are working with, compare yourself to a different reference group and set higher standards. You can exceed the expectations of your boss or co-workers, and become self-directed and more creative. Raising your goals not only allows you to give more to the world, but to feel happier yourself. Consider raising the *quality* of what you are doing as well as the *quantity.*

Another approach is to consider looking at your job from a whole different perspective. What is missing that could make your unit more effective meeting the needs of others? What could you invent, initiate, or propose that would make a difference in the lives of those you serve? Find the answer to that question and you may create a whole new--more exciting--project for yourself.

(2) Become MORE ATTACHED to one goal or plan. If you choose to keep a goal or activity, but find yourself understimulated by it, *increase your caring about it.* Learn more about it, get better acquainted with it, and learn how it might make your life or the world better. Focus on its positives. If there are negatives that are turning you off, learn to understand and accept them better.

How can you make the activity more enjoyable or meaningful? Focus on the *quality* of your work and view it as a *work of art* that will be beautiful to you.

(3) Focus on OUTCOME goals. When you are feeling overconfident, bored, or apathetic, focus on the potential outcomes. If you want to *increase arousal* during some activity, then focus on *important values* which can be affected by success or failure of that activity.

For example, if you are having trouble getting something done due to lack of interest or time conflicts, focus on positive and negative *consequences* relating to important values. *Focusing on the difficulties or uncertainties* of getting what we want increases our arousal. Remind yourself what will happen if you perform at an adequate level and what will happen if you do not. What are the internal and external consequences? What are the career, financial, or interpersonal consequences? How will it affect other people's lives? What will you think of yourself later if you did or did not do your best?

(4) Focus on STATIC, one-shot goals. What if you have started to lose sight of your long-term goals or your dynamic, growth-oriented goals? Challenging short-term, static goals can renew your interest. You might make a game of what you are doing to stimulate your interest. Find a way to measure progress--keep score. Introduce a frame of reference for comparing your progress.

You may want to introduce friendly competition into an otherwise boring activity to make it more challenging. Then winning can be a static goal which adds stimulation to the activity. Or, you may want to establish a challenging yardstick to beat--such as your own past performance. We can also make a contract with ourselves that we will get some reinforcement contingent upon our actions. That is another way to raise the stakes and our arousal by creating a static goal (such as getting the reward).

(5) Focus on COMPLEX, LARGE-STEP goals If you have become bogged down in too much detail, then you may get bored. Try focusing on larger or more complex tasks. Focus more on the big picture. See if that larger perspective suggests new approaches or new tasks.

Converting simple tasks into more complex, interesting ones. One way to make a task more complex is to *pay more attention to details and to create many small tasks* from a task that someone else might consider a simple task. When most of us look at a bug, we just glance at it and lose interest. A bug is just a bug. However, a bug biologist I know is fascinated with bugs. He sees much more in bugs than you or I. He loves bugs. He could study bugs for hours and never get bugged. An activity that drives a person bugs can become fascinating when that person learns to look at its complexity and find the beauty in it.

More concentration, attention to details, and personal involvement can overcome boredom. In our daily lives and our work, many of us find that significant amounts of our time are spent in a state of boredom or understimulation. We may rarely feel truly challenged and excited about our work. In his book, *Skillful Means--Patterns for Success*, Tarthang Tulku (1991) summarizes the problem:

> **we rarely put our hearts and minds fully into our work;**
> **in fact, working just enough to get by has become the norm.**
> **Most people do not expect to like their work, much less to do it well,**
> **for work is commonly considered as nothing more than a means to an end. . .**
> **This kind of self-centered motivation makes it difficult to express and**
> **develop our human potential through our work.** (p. xix)

Tulku further believes that a process of (1) developing inner clarity, (2) concentrating intensely, and (3) considering the effects of our actions from a *broad perspective* will greatly increase our interest and performance--even when we are doing simple tasks. Remember, a task is only a task--it is never boring in itself. "Bored" describes our reaction to the task. By changing our reaction to the task, we can eliminate our boredom. Tulku gives an exercise in "lighthearted concentration" that provides some instruction for us.

You can develop this concentration at work by doing one task at a time, devoting all of your attention to what you are doing, being aware of each detail involved.

GOAL FLEXIBILITY AND HAPPINESS

In his review of research on factors related to happiness, Ed Diener (2002) says, "Thus, one determinant of people's adaptation to conditions often might be the extent to which they alter their goals when new circumstances prevail. Thus, goal flexibility may be a key to [happiness] in adverse circumstances."

PRACTICE: Examine an area of boredom or depression. (1) Identify an underarousal problem area. (2) Ask yourself how much your underarousal is due to avoiding stressful situations and how much is due to being in understimulating situations. Explore your emotions to find underlying fears. (3) Use the methods in this chapter--especially in the last section--to deal with this situation.

SUMMARY--MENTAL CONTROL STRATEGY 4:

Harmonious functioning (and happiness) require
an optimally challenging match between tasks and abilities.
Adjusting goals and expectations adjusts the level of challenge like a thermostat.
If you want to *lower arousal*--when too anxious, angry, afraid, or confused,
choose goals that are lower, have alternatives, process-oriented,
dynamic, and simpler (LAPDS).
If you want to *raise arousal*--when too bored, depressed, or apathetic,
choose goals that are higher, involving, outcome-oriented, static, and complex.
Remember to make *multiple* goals and expectations to cover all outcomes--
Go for the Gold, but be prepared for the worst!

Mental Control Strategy 5:
OPTIMISM--You can be happy *no matter what happens*

Interviewing for a job, waiting to hear the results of a test for cancer, or discussing a serious relationship problem can create a high level of anxiety. These situations involve *uncertainty about vitally important outcomes.* In situations such as these, how do we adjust the thermostat to get into the zone of harmonious functioning?

If we believe that we will get what we want, then we feel more confident. The result of too much uncertainty is anxiety (too much challenge to obtain a state of harmonious functioning.) For most important goals in life, we want more certainty and confidence--not less. We want to feel calmer and less stress--not more.

To increase our mental control over an outcome, it is unnecessary to know that we will *obtain the exact outcome we want*. We simply need to increase our belief that we will get *some outcome that we can be happy with* (or at least accept). That optimism will give us increased mental control over our emotions.

Deep optimism **depends upon confidence that our ultimate concerns will be satisfied.** If we are confident that we and others can be happy *despite* not getting the job we want, the relationship we want, or the house we want, then we will *remain optimistic and in control of our emotions.*

However, the more threatening an event is *to our ultimate concerns* and the more doubt we have that our ultimate concerns will be satisfied, the *more pessimistic and upset we will be.*

Deep **optimism** refers to our **ultimate concerns**--confidence that ultimately we will be happy and the world will be ok. There are two basic sources for optimism--confidence in ourselves and confidence in forces outside ourselves.

OPTIMISM BASED UPON *OUR CONTROL* OF OUTCOMES
Answer the following questions:
1. Fate is more in control of my life than I am. (True or False)
2. Other people seem to have more influence over what happens to me than I do. (True or False)
3. Luck or chance plays a dominant role in affecting my life. (True or False)

Believing *we control outcomes* increases calmness and motivation. Exaggerated beliefs that *external causes*--nature, luck, fate, other people, or the weather control the outcomes we want can lead to a "why try," apathetic attitude. We can slip into the role of being a weak victim of these powerful external powers. We often learn this attitude from parents who played the role of victim.

The more we believe that *we can control the outcomes*, the more optimistic and confident *we will feel*. Believing that *we can control the satisfaction of our ultimate concerns* helps produce deep, pervasive optimism. Knowing that our happiness is determined by our thoughts and knowing that we can control our thoughts is a pillar of that deep optimism.

Accurate beliefs about internal versus external control. Dr. Julian Rotter was one of the first psychologists to recognize the importance of whether we believe we are internally or externally controlled (Rotter, 1954). More recently, Ryan and Deci (2000) present a well-supported *self-determination theory* that is consistent many of the ideas presented below.

If we believe external forces control our important outcomes, then we don't have to work hard, face negative outcomes, or take the blame if we don't get the results we want. Thus, avoidance of responsibility and avoidance of anxiety can be powerful reinforcers for beliefs in external control.

The down side of exaggerated external control beliefs is that we tell ourselves we are weak victims. That message undermines our confidence in ourselves and decreases our chances of success. (See Chapter 6.)

It is also possible to hold exaggerated beliefs that we *control external events more than we actually do*. To believe that we need to almost completely control outcomes is not only a serious logical error, but is often the root of prolonged unhappiness. A distorted belief in total control may give us a feeling of power. However, this distorted belief in power also has some of the following negative consequences.

• Feel *too responsible* for the outcomes--producing high worry and guilt.
• Not allow others to take responsibility and control (*codependency*)--placing an extra burden on us and limiting others' growth.
• Become domineering and manipulative.
• Develop too high expectations--increasing anxiety and reducing performance.
• Become overconfident--also potentially reducing performance.

An accurate causal analysis leads to realistic confidence–think MULTIPLE-CAUSATION. Almost all outcomes are caused by *many factors*--both internal and external--operating together in complex ways. Most of us tend to *oversimplify our thinking* and focus on only one or two causal factors. We may think someone else is the entire cause of the problem; or, conversely, attribute to ourselves such superhuman powers.

We are never entirely to blame for anything. Nor is anyone else. *Stop wasting your time trying to find who's to blame--instead try to find the multiple-causes of the problem.*

Optimism based upon *our ability to influence* life events. A client came in because she said that couldn't make a commitment to get married although she was happy in her long-term relationship and wanted to continue it. In essence she *was not confident that she would be happy if she got married.*

When we examined the feelings, experiences, and beliefs about marriage, she made the comment, "I have never known a couple who were happily married." No wonder she was not looking forward to getting married! My client had grown up with parents who were unhappy with each other and she certainly did not want that. She had no positive models for a happy marriage.

In order for her to increase her optimism, she developed a *mental model* for what *her* happy marriage could be like. She thought about how she and her lover could *together create a happy marriage.* Since her model was a lot like her current relationship, her confidence that they could be happily married increased. She had successfully *replaced a negative view* of marriage with a realistic, positive one.

I have had many clients who have felt devastated by a breakup because they thought they would never be happy again. However, once they realize that they *have the qualities necessary* to attract someone at least as good as their last lover and *have the qualities necessary* to do their half to create a happy relationship, they feel optimistic again. In these cases their optimism was based upon their understanding of the situation and their confidence that *they could perform the steps necessary for getting the results they wanted.*

Our happiness is *more controlled by internal factors*–which we can control. We have internal and external routes to happiness. However, our emotions are *most directly affected by internal factors.* We can learn how to get internal control over our emotions. We can learn how to choose to be happy in any situation. This confidence is the basis of optimism--it helps us rise above life's daily difficulties as if floating on a cloud over life's peaks and valleys. This bottom-line security is based upon realistic knowledge that we can *rise above any situation.*

Being happy by accepting the worst possible events. Sometimes, *we have little control over important outcomes.* If we can feel good about *all* of the possible outcomes-- including the *worst* ones--then we will get mental control over our emotions.

For example, a client was facing a difficult and serious operation for life-threatening cancer. She knew that her beliefs, emotions, and behavior could affect the outcome. She did her best to maximize her positive state of mind and her health. Yet underneath, she still had an overwhelming fear of dying and knew this fear of dying could actually increase her chances of dying.

She also knew that her health would be affected by many *factors beyond her control.* How could she overcome a fear of dying when she knew there was a high chance of dying no matter what she did?

How could she feel calm *when so much of the outcome was out of her control?* There are two answers--the first is that she would feel better to the degree that she could trust *the external powers that were in control* to help her get well. If she believed the physicians or God was in control, then she would be calm to the degree that she could trust that they would heal her. Hearing positive stories of how others had survived helped comfort her.

Additionally, she still needed to face the worst possible outcome. She needed to *get mental control* of her fear of dying. We have many ways to deal with fears of death or other uncontrollable outcomes (see world view Chapter 4). Changing her view of life as well as death was necessary. Instead of *deficit motivation,* feeling sorry for herself, and focusing on what death would mean that *she could not have,* she began to focus on *abundance motivation* and *appreciate all that life had already given her.* She accepted the inevitability of her eventual death and accepted that possibility that it might occur soon.

Whenever she would get fearful about death, she would focus on moments of happiness throughout her life to feel gratitude instead of resentment. It worked--she felt much better. At last report, over a year later, the immediate cancer threat was gone and she was in better health.

DEEP OPTIMISM BASED UPON TRUST IN BENEVOLENT FORCES

If we believe that some *deep, unchangeable forces* will cause our ultimate concerns to be met, then our *optimism will be deep, pervasive, and enduring.* One such belief is that a benevolent Supreme Being is in charge of the universe. Another is that we are in harmony with the laws of the universe and that harmony is sufficient to get our ultimate concerns' met.

If, on the other hand, we believe that the world is basically a dark and capricious place, that the built-in forces of the world will only randomly provide happiness, or that these forces are out to get us, then our *pessimistic view of life will be deep, pervasive, and enduring.*

If you have developed a pessimistic philosophy that the negative forces usually win and that happiness is elusive--at least for you, then that philosophy is an underlying source of your resentment, suspiciousness, pessimism, and depression. You may believe that your views are a true and accurate picture of the world. However, if you do, challenge these beliefs and try rereading Chapters 1-4.

When you have little external control, put your trust in benevolent forces. When you recognize that you cannot control important events, put *your trust in powerful, benevolent forces*--whether they are God, Nature, Evolution, Society, your doctor, or a friend. Deep optimism is *not* that we will get *exactly what we want,* but that we can find *some way to be happy no matter what happens.*

Following is a sample of comforting statements that have worked for others when they felt that an outcome was outside their control.

- **"Let go and let God"** take care of the problem--it is outside my control or responsibility.
- **"That which does not kill me, makes me stronger . . .He who has a *why* to live for can bear almost any *how.*"**--Nietzsche
- "Now this, monks, is the noble truth of the way that leads to cessation of pain . . . abandonment, forsaking, release, non-attachment." Buddha (Burtt, 1982)
- **"Trust the creative forces in every atom, cell, and living creature."**
- **"Everything in the universe has a purpose."** "There are no accidents, everything I am experiencing is in some way necessary for me to move ahead to the next step. . . Rather than asking the "Why me?" question, you begin to ask, 'What is in this experience that I can use in a beneficial way?'"-Dr. Wayne Dyer, *Real Magic, pp. 6-7.*
- "When a man finds that it is his destiny to suffer he will have to accept his suffering as his task; his single and unique task. . .**His unique opportunity lies in the way in which he bears his burden**. . .What you have experienced, no power on earth can take from you." -- Dr. Victor Frankl, *Man's Search For Meaning, p. 123-125.*
- **"The human spirit can "rise above" any hardship to find happiness."**
- **"Happiness is a state of mind we can create by harmonious thoughts."** If we can find anything interesting or fun to think about or to do, we can get back into the zone.
- **"The Lord is my shepherd, I shall not be in want**. . .for even though I walk through the valley of the shadow of death, I will fear no evil, for you are with me. . . Surely goodness and mercy will follow me all the days of my life, and I will dwell in the house of the Lord forever." *Psalm 23*

PRACTICE: Reframing. Think of 1-3 negative or pessimistic thoughts that inhibit you or create negative feelings. Then think of new beliefs or thoughts that reflect Higher Self beliefs. This is reframing and "rising above" old beliefs.

SUMMARY: MENTAL CONTROL STRATEGY 5: OPTIMISM

Realistic optimism is not based upon fooling ourselves
that we will get everything we want.
It is based upon valid beliefs that we can find meaning and be happy
either if we get what we want or if we do not.

Mental Control Strategy 6:
FOCUS--Keep your eye on the ball to funnel your energy

Dr. Maslow associated the peak experiences so often felt by his self-actualizing people with periods of intense concentration and growth.

Apparently the acute mystic or peak experience
is a tremendous intensification of any of the experiences
in which there is a loss of self or transcendence of it;
e.g., problem-centering, intense concentration, . . .
intense sensuous experience, self-forgetful
and intense enjoyment of music or art. (Abraham Maslow, 1954, p. 165)

I once saw a book in which a researcher examined photographs of some of the best baseball hitters of all time. He compared photos of the best hitters swinging at the ball to photos of average hitters. The great hitters such as Ted Williams, Mickey Mantle, and Henry Aaron had their eyes glued to the ball as they were swinging. The eyes of the other major league players were typically looking toward the pitcher, first base, or anyplace except the ball. What is true in baseball is true in life. If you want to do well at something, you've got to keep your eye on the ball.

A member of singer/songwriter Garth Brook's inner circle described him as so focused when he is writing that an explosion could go off right next to him and he would never hear it. By keeping his attention focused on his writing, Garth Brooks could concentrate his mental powers on creating his best music.

This type of concentration usually results from total immersion in the subject and a loss of time perspective. Dr. Maslow called this characteristic problem-centering, and believed it to be one of the most important characteristics of self-actualizing people. It is also a direct cause of achieving states of loss of self, happiness, and peak experience.

PROBLEM-FOCUS VERSUS SOLUTION-FOCUS

A major university decided to form study groups to solve a variety of important problems at the university. Half the groups were told to *find all of the problems* they could and make reports about them. The other half of the groups were not told anything about finding problems. They were instructed to focus on *finding solutions* to whatever problems they thought might exist.

The *problem-focus* groups explored the problems thoroughly and became increasing discouraged about what a mess the university was in. Attendance dropped and one-by-one the groups disintegrated. Few reports were filed.

The *solution-focus* groups had quite different results. Groups quickly found a few problems members thought were important. However, they spent little time dwelling on the problems. Instead, they started *focusing on solutions*. Members made many positive suggestions and became enthusiastic about them. People enjoyed going to meetings, and some groups lasted for several years. The solution-focus groups contributed to many changes in their university.

Individuals are much the same way. We all know complainers--people who are constantly focusing on their problems and play the role of victim. They seem to seek sympathy. They may want validation that the situation is so impossible, they have no responsibility to improve it. They may fear that--despite their disadvantages--they could have solved their problems and achieved a happier life. It's easy to slip into that mode of thinking.

Do you ever find yourself complaining repeatedly about the same issue, end up feeling sorry for yourself, and slip into the victim role? Change your focus from the *problems, disadvantages, and roadblocks* to focus on your *resources, constructive ideas, and potential solutions* to improve the situation. You will experience an immediate improvement in attitude and begin to make genuine progress.

> **PRACTICE: Make progress on an impossible problem**. Think of a problem which you have given up on or a problem you constantly complain about.
> (1) List the **external barriers** (factors outside yourself) which are contributing to the problem or are barriers to your solving the problem.
> (2) List the **internal barriers** (your beliefs, motivation, lack of training or experience, disabilities, etc) which are barriers to solving the problem.
> (3) List the **external resources**--external factors or resources (people, money, job, educational opportunities, etc) which are available to help you.
> (4) List your **internal resources** that can help you (your intelligence, motivation, experience, persistence, ability to learn, time, etc.).
> (5) For each external and internal barrier list **resources and ideas that can help you overcome** that limitation.
> (6) List potential **new solutions**, and ideas of how to follow up on them (example, get more information).

FOCUSING ON THE BALL CAN HELP US OVERCOME ANXIETY

Giving an important speech, confronting a powerful person, or performing a difficult task under great pressure can lead to high anxiety. **Performance anxiety** means anxiety in a situation where optimal performance seems important. It usually involves evaluation by others and ourselves. (Expectations and goals are key parts--see strategy 4--to keep in the zone.)

Performance anxiety produces interfering thoughts. There are many types of performance anxiety, but they have similar causes. Test anxiety is a good example and is common among students. Research and my clinical observation indicate that people who have test anxiety spend much of their test time thinking negative thoughts. These negative thoughts may involve possible consequences of not doing well on the test, of self put-downs, of thinking how they are doomed to fail, or of many other negative themes.

It is not just the negativism of these thoughts that reduces student's chances of doing well on the test. In addition, they may spend 10 to 30 minutes out of a 50-minute test hour focusing on these negative thoughts. That leaves them *only 20 to 40 minutes to focus on the content of the test and search their memory for answers*. Their classmates have the whole 50 minutes!

Control focus to prime and control your brain's search for memory associations. If you focus on the word "apple," your memory naturally begins to search for related associations, such as the visual image of an apple and taste of an apple. If you focus on negative themes, your memory will produce associated thoughts such as previous failures or terrible things that

246 / Dr. Tom G. Stevens

could happen if you don't do well. Even prolonged debating with yourself to generate positive thoughts can interfere with keeping your eye on the ball in many performance situations.

You control your brain's search and priming of content-related memories by controlling your focus of attention. If you direct your focus to the *actual content* of the test, speech, or other performance, then your memory will naturally search for associations related to the performance. *You will recall the content necessary to answer the questions.*

Refocus on the ball during a task to overcome anxiety. Use the following steps to *overcome performance anxiety* and *maximize concentration* during the performance.

(1) Observe your focus. During the performance, let your Higher Self (or inner observer) partly be alert to the occurrence of negative or other interfering thoughts. Examples: "What will everyone think of me?" "What if I fail?" "This can't be happening to me." "Why can't I remember this?" "I worked so hard." "This is terrible." "I can't cope with this." "I don't know what to do." "I'm a failure." "That is so stupid." "What's the matter with me?"

(2) Refocus on the content. When you observe interfering thoughts, remember:
• These thoughts are *interfering with your focus on the content* and preventing success.
• You do not have time to deal with the underlying issues now; you can *deal with them later.*
• You can repeat short pre-planned positive statements to yourself (see 3).
• Focus your attention on any part of the actual *content of the current task that will get you re-engaged* in the immediate task. This new focus will even help you *remember "forgotten" material* that you couldn't recall when you were focusing on negative thoughts, because the new focus primes related memories.

(3) Later, examine underlying issues. At times outside the performance situation or during breaks, examine the interfering thoughts. What were *the content and themes of* the interfering thoughts? Follow your feelings [self-exploration Chapter 2] to get to the underlying subparts and issues that are producing the interfering thoughts. Also, see the HARMONY strategy 2 above. Write a few short statements that cope with underlying themes. You can use these later in the target performance situation.

Competing parts of ourselves generate conflicting thoughts. Any thoughts that change our focus from the primary task at hand can interfere with our current performance--not only negative thoughts, even pleasant ones. The sources of these thoughts are cognitive systems. Distracting thoughts can affect performance.

Negotiating with our subparts to reduce interfering thoughts. If we are in the midst of giving a speech, a serious discussion, taking an exam, playing ball, or writing a proposal, then we certainly cannot resolve all of our underlying conflicts then! It might take a while to resolve these issues. But, what can we do right now to improve our focus? One way is to temporarily focus back on our goals, values, or reasons why we are doing what we are doing right now. We can ask ourselves, *"What do I want to be doing right now?"* considering all of my feelings and subparts.

No matter how pressing the immediate situation may be, we can remind ourselves, "*I am free to do whatever my other subpart (that is trying to interfere) wants to do instead.*" After considering the main factors, we can make a *fresh decision now* about whether we choose to continue the match, meeting, exam, or writing. If we decide to continue and the interfering thoughts continue, we can remind ourselves why we made this decision to forge ahead.

To negotiate with the subpart that is generating the interfering thoughts, we can schedule a time to attend to that subpart and the issues it is raising. We can even write down thoughts we are getting from it so that we can get back in touch with those thoughts later. Negotiating with the troublesome subpart can help reassure it, and that can help quiet it for a while. However, if the executive self later breaks its promises to other subparts, then they will not trust it and will not be put off so easily in the future.

What is the ball? Where do we focus for maximum performance? This is a complex issue and will depend upon the specific task we are engaged in. The rules I follow for directing my attention when I am playing tennis may bear little resemblance to the rules I follow for directing my attention when I am writing this book. Directing our focus is part of the skill we learn as we move from novice to expert in any task. Learning where to focus attention is a skill that helps make a superstar athlete better than their rivals.

• **Focus on *deep content* and connect to it to maximize interest and learning.** I once had a student who sat in the middle of my psychology class, closed his eyes during my lectures, and never took a note. It used to annoy me, because I thought he was sleeping in my class. Yet, when I graded the first exam, I was amazed: he had the highest grade in the class!

I couldn't believe it, so I asked him how he did it. He said that during my lectures he would focus his attention on what I was saying and try to visualize it and think of ways he could apply it to his life. He said he didn't need to take notes, because he focused so well it seemed easy to remember what he needed on the exams.

Contrast his approach with students who spend most of their time focused on taking notes or on thoughts that are totally unrelated to the lecture. They may rarely focus on the deeper content of the lecture or rarely attempt to assimilate it. They never learn the material in the first place.

Later that student may try to memorize it in some unproductive and boring rote fashion. Understimulation leads to poor learning and memory. On the other hand, the successful student concentrates on *understanding the lecture's or book's deeper meaning and understanding how to apply it to new situations*. This intense focus and struggle to understand the material creates harmonious functioning and its big three interwoven outcomes--peak learning, peak performance, and peak happiness.

• **Focus on what you *want to say* to overcome self-expression or speech anxiety.** A client came to me who had an ironic problem. She was a successful teacher who spoke in front of her students every day with great confidence--even when being evaluated by her principal.

Yet she was currently taking a graduate class that required her to speak in front of the class. She was terrified. She had a history of being terrified of speaking in front of her peers. Why was this so? She could teach children confidently with her peers present or even with a principal present who had to make a decision about her job security! Why couldn't she speak to a group of fellow college students with only a grade at stake?

After much inquiry, we found out that the main difference between her teaching situation and her speaking to a college class was that in the first instance she felt like *what she had to say was important*. She really wanted to teach the children the things *she believed they needed to learn*. Therefore, she would lose herself and focus all of her attention on her goal of helping the students learn the material.

In the college class, she was required to give a speech on a topic she had little interest in, knew little about, and thought would bore the other students. Therefore, her *mind* focused on her own fears about evaluations by her peers and her instructors. She could not get lost in *delivering a message she thought was important*. She rewrote her speech into one she *really wanted to tell her classmates*. Focusing on what she *wanted to tell them* reduced her anxiety so much that she delivered the speech confidently.

This method works with most people when they feel anxiety about talking with others. A salesperson who first sold himself on his product and was honest with customers became more confident and persuasive. People afraid of talking to strangers have become more outgoing and confident. They focus on *their genuine interests* instead of making a good impression. They ask themselves, "What do I want to know about this person--or learn from this person?" and "What would I like to tell them about me or talk about?"

The next time you feel anxious about talking with someone (or giving a speech), focus on what you want to *learn* from them and what you want to *say*– not on any *outcome* (focus on process goals).

FOCUS ON YOUR ULTIMATE CONCERN FOR CLEAR INNER DIRECTION

In the big game which is life, keeping your eye on the ball means focusing on your ultimate concerns. My ultimate concern is the greatest happiness for myself and others over time. Happiness is partially a measure of the harmony in our mind-body subparts. If all of my subparts such as psychologist, athlete, husband, artist, and child are in harmony, then I will experience happiness.

People elevate many different *means* to happiness above the *end* goal happiness. These means may include a love relationship, immediate pleasure, money, job status, family, or security. By not keeping their eye on the ball, they start making these *means* to happiness into *ends*. Consequently, they make decisions that undermine their happiness. A major cause of my clients' unhappiness is their making family or relationship an ultimate concern. They become obsessed with trying to gain acceptance--no matter how dysfunctional the relationship. They lose sight of their own happiness.

I keep reminding myself that overall happiness for self and others is my ultimate concern. I am also *most responsible* for my own happiness. If there is a prolonged conflict between my family, my wife, my job, my recreation, my security, or anything else and my ultimate concern, then I will put my ultimate concern first. Sherry does the same, and it helps create a very happy marriage for both of us.

Focus on your ultimate concern to provide a beacon to lead you through fog, currents that take you adrift, and violent storms. It will provide meaning for your life and help keep you in the zone of harmonious functioning.

YOU CAN ACHIEVE MENTAL CONTROL OF YOUR EMOTIONS
AND INCREASE PERFORMANCE

I use these six mental control strategies almost every day with my clients and with myself to get control of emotions. If you are not currently using these mental control strategies, learning them and using them habitually will make a significant difference in your life. You will be able to adjust your emotions like a thermostat. You can turn down the challenge when your emotions are too hot, and turn up the challenge when your emotions are too cold. Spend much more of your life in the zone of harmonious functioning.

Review the figure of the harmonious functioning model. Then etch the SIX Harmonious Thinking mental control strategies in your mind. Perhaps you would like to learn a little memory trick to help you remember the six strategies. When I was a child, my mother read me a story about the *Little Engine That Could*. This little Choo Choo had to carry a load of toys for all the children at Christmas up and down steep hills. When it came to a hill that seemed too overwhelming, it repeated the message, "I think I can, I think I can" over and over again--until it reached the top of the hill.

> **Think of *The Little Engine That Could* and watch it "chug off" saying**
> **"I think I can, I think I can." Use the acronym, CHUG-OFF.**
> **C=Choice; H=Harmony; U=Understanding; G=Goals & expectations;**
> **O=Optimism; and F=Focus (drop final "F").**
> **Use it to remember the six mental control strategies.**

PRACTICE 1: Use this chapter to overcome a difficult emotional situation. (1) Think of a situation, person, or issue where you would like to get better emotional control (or performance). Or think of an emotion you have trouble dealing with. (2) Is the emotion involved primarily an overarousal emotion, an underarousal emotion, or sometimes one then the other? (3) Apply the six Harmonious Thinking Strategies. Note that the problem may be solved by just one of the six--or it could take all six.

PRACTICE 2: Memorize the CHUG-OF parts and practice using them intensely until they become habitual! Put up a list on the wall, carry a list in your billfold or purse. Go back and refer to parts of this chapter like a reference book when you need it. This--more than almost any other chapter--is useful on a daily basis for coping with unpleasant emotions.

PRACTICE 3: Study the Harmonious Functioning Model diagram below until you understand each part. This exercise will help you understand and be able to visualize the HF model. Mental imagery is an excellent way to understand and remember sets of complex ideas. Try to redraw it from memory.

EFFECTS:

CONFUSION, SEARCH
1. Poor Learning
2. Poor Performance
3. **OVERAROUSAL EMOTIONS:** Anxiety, Confusion, Anger, etc
* Overwhelmed, confused, frantic (negative) interfering thoughts. Overwhelms ability to understand or cope with input.)

DELAYED EFFECTS:
* Dislike, Avoid, or Fear Activity
* Lower Confidence & Self-Esteem
* Lower Immune System & Health

"BIG 3" OUTCOMES:
1. Peak Learning
2. Peak Performance
3. Peak Interest & Happiness
* Optimal Arousal & Energy (Happiness zone varies from tranquil to highly excited states)

DELAYED EFFECTS:
* Value Activity (Intrinsic Interest)
* Confidence & Self-Esteem
* Physical Health (brain & body)

TUNED-OUT, "NUMB"
1. Poor Learning
2. Poor Performance
3. **UNDERAROUSAL EMOTIONS:** Bored, depressed, grief, lonely
* Low energy, feel tired
* Nothing seems interesting
* Runaway Emotions Cycle? (Deep depression, etc)

DELAYED EFFECTS:
* Dislike Activity, General Apathy
* Lower Confidence & Self-Esteem
* Lowered Immunity & Health

LEVEL of CHALLENGE:

"ABOVE THE ZONE"--

OVERSTIMULATION: (Too Challenging, Complex, Conflicting, or Difficult-- Overwhelms ability to understand or cope with input.)

* The IMPORTANCE of the underlying VALUES or biological NEEDS "raises the stakes" & increases arousal

"IN THE ZONE" of HARMONIOUS FUNCTIONING: (Optimally Challenging, System functioning "as it was designed" for maximum health)

Optimal MATCH between:
(1) INPUT Complexity, Difficulty, Newness, Danger, Ambiguity, etc

(2) COPING ABILITY--Skills, Knowledge, Understanding, Expectations, Goals, Beliefs, Ability to structure or cope with overstimulation

"BELOW THE ZONE"-- UNDERSTIMULATION: (Too Little Challenge-- Too simple, easy, redundant, limited growth potential)
* Often caused by:
1-Loss & goallessness
2-Avoidance of situations which are "above the zone" &produce too much anxiety.
3-Too much structure or overcontrol of input.

SIX HARMONIOUS THINKING Mental Control Strategies:

1. CHOICE of Episode: Replace or Convert Episodes?
* Do what you love or
* Learn to love what you are doing

2. HARMONY of Motives & Parts of Self:
* Do I look forward to doing it?
* Resolve Inner Conflicts

3. UNDERSTANDING: Creating a Road Map to Success. (Right knowledge, skills, & plans)

4. GOALS (and Expectations):
1-Goal & expectation LEVELS
2-ALTERNATIVE goals & plans vs. very ATTACHED to one
3-PROCESS vs. OUTCOME goals
4-DYNAMIC vs. STATIC goals
5-SIMPLE, SMALL-STEP vs. COMPLEX, LARGE-STEP

(Think LAPDS to recall the 5)

5. OPTIMISM-- that we can be happy with any outcome! (Based on confidence that we can achieve a happy mental state even in the worst situation.)

6. FOCUS Keep your eye on the ball!

(Think CHUG-OF to recall the 6)

HIGHER BRAIN CENTERS:

HIGHER SELF:
* Ultimate Concern is HAPPINESS for self & others
* Clear BOUNDARIES of control & responsibility
* Broad PERSPECTIVE of time & references (Eg All people)
* ABUNDANCE THINKING- (Gratitude, "ZERO" expectations of what we will receive)
* UNCONDITIONAL LOVE for self and others: Giving out of love and empathy without expectation of receiving vs. out of obligation--or as a trade

EXECUTIVE SKILLS
* Self-Exploration
* Problem-Solving
* Conflict Resolution
 ->Negotiating "Win-Win" solutions between parts of self or with others
* Goal-Setting & Planning
 ->Achievement Excellence Cycle
 ->O-PATSM System
* Emotional Coping Skills

PARTS OF SELF:
Cognitive Systems, Life Themes, Roles, Mental Models, Body, Reference Groups, etc
* Each is a potential source of harmonious functioning.
* Aware of Self Parts?
* Values Checklist?

EXAMPLES:
"Inner Child" "Explorer"
"Inner Parent" "Therapist"
"Achiever" "Helper"
"Artist" "Scientist" "Friend"
"Lover" "Tennis Player"

The SIX HARMONIOUS THINKING Mental Control Strategies and   Tom G. Stevens PhD

HARMONIOUS FUNCTIONING MODEL OF EMOTIONS & PERFORMANCE

SHAQ Research Results: Emotional Coping Habits

The Emotional Coping scale asks, *how often do you respond to being upset with the following response?* The users check the percentage of time they respond with a particular type of response (see subscales below). The Emotional Coping scale correlated with Happiness, .66; with Low Depression, .60; with Low Anxiety, .51; with Low Anger-Aggression, .49; with good Relationships, .42; with Health, .49; with Income, .13; with Education, .14; and with college GPA, .14.

Emotional Coping consists of the following six subscales.
1. Problem-solve, self-explore, talk subscale correlated with Happiness, .48; with Low Depression, .28; with Low Anxiety, .22; with Low Anger-Aggr, .29; with good Relationships, .42; with Health, .26; with Education, .10; and with college GPA, .11.
2. Positive thoughts, philosophical view, pep-talk subscale correlated with Happiness, .57; with Low Depression, .50; with Low Anxiety, .36; with Low Anger-Aggr, .31; with good Relationships, .36; with Health, .28; with Income, .05; with Education, .08; and with college GPA, .05.
3. Positive acts, fun, exercise. subscale correlated with Happiness, .36; with Low Depression, .24; with Low Anxiety, .14; with Low Anger-Aggr, .21; with good Relationships, .25; and with Health, .29.
4. Not anger, blame, withdraw subscale correlated with Happiness, .49; with Low Depression, .53; with Low Anxiety, .48; with Low Anger-Aggr, .45 with good Relationships, .27; with Health, .26; with Income, .13; with Education, .08; and with college GPA, .09.
5. Not smoke, drugs subscale correlated with Happiness, .19; with Low Depression, .29; with Low Anxiety, .33; with Low Anger-Aggr, .26; with good Relationships, .07; with Health, .64; with Income, .07; with Education, .18; and with college GPA, .11.
6. Not eat item correlated with Happiness, .20; with Low Depression, .27; with Low Anxiety, .22; with Low Anger-Aggr, .21; with good Relationships, .07; with Health, .24; with Income, .10.

Positive responses such as problem-solving, exploring, positive thoughts, reframing with Higher Self or other positive beliefs, doing positive engaging activities, and avoiding unproductive, hostile, damaging, or addictive thoughts and actions are some of the best ways to get control of emotions.

As you can see, how we respond to daily negative emotions may have strong effects on our overall happiness, negative emotions, relationships, health, and is even related to income and educational achievement.

Note: For all correlations, p < .0001 and Ns ranged from 2704 to 3226.

Happiness is *not* caused by external conditions.
Happiness measures the harmonious functioning of our brain--
how optimally it is challenged and how much it is learning.
Overchallenge causes overarousal emotions like anxiety and anger.
Underchallenge causes underarousal emotions
like boredom and depression.
We can adjust our emotions like a thermostat
by adjusting the challenge level.
Belief in mental control seems like magic,
because that belief alone helps get control.
The six mental control strategies give you
basic tools to achieve mental control.
Learn how to CHUG-OFF
when you need to adjust your emotional thermostat.
CHOICE to replace or convert the situation,
HARMONY of motives through self-exploration,
UNDERSTANDING the situation and creating a road map,
GOALS (to lower anxiety, set goals LAPDS--
lower, alternative, process, dynamic, , simple),
OPTIMISM that I can eventually be happy
no matter what the outcome, and
FOCUS on the ball and ultimate concern.
Through strengthening your Higher Self and increased mental control,
YOU CAN CHOOSE TO BE HAPPY.

CHAPTER 9

CREATE A BETTER WORLD
FOR YOURSELF AND OTHERS:

Get control of your time and yourself
to accomplish more and have more fun!

\\

FEELING IN CONTROL OF OUR LIVES VERSUS FEELING HELPLESS

George owns a thriving business and has lots of money. Yet, he feels that his life is out of control and feels helpless to do anything about it. Happiness has eluded him and life seems to have little meaning. He has this feeling of powerlessness despite years of being the boss, having others respect him, and having so much business and financial success.

On the other hand, Josie Fullerton is 92 years old and lives in a retirement home. She has little money or other signs of power or influence. Yet Josie is happy, exudes warmth and joy, and says that she has everything she needs. She is grateful for all she has and feels at peace with the world. How can it be that George, with so much external power and resources, can *feel* helpless, while Josie, with so little external power and resources, can feel so much control?

Feeling in control depends on control of values and *emotions.* The reason for this paradox is that the *overall feeling of control* is not necessarily related to how much *actual external power* we have; it is more related to how much control we have over our *emotions* and the satisfaction of our *values.* Even though George owns a business and makes a lot of money, he does not enjoy his work, does not find it challenging, and does not feel he is contributing adequately to society. Important values are not being satisfied, and he feels powerless to do anything about it. He's an unhappy man.

George even feels trapped by his money and success; because he thinks he could not change a career that has brought him so much financial success. In addition, George is not happy in his marriage and has little time for recreation or other interests that contribute to his happiness. In short, instead of his business being an asset to his happiness, he lets his business control him.

This is another example of choosing an ultimate concern (business success) which undermined happiness. If we want to be happy, then we must give happiness priority over lesser things.

On the other hand, Josie puts happiness first. She loves to read, visit with people, play bridge, knit, do hospital volunteer work, travel, and appreciate beauty of all sorts. Josie loves to learn and help others. She had a philosophy of life that helped her have a positive way of viewing the world. Josie's sense of control in her life was based on her confidence that she could make herself happy--even after losing her lifetime partner of more than 64 years. Josie was recently elected president of her retirement association. When I asked her what the secret to her longevity was she said, "Being happy. Happy people live longer!" Research evidence supports Josie's contention.

CHANGING OUR ACTIONS AND ENVIRONMENTS TO FIND HAPPINESS

In past chapters we have seen that we can choose to be happy by choosing many *internal routes to happiness* such as developing our Higher Selves, world views, and self-esteem. We have learned about how to get more internal control and get more mental control of emotions so that we will spend more time in the zone of harmonious functioning.

In this chapter, the focus is on *external routes* to happiness. How can you find the physical and social environments that make you happiest? How can you achieve your goals? How can you have a significant impact on the world? The O-PATSM system has helped many people achieve more control of their lives.

I assume that goals of good time management are to *maximize our time feeling happy* and to *maximize our positive impact*. To maximize our happiness and productivity, we need to become *conscious* of both our *values* (that underlie happiness) and our *habits* (that create our impact). Our values serve as our beacons and our habits as our ships to take us where we want to go.

AUTOMATIC HABITS--HABITS CONSUME MOST OF OUR TIME

Have you ever been driving down the freeway and suddenly realized that for the past 5 miles you have been totally unaware of your driving? Scary isn't it? Did you wonder how you drove so far without having an accident? This is an example of how powerful automatic habits can be.

Much of what we do in a typical day is fairly automatic. Much of our behavior could almost be described as a series of stimulus-response types of interactions with our environment.

Think about a typical day and how many automatic habits you have. The first stimulus is the alarm clock. That clock may stimulate thoughts of work and a programmed routine of getting dressed and eating breakfast. At work, you have a whole series of automated work habits--including interpersonal habits such as automated greetings. Most of these situations take little conscious thought and problem-solving.

Automatic habits tend to continue as long as they *minimally* satisfy our values. Habits become habits because they are **reinforced** by meeting our values at some minimal level. We develop habits of eating breakfast and kissing our loved ones because these habits are reinforced by satisfying important values. We get up in the morning and get to work on time so that we will avoid the **punishment** of embarrassment and eventually being fired. The fear of these consequences may be part of what creates our anxiety as we weave in and out of traffic desperately trying to beat the clock.

The executive self creates automatic habits to increase efficiency. When I first learned to type, the process was painstaking. I had to look at a book above the typewriter and consciously calculate hitting each key. Yet, now as I type these words I just think the word and my fingers automatically type them on the screen. What a miracle!

That miracle is my cognitive brain programming the habits in the automatic habit brain. Once the habits are programmed, they are remembered forever.

Habits are automated, efficient routines to meet our values. Imagine how complex life would be if we did not have an automatic route to work. What if every day we had to read a map and plot the route to work? What if we had to carefully ponder everything we said to people? With automatic habits we just push an internal button and a programmed sequence of thoughts or behaviors emerge. They perform tasks to satisfy our values.

Too much routine can cause boredom and depression. If our lives become too programmed or routine, they may become stagnant, boring, and *depressing*. To spend more time in the zone of harmonious functioning (happy), we need to optimize challenge, change, and complexity (Chapter 7).

There is another problem with becoming too programmed. Recall that habits may continue as long as they meet a *minimal* level of satisfaction. Perhaps our values are being met minimally, but we could be a lot happier. To *maximize* our happiness, we need to use the conscious part of our brain--our inner executive (and Higher Self). We need a system like O-PATSM to *consciously* make sure we are getting our values met.

For example, Gloria was an divorced college student and mother. She was busy and was accomplishing a lot. During a typical day, she attended classes and then went to work. After work, she picked up her two children, attended to them, and studied every free minute before bed. On weekends she did her chores, was a mother, studied, and worked.

The habits she developed were efficient for meeting her basic goals. She wanted to be a good mother, get her college degree, and be able to provide a minimal standard of living for herself and her children. She was meeting all these goals and was pleased with herself. Her accomplishments had been a big confidence booster.

So what is wrong with this picture? What is wrong is that Gloria could have been happier than meeting her minimal basic goals. Gloria said, "I'm so busy doing the things I need to do that I never take 5 minutes for myself to think about being happier." Even though she was busy--she spent a lot of time daydreaming, worrying, or working slowly. Her mild depression from so many unsatisfied values had reduced her energy and efficiency. She had even begun to resent her children. She felt trapped.

The O-PATSM system helped Gloria get *conscious control* of her life. Gloria took my self-management workshop because she wondered if she could be happier. Once Gloria used the O-PATSM self-management system for awhile, she realized she could still meet her basic goals *and* enjoy life a lot more.

Following the O-PATSM system, Gloria listed her basic values and 6-month objectives in each life area. The values and objectives she listed reflected several higher and more fun values she had been ignoring. She held weekly self-management sessions to consciously plan and prioritize her to-do lists for the following week. The to-do *priorities* were based upon her values and objectives checklists.

Getting life in balance. Finally, she used her to-do lists moment-to-moment to remind her of the little extra things she had been omitting from her life. These little extras added joy where there had been little. These extras included time to herself, nature walks, pleasure reading, aerobic dancing, calling friends, attending social events, and dating. As a result of feeling happier, she became more efficient doing everything from housework to homework. Gloria learned how to spend more of her time doing what she wanted--she was *happier and more productive*.

BALANCE VALUE SATISFACTION TO ACHIEVE INNER HARMONY--
One value versus another?
Self versus others?
Now versus the future?

When an automobile wheel is out of balance, it shakes the entire car. If one value is not getting met, it can shake our inner harmony. Knowing that we are not caring for ourselves, knowing that we are hurting others, or knowing that we are not providing for our future can create serious disharmony and anxiety. Our research with the Life Skills Questionnaire found a correlation of .50 between life area balance and overall happiness the past three years.

BALANCE BETWEEN PARTS OF OURSELVES

I will never forget the man in his early 50's who approached me after one of my first self-management workshops. He told me that he owned an accounting firm. He said that he had gotten a great deal out of my workshop, but that I would never believe his story about *what* he had learned.

He said, "I have used O-PATSM-like principles for over 20 years in my business, and these principles are responsible for my success. The reason I took your self-management workshop was because my personal life has *not* been so successful. The strange thing is that, in all these years, it never occurred to me to use the same principles that worked so well in business to manage my personal life. Now I can see why I haven't been happy." He gave the example of his social life. He said that he had no real friends--only business contacts. He had always left the social planning to his wife, so *their* friends were really *her* friends. The O-PATSM system helped him get control.

For a balanced life, I value *each area of my life.* If we want to be happy in each area of our lives, we must take *conscious* control of each area of our lives. We will each have a list of life areas that works best for us. A sample list of life areas might include some (or all) of the following. Make your own list now.

- career
- relationships
- self-development and spiritual
- health and physical activity
- recreation, travel
- finances
- maintenance and chores
- organizations and special activities

BALANCE BETWEEN PRESENT AND FUTURE SATISFACTION OF VALUES

What do terms like ego strength, will power, and self-discipline all have in common? They usually refer to some sort of inner strength that allows a person to work toward *distant future goals*, even though the person has to endure pain or give up pleasure now in order to reach that goal.

Every major religion, many philosophers, and most psychologists have recognized the importance of will power for achieving distant goals. The psychologist Dr. David McClelland (1991, 1961) is renowned for his decades long study of achievement motivation for individuals and societies. He found that societies espousing values related to postponing immediate enjoyment for future benefits and other achievement values tend to achieve more.

If we want our personal worlds to be more like our ideals, then we must invest energy now into creating that world. We can save money to buy a car or house instead of spending it for fun now. We can go to college to have the career and benefits we want instead of getting a job and having more money now. Investing in the future has many great advantages. Many people have not learned the lesson of delaying pleasures for future benefits. If you are one, perhaps too little focus on the future is why you are in a mess now.

Other people invest *so much* effort toward future goals that they undermine their own efforts. For example, some students spend so much time working, taking care of others, going to school, and *not taking care of current values* that they burn out and quit. If they had balanced future happiness with current happiness better, they would not have lost motivation and eventually would have reached their goals.

A second danger of becoming too future-oriented is developing this future orientation into a lifestyle. These people live their entire lives working toward the future-- feeling unhappy and deprived. They may overvalue frugality, self-discipline, or self-sacrifice. These habits should be *means* to happiness, not ends in themselves. These people may never reap the harvest from their work. Instead, the only benefits they may reap are of being a martyr or feeling superior to others who enjoy life. Not much compensation!

Other people are able to give a disproportionate amount of energy for *limited amounts of time--if they can motivate themselves to keep going.* For example I knew of one student who worked 40 hours per week, spent almost 40 hours per week on schoolwork, and commuted over 10 hours per week. He was saving money toward buying a house. He did this for almost 6 years. He said that he averaged sleeping about 4 hours each night.

He was mildly depressed much of the time. I helped him clarify that he was choosing to remain less happy, because he was denying many of his important values and parts of himself for so long.

> **PRACTICE:** Look at the balance in your life between investing in the *present* and investing in the *future.* In what areas are you giving too little attention to future needs and values? In what areas are you giving too little attention to current needs and values?

CLARIFYING VALUES--MAKE A VALUES CHECKLIST

I assume that at least one of your ultimate concerns (top goals) is to be happy. We have seen how the satisfaction of values is necessary for happiness. These values range from *basic biological values* such as food and sex to *higher values* such as Maslow's meta-values (beauty, truth, wholeness, etc.).

Use your values checklist for making decisions and planning your time. If you want to *consciously oversee* that your values are being satisfied, first clarify what your important values are. Use your values checklist for every important decision--including career decisions, relationships decisions, and activity decisions. Choose the alternative you think will *maximize the overall satisfaction of your values.*

Values can be hidden from our normal awareness. Our values are our enduring, underlying needs and wants. When I ask you to list your values, you probably won't list them all, because values are more hidden from consciousness that immediate goals.

Values can be on different levels. Value is a term that can be applied to many different levels of objects and activities. For example I value playing tennis. Tennis is a *specific, concrete* lower level value activity. It is easy to be aware that we like a specific activity such as tennis. My higher level, more general values that *make* tennis so important include physical activity, health, socializing, learning, and being outdoors.

Believing that we can *always* create alternative routes to happiness increases our *self-confidence.* What happens when an important relationship suddenly ends? We normally feel a great sense of *loss* and *grief*, because important values which have been getting satisfied are suddenly *not being satisfied.* The extreme anxiety and depression people feel after such a loss is a problem common to many of my clients. How can they be happy again?

**To overcome a loss, first find substitute activities or objects
that meet the *same underlying values.***

The first step is to identify the *values that were being satisfied* by the lost person, object, or activity. Common values include companionship, communication, understanding, caring, sex, financial help, emotional support, doing chores, taking care of business affairs, or many others. We can become *so dependent on someone else* for satisfying these values that we may come to falsely believe that we cannot get these values met without that person. We do not realize what inner powers we already have and can develop for *getting these values met ourselves* (or with different people's help).

Once we realize that there are many routes to happiness--many ways we can meet our underlying values--then we instantly have a greater sense of inner strength and power.

TECHNIQUES FOR CLARIFYING IMPORTANT UNDERLYING VALUES

How we can discover these hidden, unconscious values? First, think of the values that *are* conscious. Some of your most important values are obvious and you can just list them once you understand what a value is. However, other values are difficult to identify. In the following sections, I will describe a number of values clarification methods. *Use these values clarification methods to make your own values checklist.*

Follow your emotions to underlying values. Since your emotions are so closely linked to your values satisfaction, you can follow them to find underlying values. Focus on your emotions and focus on thoughts and images that are associated with these emotions to give you clues about underlying values. A good psychotherapist knows this technique well. Instead of avoiding thoughts and images that produce strong emotions, focus on the thoughts and images producing the strongest emotions. (See the self-exploration method in Chapter 2.)

Actively fantasize and observe the dreams and themes that interest you. In an experiment during World War II, prisoners in a state prison volunteered for research on starvation. After days of bread and water diets, their attention was constantly focused upon food. They dreamed about food, they fantasized about food, and they talked about food with each other constantly. In other words, when an important value is not being met, it tends to emerge in the *themes* of our thoughts, dreams, and actions.

What themes attract you in movies and TV shows? What do you like to read and talk about? What do you think about when your mind is free to wonder? Do you have active fantasies or dreams? If you constantly watch romantic or adventure movies, then they reflect your values. *You may not be getting some underlying value adequately satisfied.* Watching those movies is one way to get more romance or adventure in your life.

Similarly, notice the themes that turn you off. What are you avoiding? Perhaps you are getting *too much* of something. Or perhaps you are not facing a fear you need to overcome. Maybe you can reduce your unhappiness through self-exploration.

Actively dreaming and fantasizing can be the first step to creating a world more like our dreams--at least in ways which meet the *same underlying values.* Martin Luther King's "Dream for America" not only was a powerful motivator for himself, but even helped create a world that was more like his dream.

What are your fantasies and dreams? If they seem silly, impractical, or that no one would value them, try questioning those self-doubts. If--after examination--they still seem impractical, (1) identify the underlying values and (2) create more practical dreams and goals (that will meet those underlying values).

Value *expectations* affect our happiness. To get over negative emotions, identify (1) *which values are not being met* and (2) your *value expectation levels* for each value. Two people may make $40.000 per year, one is very happy with that income and one is very unhappy with it because their expectation levels are different. One person thinks they need or should be making $30,000 and the other $50.000. Their expectation levels are almost as important as their actual salaries in determining their overall satisfaction in this value area. As you identify different values and goals, examine your *goal and expectation levels.* (See Chapter 8 to see how to change those levels.)

    PRACTICE: Values Clarification Exercises.
    (1) *Make a values checklist.* List as many important general, underlying values as you can think of off the top of your head. First, list your different life areas such as your career, people, your body and mind, your possessions, the world around you, your recreation and other interests, etc. Then, list values under each life area. During each of the following exercises, when you think of a new value, add it to your values checklist.
    (2) **Think about how you spend your time.** Ask yourself why you spend so much time doing what you do? What values are being satisfied (or you hope will be satisfied in the future) from each important activity?
    (3) **What do you spend your money for?** What would you add to your life if you had 10 million dollars? (Your spending reflects your values.)
    (4) **If you could have one special, unlimited talent be given to you, what would it be?** What values would it help you satisfy?
    (5) **Think of times in your life when you were the happiest.** Picture them clearly and follow your feelings to see what values were being satisfied. Which are not being satisfied now?

WE CAN CHANGE OUR VALUES AND INTERESTS
to make life happier and more productive

VALUES TEND TO LAST, BUT CAN BE CHANGED RADICALLY

Do you still enjoy the same activities you did 10 years ago? The same music? What about the types of people? Research has shown that people's general interests, attitudes, and other preferences tend to persist for many years. On the other hand, it is possible for our interests to change radically.

We can change our values and interests with new knowledge and skills. Does your life seem too monotonous, too hum-drum? Do you want more zest and fun? Perhaps you need some new interesting activities. We need knowledge and skill to enjoy many things in life. Certainly we cannot enjoy talking with a Frenchman unless we can speak French. We cannot enjoy playing tennis unless we know how to play. We cannot enjoy classical music, unless we can perceive the more subtle music patterns and appreciate them.

Frequently, clients' primary complaint is that they are depressed or feel that they cannot enjoy being alone. Often, they *only enjoy activities involving other people.* Sometimes, they have trouble thinking of anything they enjoy alone at all! They are very dependent upon other people for their enjoyment in life. Therefore, they are susceptible to being controlled by others.

In contrast, people who have developed their own interests and enjoy solitary activities are rarely needy--they tend to be much more independent. The greater the variety of interests, the less dependent they are upon any particular person, economic situation, or any other factor. In short *a person with many interests has more routes to happiness available--and is less dependent upon one route.* Learn how to be self-entertaining!

We can change our values by changing our beliefs and reconditioning ourselves. When I was a child, I disliked fish and loved beef. However, once I learned about the health advantages of fish, I decided to try to like fish better. I used a technique of gradual association with positive things I already liked. I started with mild-tasting fish combined with sauces or other seasonings that largely took away all of the fish taste and left a pleasant seasoned taste.

In addition I told myself how healthy fish is. I pictured it helping clear my arteries and pictured animal fats clogging my arteries. I was so successful that today I like fish better than beef and even eat fairly strong-tasting fish.

We can learn to recondition our tastes--*to dislike sources of bad habits.* For example, I led a stop smoking group in which we used a rapid-smoking aversive conditioning technique to help people lose their attraction to the taste of cigarette smoke. People smoked one cigarette after another in a small room until each person felt almost sick at their stomach. This conditioning experience helped them lose some of their positive taste for smoking and made quitting much easier.

We also asked people to examine reasons *why* they smoked and examine basic beliefs related to smoking. For example, some people had always thought of themselves as being independent, rebellious, or outgoing and had associated this self-image with smoking. Once they realized that they would be more independent and possibly even more respected by *not* smoking, this change in beliefs also contributed to their quitting.

Six months later, over 70% of the people were still abstainate. These value change techniques are effective. The stop smoking programs that use these techniques achieve the best results of any reported in the research literature on smoking cessation.

How can we develop new interests? "I can *learn to enjoy* this." Do you assume that your interests are unchangeable? Do you assume that because you never liked something, you never will? These assumptions, alone, can prevent you from growing and developing new interests. If you have assumptions such as these, then the first step is to question them. My own view is that if one healthy person can enjoy an activity, then *almost anyone can probably learn to enjoy it*--if they are willing to learn *how* to enjoy it.

If we don't enjoy something, it is because we can't create the *mental state* of someone who does enjoy it. Appreciation requires learning. I would not say to myself, "I will never enjoy opera." I will only say that I don't care for it much now, but that I think I could learn to like it if I chose to take the time and energy required *to learn how.*

After you overcome your belief that you cannot learn to enjoy something, then it is time to begin learning how to enjoy it. Learning may require reading, taking lessons, practicing, and playing. Find people who like the activity and interview them. What do they like so much about it? How did they learn to like it? Arranging to have a surplus of overall positive versus negative experiences with the activity is very important.

> **PRACTICE: Inventory of Interests--stretch your likes.** (1) Take an inventory of your current interests. Do you have enough activities that you truly enjoy doing alone? With others? If not, then think of some that you might like to try. (2) Think of at least one potential new activity you want to enjoy more. Plan to increase that interest. Take lessons, interview people who love it, or read about it.

YOUR PERSONAL WORLD--You can make it a happier place!

THE "GOOD LIFE"--EXTERNAL ROUTES TO HAPPINESS
What is your dream of *La Dolce Vita*--the good life? When I was 16, the good life meant someday having a wife who is beautiful, charming, loving, understanding, romantic, and fun. It was having an interesting career, being the best at something, making a lot of money, and having time to play. The good life meant travel, friends, sports, and fun in my free time. I wanted to live in a beautiful home in a beautiful, interesting area. Even though I now know that I don't *need* these things to be happy, I still *prefer* them; and I still believe that these external routes contribute to my happiness.

We create our personal worlds (within limits). Happily, most of my teenage dreams have come true. These dreams have provided direction for the decisions, goals, and actions I have taken to create the personal world I so love today. In addition, seeing my dreams come true gives me a sense of satisfaction and accomplishment.

WE LIVE IN UNIQUE PERSONAL WORLDS
My first image of my personal world must have been a room full of bright lights and a giant wearing a white mask and rubber gloves. It must have been quite a shock. My personal external world suddenly expanded from my mother's womb to a place filled with strange images that I have been coping with since.

Now, my personal external world consists of my home, my neighborhood, my wife Sherry, my family, other people, my work environment, tennis courts, restaurants, and my natural environment. My more immediate personal world environment also consists of books, music, TV, movies, and journals. Media are windows to an even larger personal world.

Zones of influence in our personal worlds. The actions of Mikail Gorbachev ended the Cold War, and affected my life half a world away. Any event, anywhere, could potentially influence my life. However, events occurring in my immediate zones of influence (such as my family and job) normally have greater impact on me. What are the zones of influence in your personal world?

Choosing our *boundaries* and priorities gives us more control of our lives. As a child, I had little choice about who my parents were or where I would live. But, as an adult, I have a wide range of choices about where I want to be, what activities I want to be in, and who I want to be with. Clarifying my boundaries and prioritizing my zones of influence helps me make decisions and helps me emotionally let go of less important areas. I choose to make my wife more important than my friends, and make my friends more important than my acquaintances--and so forth. We cannot be all things to all people.

Personal worlds can vary dramatically. Sometimes we fail to recognize how different various people's worlds can be, and how these differences can dramatically affect their thinking and behavior. Put yourself in a day of the life of several different people--such as a family member, a homeless person, a corporation president, a physician, a factory worker, your boss, or a convict.

Understanding people's personal worlds is necessary to understand the person and the issues they must deal with to be happy. The insights gained can help us create a happier personal world. Experiencing other people's worlds has been an interesting benefit of being a psychologist.

PRACTICE 1: What is your current personal world? What are the main environments in your personal world? Does each environment seem powerful when you are in it--almost as if the others didn't exist? Where do you usually feel happiest? Where, the unhappiest? How do your feelings, thoughts, and behaviors differ in these different environments? What can you learn from this comparison that will help you create a happier personal world?

PRACTICE 2: What is your image of the good life? Get in touch with your current and past images of the kind of personal world (life) you want (family, home, work, play, community, etc.). (**Warning:** From past chapters I hope it is clear that becoming too attached to any specific goal can lead to unnecessary anxiety and pain. Become aware of several routes to happiness and productivity--if one becomes blocked you can create another.) Develop a variety of scenarios and *prioritize them.*

THE VALUE OF HEALTH:
YOU CAN CHOOSE TO MAXIMIZE YOUR HEALTH

As my friend Jack says, "It's a great day whenever you wake up on the right side of the grass." While this is not a book on health, it is a book on how to maximize happiness and well-being. Health and longevity are vital for well-being and maximizing happiness. Research strongly supports the value of healthy habits including exercise and good nutrition for good health, longevity, and happiness. By integrating good health habits into your daily routine, you can maximize your health, longevity, and happiness. Studies have even shown that *regular vigorous exercise alone* can be as effective as medication in reducing clinical depression (Babyak, et al., 2000). Following is a list of health guidelines that is strongly supported by current search. Sherry and I follow them all. If you love yourself, then you will care for each cell in your body, and live as healthily has possible.

•**Regular vigorous exercise.** At least 20-30 minutes daily; better, an hour or more. Also, spread at least mild exercise throughout the day. Use weight-bearing exercises multiple times per week to make sure that you exercise all muscle groups and do full-range of movement to help all joints.

•**Healthy diet.** Adequate complete protein, low-fat/adequate Omega 3 fats and other good fats, lots of dark fruit and vegetables, multi-grains, fiber, etc. Drink tea and coffee. Eat low-fat chocolate, and other beneficial foods. Keep alcohol to one drink daily—best drink red wine. Control calories to keep weight in ideal range.

•**Supplements.** *Adequate minerals and trace minerals*—most don't get enough in our diet. Omega 3 fatty acids, proper amounts of all vitamins, CQ10, Alpha Lipoic Acid, vision supplements, amino acids, additional supplements supported by research. Go to Life Extension Foundation, www.lef.org, or other respected sources for good information.

•**Eliminate drugs and medication.** All recreational drugs (including marijuana) have serious, negative effects on health and psychological well-being. Do not use drugs and do not smoke! Even prescribed medications have negative side effects and in many cases can be replaced by good exercise, diet, and supplements. Be cautious and get advice from alternative medicine sources as well as traditional physicians.

•**Keep weight low.** Get to the low side of recommendations for your height. Research on caloric restriction seems to show great longevity benefits.

•**Safety counts.** Risk-takers tend to have lower longevity! If you take a risk that kills 1/10,000 of the time, that seems like pretty good odds—right? But what happens to your odds if you do it weekly or daily for 10 to 20 years? Wear seat belts, don't do dumb things, and think about safety in all situations where some risk might be present. Plan what you would do in worst case scenarios.

•**Get enough sleep.** Studies show 7-8 hours/night is associated with better health and greater longevity.

A mountain of research evidence supports the health, happiness, and longevity benefits of the above habits. Good health and safety habits are an essential part of good self-management.

One of my top goals has been to maximize my health and longevity. While I've always enjoyed sports, I took up tennis at age 30 and have played several times weekly for many years. Currently, I play tennis, ride my bike vigorously an hour, swim vigorously an hour, or walk several miles almost every day. My wife, Sherry, does all this except play tennis. We eat healthily and take nutritional supplements supported by health research. Our health habits have helped keep us young and energetic in appearance and activities. We see many people our age who haven't lived healthy becoming sick, disabled, or limited.

The years and decades multiply the effects of small differences in daily habits. For example, how did one beautiful 120-pound 20-year old become a 200-pound 60-year old while another stayed at 120 pounds? Twenty extra calories a day is about two extra pounds per year. In 4 years that's only 8 pounds, but in 20 years it's 40 pounds, and in 40 years it's 80 pounds. A secret to controlling weight is keeping it within a 3-5 pound range. When it gets near the upper limit, put on the brakes and get into gear.

Small daily health habits add together over the years to make the difference between health and sickness and between life and death.

> Every cell in our bodies is important to our overall health, and
> each cell has very specific needs for nutrition and exercise.
> Our daily nutrition and exercise habits
> add together to create huge effects on our health and happiness.
> Make your health an important life area
> in your *Personal Objectives List* (see below)
> and get started now!

SHAQ Research Results: Health Habits

First, good health correlates well with happiness and other outcomes. The Health Outcomes Scale correlated with Happiness, .40; with Low Depression, .38; with Low Anxiety, .34; with Low Anger-Aggr, .39; with good Relationships, .21; with Income, .09; with Education, .12; and with college GPA, .12.

While health was not a central focus of the SHAQ research, SHAQ did produce some interesting health-related data. I have already presented a great deal of data relating almost every SHAQ scale so far to the Health Outcomes scale. In this section I present data relating health habits to important outcomes.

The five Health subscales follow:

1. Physical Conditioning correlated with Happiness, .43; with Low Depression, .30 with Low Anxiety, .25; with Low Anger-Aggr, .28; with Relationships, .28; with Income, .08; with Education, .06; and with college GPA, .06.

Healthwise, physical conditioning correlated with Low Illness, .32 and with Low Weight, .43.

2. Good Nutrition Habits correlated with Happiness, .39; with Low Depression, .25 with Low Anxiety, .23; with Low Anger-Aggr, .26; with Relationships, .24; with Income, .10; with Education, 18, and with college GPA, .14.

Healthwise, good diet correlated with Low Illness, .21, with low weight, .26; and with physical conditioning, .43.

3. Hours Sleep correlated with Happiness, .33; with Low Depression, .19 with Low Anxiety, .14; with Low Anger-Aggr, .27; and with Relationships, .31.

Healthwise, hours sleep correlated with Low Illness, .22, with low weight, .19; with physical conditioning, .35; and with healthy diet, .29.

4. Low Weight correlated with Happiness, .22; with Low Depression, .19 with Low Anxiety, .09; with Low Anger-Aggr, .17; with Relationships, .13; and with college GPA, .06.

Healthwise, low weight correlated with Low Illness, .15 and with physical conditioning, .43.

5. Low Addictive Habits (low alcohol, no cigarettes, no drugs) correlated with Happiness, .23; with Low Depression, .24 with Low Anxiety, .21; with Low Anger-Aggr, .24; with Relationships, .12; with Income, .03; with Education, .12; and with college GPA, .11.

Healthwise, Low Addictive Habits correlated with Low Illness, .16 and with physical conditioning, .18.

As we have found in all areas so far, good seems to correlate with good. Good exercise, diet, sleep, and non-addictive habits correlate not only with each other but with lower rates of illness, greater happiness, and lower negative emotions. In this case, it seems likely that there are strong mutually causative forces at play. People who value themselves and their own happiness tend to value health and have healthier habits. The resulting better health contributes to their happiness, continued health, and reinforces the underlying values and habits.

Note: For all correlations, $p < .0001$ and Ns ranged from 1908 to 3179. All ratings are self-report.

CREATING A BETTER WORLD AS A GIFT OF LOVE--AND A MESSAGE TO OURSELVES
A world full of potential awaits us.
We were given many talents and an almost unlimited potential to learn new ones.
We were given many resources and opportunities.
Our most powerful motives move us to learn and create.
Our sense of inner harmony cannot be complete as long as we see needs or
potentials in our environment that shout for our attention.
Love and productivity directed externally is not only a moral good,
but is a necessary part of achieving inner peace and happiness.
We may not greatly impact the whole world,
but we can profoundly affect our personal worlds.

We may be so focused on ourselves that we overlook one of the greatest sources of happiness--giving to others. *Loving, creating, and giving can bring internal satisfaction to the giver even though there is no external reward.* As we grow, our caring about the external world grows. Our caring may start with loving "mama" and "dada" and expand to our siblings, friends, communities, and the natural environment.

Altruism simply means that we genuinely care about other people and our world. It is based upon empathy: when we see hurt, we hurt a little; and when we see happiness, we feel a little happier. Whenever I consider a new activity, one of my main criteria is, "*How much positive impact will it have on the world--especially the happiness of others?*"

Giving without expectation of reward improves self-esteem. When we give without anticipating any benefit from it, then we give ourselves a subtle message that we have *abundance and power.* That message raises self-esteem.

If I approach life as if I need to get all that I can from others ("take, take, take"), then I give the message that I am needy and dependent, because I am too inadequate to take care of myself and make myself happy.

FROM DREAMS TO REALITY:

Get a clear idea, and then focus on your goals--persistently!

ACHIEVING EXCELLENCE CYCLE--ACHIEVING DISTANT DREAMS AND GOALS

Frank Sinatra grew up in an Italian section of Philadelphia. His parents actively discouraged him from going into a singing career. His father wanted him to do something practical that would produce a steady income. Yet, he loved to sing and developed great confidence from his enthusiastic audiences. Early in life, he set a goal to become the best and developed a belief that he could. He didn't do it because he should, he did it because he wanted to. He told his parents that he could make it to the top--even though he still was unknown.

Although there are many routes to successful accomplishment, Frank Sinatra's life seems to fit a familiar pattern that can help you maximize your own potential. People who achieve extraordinary levels of success often use a process that I call the **Achieving Excellence Cycle.** Follow these steps to reach your dreams.

(1) Fantasize about what you want. Develop highly valued and emotional fantasies or dreams about the future, whether they seem realistic or not. Then, move from fantasy to clearer, more realistic visions.

(2) Explore to achieve harmony of motives. Self-explore and list your values and abilities. Explore external sources of information. Begin to let each important part of yourself think about your fantasies and have input to your ultimate goals. Move from visions to clearer goals. Aim to satisfy a *variety* of values (and parts of yourself) from one clear dream.

(3) Set high, but realistic, distant goals. Set *high distant goals* based upon the dreams. If the dreams are true to your inner values, they will automatically generate persistent motivation. Make growth, learning, and achievement motivation a high priority. Frank Sinatra had to learn *how* to sing and perform before he could become famous.

(4) Develop intermediate outcome and process goals. Focus on *step-by-step realistic, interesting, and challenging goals.* Work with great effort and confidence toward reaching those immediate goals. If a goal seems too difficult or vague, break it into smaller, simpler, behavioral goals. Use outcome goals to choose process goals, but *focus on process goals and growth-oriented goals* (especially if the outcomes are uncertain or remote). (See rise above chapter; strategy 4.)

(5) Monitor progress toward goals and modify whatever is necessary. Successfully achieving internal standards increases self-confidence. Positive feedback also increases confidence too. However, after *developing a certain level of internal control and self-confidence*, we become less dependent upon outside feedback. Frank Sinatra probably needed the praises of his audiences when he was young; but early, he developed an *internal evaluator* that kept him going--even when the outside world soured on his music and many thought his career was finished. His continued persistence led to renewed success for over 40 more years!

    Failure is common and a part of the learning and growth process. Regularly revise goals and plans to make them more realistic. The more difficulty you have achieving outcome goals, the more you need to focus on learning and process goals. Also, review alternative goals in case the entire enterprise does not work out. The O-PATSM system will provide a way of setting goals and monitoring progress.

(6) STAY IN THE ZONE--Focus on *learning, growth, excellence, and enjoyment of the process.* External goals such as making money are less important. If you stay in the zone of harmonious functioning, you will be making maximum progress most of the time because you will be in a state of peak learning, peak performance, and peak happiness.

    Functioning harmoniously will give you more motivation to persist–despite difficulties--to be successful. It will boost your self-confidence, love, and energy for persisting. *Use the six **CHUG-OF** harmonious thinking mental control strategies (from Chapter 8) to stay in the zone.* Use them to adjust your emotions and arousal like you adjust a thermostat when they drift into the states of overarousal and underarousal.

Be the best *you* can be--express yourself and do what you love. Self-actualizing people focus on learning to be the best they can be at expressing their own unique styles and interests. Frank Sinatra continued to sing and perform even when he was down and out after enjoying success for many years. He kept singing and performing even into his 80's when he had all the money and success anyone could ever want. He could do whatever he wanted. He had tried retirement (over 25 years before), but found he loved performing too much to quit.

We can learn from people who have achieved extraordinary levels of success. In the area of music, Frank Sinatra seemed to have reached some state of harmonious functioning that has had powerful effects upon his own life and the lives of millions. Maslow's self-actualizing people seemed to have had similar experiences of love for their work, which lead to extraordinary success.

**To achieve high levels of excellence and impact,
focus on developing yourself and
on developing your love and expertise for your enterprise.**

How much we achieve will also depend on what resources we start with. Even our best efforts will not guarantee excellence or impact, but we can do *our personal best*. We can use the resources and talents we *were* given to make the world a little better place for ourselves and others.

Develop your achievement motivation--it makes pursuing goals more fun! The process of meeting goals can be rewarding in itself. It also increases our self-esteem and control over our lives. The more positive experiences and beliefs that we associate with achieving goals, the more attractive achieving *per se* can become. Research has shown that achievement motivation tends to increase high achievement.

My own earlier experiences helped make achieving goals important for me. My mom and friends got excited when my team won a baseball game or when I played well. They praised me for getting good grades, and Mom was proud when I converted a back porch to a den. Consequently, I felt proud of my accomplishments. They helped me develop a greater desire to achieve goals and value achievement for its own value.

Many parents are too overprotective. They do not give their children enough responsibility or let them receive natural consequences. On the other hand, many parents are overly critical and punitive. Or, they view failure as something terrible instead of viewing failure as a learning experience. Being overprotective and being too punitive both tend to increase *fear of failure*. Research has shown that people who are motivated more by *fear of failure* than achievement motivation tend to *underachieve*.

The more positive associations we develop about achievement *per se* the more we tend to be motivated to do well at *whatever we attempt*. The more *difficult* the goals we achieve, the more we develop confidence that we can achieve success in difficult situations *in general*.

Frank Sinatra developed confidence from overcoming difficulties. His father put obstacles in his way and his rebellious subparts were stimulated to show his father that he could succeed. That does not work for everyone, but it worked for him.

The psychologist Dr. David McClelland has achieved great prominence for his research on achievement motivation. In a recent review of research on achievement motivation, he stated that one of the greatest factors for building achievement motivation is *overcoming a series of difficult goals* to obtain only *small to moderate* amounts of reward. Not being over-rewarded for achievement seems to get people into the habit of working persistently toward important goals--even during lean times.

PRACTICE: Are you motivated more by *fear of failure* or *achievement motivation*?
Complete the following questionnaire:
•When you set goals, are you more worried about *failing* and think more about avoiding a failure than about the joys of success?
•Do you tend to set overly easy or extremely high goals?
•Do you often give up or lose motivation short of attaining your goals?
• Are you easily sidetracked when pursuing goals?
•Are you easily discouraged by any failure or negative feedback?
•Does it take much external support or success to keep you pursuing a goal?
•Yes" on any of the above are signs of too high a fear of failure and too low achievement motivation.]
•When you set a goal, are you excited about reaching your goals?
•Are you determined to reach your goal--just because you set the goal?
•Does it feel good to reach a goal--just because you reached your goal?
•Do you make *any goal* important and strive hard for it--even if you are not very interested in the goal *content*? Do you value high grades in *all* subjects (versus only those you like)?
•Do you tend to set realistic, moderately difficult goals?
•Do you tend to underestimate how easy it is to reach your goals?
["Yes" on most of the above are signs of high achievement motivation.]

Try some of the suggestions in this chapter (achievement process and O-PATSM), and re-read the self-esteem and internal control chapters (5 and 6) to get more achievement motivation and internal control.

IT PAYS TO WORK TOWARD HIGH-RISK GOALS:
WE ARE PART OF A LARGER PROCESS

Some of our dreams and goals might seem so distant or difficult to reach that we fear we may never reach them. We may not. Does it mean that people who spend their lives working toward big goals--and never reach them--are failures? That they are failures as people?

Unless we can accept the possibility of not reaching big, long term goals, then we will be doomed to either not setting difficult goals or to feeling high levels of anxiety. How can we accept the possibility that we may work very hard, very long--and still not achieve the goal? How can a scientist spend his life looking for an AIDS cure--and never find it?

Ideally, I would like this book to help millions of people live happier lives, to make a lot of money, and to create new options for me. When I was thinking about writing it, I realized that getting it written and published would take hundreds of hours. I knew that if I devoted the same amount of time to extra teaching and counseling, I could make thousands of dollars. I also knew that there were huge odds against the book ever being published, much less being a big success.

However, I set other goals that I have a high chance of obtaining. One goal is to write for my own knowledge development. Another goal is to see my own ideas about how to be happy in print. I have been accumulating this knowledge for many years and am determined to record them. I know they can help people. Finally, the most important goal is for this book to help my students, clients, and other readers lead happier lives.

Together we can accomplish miracles that no one can accomplish alone. Thousands of scientists searched for a polio cure, but only Dr. Jonas Salk found it. Were the rest of their efforts wasted? Of course not. Many contributed to the knowledge that led to Dr. Salk's discovery. What if Dr. Jonas Salk had looked at the odds against finding a cure and given up?

Whenever we work toward some important goal that matters for humankind, we are *part of a larger group* working to accomplish a similar goal. Though we are part of a group, we each have something unique to contribute. We have a different point-of-view and approach. If we do not pursue it, no one else can exactly duplicate it and something will be lost.

Even if we do not reach our highest goals,
the bigger social goal will never be achieved without the efforts
of many people like us working to achieve it.
We are part of a larger harmonious group process achieving miracles--
like finding a cure to polio or dismantling the iron curtain.
These miracles could not happen if only a few people pursued the goal.

As I write, I am part of a larger process involving many people working toward human enlightenment. Thousands of potential authors have ideas they want to publish--ideas they believe can help people. If all of us let the *high risk keep us from writing, then no books would ever be written.* However, if most of us write our books, then *some* books will survive the odds and will help enlighten millions of people. *Even if my book is not chosen, my writing is part of a larger group writing process which must happen if humankind is to be enlightened.* Repeating that thought to myself increases my motivation to write!

THE O-PATSM SYSTEM:

From dreams and values to actions--creating the worlds we want

THE VALUES-ACTION GAP

Do any of the following apply to you?
• Are you too busy? Do you feel overwhelmed with too many things to do?
• Does your life ever feel out of control?
• Do you often feel disorganized? Do you have trouble setting priorities?
• Is your life out of balance? Do you neglect one or more life areas?
• Do you worry about accomplishing enough or about being more successful?
• Do you lack enough decisiveness, self-discipline, or self-motivation?
• Do you ever feel adrift--like a small sailboat in a storm--to be thrown here and there by powerful outside forces? Do you long to have a course you can follow consistently?

"Yes" answers to any of these questions may indicate that your self-management system is in need of repair or that you need to find a whole new system. Several "yes" answers may indicate that you don't have a good, *conscious,* daily self-management system.

Most of us have a values-action gap. By values-action gap, I mean that there may be little or *no conscious connection* between our daily actions and the satisfaction of our values and goals. We may spend most of our time *reacting* to situations instead of *consciously planning* our time and actions--to see that our values are adequately met. The values-action gap often causes unhappiness in one or more life areas.

If we don't regularly check in with the Higher Self to see how we want to spend our time in each area of our life, then we will not have any *internal direction based upon our highest goals.* The Higher Self can help us resist the external forces around us that are attempting to influence our time and actions. Family, friends, employers, teachers, and many others are constantly giving us messages to get us to spend our time in ways that *they prefer.* What is the source of our internal messages that provide us with internal direction? Often these quiet inner voices get drowned out in the face of the external demands.

Has there ever been a time in your life when you decided to make some changes, but later discovered that you had forgotten all about the resolutions you had made just a few weeks before? Perhaps you lacked a good self-management system to remind you of your goals each day. Learn to be proactive not reactive!

**The little voice from within--representing your innermost desires—
may be weak compared to the loud demands
from your external environment.
Develop your internal compass to keep you on course.**

THE VALUES-EMOTIONS LINK:
GET CONTROL OF VALUES TO GET CONTROL OF EMOTIONS

One of my clients, a woman in her mid twenties, had been battling severe depression and suicidal thoughts for many years. She had been hospitalized for depression more than once. While she was a student at the university, I counseled with her on and off for several years and she had steadily improved. Three years after leaving the university, she came back to see me, and told me about how happy she was and how well she had beaten her depression.

I asked her what had been the biggest factor in overcoming her depression. She said, "Using the O-PATSM system." I was shocked. Because, during her appointments, we had focused on her interpersonal relationships. I had only casually recommended to her one day that she read the O-PATSM manual. I wasn't even aware she had been using the system.

When I asked her why O-PATSM was so important to her, she replied, "The main reason I was depressed was that I always felt like my life was out of control. Using *the O-PATSM system gave me control of my life.* For the first time, I could figure out what I wanted, set goals, and get what I wanted. I didn't have to please anyone else or depend on anyone else--just me."

O-PATSM BRIDGES THE GAP BETWEEN VALUES AND ACTIONS

The O-PATSM system gives us the conscious bridge to the values-action gap that we need to maintain conscious *internal control* of our lives. We have *written lists* of each stage of the process that we can keep checking. They remind us of what we said were our values and goals when we took time to look at the big picture. Study the O-PATSM figure now to see the different parts of the O-PATSM system and to see how they connect with each other to bridge the gap between our values and our actions. My research with the Life Skills Questionnaire found that just using parts of the PATSM system correlated .38 with overall happiness for the past three years.

A *checklist* for each part acts as a perfect memory device and keeps us accountable to ourselves. Each O-PATSM link can serve as a perfect memory so we don't lose sight of our beacons. Each checklist is a reminder of what we said was important during times when we had a better perspective on our lives. O-PATSM gives us more internal control over the external forces that are constantly interfering with our priorities.

To use O-PATSM, complete the following steps:
Step 1: **Clarify values and dreams.** Create a **values checklist**.
Step 2: **Write goals and objectives.** Every few months create a written set of goals and objectives and a written **average weekly schedule**--based upon satisfying *all* of the values on your values checklist.
Step 3: **Hold regular self-management sessions**--and create a new written, **prioritized to-do list**, which covers your important to-dos from each area of your life.

Step 4: Consult the to-do lists before you decide upon activities. Use this to-do list on a moment-to-moment basis to set priorities and decide what you want to do next.

Since we check each item from the past week's to-do lists as we make our new weekly to-do lists, we cannot forget any to-do for very long. Likewise, we check all of our objectives weekly to see what progress we are making on them. Thus, we have a complete accountability system for sticking to our important values and goals. We know what progress we are making. Our lists remind us of what we really want.

Completing important tasks and making progress on goals increase our confidence and motivation to accomplish even more. In the long run, this process can dramatically affect our self-esteem.

We may not get everything done on our to-do lists; but as long as we keep doing the highest priority items first, then we will make sure that we get the most important things done. And we will spend *most of our time engaged in "A" priority activities.* Our lives will be spent in "A" quality time–being productive *and* having fun! What more can we ask from life?

O-PATSM--an acronym for good self-management. To help you remember the key aspects of this self-management system, remember the meaning of each O-PATSM letter.

OPATSM TIME MANAGEMENT SYSTEM

O = OBJECTIVES. Write them at least once a year and use weekly to make to-do lists.
P = PRIORITIES. Prioritize *all* objectives and to-do's. Do highest priority *first and best.*
A = All life AREAS. Take good care of yourself in every life area--achieve balance.
T = TO-DO lists. Make weekly and daily lists. Keep with you and use at all times.
S = SELF-MANAGEMENT SESSIONS. Take 1 hour each week to get control of your life: make that time sacred!
M = MOMENT-TO-MOMENT use of the system. What do you want to do right now?

The above is an overview of O-PATSM. In the next sections I will provide the details you need to make this system work for you. Study the O-PATSM diagram on the next page.

RULES FOR SETTING PRIORITIES

Learning how to set priorities is a crucial aspect of the O-PATSM system. We need to be setting priorities constantly--while writing goals and objectives, while writing weekly to-do's and during moment-to-moment decisions about what do in the next time frame. Following is a list of guidelines. *Learn these well* so that you can begin to establish them as automatic habits.

1. Prioritize all activities "A," "B," or "C" by how much they contribute to your overall happiness. You may want to use finer divisions of priorities if needed such as A+, A-, etc or A1, A2, etc. The highest priority activity is the one which contributes most to the overall happiness of yourself and others over the longest period of time.

2. Recognize that "A"'s provide the most satisfaction of your values over time. That is the definition of an "A" activity. Balance immediate versus long-range values and self- versus other-oriented values. Try giving high priority to *some* items from every major life area.

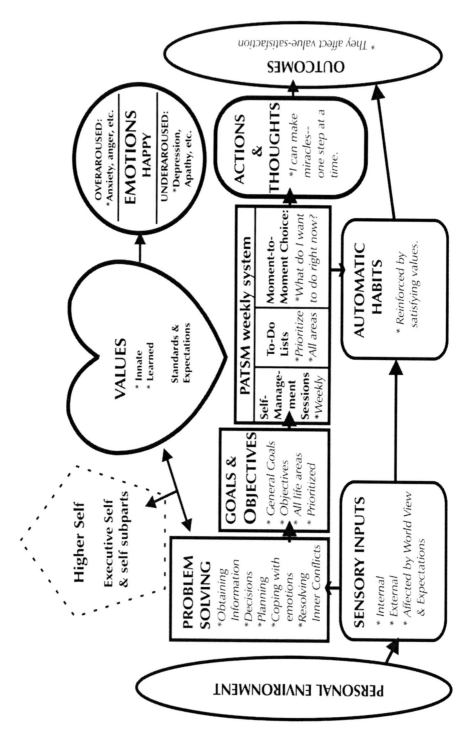

O-PATSM System Bridges GAP Between Values and Actions

3. Spend as *much time on the* "A"s and as *little time on the* "C"s as possible. Recognize that you can't do everything. You probably don't have enough time to accomplish everything you would like. A restatement of my ultimate goal of happiness is to spend as much of my time as possible *doing "A" activities* and as little time as possible doing "C" activities. (These are *process goals*.)

If you can't be productive or have fun, then why do it? Try applying your priorities to how you spend other resources--such as your *energy* and money.

4. Do "A"s *as well as possible*, and the "C"s *as quickly as possible*--or not at all--or get others (to whom they are important) to do them. A high "A" activity or goal is worth the resources required to do it at a high level of quality, a "C" activity is not. Compulsive, over-perfectionistic people are ineffective because they waste so much time on the "C"s.

On the other hand, other people do their "A"'s quickly or poorly. Or, they may avoid doing the "A"s because they seem too overwhelming or unpleasant. These people become sloppy or erratic. They are ineffective doing the most important things in their lives. They often feel like failures or "losers."

The ideal is to be perfectionistic on the highest "A"'s and to be "quick and dirty" on the "C"s. Or, don't do them at all. If the activity *is* important to someone else, normally let that person be responsible for getting it done.

5. Discriminate between *your true priorities and others' priorities* (for you). Act accordingly. Balancing your own values against the requests, demands, and needs of others who you may care a great deal about is difficult. *Assertiveness* includes the ability to pursue your own values actively--even in the face of opposition, ridicule, or threats. In addition, assertiveness means caring about others and their values and needs.

6. Spend one hour each week planning how to spend the other 112 waking hours. This is the best investment you can make of your time, because it determines how effective and happy you will be with the other 111 hours. Just a 1% increase in effectiveness and happiness more than repays that one hour.

Where To Put Your Objectives, ToDo (Task) Lists, Calendar, and Reminders

For many years I wrote my values list, objectives, tentative schedule, and my special projects using pen and paper. I kept my weekly ToDo lists in a small calendar organized by the week. I carried it in my back pocket everywhere.

Now I keep all information on my handheld computing device that is also a phone, etc. It comes with a task-list, calendar, address book, built-in alarm/reminders settable for both calendar and task list items. I have adapted its task priority system to my own system. I keep objectives lists and other important lists in the memo application--each list is a separate "memo."

Now if I want to write a task (or ToDo), I enter it on the task list with a priority. I may also enter a reminder date or even a recurrent reminder. That way I can't ever forget the task by a particular date.

Besides being more organized and getting reminders, this electronic wonder also allows me to backup all my data, so I don't have to fear losing it.

USING O-PATSM STEP-BY-STEP:
HOW TO GET CONTROL OF YOUR TIME STARTING NOW

Are you ready to start testing the O-PATSM system in your own life? I suggest that you try it for a minimum of four weeks. If you are ready to start, follow steps 1-4 below.

STEP 1: CLARIFY VALUES AND DREAMS

First, make a written values checklist as described earlier. This process includes prioritizing your values and understanding your ideal and minimal expectations.

STEP 2: WRITE GOALS AND OBJECTIVES

Make written lists of general long-term goals and more immediate and specific goals (objectives). Every 3-6 months, revise your objective lists. The objectives should be **specific, time limited, and clear** about what to do to meet them. For example, write "I will play tennis an average of 3 times per week" not "I will get more active."

6-MONTHS PERSONAL OBJECTIVES EXAMPLE
(With priorities, life areas, and objectives)

Writing
A   1. Complete rough draft of book by end of January.
A   2. Read at least 2 books on writing style and publishing. ETC

Social
B+   1.Activity with another couple at least average 2/month.
B+   2.Socialize with work friends at least 30 minutes, 2-3/wk.
A 3.See close friends for lunch, etc. 2-3/month.   ETC

Health & Physical Activity
A   1.Play or practice tennis 3 to 5 times per week.
B+   2.Do 5-minute warm-up exercises each morning.
A-   3.Get at least 30 minutes of physical activity each day.
A   4. Get regular checkups
B 5. Read health articles and subscribe to heath magazine   ETC

Sherry
A   1 Have nights high quality time Wed, Fri, Sat.nights
A   2. Sunday day together doing what we feel like
A   3.Take weekend vacation at least once per 12 weeks.
A-   4.Go to concerts, dance, plays, etc. at least 1 per month.
A   5. Vacations: Summer to Maui, Winter: Skiing 10+ days ETC

Self-Development
A   1.Plan in relaxation or safety-valve periods each day.
B+   2.Speak more concisely and focus on results more.
A   3. Focus on improving writing skills
A   4. Keep working on development of Life themes and generating positive thoughts. ETC
OTHER OF MY LIFE AREAS INCLUDE Family-Friends, Career, Financial, Home Maintenance, etc.

Prioritize all objectives and to-dos "A," "B," or "C" according to how important they are for satisfying your values, these priorities can empower your decisions later about what will make you the happiest. (See 6-Month Objectives Example.)

TYPICAL WEEKLY SCHEDULE EXAMPLE

TIME	MONDAY	TUESDAY	WEDNESDAY	THURSDAY	ETC
7am ------ GET UP SLEEPY HEAD, WAKE-UP EXERCISE, EAT, ETC -----------------					
8am	Self-Mangmt Session	Appointments	Appointments	Appointments	
9am	Appointments	Crisis Hour	Appointments	Appointments	
10am	Appointments	Appointments	Staff Meeting	Appointments	
11am	Appointments	Workshops	Meetings	Workshops	
12am	Lunch	Lunch	Lunch	Lunch	
1pm	Admin	Special Projects	Supervision	Special Projects	
2pm	Appointments	Special Projects	Univ Planning Committee	Special Projects	
3pm	Crisis Hour	Special Projects	"	Special Projects	
4pm	Appointments	Special Projects	"	Special Projects	
5pm	Appointments	Special Projects	Chores	Special Projects	
6pm	Class	Tennis	Sherry/Nite-out	Tennis	
7pm	Class	Tennis	"	Tennis	
8pm	Dinner, etc	Dinner, etc	"	Dinner, etc	
9pm	Relax, etc	Relax, etc	Relax, etc	Relax, etc	
10pm	"	"	"	"	
11pm	BEDTIME--->>				

Make a Typical Weekly Schedule. Make a schedule that will list every waking hour of every day Monday through Sunday. I generally make only one of these per semester. On that schedule I list all of my regular activities such as work activities like appointment times, classes, regular meetings, and creative time. I also list all of my regular personal life activities such as reserved times for Sherry, my tennis times, my chore times, and my thinking or alone times. This schedule is flexible, but serves as a useful guideline to make sure I have a regular time in my schedule for my "A" activities. My schedule is a powerful rudder for resisting outside forces.

Making this schedule in itself requires some practical resolution of inner conflicts. Your inner conflicts often make themselves felt most in conflicts over how you spend your time. Create a typical weekly schedule that embeds the conflict resolution into your life (and helps break old habits).

For example, if I build tennis into my schedule, I assure that my inner tennis player and my inner health expert will get their needs met. Writing a typical weekly schedule is a necessary part of writing objectives, because I cannot play tennis three times per week unless I can build those times into my schedule. If I cannot find the three times without interfering with some other goals too much, then I must compromise and only play tennis two times per week. (See Proposed Weekly Schedule figure.)

STEP 3: HOLD REGULAR SELF-MANAGEMENT SESSIONS ONCE PER WEEK

Find a time on your schedule that you make "sacred" for your weekly self-management sessions. Possibly use an hour of "work time" for planning. At that time, do the following:

(1) **Review last week's to-dos.** Review and check off what you have accomplished on the past week's to-do list. Re-write (at a later time) or eliminate items you have not completed.

(2) **Make your new to-do list for the coming week.** Consult your list of objectives as you write your prioritized to-dos. This is critical in bridging the values-action gap. Prioritize all to-dos and make sure you cover every life area.

(3) **Check in with your current feelings.** Since your feelings reflect your current value satisfaction and your feelings about the future, they can help you see if you are overlooking any important issues. As a result of checking your feelings, you may want to modify your objectives or change your to-dos for the week.

Organizing your task lists. Many people only need to keep one overall task list. However, there are often advantages to keeping several lists or sublists. Following are some examples.

1. Ongoing task lists or to-do lists include to-dos that can be done any time or any time that week. All should be prioritized (and organized into areas for complex task lists).

2. Daily to-do lists include to-dos that are targeted for specific days (E.g. appointments, deadlines, activities, etc.) Put under specific days on your calendar. In my electronic device, I often put these items in the calendar section along with appointments or events.

3. Sublists divide to-dos into types. I recommend separate lists for work, personal, phone calls/internet, errands, or special meetings, projects, or agendas.

4. Other lists: This book is my **MASTER LIST.** Other lists include goals/objectives, lesson plans, special projects (see two-dimensional list figure below), shopping lists, and detailed agendas. These may be kept as memos or special documents in electronic devices.

5. Set alarms/reminders on electronic devices to remind you at the right time.

STEP 4: CONSULT THE TO-DO LISTS BEFORE DECIDING ON ACTIVITIES

The final part of bridging the values-action gap is using your to-do list in your daily moment-to-moment life. Follow these simple rules.

•**Do the highest priority items first!** This is at the heart of good time management. If you do the highest priority items first, then you will spend most of *your life in high priority and high quality activities.* If you spend your time on low priority activities, you may never get to the most productive and enjoyable times of your life.

•**Do the highest priority activities with *high quality* and spend *more time* on them. Do the lower priority activities as quickly as possible**, put them off, or don't do them at all.

•**"What am I going to do now?"** *This is the most important question in your life!* Because "right now" is all that you can ever control. Your current thoughts and actions determine the outcomes that you will have to live with in future moments. The most important answer to that question is, "*I will choose the alternative that I think will create the most overall happiness.*"

If your values, goals, 6-month objectives, and to-do's are well thought out and reflect your ultimate concern, then the item marked with an "A" on your to-do list will contribute most to that ultimate happiness. Get in the habit of looking at your list before making decisions about what to do next--because your list represents the quiet, inner voice of your dreams.

One step at a time, one day at a time. These little decisions about what we will think and do right now usually seem insignificant at the time, but these are the decisions that--when added together over a longer period of time--have huge effects on our life. Saying little loving remarks an extra few times per day can have dramatic effects over a longer period of time.

Smoking cigarettes 20 times a day can have dramatic effects on our health. Putting a little extra time into studying each day can make the difference between an "A" and a "C" at the end of the semester. These little actions make the difference between a happy marriage and a divorce, between life and death, and between getting the job you want or not.

To attain your dreams, take one small step each week. A friend of mine, who was a 50-plus year old woman had a dream for many years to climb Mt. Everest--even though she had never done any mountain climbing. However, she had assumed she was too old. One day, she questioned that assumption. She decided to go as far toward her goal as possible, and decided to *not* let negative assumptions stop her.

That week she bought a pair of mountain climbing boots and enrolled in a mountain climbing class. She has since climbed a number of mountains and loves it. Some day she may make it part way up Mt. Everest! Dreams--even impractical ones--can come true if we take one-step at a time.

YOU CAN ACCOMPLISH MORE *AND* HAVE MORE FUN!

By *consciously* focusing and planning to get your values met, you increase the odds that you will actually get them met. You will probably begin to see improvements in every area of your life. This may seem like a miracle as if we are creating more time, but it isn't.

> **PRACTICE: Try using O-PATSM for at least one month**. Consider the time-management system you have been using. Try using the O-PATSM system for one month. This was the challenge I made to several thousand students who took my self-management workshops. After trying it for one month, their follow-up ratings of O-PATSM's "overall usefulness" averaged over 8.0 on a 9-point scale. They also rated over a 90% probability that they would continue to use O-PATSM. To use O-PATSM, *carefully follow this chapter's instructions.*

Two-Dimensional To-Do List--to track several task areas
(College student example tracking classes for semester)

CLASS DATE	ENGLISH	MATH	CHEMISTRY	PERSONAL
MON, Oct 22	A-Write Essay	B-Ch12		can
TUE, Oct 23	A-Finish Ch9	A-Problems DUE		put
WED, Oct 24		A-Exam Review 1	A-Read Ch5	personal
THUR, Oct 25		A-Exam Review 2		tasks
FRI, Oct 26	A-Essay DUE	A+EXAM		here or
SAT, Oct 27				elsewhere
SUN, Oct 28	A-Read Ch10	A-Start Ch13	A-Do Lab Problems	
etc				
Repeat Each				
Week				

STUDENTS: (1) Make a "blank" to-do book for the entire semester; (2) fill in the due dates of all assignments from course syllabi, (3) do the detail for the next week during your self-management session, (4) update each time you study.

MANAGERS AND OTHER PROFESSIONALS can use the same two-dimensional format to organize complex projects, businesses, etc. For example, a small business owner might use headings such as *Marketing, Personnel, Legal, Financial, Customers,* etc. List the days/dates along the vertical axis and the task areas (example: marketing, finance, personnel, operations) along the horizontal axis.

HURRY SICKNESS--TOO MUCH TO DO, TOO LITTLE TIME

Do you have too much to do and too little time to do it? Do you feel too stressed, anxious, or guilty about not getting more done? If so, you sound like hundreds of people from all types of professions who have taken my self-management workshops.

A woman who held a high executive position told me that as she had been more and more successful in her work, but had begun to suffer from hurry sickness. She rushed through almost everything she did and therefore even many of the fun things in life had become chores to her that she would just rush through. As she had taken on more and more responsibilities at work, she had less and less time for herself.

She felt good about her work, but overall was feeling more stressed and less happy as a person. Ultimately, she *added more time for herself and her family* (by spending less personal time on her work). It was a big gamble for her. She had assumed that it was essential for her to spend all of this extra time on her job. She had a huge fear of failing at her job if she took this risk.

She took the risk. She used O-PATSM and got more assertive about setting priorities at work. She focused more on *quality instead of quantity.* She also focused more on *doing what she thought was important versus doing what others expected.* The quality of her life improved dramatically!

If we add activities, we must subtract something. It may seem too obvious to say that we only have a fixed amount of time, but we may often forget that fact when we make new commitments. Often we add something and fool ourselves into thinking we are not subtracting something--only to find that we are subtracting peace of mind. Ask yourself,

"What will be the costs of adding that new activity?" I prefer to *choose* what I will subtract--instead of leaving it to chance.

If I am considering teaching an extra class, I ask myself how working 12 hours on Mondays, reducing tennis once a week, and taking time away from my chore time on Saturday afternoons will affect my happiness for the semester. How can I juggle my schedule to reduce the impact of adding this class? How do these loses compare to the gains?

What if we have too many responsibilities and too little time for ourselves? In one of my classes, a woman raised her hand and was visibly angry when I said it was possible to have fun, enjoy life, *and* be very productive. She said, "Dr. Stevens, you may have time to play tennis, go out, and travel a lot, but I have too many responsibilities to have any time for myself or for playing. I am a professional and when I come home every day I have to take care of three children, feed my family, do the dishes, clean-up after everyone, and put the kids to bed. On the weekends I shop, do the laundry, clean the house, work in the yard, go to my kids activities, and lots more. You tell me how am I going to find any time to have fun!"

Before I could answer, another woman sitting right behind her raised her hand. She said, "Dr. Stevens I would like to say something to this lady." She turned to her and said, "I also work full time as a professional and I have five children and a husband. But I still do almost all of the things that Dr. Stevens does to enjoy life. I play tennis twice or more a week, go out with my husband once or twice a week, travel a lot, and have time for myself. Would you like to know how I do this?"

The first woman was very interested, so she continued, "In my family, I don't do many things *for* people. Instead, I am the household manager. We all take care of ourselves and have chores that contribute to the whole family. My job is to organize it all and to follow-up. The result is that everyone has learned to be cooperative and independent. My children have learned how to take responsibility for themselves, do very well in school, and get their chores done without my saying much."

The first woman had been taking care of everyone in her family and had never learned how to be assertive about getting everyone organized or learned to at least do no more than her share. The second woman and her family had learned to *prioritize their activities.* They spent as much time as possible in *quality activities* and tried to get their chores done as efficiently as possible. *All did their share, so no one had too much to do.*

Do you have too little time for yourself--and for fun? I play tennis three or more times per week, spend at least three or more quality nights with my wife Sherry, take a full day with Sherry on the weekend, visit with friends, spend time with children, and work outside my job time on creative activities such as my book. In addition, Sherry and I split the chores pretty evenly.

Sherry also works full time and has a schedule similar to mine. Almost all of our time is spent in interesting or fun activities. Yet, we have also learned to normally avoid scheduling so much that we feel too rushed. Several good friends have said that we lead the best lives of anyone they know. We appreciate those comments very much.

The principles of the O-PATSM system and *balancing activities* are major factors in why this all works so well for us. Each day typically includes challenging mental activity, interpersonal activity, and physical activity. In addition, we spend time in beautiful settings, give and receive affection, eat well, sleep well, and spend time alone.

SHAQ Research Results: Self-Management Habits

The Self-Management scale was designed to test the main aspects of the OPATSM system and some self-development habits. This scale correlated with Happiness, .66; with Low Depression, .40; with Low Anxiety, .32; with Low Anger-Aggr, .38; with good Relationships, .50; with Health, 47; with Income, .10; with Education, .14; and with college GPA, .20.

The four self-management subscales follow.
1. OPATSM time-management habits correlated with Happiness, .41; with Low Depression, .20 with Low Anxiety, .11; with Low Anger-Aggr, .13; with Relationships, .35; with Health, .26 with Income, .02; with Education, .07; and with college GPA, .11.
2. Busy, efficient task accomplishment correlated with Happiness, .55; with Low Depression, .39; with Low Anxiety, .30; with Low Anger-Aggr, .28; with Relationships, .34; with Health, 29; with Income, .07; with Education, .06; and with **college GPA, .08.**
3. Self-health care correlated with Happiness, .46; with Low Depression, .27 with Low Anxiety, .22; with Low Anger-Aggr, .28; with Relationships, .33; with Health, .59; with Income, .09; with Education, .13; and with college GPA, .14.
4. Self-development, habit change correlated with Happiness, .56; with Low Depression, .30 with Low Anxiety, .23; with Low Anger-Aggr, .35; with Relationships, .42; with Health, 35; with Income, .09; with Education, .15; and with college GPA, .17.

Self-management is a key factor associated with happiness and less negative emotions. It also has surprisingly high correlations with relationships and is associated with health, income, and educational outcomes. However, our data show that few people really follow all or even most of the OPATSM system practices. Therefore, I think that the data actually underestimates the value of putting all of those elements together—especially in the areas of career and academic success.

Note: For all correlations, $p < .0001$ and Ns ranged from 1448 to 3226.

Our year has various times where we may focus more on one interest than another-- skiing, spring plays and concerts, summer travel to Maui or elsewhere, the Hollywood Bowl season, fall romantic dinners by the fire and TV mysteries, and finally, the holiday season. These activities contribute to values of romance, beauty, creativity, exploration, sports, travel, family, and friends. I hope your life is (or will be) at least as interesting and fun. O-PATSM can help!

Clarify your values,
develop a variety of interests and routes to happiness,
reflect and plan regularly, and
spend as much time as possible in high quality activities.
If you do, you can overcome the external forces pushing you off course,
and you will become more internally controlled.
One day at a time,
you will create a better world for yourself and others.

EPILOGUE[30]

Our mental structures have the power
to create choice
where no choice previously existed
(when we were ruled by biological and environmental
forces beyond mental control).
These mental structures are the keys to controlling
our lives and our emotions.
Making happiness for self and others
an ultimate concern;
valuing love, truth, harmony, beauty, and other metavalues
above transient events and objects;
developing our Happiness Quotient;
learning many internal and external routes to happiness;
getting mental control of the CHUG-OF conditions
(Choice, Harmony, Understanding,
Goal-challenge, Optimism and Focus);
and using the OPATSM system
give us the power
to rise above anxiety, anger, and depression and
to choose to be happy.

---

[30] This is the location of the Epilogue in the First Edition. I have left it here because I think this location is still appropriate though it precedes the added Chapter 10.

SUCCESS and HAPPINESS ATTRIBUTES QUESTIONNAIRE (SHAQ) RESEARCH and BOOK CONCLUSIONS

\\\

What are the most important factors for overcoming negative emotions and leading a happy life? I used four perspectives to discover these factors—philosophical-spiritual, scientific-psychological, psychotherapeutic, and personal. I wrote the first edition of this book to share those inner secrets of happiness.

Since writing the first edition, new evidence about ideas in this book has impelled me to write this revision. I have received many emails from people worldwide telling me how reading this book has changed their lives. However, I also wanted scientific evidence. Therefore, I designed the *Success and Happiness Attributes Questionnaire (SHAQ)* by going through the book chapter-by-chapter and creating questions from the ideas in each chapter. Such a thorough scientific test of ideas in a self-help book is rare, but I think it is important. I then gathered data from more than 3400 people who completed SHAQ (free) on my website.

The research results support SHAQ's reliability, validity, and utility as a questionnaire. More importantly, the results so strongly supported the ideas in this book that they surprised even me. It seems clear from the results that learnable, internal factors are the main determinants of people's happiness ratings.

As you have seen, I have included the research results side-by-side with their associated values, beliefs, and skills in each chapter. This chapter summarizes the main factors that the SHAQ data has linked to overall happiness, less negative emotions, good relationships, health, and other life success outcomes.

Are demographic factors important? Do factors like sex, age, religion, occupation, and ethnicity have significant effects on happiness and other outcomes? I found only weak or non-significant correlations in almost all cases. However, some *values and beliefs* espoused by religions were important factors (see below and Appendix F).

Overview of SHAQ Research Data Results

SHAQ has 81 scales and subscales reflecting the complexity of key cognitive factors influencing happiness and success. SHAQ's scales are reliable.[31] Overall happiness, depression, anxiety, anger, health, relationship outcomes, highest personal income, academic achievement, and other factors were measured by outcome scales that proved to be reliable and face valid.

The SHAQ scales had moderate to high positive correlations with almost all outcome measures. SHAQ's main 56 subscales had surprisingly high multiple correlations with the **emotional outcomes:** with Overall Happiness, $R = .87$, EffectSize[32] $= .75$; with Low Depression, $R = .73$, EffectSize $= .53$; with Low Anxiety, $R = .68$, EffectSize $= .43$; with Low Anger-Aggression, $R = .70$, EffectSize $= .49$.[33] For the subjects who completed all 70 subscales--including the academic scales[34], $R = .90$, EffectSize $= .81$ for Overall Happiness.

In addition, the 56 SHAQ subscales[32] correlated with the **Relationship Outcomes scale**, $R = .70$, EffectSize $= .47$; with the **Health Outcomes scale**, $R = .82$, EffectSize $= .67$; with **Highest Income**, $R = .49$, EffectSize $= .24$; and with **Educational Attainment**, $R = .46$, EffectSize $= .21$. **Behavioral measures** used as outcomes also yielded good results. For example, for a Major Depression Checklist, $R = .60$, EffectSize $= .36$; Amount of Therapy for Depression, $R = .45$, EffectSize $= .20$; and Amount of Medication for Depression, $R = .41$, EffectSize $= .17$.

Factor analyses demonstrated the scales' and subscales' relative autonomy from each other.[35] **Users rated the interest and usefulness** of SHAQ with a mean of 6.1 of a possible 7.0 rating.

More specific results of SHAQ's scales and subscales are found near the end of each chapter and in other locations--see the Index of SHAQ results below for page numbers. (For more research detail, see Stevens, 2009.)

YOU *CAN* CHOOSE TO BE HAPPY

Determinates of our happiness and other emotions can be divided into four types—(1) heredity, (2) relatively stable personality factors, (3) situational-environmental factors, and (4) learned-cognitive factors. These four overlap.

Heredity and general personality traits resistant to dramatic change are important factors associated with happiness and negative emotions.[36] Due to their stability, they're often not the best target for getting control of emotions.

Researchers have also found strong evidence that we all have a happiness *set-point* that remains relatively stable irrespective of circumstances. For example people who win the lottery or suffer life-changing disabilities tend to return to the level of happiness near the one before these life-changing events. That is good news for those experiencing negative circumstances, but bad news for those experiencing good circumstances. Therefore, changing circumstances *alone* isn't the best way to change happiness levels.

---

[31] Cronbach alphas were $> .80$ for almost all main scales and subscales > 5 items.

[32] *EffectSize* (R^2) is the effect percentage accounted for. Example: if factor X is 100% the cause of factor Y, the EffectSize$=1.00$; 50% of the effect is EffectSize$=.50$.

[33] Number of subjects (N) $= 1123$ for those analyses—users taking all scales. Correlations with Ns near 3400 were consistent with those from the smaller sample of 1123 users taking all the scales.

[34] Number of subjects (N) $=224$.

[35] Varimax rotation; non-orthogonal factors.

[36] A meta-analysis of 137 studies found several general personality factors to be significantly associated with happiness and/or negative emotions. These include the Big 5 traits of low neuroticism, extraversion, and agreeableness; self-esteem; internal control; and hardiness (DeNeve & Harris, 1998).

Though this emotional set-point is important, both research and anecdotal-clinical evidence shows *we can change that set-point*. For example, as people age, they tend to get happier. [37] I have experienced set-point changes in my own life and have seen changes among many clients and acquaintances. Haven't you seen people become happier or unhappier for prolonged time periods?

We can choose to be happy (and change our *happiness set-point*) best by learning how to change the learned-cognitive factors. This book and the SHAQ research have detailed many specific emotion-affecting values, beliefs, skills, and habits that we can learn and control. Step-by-step instructions were often provided.

You can adopt these happiness-influencing factors if you choose. Even if you've had chronic problems with anxiety, anger, or depression, using strategies such as adjusting goals-expectations, reframing with Higher Self beliefs, or even exercising regularly can provide means to "rise above" these negative emotions. Thus, you really, really can choose to be happy. This isn't a choice you can make just once; you must make it over and over again to establish a new happiness set-point.

Choice of ultimate concern and top values are primary factors. My research supported the book's assertion that time-honored, internally centered values are among the most important contributors to happiness, to lower negative emotions, to better relationships, to better health, and to other success factors. The more people valued mental or internally-centered values such as happiness and health for self and others; loving all people unconditionally; contributing to the world; integrity; self-development; seeking truth and knowledge; mental challenge; living a balanced life; and loving God (Higher Power), the happier and more successful they tended to be. Supportive values include honesty, beauty, kindness, playfulness, competency, efficiency, simplicity, creativity, diversity, cooperation, understanding, family, friendship, achieving goals, self-discipline, self-sufficiency, internal control, optimism, and others. My research (and that of others) shows significant moderate correlations between these values and happiness, low negative emotions, relationship success, income, health, and academic success (Stevens, 2009).

Positive existentialist psychologists, such as Victor Frankl (1969), have long suggested that having positive goals, purpose, and meaning in life is essential to happiness and success. My data supports that assertion. The data show that people with stronger commitments to almost any values we listed were happier than people with weaker commitments. Lower value scores may reflect confusion or lack of thinking about one's values as Tillich and the existentialists suggest. (SHAQ didn't test any really negative values such as "harming others" or "revenge.")

In Chapter 1, I (following several philosophers) suggested that a good choice for an ultimate concern is *happiness for self and others*. Some have argued that since happiness is a by-product of other factors, to make it a goal is counter-productive. By the same argument, to make health a goal would undermine our ability to be healthy. However, people who make health a top goal tend to exercise more, eat healthier, not smoke, and follow other health practices that clearly increase one's odds of being healthy. It's a good analogy for making happiness for self and others a top goal. At age 16, I made happiness for self and others my top goal, and I first chose to be happy by thinking positive thoughts when feeling angry. For me, fifty happy years has validated that decision. The SHAQ research supports these assertions.

---

[37] See Lyubomirsky, Sheldon, & Schkade, 2005, about set point and adaptability.

A strong Higher Self, Positive World View, Self-Worth, and Internal Control are important factors related to happiness and other positive outcomes. These four factors are the titles of four book chapters (3-6 respectively) and the titles of four SHAQ main scales. These factors are intimately related to choice of top values, but also need supportive cognitive belief-skill systems. For example, a person who makes happiness for self and others an ultimate concern will love himself/herself and others (self-worth), will tend to develop a more positive and optimistic world view, and will tend to focus on those goals despite outside pressure to do otherwise (internal control). Finally, this ultimate concern will be the center of developing a strong "Higher Self" executive cognitive system. Over time with persistent, active learning and self-development, those cognitive centers will become stronger. The SHAQ research shows strong correlations between these four scales and happiness and low negative emotions. They also correlate significantly with health, good relationships, income, and academic success.

Overcoming generalized fears such as fears of poverty, failure, rejection, illness, and death. These fears are often the flip-side of one's top values and goals. For example people whose most important value is *family* may have the greatest fear of losing their family. Since our top values have both emotional and behavioral control over us, it is important to choose them carefully. *Internally-centered values* such as happiness, love, integrity, and learning usually provide us with more control over their satisfaction. *Externally-centered values* such as career success, being loved, or wealth are less controllable, and our lack of control over them increases uncertainty and anxiety. For example, we can control our loving someone and being kind to them, but we cannot control their loving us back or treating us well. In this sense, it is often better to give than receive. The SHAQ results show sizable correlations between these low fears and emotions (happiness and low negative emotions). Means of identifying and overcoming these fears are described in Chapters 2, 4, and elsewhere.

Life Skills: self-management, emotional coping, learning, and interpersonal skills are very important. SHAQ research results strongly support the importance of these key life skill areas. SHAQ results showed greater happiness, lower negative emotions, better relationships, and better health associated with each of the following skill areas. The areas discussed in detail were:

Self-management (Chapter 9). *Values clarification and change, goal-setting, and the OPATSM self-management model* skills were presented step-by-step.

. **Emotional coping skills** (Chapter 8-elsewhere). Examples: CHUG-OF and LAPDS methods. Positive thinking, communication, action, and adjusting goals-expectations are some important types of positive coping skills examined.

Learning skills (Chapter 7) were not only associated with academic success, being happier, and having lower negative emotions but were among the best predictors of personal income. Many business leaders say continued learning and self-development were key factors in their success.

Interpersonal skills (Chapter 6, appendix E). I included detailed, key assertive intimacy and conflict-resolution beliefs and skills that our data show are important in all kinds of relationships—especially intimate ones.

Personal competency and self-confidence are important. The SHAQ research shows strong correlations between people's estimates of their competencies and outcome measures. This relationship was true for almost every type of competency measured. Self-confidence/competence is important for higher happiness and lower negative emotions. Life skills can affect emotions (1) via increased *knowledge and confidence,* (2) via *goal success,* and

(3) via creating more *positive living environments* (including work and social environments). Strengthen the *university in your head* (all areas of knowledge).

The rich get richer—good correlates with good. The overwhelming majority of SHAQ scales and subscales had significant positive correlations with each other. If a person has one functional factor, it spreads its influence to other factors (possibly by generalization and reinforcement). In Chapter 3 I discussed how a fundamental value/goal change can have far-reaching effects on the personality and behavior.

Happiness and other emotions are determined directly by complex internal cognitive dynamics—the Harmonious Functioning Model. The *Harmonious Functioning (HF) Model* (Chapter 7) is my understanding of how complex cognitive and emotional factors work together. (The cognitive system is the entire "higher" perceiving-thinking part of your brain.) The Harmonious Functioning (HF) model proposes that the "goal" of the cognitive system is to maximize learning, development, internal harmony, efficiency, and control. The brain uses emotions as feedback-motivators to obtain these goals.

If the cognitive system is processing harmoniously, then it produces positive emotions—if not, negative emotions. Cognitive subsystems constantly attempt to understand inputs by matching expectancies to them. If there is too much mismatch, then the cognitive subsystem searches for other understandings to match against the inputs. The cognitive system's search for answers creates stimulation. *Too much confusion/stimulation* produces overarousal emotions such as anxiety.

On the other hand, if inputs contain *too little new information,* then the cognitive system is understimulated and produces underarousal emotions such as apathy, boredom, or depression. These dynamics are complex. For example a person may be overwhelmed (producing anxiety), then ignore or avoid the situation. The result would probably be understimulation, apathy, and/or depression.

In this model the emotions are vital functional aspects of the cognitive system. Anxiety provides us with valuable feedback that our understandings, expectations, goals, or plans are confused or invalid and not able to adequately cope with the input situation. *We need to find new ways to cope with the input.* For example we may have inadequate plans to cope with an unexpected or difficult situation. Developing a good plan can immediately reduce anxiety. A lost and anxious driver who gets a good map can suddenly feel much better.

On the other hand, boredom, apathy, or depression tells us we are underchallenged. The underchallenge may be because we have too much routine and too little challenge. The underchallenge could be because we failed or even completed an important goal and are now *goalless.* Alternatively, we may have lost an important person, job, or other part of our life and feel empty. Depression tells us we need to set new, optimally-challenging goals and/or create more optimally-challenging situations. Finding new interests, new people, new ways of thinking, or other new goals or situations can immediately reduce boredom, apathy, and depression. It may seem amazing how a depressed person can watch a good movie, listen to beautiful music, take on a challenging task, or get into a good conversation; and suddenly their depression lifts during that activity. The depression is a wake-up call that we need to make changes.

Anxiety or depression can be catalysts for major life turning points. Anxiety and depression can be very uncomfortable; but that is their value. They motivate us to change our cognitions and life so that we can be happy.

My data is consistent with the Harmonious Functioning Model. I have also shown how the HF model (1) integrates ideas from the field of learning with the field of motivation and emotions and (2) provides a simple way to think about both good learning strategies and powerful emotion-altering tactics. For example, Chapter 7 describes learning strategies and Chapter 8 describes methods of "adjusting your emotions like adjusting a thermostat." SHAQ data supports the effectiveness of these learning methods and emotional control methods. Aristotle understood the close connection between our cognitive system and our emotions. About mental harmony, long ago he said,

Happiness, therefore, must be some form of contemplation...
He who exercises his intellect and cultivates it
seems to be both in the best state and most dear to the gods...
so that in this way too the wise man will more than any other be happy.

Book Conclusion: Do You Choose To Be Happy?

Religions have taught millions of people how to be happy. Philosophers, psychologists, books, self-help groups, and others have taught millions more. People can learn to be happier!

Maslow (1954, 1962) led a movement focusing on positive human factors and self-actualization. American Psychological Association (APA) president Martin Seligman edited the classic *American Psychologist* Special Issue on happiness and positive psychology (2000) launching the new millennium in a positive direction. The resulting positive psychology research is partially incorporated in this edition.

The SHAQ data did not find any single earthshaking factor that creates happiness alone; instead, my data paints a comprehensive picture of the *multitude of cognitive factors involved*. A person scoring high on these factors--a high *Happiness Quotient (HQ)*--will have a high chance of being happy. The good news: if only one factor were involved, our happiness would be entirely tied to that factor. The more factors involved, the less we are affected if something goes wrong with one. Thus, the more strengths we have, the greater our chances for happiness--no matter what happens to us. A higher HQ increases our ability to "rise above" negative emotions or to avoid them altogether.

SHAQ data supports the conclusion that this robust multitude of cognitions are not only important for achieving a good emotional life, they are important for achieving health, good relationships, and academic and career success.

Because of their specificity, most of these cognitions are *learnable* and *teachable* beliefs and skills, and not general, heritable traits. I have described many in detail in this book; and you can complete SHAQ (free) on my website to test yourself. Then you can begin raising your own HQ and help others too.

My SHAQ research paper has been read by experts looking for alternative explanations of the data; but currently there is no reason to believe that the data aren't what they appear to be—strongly supportive of the ideas presented here.

I have described in detail--and the SHAQ results have supported in detail—that these *controllable factors* are associated with happiness and success. The key factors are not money, status, or other external factors; they are what's inside—your values, beliefs, knowledge, skills, and habits. Top values such as happiness for self and others, love, truth, knowledge, growth, health, beauty, integrity, and productivity are central. Developing beliefs, skills, and habits supporting these values in each life area gives you a robust set of personality factors that shields you against misfortune and bad circumstances. They increase your chances for rising above difficulty to find happiness. These positive internal factors can also help you create or gravitate toward environments and people who will contribute to your happiness and success.

When I was 16, I made a decision to make happiness a top goal in my life and wrote my first "How to be Happy" guidelines. Over 50 years later, those happiness guidelines have been transformed into this book, and I'm very grateful for a happy, blessed life. I am convinced that if you follow these guidelines through the years, you can be happy and help the world become a little happier place.

Start Your *Choose to be Happy* Self-Development Program

1. Use the Choose To Be Happy Checklist (Appendix A). Put it in a central place and review it regularly. Use this book as a reference manual.
2. Use the OPATSM system weekly. Examine your top values and goals, and organize your time and your life focused upon them.
3. Complete SHAQ and examine the results and your values, beliefs, and skills. Pick a few self-development goals to focus on. Then start testing new beliefs, goals, and actions/activities to improve your life. Save your complete results and HQ score.
4. Be persistent, learn from results, and don't give up. Practice rising above difficult circumstances. Read, find role models, regularly analyze your own beliefs, thoughts, and actions related to their happiness effects and other outcomes.

These are the first steps after reading this book to take
for maximizing your happiness, health, and success.

**I wish you a healthy, happy life;
and
I hope you help spread happiness wherever you go.**

My Personal Experience

When I was an infant I couldn't *choose* to be happy,
I didn't have the cognitive structures required to make a conscious choice.
I didn't even know the word "happy."
I depended on my environment to make me happy;
my parents provided my food, care, and much of my stimulation.
Once I learned what the word "happy" meant, I had more choices.
I tried to make myself happy, but I had little knowledge of *how* to do it.
I was often happy, but it was because I was lucky—
I had a pretty good environment.
It was not because I knew much about how to make myself happy.
One day I decided to make happiness my top goal.
Over the years, I learned a lot more about how to make myself happy, and
I developed my skills.
Creating those mental structures (my Higher Self) increased
my Happiness Quotient (HQ) and my happiness power.
Now, I can choose to be happy, and I have
a good chance of being successful.
I have had a happy life for which I am very grateful.
Without knowledge, we have little choice and little power.
With knowledge, we can transcend our environment and
even our own biology to soar to new levels of living.
I hope this book has contributed to your journey to self-actualization.
I hope it has strengthened your Higher Self, so that

you can choose to be happy.

I wish you a happy life!

For daily reminders,
use *The Choose To Be Happy Checklist* in Appendix A.

For new happiness ideas or to take SHAQ—all free,
visit my website: www.csulb.edu/~tstevens

INDEX OF RESEARCH RESULTS
FOR THE SUCCESS AND HAPPINESS ATTRIBUTES
QUESTIONNAIRE (SHAQ)

Note: For a complete a paper presenting a more complete scientific presentation of the SHAQ results see Stevens, 2009, on my website, currently www.csulb.edu/~tstevens.

THE CHOOSE TO BE HAPPY CHECKLIST

Do you know that you can choose to be happy? You can't just say to yourself, "Be happy", and magically become happy. However, you can choose values, beliefs, thoughts, and actions that will lead to happiness. This list of key happiness tips is from my book--*You Can Choose To Be Happy*.

☐ **1. CHOOSE TO BE HAPPY BY MAKING HAPPINESS (for self and others) YOUR TOP GOAL.** If you make values like money, success, a good lifestyle, or even family approval your top goal in life--yet are not happy--what have you gained? Aristotle, Buddha and other great thinkers said that only happiness is worthy of being our top goal. To maximize your chances of being happy, make *overall happiness for yourself and others* your top goal (ultimate concern) in life. Integrate all other goals around that central goal. Happiness is different from pleasure. It isn't shortsighted or selfish the way pleasure is. Happiness requires love, enlightenment, truth, getting higher needs met, and inner harmony.

You are responsible for your own happiness. No other person or external condition can make you happy or unhappy. You control your own happiness by your thoughts and actions. Your happiness is in the palm of your hand. You can choose to be happy by developing your *Happiness Quotient (HQ)*--learning functional beliefs and life skills and learning both *internal* and *external routes to happiness*. (Chapters 1,2)

☐ **2. LOVE SELF AND OTHERS UNCONDITIONALLY.** Love and happiness go hand in hand. The feeling of love is a happy feeling--perhaps even the essence of happiness. Loving someone means making his or her health and happiness a high priority. Choosing to make happiness for self and others your ultimate concern is the practical application of loving self and others. To develop your own self-love (self-esteem), take good care of yourself in all life areas--health, career, relationships, recreation, finances, spiritual life, etc.

An important element of self-esteem and happiness is loving yourself and others *unconditionally*. Unconditional love can overcome the criticism, negativity, and dysfunctional treatment from others. Loving self and others *unconditionally* means finding something beautiful and worthwhile in ourselves and others *no matter what we are or what we have done*. No matter how unintelligent, ugly, uneducated, poor, or sick we are. No matter how much we have failed or done bad or stupid things. No matter what anyone thinks of us. No matter if no one else in the world likes us or not. No matter what--we are still *worthy of our own love and still worthy of making happiness a top goal.*

To love yourself unconditionally (1) find a philosophy of life that appreciates *all human beings*, (2) *continually choose* to make health and happiness top goals, and (3)use the *self-acceptance process* to accept and forgive the worst aspects of yourself and others. Cleanse your emotions from recurring feelings of resentment and guilt. Face the worst incidents head on. Empathy is the best cure for anger and guilt. First, understand possible *causes*. Understand *why* people do harmful things, and understand that destructive people are not happy people--they constantly pay for their harm to others. The dysfunctional beliefs that hurt victims hurt perpetrators. Choosing to focus on unfairness or getting even only generates more pain for you--worsening the original injury. Instead, focus on acceptance and make your own life as happy as possible. Then, the past will not matter so much, "Let go and let God." (Chapter 5--also Appendix on Anger)

□ **3. SEEK TIMELESS, MENTAL (or Spiritual) VALUES.** As soon as you choose an important goal, you give it power over your life. If you choose to make an *Externally-Centered (EC)* value like money a top goal, then instantly you give money power over your emotions. Anyone controlling your income can control you and your emotions. Uncertainty over money will create high anxiety. If you make *Internally-Centered (IC)* timeless, mental values like happiness, truth, beauty, knowledge, and love primary values, then *you* have much more control over your own destiny. You can fulfill these values in many ways that don't depend on other people or ups and downs of everyday life.

Make *seeking truth and knowledge* close companions to choosing happiness for self and others as your top goal. Seeking truth and knowledge is a primary motive of the brain. Avoiding the truth automatically causes repression and internal conflict. We can't completely hide the truth--some part of our brain knows the truth and will undermine our happiness until we integrate that truth into our lives.

Make **personal growth** a top value. It goes hand-in-hand with seeking truth and happiness. Actively seek sources that can help you learn how to be happy--people, books, classes, etc. People who thirst for growth can learn to lead the happiest lives. Other top values of Maslow's self-actualized people included **beauty, simplicity, uniqueness, self-sufficiency, wholeness, playfulness, richness, completion, justice, aliveness, and goodness.** We can satisfy these general values no matter how poor or alone we might become. They depend primarily on our mental powers--not on outside forces.

Do not become *overly attached* **to any** *particular* **goal, person, event, or external condition.** Doing so immediately creates anxiety, because it means that too much can be lost by putting all our eggs in one basket. Instead, make enduring mental or spiritual states your top values. (Chapter 1)

□ **4. DEVELOP YOUR PHILOSOPHY OF LIFE AND BUILD A STRONG HIGHER SELF.** Your brain creates parts of you that are like little people inside you--your inner child, inner parent, and parts representing all your life roles (child, parent, student, professional, lover, athlete, artist, etc.). Keeping your inner subparts operating as a harmonious group is essential to happiness.

Your Higher Self is your Inner Hero that loves unconditionally and automatically makes happiness for you and others a top goal. If you don't listen to it and follow its direction, it will remain weak and ineffectual. If you do, it will manage your life like a good executive of a corporation or conductor of an orchestra. Self-actualized people have strong, integrated Higher Selves. Developing a strong, positive philosophy of life builds your Inner Hero. (Chapter 3)

□ **5. SEEK EMPATHY AND BALANCE.** Learn to understand and respect each point-of-view of each inner part. Seek the same deep empathy for others. Learn how to weigh the value of each point-of-view for truth and happiness. We can learn from any point-of-view, even if that learning means we learn of its destructive power and learn how to overcome it.

A strong Higher Self acting like an inner conductor can create the proper balance between inner subparts. It can create the *inner harmony* essential to happiness. Learn your own proper balance between potential inner conflicts such as work versus play; giving versus receiving; or focusing on the past versus the present versus the future. Try achieving balance between mental, physical, social, and other activities each day--or at least each week.

☐ **6. OVERCOME YOUR GREATEST FEARS, and LEARN THAT YOU CAN BE HAPPY IN ANY SITUATION.** What are your greatest fears--poverty, loneliness, rejection, failure, blindness, sickness, death? As long as these fears remain hidden and unresolved, little daily reminders of them--such as a poor grade or a rejection--will haunt you and reduce your happiness each day.

Use the self-exploration process (Chapter 2) *to discover and face every important fear in your life.* Develop plans and clearly imagine what you would *think and do* to make yourself happy in that awful situation. You may need to find out how others have successfully coped with those situations. Victor Frankl overcame Auschwitz and Genevieve overcame a year in a full body cast. They showed that an active mental life filled with positive mental activities and thoughts can sustain a will to live and even create happiness in the worst of situations. Genevieve said it became one of her happiest years. After that year she said, "I used to be a fearful person. However, after that year, I knew I could overcome anything."

Once you overcome your deepest fears, then you can face each day with new confidence and calmness. You will immunize yourself to those daily negative reminders. (Chapter 4)

☐ **7. USE ABUNDANCE THINKING--Set Zero Expectations about what you will receive.** Overcome deficit (entitlement) thinking--that others (or the world) owe you something. Thinking you are entitled to more than you have leads to feeling deprived and resentful. Some people spend their lives feeling like victims. What a waste! If you learn to view every moment and everything you receive as gifts to appreciate and be grateful for, then you will be happy. *Hope for the best, be prepared for the worst, expect something between, and be grateful for all that you receive.* (Chapter 4)

☐ **8. MONITOR YOUR EMOTIONS, SELF-EXPLORE THE CORE ISSUES, AND RATIONALLY SOLVE YOUR PROBLEMS.** Be your own psychologist and discover the deeper causes of your feelings. Use the *self-exploration process* to follow your emotions to the heart of any problem affecting your happiness. Focus on the emotion, note associated thoughts and images, and track the general, underlying *themes* of your thoughts. Once you discover the root causes of your problems, use your higher beliefs and a good *problem-solving process* to resolve the problem. Choose to be happy by choosing the alternative that maximizes happiness.

Replace unproductive and negative beliefs and themes with more constructive ones. Cultivate interests in positive philosophies and activities. Choose beliefs that are consistent with your overall goals of seeking happiness and truth. (Chapters 2, 3)

☐ **9. REPLACE EXTERNAL CONTROL with INTERNAL CONTROL.** Recognize the forces in your life--family, peers, media, or authorities that want to influence your thoughts and actions. Observe these external influences and learn how they control you. Develop the inner parts of yourself--such as your Higher Self, values, and interests--to give you strong inner goals and direction. Learn assertive--not nonassertive or aggressive--means for dealing with external control. Assertion means balancing empathy for others with empathy for self and seeking win-win solutions through constructive communication and negotiation.

Clarify boundaries of responsibility. If you feel overly responsible for other people's happiness or for events in the world beyond your control, then emotions like guilt, anxiety, and pressure will remain out of your control. Learn what codependence is and how to control it. (Chapter 6)

☐ **10. LEARN THE HARMONIOUS FUNCTIONING MODEL to understand your emotions and perform at peak motivation.** The harmonious functioning model is a breakthrough for understanding the basic causes of happiness and motivation. Your *higher brain's* fundamental motive is to learn, process information, and perform complex tasks. It seeks an optimal level of challenge (match between task complexity/difficulty and your abilities). When there is *too much challenge,* your higher brain produces overarousal emotions like anxiety and confusion. When there is *too little challenge,* your higher brain produces underarousal emotions like depression and apathy. Only during optimal challenge do you get in the zone of harmonious functioning and produce maximum interest, happiness, learning, and performance.

Inner conflict also causes overarousal, while inner harmony leads to happiness. One reason why happiness is such a worthy top-goal of life is that your brain regularly measures how well your life is going in every life area. Your brain uses emotions as feedback (and as your most powerful natural motivator) to get your conscious mind to fix whatever is wrong (including concerns for other people and the future).

When your mind has inner harmony, it creates *peak learning, peak performance, and peak happiness.* Over time, harmonious functioning increases love of the activity, self-esteem, and health. (Chapter 7)

☐ **11. USE THE SIX HARMONIOUS FUNCTIONING *CHUG-OF* MENTAL CONTROL STRATEGIES to rise above anxiety, anger, and depression.** Learn to adjust your emotions like you adjust a thermostat. If your emotions are too hot (such as anxiety or anger), you can cool them off and get calmer. If your emotions are too cold (such as boredom or depression), you can heat them up to attain harmonious functioning.

Spend more of your life in the zone of harmonious functioning. These strategies can give you *immediately improved mental control* of your emotions. **You can choose to be happy by choosing to use one or more of these strategies.** (Chapter 8)

**SIX HARMONIOUS FUNCTIONING mental control strategies
to RISE ABOVE negative emotions (think of *CHUG-OF* to remember):**

1. **CHOICE.** *Replace or convert* the situation. Do what you enjoy or enjoy what you do!
2. **HARMONY** of motives. Resolve inner conflicts between parts of yourself to look forward to activities--instead of trying to motivate yourself by rules, " shoulds," threats, or self abuse.
3. **UNDERSTANDING.** Understand, create a mental map, build skills, and develop plans.
4. **GOALS and EXPECTATIONS.** Keep the task challenging--not too much or too little.
5. **OPTIMISM.** Clarify how you can realistically be happy no matter what outcome occurs.
6. **FOCUS.** Keep your eye on the ball and persist--and always remember your top goals.

Mental control strategy 4: Goals and Expectations is especially useful. If you are *overaroused or overchallenged*, use the methods in the first column. If you are *underaroused or underchallenged*, use the methods in the second column. (Think **LAPDS** to recall the five goal dimensions.)

To DECREASE emotional arousal and reduce stress, anxiety, and anger: (Decrease challenge and		*To INCREASE emotional arousal and reduce boredom and depression:* (Increase challenge and attachment)
(1) Lower goal and expectation	<=>	Raise goal and expectation LEVELS
(2) Develop <u>A</u>LTERNATIVE goals and plans	<=>	Get MORE ATTACHED to one goal
(3) Focus on <u>P</u>ROCESS goals	<=>	Focus on OUTCOME goals
(4) Focus on <u>D</u>YNAMIC, growth-goals	<=>	Focus on STATIC, one-shot oriented goals
(5) Focus on <u>S</u>IMPLE, SMALL-STEP goals.	<=>	Focus on COMPLEX, LARGE-STEP goals

Process goals focus on what you *can directly control*--your own thoughts, statements, and actions. **Outcome goals** focus on results that you cannot directly control--such as other people's reactions to you, grades, or income. Focus on process goals except when planning (and during underarousal).

☐ **12. DEVELOP YOUR SELF-MANAGEMENT SKILLS to get more control of your time and your personal world--Use the O-PATSM System**. This system focuses on *external routes to happiness*--how you can get more control of your time, your actions, and the world around you. (Chapter 9)

THE STEPS FOR USING O-PATSM:
STEP 1: Clarify values (and dreams). Make a written values checklist.
STEP 2: Write goals and objectives. Make written lists of general long-term goals and more immediate, specific goals (objectives). **Prioritize all objectives and to-dos with "A," "B," or "C." Make a "Typical Weekly Schedule." Get a to-do book** that you can carry with you at all times and get to within 3 seconds.
STEP 3: Hold regular self-management sessions (once per week).
STEP 4: Consult the to-do lists as you decide upon actions.
   • Do the highest priority items first!
   • Do the highest priority activities with *high quality* and with more time.
   • "What am I going to think and do right now?" *This is the most important question in your life!* Because "right now" is all that you can ever control.
Choose the alternative maximizing overall happiness for self and others.

One step at a time, one day at a time. These little decisions about what you will think and do now may seem insignificant at the time. However, added together over a long period of time, they have huge effects on your life.
   Using O-PATSM, *YOU CAN ACCOMPLISH MORE AND HAVE MORE FUN!*

☐ **13. DEVELOP YOUR KNOWLEDGE AND SKILLS IN EACH IMPORTANT LIFE AREA** to increase personal success and confidence--especially thinking, self-management, and interpersonal skills. (Chapter 5)

☐ **14. DEVELOP LOVING, DEMOCRATIC, AND ASSERTIVE INTERPERSONAL BELIEFS AND SKILLS.** Balance empathy, understanding, and love of self with that of others. Learn how to live without "shoulds" and obligation. Learn to give out of genuine empathy and caring instead. Seek Win--Win Solutions (Chapter 6, Appendix E)

☐ **15. CREATE POSITIVE LIFE THEMES, SCRIPTS, and ROLES.** Learn how you can create the you that you want to be, and spend most of your time focused on positive interests and themes. Focus on creating positives in the world instead of avoiding negatives. (Chapter 4)

☐ **16. DEVELOP YOUR OWN SET OF "HOW TO BE HAPPY" PRINCIPLES and use them daily.** h

    PRACTICE: Use this list regularly. Photocopy this list and post it where you will see it daily. Review it regularly and reread book sections as needed.

==> I hope living by these principles makes you as happy as it has me, let me know

OVERCOME ANGER AND AGGRESSION

ANGER IS AN EMOTION THAT FOCUSES ON GETTING CONTROL

Someone calls you an inconsiderate idiot, and you feel angry. Someone cuts in front of you on the freeway, and you feel angry. Someone attacks your friend, and you feel angry. Someone tells you that you will not get the pay increase you think you deserve, and you feel angry. What causes you to feel anger? What do all of these situations have in common?

Underlying anger is caused by a perceived *loss of control* over factors affecting important values. The values in the above examples might be pride, getting someplace on time, someone you love, money, or being treated fairly--we are *frustrated* about not getting what we want or expect.

When we are angry, we usually think we know what *caused* the problem. We have some target for our anger. It may be the person criticizing you, the person who cut you off on the freeway, an attacker, your boss, or even yourself. When angry, we may hope that a burst of energy aimed at the threat will defeat it. Or we may hope that a burst of energy will break the barrier stopping us from meeting our goal.

Anger can be used constructively at times. It can give us energy we need to fight back if physically attacked. However, for most situations it merely clouds our judgment and creates extra stress. If anger prompts aggressive behavior toward other people, it can permanently harm relationships--especially with those we love. Prolonged or frequent resentment (mild anger) has been shown to be a significant cause of cardiovascular problems and heart attacks. It is the villain behind type A behavior.

HOSTILITY MEANS NOT ACCEPTING THE UNCHANGEABLE

What do the following examples of hostility have in common? Yelling at a cop for giving you a ticket. Kicking in a door that is broken. Blaming all your troubles on how your parents raised you. Refusing to accept that a relationship is over when it clearly is. Throwing a temper tantrum after losing a game. Continuing to beat yourself up after you learned your lesson.

As destructive as anger can be at times, it is not nearly as bad as hostility. Dr. George Kelly believed that the underlying cause of all hostility is *not adequately accepting unchangeable aspects of reality*. Hostility means not accepting reality. Hostility is maintaining a goal even after it is clear it can't be reached. Hostility is doing something desperate to get things right--despite reality. Hostility just hurts you and others. The only healthy response to a "done deed" reality is to accept it and try to understand it. Dr. Maslow's self-actualized people accepted life's hardships and people's shortcomings the way they accepted water as being wet. If you believe that *you can choose to be happy* and have learned the methods in this book, you know that you can be happy in the future--no matter what. So, accept the past, forgive, let go, and move on.

GET CONTROL OF ANGER-PRODUCING
BELIEFS AND THOUGHTS

Anger is caused by your inability to mentally cope with some situation. If you have a persistent problem with anger, then you either have important *underlying issues* that you have not yet resolved, or you are using *emotional coping methods* that are ineffective.

There are many internal and external methods for coping with anger. Most methods that help control *any* negative emotion also help with anger. Perceived *loss of control* for getting *important values met* causes anger. To get over your anger, it is helpful to *identify* those important values and to understand why you may lack confidence in your own ability to be happy.

Blaming others (or yourself) and remaining angry may appear the easy way out. Finding new ways to think about the situation and make yourself happy requires skillful effort. If you want to reduce your anger, consider each of the following issues or techniques for regaining mental control.

1. EXPLORE EMOTIONS OF HURT AND FEAR UNDERLYING THE ANGER

Remember that anger stems from fear and a sense of helplessness. Some important value or goal is threatened and you feel that you are losing control of the situation. You may not want to admit feeling hurt or fear. (You may think such an admission is a sign of weakness.) Yet these are the underlying feelings that will help you identify *which values and goals are being threatened.*

The real threat may not be the *surface issue* (being late to the movie) as much as the *underlying issue* (not being important to someone you love or being mistreated). Identifying emotions of *fear* and *hurt* will open the door to these underlying issues. Once you get in touch with the fear and hurt, what images, thoughts, and underlying issues are associated with (and may cause them)? (Self-exploration; Chapter 2.)

2. DEVELOP EMPATHETIC UNDERSTANDING

My sexually abused client found that developing a *deeper, empathetic understanding* of her father and developing an *unconditional caring* for him as a person were keys to defusing her anger.

If you choose to decrease your anger at someone, the first step is to make every effort to see the situation *from his or her point of view.* You might begin by asking them to explain their point of view. Encourage them to talk about underlying assumptions, beliefs, or background factors that may have led them to the point- of-view or behavior you are upset about. Summarize what they say and state what their emotions are from *their point of view* so that they agree you understand them. Understanding their situation, point of view, and the causes of their beliefs and behavior is usually the major hurdle to get control of anger.

Forgiving is not forgetting, it is remembering and letting go.
(Claudia Black, 1989)

If it is impossible to have that kind of conversation with someone, then try to imagine an **understanding scenario** that allows you to defuse your anger. From my experience of dealing with people with similar situations, I try to imagine what they might have been thinking and why.

If you do not know the person well enough to know what their motives were, then what can you do? Recall the client who was so filled with anger after being raped by a masked man she would never see again. We looked at what we knew about human nature in general. Can you accept human nature as it really is? Can you accept that gang killings, child abuse, theft of belongings, inconsiderate behavior, or other damaging events affect you and others--without getting too upset about them? Can you accept that some · people will take advantage of you and get away with it? To be able to control our anger despite tragic events, we must each find a way to deal with the dark side of life. Issues of injustice, unfairness, and entitlements are discussed below (Chapters 4, 8).

3. ASSUME THE BEST INTENTIONS WHENEVER POSSIBLE

To the degree that Mike believes his wife's underlying motives for being late were aimed at harming him, then his anger increases. If he dwells on thoughts like, "She doesn't care about me,""She's inconsiderate," "I wouldn't do that to her," or "She's so selfish," then they will add fuel to his anger.

Instead, he can interpret her *underlying intentions* as a legitimate need to take care of herself. He can *focus more on evidence from the present and past that she loves him* and is not primarily trying to hurt him. How he chooses to think will increase or decrease his anger. Try to assume the best intentions from people until you have repeated indications that they seem to have other motives.

As a psychologist who has seen hundreds of clients, I have discovered that even the most hostile people are usually *not trying to hurt others*. Instead, they primarily want *to protect or defend themselves* and to meet their own values. The most hostile people are often people who have experienced a lot of abuse and criticism and are very sensitive to it. That insight helps dissipate anger.

That insight does *not* necessarily mean that I will refrain from using consequences to discourage hostile behavior. But it does mean that I can deal with the person much more calmly and effectively.

How does the insight that people are usually aggressive to defend themselves apply to less hostile people? If a person who normally cares about you is angry or purposely harms you, then he (or she) is probably doing it out of defensiveness or *fairness!* He probably thinks that you did something to him first, and he is just defending himself, getting even, or trying to teach a lesson so you won't harm him again. In short, he is probably operating under the same reasons that *you* are when *you* perpetuate the cycle of conflict! He is *assuming the worst intentions of you*--that you don't care about him or that you tried to intentionally hurt him.

4. IS FAIRNESS OR JUSTICE AN UNDERLYING ISSUE?

So often our expectations are the keys to our feelings. We may not accept that others are imperfect or that we are imperfect. Bad, evil, unfair things happen billions of times daily. It is natural to feel negative emotions such as anger in response to events we label bad or unfair.

Fairness versus Happiness doctrines. The **fairness doctrine** states, "Life should always be fair and exactly equal for everyone." If we have developed too many expectations based upon this fairness doctrine, then we are doomed to a life filled with misery. In the worst cases people spend much of their life calculating fairness, balancing what they have received versus what they have given, and maintaining some sort of self-created accounting system that is based entirely on ideas of fairness. This fairness belief system may have little correspondence to outside reality.

What is fair about some people being born into happy, prosperous families and living prosperous, long, happy lives while other people are born into miserable situations and die young after leading a life filled with suffering? Unfairness is all around us. I recommend abandoning the fairness doctrine.

It can be replaced with the **happiness doctrine**. It states that *I will choose that which contributes most to my and others' happiness.* I accept that my life and all my options are a gift. If I compare my gifts to others'--especially to those that have more--I will only reduce my appreciation of my own gifts.

There is some justice in this world. What I have been saying about fairness is that rigidly holding on to a fairness doctrine can undermine our happiness. However, people wonder that if they do not hold on to the fairness doctrine, then there will be no justice or consequences.

I ask those people to remember that we live in a *world controlled by natural laws which we cannot break*. Natural laws *do* provide some measure of natural consequences--of rewards and punishments for our actions. Society can also create laws which provide additional rewards and punishments. Frequently the guilty seem to go unpunished. How do we control our anger when we see such miscarriages of justice?

Psychological Justice. Psychological laws are particularly effective as natural punishments. People who take advantage of other people are punished by natural reactions--such as lack of real intimacy and love in their life. They are punished by their Higher Self, which sees the evil or harm they do to others and produces guilt through natural empathy with others. They are punished by their own anger and negative beliefs--which torment them with conflict, anger, and anxiety. They are too busy feeling anger to feel happy.

For example, Stalin and Hitler are two men who may share the distinction of causing more harm to more people than any other men in history. Some have said that these men were examples of how *evil power can pay*--as if to prove that there is no justice. However, while both men achieved great worldly wealth and power, both men *lived highly tormented lives*. Understanding how difficult it is for harmful people to be happy people helps me *let go of some of my anger* when something appears unjust.

Accept reality and forgive. Some of our anger may stem from a belief that others have unfairly received more than we have. We might resent people who have more money, beauty, success, or happiness--especially if we don't think they deserve it. We might feel that life has given us a bum deal if we follow the fairness doctrine. How do we get over anger at someone who got something they did not deserve? The fairness doctrine says that people should get only what they deserve.

The happiness doctrine says that in order to be happy we must accept that things do not always appear to be fair. I will hope that both the other person and I can learn to be happy with what we have each received--even though it may not be equal or fair. Who knows what the ultimate affects of their advantages may be? Many poor people are happier than many rich people. Which doctrine will help you get most control of your anger and feel happiest?

We have seen how my sexually-abused client was able to get rid of her deep anger through understanding and forgiveness. Understanding and forgiveness are necessary ingredients to any anger-reduction formula.

We may also have trouble forgiving ourselves. We might be angry at ourselves because we are still living with the consequences of bad choices we made earlier in our lives. We may think we are so bad or stupid that we don't deserve to be happy. How can we forgive ourselves for messing up our lives? We may blame our parents or even God for making us the kind of people that failed. It may all seem so unfair. How do we get over blaming ourselves or others for our misfortunes?

The fairness doctrine says that we should only receive that which we deserve. The fairness doctrine says that someone who has more than they deserve should have the extra taken away, while those who have less than they deserve should receive more. This doctrine says we should only be happy when the accounts are all balanced. Until then, we should be spending our lives balancing the scales--and that will never happen.

The happiness doctrine says: 1–forget about fairness accounting; 2--accept life as it is now; 3--love ourselves and others unconditionally--make our own (and others') happiness the top goal; and 4--act accordingly. Blaming ourselves or others, guilt, worry, accounting, resentful feelings, and other unproductive negative thoughts are just barriers to our being happy.

[Note: Accepting the happiness doctrine does not imply that we will not be assertive about enforcing contracts or other agreements that have been made with others. We can build rewards and punishments into contracts and take actions that reward and punish others to motivate them if necessary. That is not the same as enforcing a contract out of fairness or to get even.]

> I would rather we be *unequally happy* (whether we deserve it or not)
> than be *equally unhappy* (even if we get what we deserve)!

5. ARE YOU HOLDING ON TO THE ANGER OR HURT FOR MOTIVATION?

Do you hold on to your anger or feelings of being hurt in order to *punish the person?* Do you want to punish the person to get even (operating out of a fairness doctrine)? Perhaps you can begin to see how the fairness doctrine does not work well. You may think that you should punish them by holding on to your anger. Holding on to anger or hurt can only hurt you!

If your goal is *to change someone's behavior*, you may use rewards and punishments to affect behavior. However, you don't administer the consequences out of a sense of revenge or anger. Do it caringly--as a way of helping them learn. Wait until you are calm. Stating your reasons calmly is much more effective than punishment given out of anger! (In most situations, rewards are more effective than punishments.)

> **PRACTICE: Make a Blame-list.** Make a blame list toward yourself and others. Try replacing the fairness doctrine with the happiness doctrine in dealing with the problems underlying each blame. Empathize with the other person, accept the reality of the situation, and focus on maximizing happiness for the future for each important item on the list.

6. EXAMINE UNDERLYING EXPECTATIONS

Unfulfilled expectations can lead to anger. What are your expectations of yourself and others for this situation? Are you expecting more than is realistic *for this person in this particular situation?*

Examine your underlying expectations about what you need to be happy and live the type of life you want. Examine your expectations for others. Perhaps you have higher (or different) standards than others. Perhaps you expect others to follow them as well as yourself. You may even be right. However, these are *your expectations of others*--not theirs. They are who they are, and one root of anger is *not accepting people (or events) as they are.*

Entitlement thinking and high expectations about what we should receive cause a feeling of being in a hole. They cause some people to see themselves as victims and view the world negatively. These expectations are the cause of a deep sense of powerlessness and prolonged resentment about being treated unfairly. They are the deepest source of many people's anger. (Chapter 4)

==> *Use the LAPDS dimensions (from Goals in Chapter 8) to adjust expectations and goals.*

7. CHOOSE HAPPINESS INSTEAD OF ANGER--
"MY ANGER HURTS ME MORE THAN IT HURTS YOU"

Holding on to anger has other self-destructive consequences. These consequences include negative effects on your body and taking away from your enjoyment of the present moment. You cannot feel angry and happy at the same time--it's impossible! Therefore, you have a choice--anger *or* happiness!

People who habitually choose anger over happiness lead frustrated, angry lives--not happy ones. Remind yourself of these consequences to get more control of your anger. Say to yourself, "Self, why choose anger when I can choose to think thoughts that produce happiness?" Use these eight methods to control anger. Also, refer to other powerful techniques from the book--especially the six harmonious functioning mental control strategies from Chapter 8 (CHUG-OF: Choice, Harmony, Understanding, Goals & expectations, Optimism, and Focus).

8. REMEMBER, "IT'S THE WAY OF THINGS"

My wife Sherry and I have developed a simple formula for overcoming anger, which we often use when we face something unchangeable. It comes from Winnie the Pooh Bear's philosophy of life (Benjamin Hoff, *The Tao of Pooh*). When something goes wrong that is out of his control, Pooh Bear says simply, "It's the way of things." We cannot change the world and the forces which operate it, and we can't even change many things about ourselves or other aspects of our life--especially our past. So just remember--even though we can never understand it all--the most basic understanding of all is--"It's the way of things."

PRACTICE: Develop a mental control plan to deal with anger (and hostility). (1) Think of one or more situations where you get angry. **(2)** Use the above methods to mentally role-play overcoming the anger in that situation. **(3)** Develop your own list or mental thought plan (based on these methods) of what you will say to yourself when you feel angry.

ACTION METHODS FOR REDUCING ANGER

WARNING: AGGRESSIVE EXPRESSION OF ANGER
CAN DO PERMANENT DAMAGE TO RELATIONSHIPS

---

1. THINK--"AGGRESSION WILL DRIVE A WEDGE BETWEEN US"

Think about someone who severely attacked you physically or verbally. What was that experience like? The fear, hurt, and anger of that memory can stay with you the rest of your life. The aggression may create some small measure of *lasting resentment and distance* between you and the person who delivered the attack. The aggression can cause lowered trust and a *lasting fear* that they may hurt you again.

The same lesson can be applied when you hurt someone else--whether you mean it or not. *You may be conditioning your partner to fear or resent you instead of loving you!* Fear and resentment are incompatible with love.

Is this kind of *permanent damage* what you want when you are verbally or physically aggressive toward someone you care about? You can hurt and alienate your partner with even mild name-calling or negative labeling. (It will also probably escalate the conflict.) The effect can be greatly exaggerated with someone who is sensitive to criticism or anger.

Visualize a big STOP SIGN! Think about the consequences before you attack someone or speak out of anger. Instead, try empathy; assume their best intentions; and be calm and diplomatic.

> **PRACTICE: Are you driving nails in the coffin of a relationship?** Think about your expression of anger in your most important relationship(s). Are you driving a *small wedge of permanent distance* between you and your loved one each time you hurt them? Picture that wedge each time you are tempted to attack. Instead, choose constructive expressions of anger (such as talking about feelings and issues).

2. BE ASSERTIVE--SEEK "WIN-WIN" SOLUTIONS

If you are angry at someone, focus on your top goal in life--to maximize happiness for yourself and others. *Choosing* love and happiness--even when you feel angry--strengthens your Higher Self.

Focus on loving yourself. Reach deep inside and find the part of you (your Higher Self) that loves this other person unconditionally (*i.e.* no matter what they have done). Focus on those feelings of love and on the goal of seeking a "win-win" solution. Try to understand their point of view as well as your own. If you are successful in producing a win-win solution, you will have a triple win: 1-getting your own original needs met, 2-eliminating your own self-destructive anger toward the other, plus possibly 3-getting the other person to feel closer to you (winning them over). The best way to eliminate an enemy is to make him or her your friend!

3. TAKE A "TIME-OUT" IF SOMEONE GETS TOO UPSET

Observe your own emotions when you are in a frustrating situation. If you see that you are starting to feel too angry, anxious, or guilty, then take a time-out. A time-out means that you both stop talking or that you separate long enough to think about it, calm down, and get your control back. Time-outs can be effective even if they are only one to five minutes long. Use your time out to clarify what you want or how you want to deal with the other person.

To take a time-out, you might say, "I need some time to think about what we have been talking about. I would like to continue our conversation [in a few minutes, at a later time, etc.]." If the other person doesn't want you to leave, insist and leave anyway.

Similarly, if you observe that the other person is getting too upset and is not dealing constructively with the situation, take a time-out. You could say the same thing as before, or say, "It looks like we're both getting upset, and if we can't discuss this more calmly, then I will need to take a time-out."

Take the time-out in the *early stages* of a conflict, don't wait until it has gotten destructive. Take time-outs as often as is necessary to keep things reasonably calm and productive. (See Chapter 6.)

4. FIND CONSTRUCTIVE WAYS TO RELEASE YOUR HIGH ENERGY AND AROUSAL

You have heard the expression, "Get your anger out to get rid of it." Freud used the analogy of a steam pot that will burst if the energy is not released. To some degree the analogy is accurate.

Anger causes high levels of arousal and energy--energetic activity releases it. Research has supported the idea that anger leads to a high arousal, high energy state that can last for hours--or even longer. During that time, we are more prone to renewed anger. Energetic activities use the energy and help dissipate that extra arousal. Therefore, in addition to internal methods of reducing anger, it is important to dissipate anger by energetic actions. Try exercise, walking, running, sports, physical labor, or other energetic activities--especially those that make you feel good.

5. CHOOSE CONSTRUCTIVE (NOT SELF-DESTRUCTIVE) EXPRESSIONS OF ANGER

Many people take Freud's analogy farther. They believe that in order to get rid of their anger, they must get their *aggression* out by doing something destructive or harmful to some other person or some thing. Many people--even some therapists--mistakenly believe that aggressive or confrontive expressions of anger are the only way that we can get our anger out. We have to take it out on someone or some thing. Research has shown that this belief is not true.[38]

It is true that any energetic behavior reduces anger by dissipating the arousal. It is also true that the resulting good feeling reinforces the destructive behavior. However, reinforcing aggressive behavior means that it will become a *stronger habit*. People using aggressive behavior to get rid of their anger tend to become more--not less--aggressive. Research supports this conclusion. A better way to reduce anger is *to do something constructive and energetic* such as exercise, sports, or doing something physically active that helps solve the problem.

What about "honest" aggressive behavior? How would you feel if someone called you stupid, selfish, or a string of other negatives and then said, "I just wanted to be honest about how I feel?" How would you feel? How constructive was it to the relationship?

The aggressive statement may have been honest in the sense that it reported their thoughts at *an angry moment*. However, was it the whole picture? Or was their "honesty" just a series of anger-induced thoughts that were intended to hurt you in order to get even for some perceived harm?

Wouldn't it be more constructive if the person told you that he or she cares about you, but is angry over something you did? Wouldn't it be more constructive if the person took time to listen to your point-of-view and work on constructive solutions to the problem? Which approach is better? Aggressive honesty or a thoughtful, assertive honesty?

> **PRACTICE 1: (1) List your self-destructive expressions of anger and replace them with constructive expressions.** List ways you deal with frustrating situations. What thoughts increase your anger? Which words or actions are harmful to others, your relationships, or yourself? (Examples: Yelling, swearing, attacking, throwing things, eating, smoking, drugs, avoiding the problem, or taking it out on someone else.) What thoughts and actions would be more constructive?

---

[38] See Carol Tavris' book, *Anger, the Misunderstood Emotion*, for a good summary of research demonstrating how people *learn* to respond aggressively or constructively to anger. Either expression of anger can reduce the anger's arousal, either can be reinforcing; but aggressive responses tend to make people *more aggressive*.

(2) List energetic activities to reduce anger's arousal. Sports, exercise, biking, walking, running, doing chores, laughing, and even (constructive) talking can help reduce anger's arousal. The more vigorous the activity, the more effective.

PRACTICE 2: Develop a plan for assertive (not aggressive or passive) conflict resolution. Follow the suggestions above (and in Chapter 6) to develop a plan of how to deal assertively with situations where you tend to be angry and aggressive (or nonassertive). Seek win-win solutions.

CHANGE AGGRESSION-ENHANCING PERSONAL CHARACTERISTICS

Anderson and Bushman's review article, *Human Aggression* (2002) describes factors research has shown to increase aggression. These factors include values and beliefs, family and social influences, previoius reinforment for aggressive behavior, confidence in ones aggressive "abilities," a sense of entitlement, and other factors. Each chapter in this book has lessons that can help counteract those basic inner aggression-causing factors. The Happiness Checklist (Appendix A) summarizes some of them. *Make a major life goal and project to identify and modify these predispositions.*

To overcome anger and aggression,
choose EMPATHETIC UNDERSTANDING
over assuming the worst intentions;
choose UNCONDITIONAL POSITIVE CARING
over insensitivity;
choose the HAPPINESS DOCTRINE
over the fairness doctrine;
choose ACCEPTING the unchangeable aspects of reality
over hostility--"it's the way of things;"
take CONSTRUCTIVE ENERGETIC ACTIONS
to help get rid of the steam inside; and
remember, there is inherent justice for harmful behaviors.
Most of all, remember,
EVERY MOMENT OF ANGER IS ONE LESS MOMENT OF HAPPINESS

THE RUNAWAY EMOTIONS CYCLE:
Overcoming Panic Attacks and Other Runaway Emotions

Sometimes emotions seem to get out of control and become very frightening--simply because they seem *out of control*. As a result, we may fear something disastrous--such as going insane, dying, or being depressed forever. These cycles of deep depression, temper tantrums, or panic attacks have one thing in common--the negative emotion increases negative thoughts--which, in turn, increase negative emotions. Each cycle increases both negative emotions and negative thoughts--until something final interrupts the cycles. If nothing else intercedes, the body will intervene--sheer exhaustion (or other state) will begin to help reduce the extremely high (or low) emotional state.

PANIC ATTACKS—A COMMON RUNAWAY EMOTIONS PHENOMENON

The negative emotion-thought feedback loop is a cause of panic attacks. One of the greatest causes of panic attacks is a feedback loop that works as follows:

1-Original anxiety cause. A person starts feeling upset about one situation. Example, Diane feels anxiety about rejection meeting someone.

2-Anxiety stimulates secondary (thoughts) reaction. When Diane notices herself feeling anxious, she notices that her heart rate is increasing and her breathing is getting tighter. This observation triggers a *secondary thought* that she might get so anxious that she can't breathe and might faint.

3-Feedback (negative thought) increases anxiety level. The *thought* that she might lose control and faint *increases her anxiety another step.*

4-Feedback loop continues until something terminates it. This escalation between thoughts about losing control and anxiety increase until something terminates it. Diane could suddenly decide to leave the situation. That might decrease her anxiety and her thoughts about losing control. She could get so anxious she faints, and her body ends the feedback cycle.

One major cause of panic attacks is the *underlying fear of the outcome*--such as going crazy, fainting, or having a heart attack. Becoming aware of what those underlying fears are and learning ways of coping with them is a major way to control panic attacks (see Chapters 4 and 8) People don't die or go crazy form panic attacks--those are serious misconceptions!

Another major cause is the feedback cycle itself. *Noticing the increases in the negative emotion* itself triggers the thoughts such as, "I'm losing control." Those secondary thoughts in turn increase the negative emotion. To break this cycle it is necessary to *quit focusing on the increases in anxiety* and *focus on more constructive thoughts and ways of solving the immediate problem*--such as Diane's talking to the stranger and overcoming her fears of rejection. It is important to remember that the *"out-of-control" thoughts and beliefs about emotions* magnifying the emotions. They are like pouring gasoline on a fire. Remember, these are *just thoughts--not the truth!* Continuing to focus on them only strengthens them.

When people get in **deep depressions** or get suicidal thoughts, they are often going through a similar process. Except, instead of anxiety, they primarily feel depression. There is a similar fear that the emotion will go on forever or get even worse until they can't stand it.

Questioning the "I can't stand it" self-statement is important. The truth is that even if they do nothing, the depression will partially lift on its own--especially if they just accept that it is ok to feel awful and be depressed for a while. Positive problem-solving, thinking, and actions can help even more.

Recognizing that *I have a choice* of whether to get more control of my emotion can help. Say to yourself, "No matter what this is doing to anyone else, this unpleasant feeling is very unpleasant to me, and I am getting sick and tired of feeling this way. I chose to accept that it is ok to feel this way--I am not going crazy, am not a lunatic, am not out of control. These are just *thoughts--not reality*. It is ok to feel that way, but *I would prefer to feel better*. I choose to think about immediate ways to feel better or get help in feeling better."

Dysfunctional beliefs about emotions help cause runaway emotions

Beliefs that negative emotions are bad, destructive, or foretell some terrible consequences are often a root cause of runaway emotions. Beliefs that emotions are *bad* are dysfunctional beliefs. They can set off a vicious runaway emotions cycle (see Appendix C). We need to identify and cleanse ourselves of all beliefs such as the following:

- **"If my anxiety (depression, etc) gets to strong,** I will...(go insane, have a heart attack, die, make everyone think I'm crazy, lose all my friends, etc.)."
- **"It is wrong to ever feel angry."** Instead try, "Anger tells me that I don't seem to be getting what I want, and I need to understand and accept the situation (or other person) better."
- **"If I feel guilty, I must be guilty."** Instead try, "If I feel guilty, I will examine my underlying beliefs are expectations. Do I want to change my behavior or my expectations? Do I need to make restitution?"
- **"Feeling depressed (or anxious) means that my feelings (or life) are out of control."** Instead, try "I may *feel* out of control or *fear* that my life is out of control, but that emotion does *not mean* that it *really is out of control*. I can get eventually get control and be happier!"
- **"Feeling fear is a sign of weakness."** Instead try, "Fear is not a sign of weakness. If I feel fear, I will try to examine why I am afraid and what I can do about it."

PRACTICE: Identify dysfunctional beliefs that you have about emotions. Look at the above examples and take each emotion--anger, depression, and anxiety. Identify any negative associations (thoughts) that you have with any of these emotions. Do you see them as *signs* of weakness, badness, incompetence, future negative outcomes, or anything else negative? If so, find more constructive beliefs and points of view to overcome these negative ones. Then use them whenever you get the negative emotions.

NEGATIVE COGNITIVE STYLES

Dr. Aaron Beck recognized that people who have chronic problems with depression, anxiety, guilt, and other negative emotions usually have a negative thinking bias. Research has supported the efficacy of cognitive therapy (called cognitive restructuring) that replaces these styles with more positive thinking.

Negative bias. Negative bias is a tendency to look at the more negative side of some event, person, object, or situation. It gives a *negative interpretation* or a *negative point of view* for looking at a situation. **Instead think:**
- I *will assume the best instead of assume the worst.*
- *Positive self-fulfilling prophesies* tend to create positive outcomes; negative self-fulfilling prophesies tend to create negative outcomes.
- Negative explanations of my own or other peoples' underlying motives cause me to intensify my anger or other negative feelings.
- Assuming the world is a hostile place creates fear, anxiety, and anger.

Negative *selective abstraction*. Selective abstraction means taking negative features of a situation out of context and exaggerating their significance. Usually it also means negating positive features. Example: A student who gets four "A"s and one "C," then focuses on the "C's."   **Instead think:**
- I will list *at least one positive feature* for each negative feature.
- I will limit my focus on negative features to constructive thoughts about how I can either *accept or change the negative features.*

Overgeneralization. When we overgeneralize, we assume far-reaching conclusions from limited data. A student made a "D" on one test. She overgeneralizes, she doesn't just think "Well, I messed up on that one test. Instead, "I may not pass the course, not ever finish college." "I must be stupid and a failure." "My whole life is ruined."   **Instead think:**
- I will put the negative event into its *proper perspective.*
- I will look for the positive aspects of every event. When I make mistakes, there is *always something positive* that comes from that event.
- These are just *overgeneralized thoughts*, not reality.

Thinking in extremes. It means exaggerating differences, dichotomous thinking. Everything is either black or white, wonderful or awful, always or never. It leads to exaggerated emotions. Catastrophizing may provide an excuse for not being able to deal with it and get rewarded by others.   **Instead think:**
- I will stop using overly dramatic or melodramatic language and replace that language with *calming language.*
- I will learn to realize that there are almost never "never," "always," 100% events. Instead I will always try to be accurate in balancing out causation.

==>**Refer especially to Chapters 1, 3, 4, 5 to increase positive thinking.**

ASSERTIVE COMMUNICATION SKILLS TO CREATE UNDERSTANDING AND INTIMACY

The process of resolving a disagreement or mutual problem involves a number of specific interpersonal skills. My wife Sherry and I developed the Stevens Relationship Questionnaire (SRQ) and found high correlations (greater than 0.70) between both the *Assertive Conflict Resolution* scale and the *Intimacy* scale and the Locke-Wallace Marital Satisfaction scale (Sherry Stevens,1988). The SRQ is now part of SHAQ (free on my website). The SHAQ research results further support the recommendations below. This Appendix provides more detail for the intimacy skills and assertive communication skills discussed in **Chapter 6.** For more detail, go to my website, **www.csulb.edu/~tstevens.**

A List of Some Key Assertive Communication Skills
SKILL 1: EXPLORING THE PROBLEM
SKILL 2: ASSERTIVE REQUEST (ERPG)--Diplomatically requesting change
SKILL 3: EMPATHETIC LISTENING
SKILL 4: PERSISTENCE IN EXPLORING THE PROBLEM
SKILL 5: ESCALATION AND DE-ESCALATION of CONFLICTS
SKILL 6: DEALING WITH AGGRESSION AND MANIPULATION--What if your partner uses negative labels or attacks you?

SKILL 1: EXPLORING THE PROBLEM ALONE
Before stating your position, use the following guidelines.
1. Recognize the problem as a mutual problem. Since the issue is upsetting *you*, it is *your problem* (no matter what your partner did to cause the problem). If you ask or state what you can do to change/help the problem *before asking* your partner to change, you can induce a cooperative situation putting pressure on your partner to match your caring, understanding, cooperative behavior.
2. Clarify what you want from the interaction *before* approaching your partner. Suggested goals include win-win outcomes, keeping the discussion on a calm, caring/loving level versus an emotional, negative one. Also, a goal can be to learn *specifically what positive behaviors you want from each other.*

SKILL 2: ASSERTIVE REQUEST (ERPG)
Whatever you want is usually best stated as a request or favor—even if you think they owe it to you. Here, "partner" can be a clerk or spouse.
ERPG is E-Empathy; R-Respect; P-Problem; G-Goal

Step 1--State *EMPATHETIC understanding* of partner's position (E). What are your partner's *feelings and thoughts related to this issue?* Possibly start by asking your partner to explain his/her feelings and thoughts about the issue. State *your most empathetic understanding of their thoughts and especially their feelings.*

Step 2--Explicitly state RESPECT and caring of partner and partner's feelings and acknowledge positive aspects of partner's position (R). "I care about your feelings," "I appreciate...," "I respect you for...," "I want you to be happy..."

Step 3--State the PROBLEM (P): Be specific, state exactly how their behavior affects you, your thoughts, and your feelings. Use neutral, descriptive words. No negative labels about yourself or partner--avoid all zingers, attacks, cynicism, and exaggerations! Describe events step-by-step in an understanding manner.

Own the problem, state it as *your problem*. After all, you are the one who is upset about it right now and want a change. Use "I feel...," "I think...," "I want..." statements to take responsibility for your own feelings and thoughts.

Step 4-State the GOAL (G)--what ideal/minimal actions do you want from your partner. How is that different from what your partner has been doing or wants?

Give as much **freedom and choice to your partner** in how or what they do to help as possible. Ask them for help and/or suggestions of how they can help and try to choose options that they are motivated to actually do--even if it means significant compromises. **Ask for their help—enlist helper motives.**

Step 5-Follow up with listening, persistence, and other assertive skills.
➔*For more help, see the more detailed guide, How to Make an Assertive Request, go to:* ***www.csulb.edu/~tstevens/assert%20req.html***

FULL ERPG EXAMPLE (Steps 1-5):
First, think through all the steps and mentally rehearse what you will say and how you would respond to things your friend might say (Step 1). Then you say, "You seem to be upset with me because you don't think that I have given you enough time lately. Is that right? [listen and respond] (Step 2). You are a good friend and I care about your feelings very much (Step 3). However, I feel pressure from your expectation that we contact each other several times/week. I am very busy, and give you all the time that I feel I can afford. I would like for us to sit down and define some guidelines that can help us both feel better about this situation (Step 4). [Then do it together, and follow the guidelines (Step 5).]

SKILL 3: EMPATHETIC RESPONSE and PROBLEM EXPLORATION

This set of skills is appropriate for all listening situations. They include when your partner is upset with you, criticizes you, comes to you for help, or just recounts daily events. If this exploration process is stopped prematurely, then the underlying issues may never get explored and resolved. **Warning**: Premature agreeing, disagreeing, offering solutions, or presenting another point-of-view can abruptly stop this necessary exploration. The five steps follow.[39]

Step 1--Identify your partner's emotions. Use your partner's body language, statements, and your own feelings to identify your partner's emotions. Ask yourself:
a. Is the emotion positive or negative?
b. What is the general type of emotion? *Negative emotions include* anxiety/ confusion,

---

[39] These steps are from Robert Carkhuff's (1969) and Robert Cash's helping skills models. Other ideas in this appendix also follow their models.

guilt, anger, or depression. *Positive emotions include* love, joy, relaxed, happy, or excited.

c. *Intensity* of the feeling? Extreme, strong, moderate, mild, or extremely mild?

d. Find an appropriate *word or phrase* to describe the feeling.

- *It is usually better to choose a feeling expression that is too mild rather than too strong. Example:* moderate anger = NOT, "you're *really angry*" or "*you're out of control*" INSTEAD "you're *feeling resentful...*" or "*pretty upset*".
- *If conflicting feelings* have been expressed, state both: **Example:** "On the one hand you feel (feeling) because (content), on the other hand you feel..."
- *If you are confused* about what your partner said, interrupt them and tell them you are confused.
- If they are talking "nonstop," frequently break in and state your empathetic summary. Say something like, "Let me see if I'm following you so far..."

Step 2--Mentally summarize content (your partner's main points)

Use *words they would use or agree with*. If you state *your response to* their position, then your partner will likely feel not understood and may argue and/or stop exploring the problem. Try to get *their approval that you understand their position. Example:* NOT: "You're saying that you were really selfish about how you spent our money." INSTEAD: "You're saying that you spent the money on purchases that you thought were important."

Step 3-State your empathetic response to your partner

Formula: "You feel (feeling), because (summary of content/causes)."

Example: "You feel **hurt** because *you think I was inconsiderate*."

Step 4--Use their feedback to correct your response if necessary.

    Positive feedback-your partner keeps exploring the problem: If your partner continues elaborating, then your empathetic response was accurate.

    Negative feedback-your partner STOPS exploring the problem: If your partner corrects you, but continues, that is OK too. However, if your partner argues with you about your interpretation or stops exploring the problem constructively, then *assume that you didn't state your partner's point-of-view adequately.* Even if you believe your partner is being dishonest, you can still say, "I hear you saying that you feel..." (If you think your partner is not being open or truthful, tell them what you think later when it's your turn to respond.)

Examples of using the empathetic listening technique. Note: *feeling* words are in **bold**, the content summary is underlined.

- "You seem very **upset** with me about my being late."
- "Are you saying that you are often **confused** because you didn't think that I told you clearly what I want?"
- "On the one hand you feel **very sad** about her leaving, but on the other you also feel **very relieved**."
- "You seem to be saying that you feel **guilty** about what you just said to me."

Step 5--Continue making empathetic responses throughout the entire discussion--especially if someone gets upset, confused, or needs time to think.

Even more useful is the general rule that *if you don't know what else to say, make an empathetic response to your partner. When you are too confused or upset yourself you can get* time to deal with your own feelings before saying something that will upset your partner more.

→ Go to Chapter 2, and read the Self-Exploration technique for more detail about exploring the problem. Use those techniques with BOTH partners.

MORE ON EMPATHETIC LISTENING and RESPONDING TO CRITICISM

• **Tell your partner that you care about her/him and her/his feelings**. Express your caring to your partner even in the midst of the most heated part of a disagreement. "Though we're upset, let's remember we still love each other."

• **Encourage your partner to be specific.** Do *not assume you understand what your partner means--especially about key points.* Try to get your partner to be especially clear about what she/he wants from you. *Example:* "I want you to be happier about this. I care about how you feel. *Please give me some examples of how you would like me to say (or do) this.*

• **Identifying central underlying issues.** How do we tell *if we are exploring the real underlying issues* that are causing most of the problems? Here are some questions to ask yourself. Is it a more **general issue** that seems related to a number of more specific situations or issues? Does something similar come up repeatedly or has it been consciously hidden repeatedly? Does the issue seem **connected to strong feelings** of either you or your partner? Is it an issue that one or both partners tend to **avoid** talking or thinking about? When you two think or talk about it, **do you get very** confused and not seem to know how to deal well with the issue? If the issue meets any of these criteria, it is probably an *important underlying issue.*

ADDITIONAL WAYS OF FINDING UNDERLYING ISSUES:

• Ask your partner to **describe other similar times or situations** that might be related to how he/she is feeling.

• Ask yourself what these similar **problem situations have in common.** Identify the underlying general issues/problems alone before the discussion.

• Ask your partner (and yourself) **when the feeling/problem started and/or when it gets worse and better**.

• Help each **take responsibility for their own thoughts, feelings, choices, and actions**. Remember that no one "Makes me feel.. ." Say to yourself, "I am responsible for my own feelings and happiness--not my partner." See Ch-6.

• *Internalize the issue* and *help your partner internalize the issue.* If you or your partner is "externalizing the problem" by blaming the other, other people, or external circumstances for the problem, then it will be helpful to gradually move in the direction of each "internalizing" the problem

• **Encourage each to stay on one main issue at a time.**

• **Suspend disagreement with your partner's position as long as possible.**

• **Avoid giving advice that is premature or not explicitly asked for.** *If in doubt about whether your partner wants your opinion or advice, ASK.*

SKILL 4: PERSISTENCE EXPLORING THE PROBLEM

Try saying this to yourself: "I care about my partner and myself and recognize that this problem and resultant hard feelings will be a thorn in our flesh until we get it under control. I will persist in working on the problem as long as I believe it is productive. I will also recognize and respect my own and my partner's limits about the length and frequency of discussions. People vary on their tolerance.

SKILL 5: ESCALATION AND DE-ESCALATION OF CONFLICTS

Escalation means "raising the stakes." Escalation usually increases the emotional intensity for both. Raising the stakes occurs when one partner makes accusations or threats or tries to manipulate the other. *De-escalation* is when the partners lower the stakes, begin to get more emotional control, and deal more constructively with the issues. **The goal is de-escalation.** Almost all of the techniques discussed in this section will generally help de-escalate the level of the conflict. Moving from "I win"--"You lose" positions to "win-win" positions can be of fundamental importance for de-escalating. Avoid use of negative labels, blaming, exaggerating, attacking, or bringing up past or irrelevant mistakes. Agreeing to change *your behavior and* making empathetic, kind, loving, and cooperative statements to your partner can be powerful de-escalators. The next section has additional suggestions.

SKILL 6: DEALING WITH AGGRESSION and MANIPULATION
If your partner begins using negative labels, attacking you, manipulating you or using aggression, you can:
• **Suspend judgment and try to get into a neutral observer mode–not a defensive or attack mode.** Suspend judgment for your own benefit. Say to yourself, "I want a successful solution for my own happiness. So attacking back will just cause unproductive escalation and fighting. It will undermine my taking good care of myself." Instead of getting defensive or attacking back, try the following:
• **Keep using the empathetic responding principles**. "I can see that you are very angry with me about ... I am sorry to see that you are so unhappy about this situation. Please continue to tell me more about why you are so angry..."
• **Get your partner to be *more specific* and *elaborate* his/her criticism more.** Getting your partner to criticize you *more* may be the opposite of what you normally do, but it can work wonders. Ask your partner questions like the following: NOT: "I don't do that, you must be nuts." INSTEAD: "I really care about how you feel, but I don't understand exactly what you mean. Can you give me some examples?" OR "Are there other situations where you think that I am being inconsiderate?" OR "If you don't like X, what would you prefer I do instead?"
• **Use the *Time Out* technique**–If you get too upset to be kind, say you need a few minutes alone and leave the situation until you can gather your composure and focus. 5 minutes, 1 hour, or even longer until both people calm down.
• **Warn your partner that you will take a time out if they do not calm down or quit using negative labels about you. Example**: Say, "Please do not talk so loud and use negative labels to describe me. I will be much more willing to continue to listen if you will just describe exactly what I did and how you feel about it instead."
• **Use the *Broken Record* technique**–In response to manipulation denying that you want what you said, keep briefly repeating your position over and over until they understand or tire. You will sound like a broken record. Use this technique carefully because it can be aggressive if not appropriately done.
• **Use negotiating with *incentives and/or consequences*..** In this case offer positive or negative consequences you will do if he/she keeps manipulating. Make contracts to provide incentives/rewards for changing key behaviors/habits.
• **Leave the relationship or reduce its level of intimacy** if you are sure that this is what you want more permanently. Never use this as a threat; it may work only once.
• **Physical attacks** are handled in an analogous way. Protect yourself and get away from your partner--creating as much space or distance from your partner as you need to feel that your safety is secure. Recognize that there is *nothing that you can do that justifies a physical attack from your partner* (except, perhaps, if you physically attacked first).
→For more on anger and aggression, go to Appendix B.

MORE GUIDELINES FOR ASSERTIVE, INTIMATE CONFLICT RESOLUTION
• Avoid *assuming* you understand your partner's feelings or thoughts—ask.
• To the extent that your partner's underlying motives are unclear, *assume the best.*
• Avoid negative or unsupportive tactics or approaches to your partner. Use *neutral, descriptive statements*--no negative labels
• *Avoid exaggerated statements,* evaluative statements, and other "zingers" toward your partner. Avoid extreme statements
• Avoid dogmatic or authoritarian statements.

IT IS OK THAT YOU AND YOUR PARTNER PERMANENTLY DISAGREE
When my partner and I cannot reach agreement, our resolution of the conflict may be *to agree to disagree.* This means we agree to understand and respect each other's position, and to avoid unnecessary discussion or zinging each other.

Separating consequences in areas of disagreement may help. For example if two people don't agree how to spend money, then separating their budgets as much as is practical can help reduce conflict and resentment.

Think of the most understanding, caring, and interpersonally skilled person you know. This is someone whom everyone admires for being
so good with people, and for sewing positive feelings wherever he/she goes.
What is it about this person that makes him/her so special?
Is it caring and empathy? Is it being assertive, diplomatic, and generating win-win solutions? Is it being a positive-thinking, happy person?
Why not choose this person as a role-model for interacting with others? Doing so may lead to interpersonal riches beyond your imagination.

APPENDIX F:

Demographic Factors and SHAQ Outcomes

Sex. The only significant findings were that females were a little happier (r =.09)[40] and had better relationships (r =.15) while males had higher incomes (r =.18).

Age. Higher age was mildly related to both low anxiety (r =.11) and low anger (r =.13). I didn't find a significant age-happiness correlation as some have. However, I found that people over 50 were slightly happier (r =.05). I also found significant relationships between being older and low depression (r =.05), low anxiety (r =.11), and low anger (r =.13). Age was one of the best predictors of income (r =.45); probably because students and younger people have not had time to advance in their careers. Similarly, higher age related to education completed (r =.25). Age was negatively related to health (r = -.07) and was not related to relationship outcomes.

Religion. Belonging to a particular religious group was only weakly related to outcome variables. Being *Jewish* (r =.06) or *Methodist* (r =.05) correlated the highest with happiness; being *agnostic* was most negatively related (r = -.09). *Fundamentalist Non-Baptists* were slightly less depressed (r =.08) and less anxious (r =.07) than other people. There were few other significant correlations. However, looking at *values* typically associated with religions, paints a different picture. Correlations with happiness, low depression, low anger, and low anxiety for *Spiritual intimacy* were .26, .12, and .05; for *Giving to others' happiness,* were .36, .14, and .11; for *Impact, change world,* were .27, .12, and .09; for *Obedience to God,* were .23, .11, and .02ns[41]; and for *Religion,* were .28, .06, and .02ns. Thus, internalized values espoused by religions were important factors. This finding is consistent with other studies showing that the positive effects of religion are present primarily for people who *internalize* the teachings.

Ethnic group and nationality. *Other Asian*[42] (r =.08) and *Mexican* (r =.08) had highest positive correlations with happiness; *European* had the most negative (r = -.05. People who spoke *other European*[43] languages were unhappy (r = -.11). *German* (r = -.09) and *other European* (r = -.13) speaking people had higher anger/aggression scores. Depression was slightly less (r =.07) among *Chinese* language and *other Asian* (r =.07), but was mostly unrelated to language, ethnicity, or religion.

Occupational category. *Students* (r =.08), *people professionals* (r =.08), *educators* (r =.07), and *managers* (r =.06) were the happiest; only *other* occupation had a negative correlation (r = -.06). *Others* were also the most depressed (r = -.06) and least healthy (r = -.08). While *students* were the happiest, they were also the most anxious (r = -.07) and the healthiest (r =.08) of the occupational groups.

---

[40] All correlations were significant at the .01 level or greater unless otherwise indicated.
[41] *ns* = correlation not statistically significant. All **N** (number of subjests) > 3000.
[42] Other Asian = not Chinese, Cambodian, Vietnamese, or Korean.
[43] Other European language = not English, Spanish, French, or German.

BRIEF BIBLIOGRAPHY

Ader, R., & Cohen, N. (1993). Psychoneuroimmunology: Conditioning and stress. *Annual Review of Psychology*, *44*, pp. 53-85.

Adler, N., & Matthews, K. (1994). Health psychology: Why do some people get sick and some stay well? *Annual Review of Psychology*, *45*, pp. 229-59.

Adolphs, R. (2009). The social brain: neural basis of social knowledge. *Annual Review of Psychology*, *60*, pp. 693-716.

Anderson, C. A., & Bushman, B. J. (2002). Human aggression. *Annual Review of Psychology*, *53*, pp. 27-51.

Anderson, J. (1983). *The architecture of cognition.* Cambridge, MA: Harvard University Press.

Austin, J. T., & Vancouver, J. B. (1996). Goal constructs in psychology: Structure, Process, and Content. *Psychological Bulletin*, *120*, 338-375.

Babyak, M., Blumenthal, J. A., Herman, S., Khatri, P., Doraiswamy, M., Moore, K., et al. (2000). Exercise treatment for major depression: Maintenance of therapeutic benefit at 10 months. *Psychosomatic Medicine*, *21*, 633-638.

Bandura, A. (1997). *Self-efficacy: The exercise of self-control.* New York: W. H. Freeman.

Banji, M. R., & Prentice, D. A. (1994). The self in social contexts. *Annual Review of Psychology*, *45*, pp. 297-332.

Barrett, L. F., Mesquita, B., Ochsner, K. N., & Gross, J. J. (2007). The experience of emotion. *Annual Review of Psychology*, *58*, pp. 373-403.

Baumeister, R. F., Smart, L., & Boden, J. M. (1996). Relation of threatened egotism to violence and aggression: The dark side of high self-esteem. *Psychological Review*, *102*, pp. 5-33.

Beattie, M. (1987). *Codependent no more.* New York: Harper and Row.

Bergin, A. E., & Richards, P. S. (2005). *A spiritual strategy for counseling and psychotherapy.* Washington, DC: American Psychological Association.

Berlyne, D. E. (1987). Arousal and reinforcement. In D. Levine, *Nebraska Symposium on Motivation.* Lincoln, NE: University of Nebraska.

Berlyne, D. E. (1960). *Conflict, arousal, and curiosity.* New York: McGraw-Hill.

Berne, E. (1964). *Games people play.* New York: Grove Press.

Black, C. (1989). *It's never too late to have a happy childhood.* New York: Valentine.

Blumental, J. (1989). Managing stress cuts heart risk. *American Heart Association.* Nov 10. Long Beach: Long Beach Press-Telegram.

Brehm, J. W., & Self, E. A. (1989). The intensity of motivation. *Annual Review of Psychology*, *40*, pp. 109-131.

Brewin, C. R. (1996). Theoretical foundations of cognitive-behavior therapy for anxiety and depression. *Annual Review of Psychology*, *47*, pp. 33-57.

Burns, D. (1980). *Feeling good: The new mood therapy.* New York: Signet Press.

Burtt, E. A. (1982). *The teachings of the compassionate buddha.* New York: Penguin Books.

Carkhuff, R. A. (1969). *Helping and human relations.* New York: Holt, Rinehart, and Winston.

Carpenter, G. A., & Grossberg, S. (1995). A neural network architecture for autonomous learning, recognition, and prediction in a nonstationary world. In S. F. Zornetzer, J. L. Davis, C. Lau, & T. McKenna, *Neural Networks and Electronic Networks.* New York: Academic Press.

Carver, C. S., & Scheier, M. F. (2002). Optimism. In C. R. Snyder, & S. J. Lopez, *Handbook of positive psychology* (pp. 231-243). New York: Oxford University Press.

Chambers, D. L., & Cillis, M. M. (1993). Cognitive therapy of anxiety disorders. *Journal of Consulting and Clinical Psychology*, *61*, 248-260.

Chang, E. C. (2001). *Optimism, pessimism, and implications for theory, research, and practice.* Washington, DC: American Psychological Association.

Clark, D. T., Beck, A. T., & Alford, B. A. (1999). *Scientific foundations of cognitive theory and therapy of depression.* New York: John Wiley.

Clark, L. A. (2007). Assessment and diagnosis of personality disorder: perennial issues and an emerging reconceptualization. *Annual Review of Psychology*, *58*, pp. 227-257.

Clark, L. A., Watson, D., & Reynolds, S. (1995). Diagnosis and classification of psychopathology: Challenges to the current system and future directions. *Annual Review of Psychology*, *46*, pp. 121-153.

Clark, M. S., & Reis, H. T. (1995). Interpersonal processes in close relationships. *Annual Review of Psychology*, *39*, pp. 609-672.

Cohen, H. (1997). Heart attack risk factors. *American Heart Association*. Nov 11. Long Beach: Press-Telegram.

Cohen, S., & Herbert, T. (1996). Health psychology: psychological factors and physical disease from the perspective of psychoneuroimmunology. *Annual Review of Psychology*, 47, pp. 113-142.

Csikszentmihalyi, M. (1990). *Flow: The psychology of optimal experience*. New York: Harper Row.

Csikszentmihalyi, M. (1988). *Optimal experience: psychological studies of flow in consciousness*. New York: Cambridge University Press.

Darley, J. M., & Shultz, T. R. (1990). judgments: their content and acquistion. *Annual Review of Psychology*, 41, pp. 525-556.

Davidson, R. J., Pizzagalli, D., Nitschke, J. B., & Putnam, K. (2002). Depression: perspectives from. *Annual Review of Psychology*, 53, pp. 545-574.

DeNeve, K., & Harris, C. (1998). The happy personality: a meta-analysis of 137 personality traits and subjective well-being. *Psychological Bulletin*, 124, 196-229.

Depue, R. A., & Iacono, W. C. (1989). Neurobehavioral aspects of affective disorders. *Annual Review of Psychology*, 40, pp. 457-492.

Diener, E. (2000). Subjective well-being: the science of happiness and a proposal for a national index. *American Psychologist*, 55, 34-43.

Digman, J. M. (1990). Personality structure: Emergence of the five-factor theory. *Annual Review of Psychology*, 41, pp. 417-440.

Dodge, K. A. (1993). Social-cognitive mechanisms in the development of conduct disorder and depression. *Annual Review of Psychology*, 44, pp. 559-584.

Dogson, K. S. (1989). A meta-analysis of the efficacy of cognitive therapy for depression. *Journal of Consulting and Clinical Psychology*, 57, 414-419.

Dyer, W. (1992). *Real magic*. New York: Harper Collins.

Dyer, W. (1976). *Your erroneous zones*. New York: Avon Books.

Eisenberg, R., & Cameron, J. (1996). Detrimental effects of reward--myth or reality. *American Psychologist*, 51, 1153-1166.

Emerson, R. W. (1991). *Self-Reliance*. New York: Crown Publishers.

Emmons, R. A. (1999). *The psychology of ultimate concerns: Motivation and spirituality in personality*. New York: Guilford Press.

Ericsson, K. A., & Lehmann, A. C. (1996). Expert and exceptional performance: Evidence of maximal adaption to task constraints. *Annual Review of Psychology*, 47, pp. 273-305.

Ford, D. H. (1987). *Humans as self-constructing living systems*. Hillsdale, NJ: Lawrence Erlbaum.

Fournier, G., & Jeanrie, C. (2003). Locus ofcontrol: Back to basics. In S. J. Lopez, & C. R. Snyder, *Positive psychological assessment: A handbook of models and measures* (pp. 139-154). Washington, DC: American Psychological Association.

Frankl, V. (1969). *Man's search for meaning*. New York: Washington Square Press.

Gelso, C. J., & Fassinger, R. E. (1990). Counseling psychology: theory and research on Interventions. *Annual Review of Psychology*, 41, pp. 355-386.

Goldfried, M. R., Greenberg, L. S., & Marmar, C. (n.d.). Individual psychotherapy: process and outcome. *Annual Review of Psychology*, 41, pp. 659-688.

Goldstein, M. J. (1988). The family and psychopathology. *Annual Review of Psychology*, 39, pp. 283-299.

Grossberg, S. (1975). A neural model of attention, reinforcement, and discrimination learning. *International Review of Neurobiology*, 18, 263-327.

Grossberg, S. (1980). Does a brain build a cognitive code? *Psychological Review*, 87, 1-51.

Grossberg, S. (1988). *Neural networks and natural intelligence*. Cambridge, MA: MIT Press.

Grossberg, S. (1982). Processing of expected and unexpected events during conditioning and attention: A psychophysiological theory. *Psychological Review*, 89, 529-572.

Grossberg, S., Commons, M. L., & Staddon, J. E. (1991). *Neural network models of conditioning and learning*. Hillsdale, NJ: Lawrence Erlbaum.

Hartup, W. W., & van Lieshout, C. F. (1995). Personality development in a social context. *Annual Review of Psychology*, 46, pp. 655-687.

Hollon, S. D., Stewart, M. O., & Strunk, D. (2006). Enduring effects for cognitive behavior therapy in the treatment of depression and anxiety. *Annual Review of Psychology*, 57, pp. 285-315.

Holyoak, K. J., & Spellman, B. A. (1993). Thinking. *Annual Review of Psychology*, 44, pp. 265-315.

Howell, R. T., & Howell, C. J. (2008). The relation of economic status to subjective well-being in developing countries: a meta-analysis. *Psychological Bulletin*, 134, 536-560.

Iacoboni, M. (2009). Empathy and mirror neurons. *Annual Review of Psychology*, 60, pp. 653-670.

Izard, C. E. (2009). Emotion theory and research: highlights, unanswered questions, and emerging issues. *Annual Review of Psychology* , 60, pp. 1-25.

Karniol, R. (1996). The motivational impact of temporal focus: Thinking about the future and the past. *Annual Review of Psychology* , 47, pp. 593-620.

Karoly, P. (1993). Mechanisms of self-regulation: A systems view. *Annual Review of Psychology* , 44, pp. 23-45.

Kelly, G. (1955). *The psychology of personal constructs.* New York: Norton.

Kessler, R. (1997). The effects of stressful life eents on depression. *Annual Review of Psychology* , 48, pp. 191-214.

Kinchia, R. A. (1992). Attention. *Annual Review of Psychology* , 43, pp. 711-742.

Knutson, J. F. (1995). Psychological characteristics of maltreated children: Putative risk factors and consequences. *Annual Review of Psychology* , 46, pp. 401-431.

Lazarus, R. S. (1993). From Psychological stress to the emotions: A history of changing outlooks. *Annual Review of Psychology* , 44, pp. 1-21.

Leary, M. R. (2007). Motivational and emotional aspects of the self. *Annual Review of Psychology* , 58, pp. 317-344.

Lebow, J. L., & Gurman, A. S. (1993). Research assessing couople and family therapy. *Annual Review of Psychology* , 44, pp. 27-57.

LeDoux, J. E. (1995). Clues fromthe brain. *Annual Review of Psychology* , 46, pp. 209-235.

Leonardo, E. D., & Hen, R. (2006). Genetics of affective and anxiety disorders. *Annual Review of Psychology* , 57, pp. 117-137.

Levine, D. S., & Leven, S. J. (1992). *Motivation, emotion, and goal direction in neural networks.* Hillsdale, NJ: Lawrence Erlbaum.

Loeber, R., & Hay, D. (1997). Key issues in the development of aggression and violence from childhood to early adulthood. *Annual Review of Psychology* , 48, pp. 339-370.

Lyubomirsky, S., King, L., & Diener, E. (2005). The benefits of frequent positive affect: does happiness lead to success? *Psychological Bulletiin* , 131, 803-355.

Lyubomirsky, S., Sheldon, K. M., & Schkade, D. (2005). Pursuing happiness: The architecture of sustainable change. *Review of General Psychology* , 9, 111-131.

Magnusson, D., & Torestad, B. (1993). A holistic view of personality. *Annual Review of Psychology* , 48, pp. 427-452.

Mandler, G., & Kessen, W. (1959). *The language of psychology.* New York: Wiley.

Marlatt, G. A., & Baer, J. S. (1988). Addictive behaviors: Etiology and treatment. *Annual Review of Psychology* , 39, pp. 223-252.

Maslow, A. H. (1954). *Motivation and personality.* New York: Harper.

Maslow, A. H. (1971). *The further reaches of human nature.* New York: Penguin Press.

Maslow, A. H. (1962). *Toward a psychology of being.* New York: Van Nostrand.

Mathews, A., & MacLeod, C. (1994). Cognitive approaches to emotion and emotional disorders. *Annual Review of Psychology* , 45, pp. 25-50.

Mayer, J. D., Roberts, R. D., & Barsade, S. G. (2008). Human abilities: emotional intelligence. *Annual Review of Psychology* , 59, pp. 507-536.

McClelland, D. C. (1961). *The achieving society.* Princeton, NJ: Van Nostrand-Reinhold.

McClelland, D. C., Atkinson, J. W., Clark, R. W., & Lowell, E. L. (1953). *The achievement motive.* New York: Appleton, Century, Crofts.

Miller, G. A., Galanter, E., & Pribram, K. H. (1960). *Plans and the structure of behavior.* New York: Holt.

Miller, G., Chen, E., & Cole, S. W. (2009). Health psychology: developing biologically plausible models linking the social world and physical health. 60, pp. 501-524.

Myers, D. G. (2000). The funds, friends, and faith of happy people. *American Psychologist* , 55, 56-67.

Myers, D. (1992). *The Pursuit of Happiness.* New York: Avon Books.

Neisser, u., Boodoo, G., Bouchard Jr., T. J., Boykin, A. W., Brody, N., Ceci, S. J., et al. (1996). Intelligence: knowns and unknowns. *American Psychologist* , 51, 77-101.

Newell, K. (1991). Motor skill acquisition. *Annual Review of Psychology* , 42, pp. 213-237.

Oatley, K., & Jenkins, J. M. (1992). Human emotions: Function and dysfunction. *Annual Review of Psychology* , 43, pp. 55-85.

O'Leary, D. K., & Smith, D. A. (1991). Marital interactions. *Annual Review of Psychology* , 42, pp. 191-212.

Pargament, K. I. (1997). *The psychology of religion and coping.* New York: Guilford Press.

Parloff, M., London, P., & Wolfe, B. (1986). Individual psychotherapy and behavior change. *Annual Review of Psychology* , 37, pp. 321-349.

Peale, N. V. (2002/1952). *The power of positive thinking.* New York: Running Press.

Peterson, C. (2000). The future of optimism. *American Psychologist , 55,* 44-55.

Petty, R. E., Wegener, D. T., & Fabrigar, L. R. (1997). Attitudes and attitude change. *Annual Review of Psyhology , 49.*

Phelps, E. A. (2006). Emotion and cognition: insights from studies of the human amygdala. *Annual Review of Psychology , 57,* pp. 27-53.

Revelle, W. (1996). Personality processes. *Annual Review of Psyhology , 46,* pp. 295-328.

Rodin, J., & Salovery, P. (1989). Health psychology. *Annual Review of Psyhology , 40,* pp. 533-57

Rogers, C. (1951). *Client-centered therapy.* New York: Houghton Miffin.

Rogers, C. (1961). *On becoming a person.* New York: Houghton Miffin.

Rose, R. J. (1996). Genes and human behavior. *Annual Review of Psychology , 46,* pp. 625-654.

Rotter, J. S. (1954). *Social learning and clinical psychology.* New York: Prentice Hall.

Russell, B. (1958). *The conquest of happiness.* New York: Bantam Books.

Rutter, M., & Silberg, J. (2002). Gene-environment interplay in relation to emotional and behavioral disturbance. *Annual Review of Psychology , 53,* pp. 463-490.

Ryan, R. M., & Deci, E. L. (2000). Self-determination theory and the facilitation of intrinsic motivation, social development, and well-being. *American Psychologist , 55,* 68-78.

Salovey, P., & Mayer, J. D. (1990). Emotional intelligence. *Imagination, Cognition, and Personality ,* 185-211.

Salovey, P., Mayer, J. D., Caruso, D., & Lopes, P. N. (2003). Measuring emotional intelligence as a set of abilities with the MSC EQ test. In S. J. Lopez, & C. R. Snyder, *Positive psychological assessment: A handbook of models and measures* (pp. 251-265). Washington, DC: American Psychological Association.

Scheirer, M. F., Carver, C., & Bridges, M. (2001). Optimism, pessimism, and subjective well-being. In E. C. Chang, *Optimism and pessimism: Implications for theory, research, and practice* (pp. 189-216). Washington, DC: American Psychological Association.

Schutz, W. C. (1967). *Joy.* New York: Grove Press.

Seligman, M. E., & Csikzentmihalyi, M. (2000). Positive psychology. *American Psychologist , 55,* 5-14.

Shank, R., & Abelson, R. (1977). *Scripts, plans, goals, and understanding.* Hillsdale, NJ: Lawrence Erlbaum.

Sherif, M., & Sherif, C. (1964). *Reference groups.* New York: Harper and Row.

Shmotkin, D. (2005). Happiness in the face of adversity: reformulating tyhe dynamic and modular bases of subjective well-being. *Review of General Psychology , 9,* 291-325.

Skinner, E. A. (2007). The development of coping. *Annual Review of Psychology , 58,* pp. 119-144.

Solso, R. L., & Massaro, D. W. (1995). *The science of mind: 2001 and beyond.* New York: Oxford Press.

Squire, L. R., Knowlton, R., & Musen, G. (1993). The structure and organization of memory. *Annual Review of Psychology , 44,* pp. 453-495.

Staats, A. S. (1968). *Learning, language, and cognition.* New York: Holt, Rinehart, and Winston.

Steel, P., Schmidt, J., & Shultz, J. (2008). Refining the relationship between personality and subjective well-being. *Psychological Bulletin , 134,* 138-161.

Stevens, S. (1988). *The relationship between scales of the Stevens/Snyder relationship questionnaire and relationship satisfaction.* (Unpublished masters thesis), California State University, Long Beach, Educational Psychology, Long Beach, CA.

Stevens, T. G. (1977). *Career and personal explorations--an effective individualized life planning course for college students.* Long Beach, CA: Office of the Chancellor, The California State University and Colleges.

Stevens, T. G. (1986). Developing a life skills assessment and referral system to screen large numbers of university students. *OCCDHE Annual Conference.* San Luis Obispo, CA.

Stevens, T. G. (2009). *Development of the success and happiness attributes questionnaire (SHAQ) to validate a cognitive model of happiness, depression, and anxiety.* Retrieved from http://www.csulb.edu/~tstevens/success/Use%20of%20SHAQ%20to%20Validate%20Model%20of%20Happiness.pdf

Stevens, T. G. (1985). *How do I decide what career or major I want? a step-by-step guide.* Long Beach, CA: Calfornia State University, LB University Bookstore.

Stevens, T. G. (1987). Large-scale life skills assessment and referral of university students. *Western Psychological Association Annual Conference.* San Francisco, CA.

Stevens, T. G. (1972). *Positive behavior change--from theory to intervention.* Monograph, University of Hawaii, Psychology.

Stevens, T. G. (1973). *The effects of covert rehearsal and reinforcement on friendly assertive behavior.* (Unpublished doctoral dissertation), University of Hawaii, Psychology, Honolulu.

Stevens, T. G. (1981). *Thee effects of self-instructional mediated learning modules on interpersonal and self-management skills.* Resources In Education.

Stevens, T. G. (1991). Use of artificial intelligence techniques in ANDY CARES--A computer advising and referral expert system. *Annual Artificial Intelligence Symposium for the California State University System.* San Luis Obispo, CA: California State University Publications.

Stevens, T. G., & Kapche, R. W. (1984). The relationship between self-management variables and smoking behavior. *Association for Advancement of Behavior Therapy Annual Convention.* San Francisco.

Stevens, T. G., & Stevens, S. B. (1995). "Taking care of self" (versus obligation)--a basis for relationship happiness.". *Western Psychological Association Annual Conference.* Los Angeles, CA.

Stevens, T. G., & Stevens, S. B. (1999). "Spiritual cognitive therapy:Targeting the core of psychological problems. *American Counseling Association World Conference.* San Diego, CA.

Tavris, C. (1982). *Anger--the misunderstood emotion.* New York: Simon and Schuster.

Teilhard de Chardin, P. (1959). *The phenomenon of man.* New York: Harper and Row.

Tillich, P. (1956). *Dynamics of faith.* New York: Harper and Row.

Tillich, P. (1967). *Systematic theology.* New York: Harper and Row.

Tillich, P. (1952). *The courage to be.* New Haven, CT: Yale University Press.

Van Lehn, K. (1996). Cognitive skill acquisition. *Annual Review of Psychology , 47*, pp. 155-181.

von Ingen, D. J., Freiheit, S. R., & Vye, C. S. (2009). From the lab to the clinic: Effectiveness of cognitive-behavioral treatments for anxiety disorders. *Professional Psychology: Research and Practice , 40*, 69-74.

Walker, B. M., & Winter, D. A. (2007). The elaboration of pesonal construct theory. *58*, pp. 453-477.

Watson, D., & Tharp, R. (1989). *Self-directed behavior change.* Pacific Grove, CA: Brookes-Cole.

Wellman, H. M., & Gelman, S. A. (1992). Cognitive development: Foundational theories of core domains. *Annual Review of Psychology , 43*, pp. 337-375.

White, N. M., & Milner, P. M. (1992). The psychology of reinforcers. *Annual Review of Psychology , 43*, pp. 443-471.

Wong, P. T., & Fry, P. (1998). *The human quest for meaning.* New York: Lawrence Erlbaum.

Zinberg, R. E., Barlow, D. H., Brown, T. A., & Hertz, R. M. (1992). Cognitive-behavioral approaches to the nature and treatment of anxiety disorders. *Annual Review of Psychology , 43*, pp. 235-267.

INDEX OF BOXES, TABLES, AND FIGURES
(Except SHAQ research related)

BIOGRAPHICAL SKETCH OF THE AUTHOR

Dr. Tom G. Stevens is a psychologist professor emeritus at California State University, Long Beach; where he worked in the Counseling and Psychological Services Center for 31 years. His four degrees include a PhD in Psychology from the University of Hawaii and a Master of Theology from the Claremont School of Theology. He was a United Methodist minister before getting his PhD. Integrating theology, philosophy, and science is a special interest of his.

His pursuit of understanding how people can learn to be happy and more productive began with a life-altering experience at age 16 when he chose to make happiness for self and others his top goal in life. Dr. Stevens' professional contributions include a number of publications and papers. He has completed research in the areas of self-management and emotional coping, interpersonal communication, career and life planning, assertion training, life skills training, habit change, and artificial intelligence. One of his research projects was a four-year study of factors contributing to the happiness and success of over 4,000 college students and persons in the community.

He also led a series of experimental studies developing self-instructional videotapes for interpersonal skills training. All ten experimental studies found positive effects. He and his wife Sherry developed a relationship questionnaire (the SRQ) which had high correlations with relationship happiness. The research supported many of their ideas about successful relationships. He also developed "ANDY" a computer program utilizing artificial intelligence to assess and advise college students. He developed a number of college classes and community workshops to help people learn self-management, career, and interpersonal skills. Thousands of people have participated in these classes and workshops (which receive high ratings from participants).

Dr. Stevens has used the term *Spiritual Cognitive Therapy* to designate a psychotherapy approach that varies from traditional cognitive therapy by focusing more upon people's top values and beliefs, because they are the core of our personality and probably are the most important long-term factors affecting our emotions and life success.

After writing the first edition of *You Can Choose To Be Happy,* he designed the *Success and Happiness Attributes Questionnaire* (SHAQ) which can be taken on the Internet free and has generated a great deal of research supporting the main ideas of this book. Many SHAQ results on 3400 people are summarized in this edition.

Dr. Stevens lives what he writes about. His favorite hobby is tennis, which he plays often. He and his wife Sherry have the kind of intimate--yet independent--relationship he writes about. Their many happy activities together include dancing, biking, swimming, music, reading, walking, and travel. They spend part of each year in their Maui paradise. Between them they have three "children" who are now adults and seven grandchildren.

Dr. Stevens believes that his greatest success is living a happy life and helping others find happiness. He has spent his life learning the secrets of how to overcome negative emotions and how to be happy, and wants to share them with as many people as possible. He wants you to know how *You Can Choose to Be Happy.*

TO ORDER THIS BOOK

To order this book, try one of the following:

(1) Internet: amazon, barnesandnoble.com or other e-Stores.
Generally 24-hour shipping is available.

(2) Local Bookstore: You may order online or at your local bookstore. It is now available through bookstores in many countries around the world (via Ingram/LSI). High shipping costs should no longer be a problem.

VISIT DR. TOM G. STEVENS' WEBSITES
for Free Self-Help and Research Results

Free Self-Help Information:

For information about the book, lots more free self-help ideas, and complete self-help manuals on relationships, emotions, assertion training, meeting people, dating, career planning, learning, etc. go to his website.

Go to website address: **www.csulb.edu/~tstevens**

(If not found in the future, search the Internet for "Tom G. Stevens PhD")

Free Success and Happiness Attributes Questionnaire (SHAQ)

Take Dr. Stevens' *Success and Happiness Attributes Questionnaire* (SHAQ) to find your *Happiness Quotient (HQ)* and your scores on the many scales summarized in this book (free). SHAQ measures values and beliefs, positive world view, self-esteem, internal control, assertiveness, intimacy, emotional coping skills, self-management skills, academic skills, and other factors vitally related to happiness, low negative emotions, good relationships, health, and success. You may save all scale and item questions and results. The results link to suggestions for improving your specific results and your HQ.

Go to website address: **www.csulb.edu/~tstevens/success**

Research Results Related to SHAQ and the Ideas in this Book

Dr. Stevens has collected a great deal of research data from SHAQ. His research supports both the validity of SHAQ and the ideas in this book. The research results have been remarkably consistent and positive. These results are based upon the responses of hundreds of people, and are growing. Many of these results are summarized in this book. However, many more are available online. Viewing these results can give you increased confidence in the ideas presented here (go to the first website above). Dr. Stevens has other professional papers available on his website as well.

DR. STEVENS WOULD LIKE TO HEAR FROM YOU

Please send your comments about the book. Dr. Stevens cares about your reactions and will respond at least once. Email him at: tstevens@csulb.edu.

Breinigsville, PA USA
06 October 2010
246812BV00002B/2/P